The World, the Flesh, and the Devil

The World, the Flesh, and the Devil

A HISTORY OF
COLONIAL
ST. LOUIS

PATRICIA CLEARY

UNIVERSITY OF MISSOURI PRESS
COLUMBIA

Copyright © 2011 by
The Curators of the University of Missouri
University of Missouri Press, Columbia, Missouri 65211
Printed and bound in the United States of America
All rights reserved
First paperback printing, 2018

ISBN 978-0-8262-2170-4 (paperback : alk. paper)

Cataloging-in-Publication data available from the Library of Congress
ISBN 978-0-8262-1913-8 (hardcover : alk. paper)

♾™ This paper meets the requirements of the
American National Standard for Permanence of Paper
for Printed Library Materials, Z39.48, 1984.

Designer: Stephanie Foley

Typefaces: AquilineTwo, Casetellar, and Garamond

FOR MY DEAREST HUGH

Contents

Illustrations

Acknowledgments

In the course of writing this book, I have acquired a variety of debts to many people, and I am delighted to have this opportunity to acknowledge their help. Many colleagues, friends, and relatives have graciously listened to me discuss the history of St. Louis, have shared their expertise on a range of subjects, and have provided hospitality as I conducted my research. It is a pleasure to thank them formally here.

My scholarly debts are vast and start with those who act as guardians of the historical record: the archivists. To the staff at the Missouri History Museum, the Lovejoy Library at Southern Illinois University–Edwardsville, the Mercantile Library in St. Louis, and the Williams Research Center at the Historic New Orleans Collection, I wish to express my admiration and appreciation for their tireless work, knowledge, and assistance. In particular, I wish to thank Dennis Northcott of the Missouri History Museum, who has been an excellent resource, as well as Molly Kodner and Anne Woodhouse, also of the MHM, Steve Kerber at the Lovejoy, and John Hoover and Gregory Ames at the Mercantile Library. Prints staff at the New-York Historical Society, the Louisiana State Museum, and the State Historical Society of Missouri proved uniformly helpful.

Over the years, many historians have provided sound advice and assistance. For reading and responding to different parts of this study, I thank the scholars who gathered at the Early Americanists Colloquium at the Huntington Library (the precursor to the USC-Early Modern Studies Institute) to discuss my work some years ago. More recently, Stephen Aron and Virginia Scharff offered excellent feedback at the Autry National Center of the American West. Steve, of UCLA and the Autry, with whom I share an interest in Missouri history, has been a supportive colleague, and I appreciate his interest in the project. Kitty Sklar invited me to present my work at the Rothermere Institute of American History at Oxford University, thereby allowing me to introduce my work to an altogether new audience. Tom Dublin ushered part of it to publication as a document project. Without the groundbreaking research done in the past few decades by Gilbert Din, William E. Foley, and Carl Ekberg, and in earlier decades by Clarence Alvord, Lawrence Kinnaird, John Francis McDermott, and Abraham P. Nasatir, and scores of others whose work I admire and cite in the notes, studies like this one would not have been possible. I would like to single out Bill Foley, professor emeritus, University of Central Missouri, Warrensburg, for a special thanks. After we met a few years ago at a Western History Association conference, Bill extended to me extraordinarily generous scholarly support, volunteering to read drafts of essays, promoting my work to editors, and sharing with me his unparalleled expertise in the history of the region. He is a model of a collegial scholar engaged in a common enterprise, and I thank him. I also owe a debt to my friend and fellow historian Andrew Hurley, whose interest in the environmental history of St. Louis first prompted me to explore its colonial period. Without the initial impetus of the collection of essays he planned, I might never have embarked on this challenging and rewarding project; I thank the Missouri History Museum for granting permission for material in that essay to be reprinted here. Finally, I thank my editor at University of Missouri Press, Clair Willcox, for his long-standing interest in the project; the readers he enlisted for their useful and welcome feedback; and Ann Youmans for her careful copyediting of the manuscript.

Financial support for this project has come from the National Endowment for the Humanities, the Missouri History Museum, the Institute for the Study of the American West at the Autry National Center, and California State University, Long Beach (CSULB). My home institution, CSULB has provided me with regular reductions to my teaching load to allow me time to work on this project, testimony to the university's ongoing commitment to and recognition of the importance of scholarship. Teaching the diverse student body at CSULB continues to challenge me to think about the uses and representations of the past.

Many colleagues at CSULB, in history and other departments, have gone out of their way to provide me with personal support, intellectual engagement, and fond friendship, especially the history department chair Nancy Quam-Wickham, who has been a champion of faculty and scholarship in the midst of dire budget crises, Sebouh Aslanian, Catherine Brooks, Susan Carlile, Jane Dabel, Kathleen DiVito, Cris Hernandez, Ali İğmen, Marie

Kelleher, Tim Keirn, Eileen Luhr, Brett Mizelle, Caitlin Murdock, Dave Neumann, Pamela Roberts, Sarah Schrank, Norbert Schürer, Lise Sedrez, David Shafer, the late Sharon Sievers, and Sean Smith. Houri Berberian has been an especially stalwart source of support and humor. Over the years, other scholars at CSULB and elsewhere have assisted with research questions, translation issues, and maps, including Nicole Albert, Vincent Del Casino Jr., Shannon Lee Dawdy, Clorinda Donato, Steve Fleck, David C. Hood, Troy Johnson, Michael Leroy Oberg, Robert Mazrim, Eric Sandweiss, Jennifer Spear, and Elliott West. Historian and judge Morris Arnold steered me to a valuable source, for which I am grateful. I also want to thank my friend and colleague Claire Emilie Martin for help with fine points of translation. Other dear friends have sustained me with food, drink, and companionship: Amy Bentley-Smith, Franz Goebel, Tim Meeks, and Kim Trimble.

My family ties to St. Louis have made this scholarly endeavor a personal project in ways I did not anticipate. I came to the study of colonial St. Louis with the questions of the historian, supplemented by the peculiar curiosity of the hometown native trying to fill in some blanks in her early education. Throughout, I have had my numerous family in mind as my potential readers. To my delight, my interest in early St. Louis has been matched by the enthusiastic response and assistance of several of my siblings, who have helped me in a variety of tangible ways. For their generous hospitality during my research trips to St. Louis, I want to extend a special thanks to my brother Mike and sister-in-law Carol Lillian Cleary; brother Kevin and sister-in-law Celeste Cleary; and nephew Mike and his wife Megan Cleary. Just saying thank you does not altogether capture how much I have enjoyed our visits. My brother Mike also accompanied me on a Cahokia Mounds excursion, sent me newspaper updates on the fate of Sugar Loaf Mound, and accepted a last-minute, long-distance research mission, heading off with alacrity to the archives. My brother Kevin drove me to the confluence of the Missouri and Mississippi, where flood waters on the northern shore of the Missouri impeded our progress and reminded me why the Spanish decided not to build a fort there in the 1760s. While I stayed at their parents' home, nephew Kevin Cleary and niece Angela Cleary displayed seemingly genuine interest in the history of St. Louis, and for that I thank them.

Family members no longer in St. Louis have contributed as well. For their help with interpreting eighteenth-century medical diagnoses, I thank my brother Tom Cleary and sister-in-law Karen R. Cleary, whose Rabideau family of origin has links to colonial French Canada and eighteenth-century

St. Louis. My sister Carol Cleary-Schultz performed reading feats, provid-ing me with impressively prompt and useful responses to chapter drafts. She, her husband Jeff Schultz, and their daughters Keira and Kelly Schultz have been delightful distractions. To my sister Kitty Cleary Adamovic, brother-in-law Larry Adamovic, and their children Meghan Adamovic, Allison Adamovic, and Jake Adamovic, I am grateful for friendship and good humor; I count on and appreciate the many kinds of support they pro-vide. To my nephew Brian Cleary, I am indebted for a variety of computer-related assistance. I will always think of Christina Cleary and the great St. Louis "re-onion" of '97. To my many other siblings, siblings-in-law, nieces, nephews, surviving aunts, uncle, and cousins, all of whom have some con-nection to St. Louis, I hope you enjoy the book. I think my parents would have been tickled by this project, and I regret that they and my brother Terry did not live to read it.

I thank my British relations, the Wilfords and the Chevalliers, for their wonderful hospitality. My mother-in-law Jan Wilford has been a source of trans-Atlantic support as well as excellent company during our mutual visits across the pond.

To my husband Hugh Wilford, I am deeply indebted and grateful. His support and assistance have been instrumental to my completion of this book. On many occasions, he has talked with me about about this proj-ect and read drafts of chapters, always responding with typically incisive commentary and advice. During a memorable summer trip spent driving through the French Pyrenees, he helped me trace the path of Pierre Laclède, the founder of St. Louis. For sharing enthusiastically in that adventure and many others, I thank him.

I dedicate this book to Hugh in appreciation of his devoted companion-ship, countless kindnesses, and essential, sustaining love.

Abbreviations

AGI-PC   Archivo General de Indias—Papeles
          Procedentes de Cuba

BLC   *Before Lewis and Clark,* Abraham Nasatir, ed.

HM   *History of Missouri,* Louis Houck

JFM   John Francis McDermott Mississippi Valley
          Research Collection, Lovejoy Library,
          Southern Illinois University at Edwardsville

MHMA   Missouri History Museum Archives (formerly
          the Missouri Historical Society)

MHML   Missouri History Museum Library

SLA   St. Louis Archives, Missouri History Museum
          Archives

SRM   *Spanish Regime in Missouri,* Louis Houck, ed.

SMV   *Spain in the Mississippi Valley,* Lawrence
          Kinnaird, ed.

The World,
the Flesh,
and the Devil

Introduction

I have a confession to make. A native St. Louisan, I spent my youth oblivious to my hometown's colonial past. I can't accuse my parents of a lack of civic pride or blame them for indifference to the city's history. My father, an immigrant of Irish and English background who lived in St. Louis from the age of three, made the place his own and was a walking compendium of information about it. My mother, born on the south side to the descendants of German and English immigrants, could not have been more of a St. Louisan if she had tried, with her typical accent and thrifty habits. Together, they showed us the city as they knew and loved it. On Sunday drives, during my childhood, we repeatedly visited two locations: the riverfront and Forest Park. At the former, walking down the large and angled cobblestones lining the river's edge, we would stare out at the Mississippi, watch it churning with branches that moved rapidly past bridge supports and gaze at barges fighting the river's swift current to move upstream. In Forest Park, our other destination, we sometimes stopped and fed the ducks in front of the Municipal Opera (the Muny, in local parlance), but more often we headed straight for the Zoo, there to delight in the barking seals and ponder the polar bears, immense and improbable creatures, particularly on sweltering summer days in the Midwest. (All of these activities—and many others in the city—I would add, were free, a fact that was and is noted proudly by St. Louisans.)

The not-so-slight, intentional hint of boosterism in my opening remarks aside, the two places I describe mark both the geographic borders of the city and the two most celebrated episodes in its history. Curving around to form the eastern boundary of St. Louis, the mighty Mississippi is muddy at this point, dirtied by silt from the Missouri River and the confluence of the two waterways just to the north. From the air, one can see the waters of two rivers, blue-gray and yellow-brown, traveling side by side in the same channel until they merge and become one, the volume nearly doubled by the addition of the meandering Missouri. I remember being impressed by the river as a child, and a little frightened of falling into it. What thrilled me especially, though, was the centerpiece of the riverfront site, the Arch, the iconic image of the city. With its gleaming silver geometry soaring 630 feet into the sky, the Arch is architect Eero Saarinen's celebration of St. Louis as the "Gateway to the West," the centerpiece of the Jefferson National Expansion Memorial. Although the famed duo of Meriwether Lewis and William Clark actually set out on their 1804 voyage of discovery through the newly acquired Louisiana Territory from St. Charles, located nearby on the Missouri River, St. Louis was the more important settlement, the place where President Thomas Jefferson sent the two men to prepare for their famed expedition up the Missouri. Here was one key to the city as I understood it then: a technological triumph symbolizing the way early champions of the West—Jefferson, Lewis, and Clark—paved the way for the nineteenth-century expansion of the United States. That is where and when the story of St. Louis seemed to begin.

The other most notable chapter in St. Louis's past took place at the western edge of the city limits. There stands Forest Park, a glorious reminder of the virtues of nineteenth-century city parks, 1,293 acres of rolling hills, gardens, waterways, bike paths, baseball diamonds, golf courses, museums, and yes, the Zoo.[1] Opened in 1876, the park witnessed its zenith of fame in 1904, as the location for the Louisiana Purchase Exposition, the months-long celebration of the centenary of the territory's acquisition, known locally simply as the World's Fair.[2] The year of the fair, when St. Louis captured the world's attention, when people and products from around the globe came to town, holds a peculiar and tenacious place in St. Louisans' civic memory. That was the city's moment in the sun, with the largest fair the world had seen, a vision of electrical palaces, fantastic fountains, 1,500 buildings, exhibitions from sixty-two countries, and over seventy-five miles of roadways.[3] The recent census of 1900 had marked St. Louis as the nation's fourth-largest city, its population of 575,238 putting it behind only New York, Philadelphia, and Chicago.[4] Impressive

---

1. Schuyler, *The New Urban Landscape;* Rosenzweig and Blackmar, *The Park and the People.*

2. The original plan for the park, by Maximillian G. Kern, was redesigned for the 1904 exposition by George Kessler, who had worked as a gardener for Central Park's designer Frederick Law Olmsted. See Fox, ed., *Where We Live,* 124.

3. Breitbart, *A World on Display.* For military, cultural, and racial dynamics at the fair, see Kramer, *The Blood of Government,* 229–84.

4. U.S. Bureau of the Census, *Twelfth Census of the United States: 1900.* "Table 6. Population of Cities Having 25,000 Inhabitants or More in 1900, at each census: 1790 to1900," 429–33, http://www2.census.gov/prod2/decennial/documents/33405927v1_TOC.pdf (accessed December 14, 2007).

domestic architecture, imposing public buildings, and a vast rail network expressed the wealth and ambition of the inhabitants of the bustling metropolis. I still take pleasure in watching Judy Garland attend the fair and sing about the delights of having it "right here in our own backyard" in 1944's Technicolor musical extravaganza. In the title song, penned in 1904 for the fair, St. Louis is pronounced "St. Loo-ee," one of the rare instances when the city's French origins are even remotely acknowledged.

When I was a child, it was clear to me that the months of the World's Fair were St. Louis's glory days, and as such the focus of school projects and source of endless trivia. We learned that ice cream cones were invented at the fair and iced tea popularized. From other lore, we believed that the neighborhood still known as Dogtown derived that nickname from the culinary habits of some of the inhabitants of the fair's Philippine exhibit in that area, the Igorots, who kept and ate dogs, and whose lunchtime dog feasts attracted significant publicity and notoriety at the fair.[5] While some of the most famed of the fair's attractions, like the giant ferris wheel, were long gone by the time I was born, dismantled and buried at the fair's conclusion, and many exhibit halls were only temporary and decayed over the course of 1904, some were built to last. The surviving structures (which our parents pointed out repeatedly) include the original part of the St. Louis Art Museum, which served as the fair's Palace of Fine Arts, as well as the gigantic birdcage at the Zoo, part of the federal government's exhibit.[6] They stand today as tangible testimony to a more than hundred-year-old civic triumph, which in turn commemorated the legacy of an event one hundred years in the past.

What do these places and moments—east and west, roiling river and sculpted park, the Corps of Discovery's exploration of the newly purchased Louisiana Territory and the centennial celebration of it—have in common, and what do they leave out? Clearly, they shape a tidy narrative arc of expansion and a civic identity tied to it. Yet they leave out all that was absent, or at best hazy, in my early education, that is, who and what came before. In the same way that the shadow of the American Revolution too often hovers over histories of colonial British America, so that the entire period becomes a dress rehearsal for revolution or a search for the forces the led to it, so, too, does St. Louis suffer from a degree of historical amnesia about who and

5. Kramer, *The Blood of Government,* 261–62, 266; Afable, "Journeys from Bontoc to the Western Fairs, 1904–1915," 446. *Where We Live* notes only that the neighborhood, first known as West Cheltenham, has been popularly called Dogtown for at least a hundred years, 118; others speculate it derives its name from mining terminology.

6. Fox , *Where We Live,* 124–25.

what preceded Lewis and Clark. The bicentennial of the Louisiana Purchase prompted a flurry of works about St. Louis, but they did not redress this glaring omission. Recent books with titles like *Before Lewis and Clark*, fine though they might be, give away the game: ultimately, it is still all about getting to Lewis and Clark. Theirs is the exciting story, the real one, or so it seems. Their setting out to explore the Missouri signaled the beginning of U.S. occupation of its newly acquired territory, a moment of looking forward to U.S. history in the region, not backward toward the colonial past.

I should note here that I am glossing over essential and impressive scholarship, in particular the studies published in recent decades by Gilbert C. Din, Carl J. Ekberg, and William E. Foley, and in an earlier generation, by John Francis McDermott, Abraham P. Nasatir, and others. Their work is the starting place for any serious inquiry into the region's eighteenth-century history and informs the narrative of this book. The crucial exception to my generalizations about historical oversight, their scholarship is not addressed by these introductory comments about the construction of historical memory and my early sense of the city, the sense of the past that limned the contours of my imagination as a child.

To the extent that I was aware of the French settlers of the 1760s and the other early French-speaking inhabitants of St. Louis, it was through street names and a few local landmarks. During my youth in the 1970s, "Laclede's Landing," where founder Pierre Laclède de Liguest decided to establish his trading post and village, was home mostly to boarded-up brick warehouses, transients, and steep, deserted streets. Urban revitalization efforts have brought restaurants and nightclubs to renovated buildings, but there is little to remind one of the city's founding generation. In the 1800s, St. Louisans, like so many other of their contemporaries, razed nearly every building from the previous century. The 1841 destruction of Laclède's original trading post, which was renovated and enlarged in 1789 by Auguste Chouteau and served as his home for decades, elicited barely any notice and no public outcry; historic preservation movements were in the infancy in nineteenth-century St. Louis.[7] Even in Boston, possessed of one of the more historically self-conscious populations in the United States, the Old State House, a centerpiece of the Freedom Trail, was nearly destroyed. Formerly the seat of royal government during the colonial period, part of the structure dates to 1713. The building was in a state of disrepair when a group of Chicagoans attempted to buy it to dismantle and reassemble in Chicago in anticipation of their own world's fair, the

---

7. Foley and Charles David Rice, "'Touch Not a Stone,'" 14–19; Ronald W. Johnson, "Historic Preservation in Missouri," 224–27.

Columbian Exposition of 1893, which commemorated Columbus's "discovery" of America four hundred years before. This Windy City overture prompted Bostonians to rally to save a piece of their heritage, organizing in 1879 to restore the Old State House and turn it into a museum.[8] By the time the world came to St. Louis in 1904, nothing of comparable significance from its colonial past was still standing.

Proximity to the river had determined where Pierre Laclède decided to establish St. Louis, and the desirability of that location continued, prompting one generation after another to tear down what stood before, building bigger and better monuments to trade, capital, and industry. As a result, the physical evidence of the colonial village is long gone, despite efforts of some city promoters to preserve it in the nineteenth century. On the site of much of the colonial village, just to the south of Laclede's Landing, is green, open space, the park where the Arch now stands as sentinel and gateway to the Mississippi and the West. Laclède's name, more than two centuries after he walked the streets of the village, is pronounced "Lacleed." And Chouteau, the surname of his partner Marie Thérèse Bourgeois and her sons Auguste and Pierre, all key figures in the city's colonial past, is said "Showtoe." One can easily spot outsiders and newcomers by their efforts to pronounce these names and others as their original proprietors once did. And the city is most definitely St. Louis, with the final "s" clearly sounded. Physically, the only bit of the village's original commons—the vast open lands for pasturage which encircled the settlement—to survive in any form is Lafayette Square, a small park on the city's near south side.

While nineteenth-century St. Louisans razed their past and contemporary ones focus little on their eighteenth-century predecessors, some responsibility for the general ignorance of the colonial period rests with historians. Since the country's inception in the 1770s, Americans have self-consciously pursued efforts to define their identity, to construct their history, and to search for the factors that have distinguished them from other peoples and nations. In the late nineteenth century, that enterprise inspired professional historians seeking to create a national narrative, one that would celebrate origins and serve to unify the people.[9] In their hands, the story became one of the successful evolution and spread of democratic institutions, derived from British antecedents and modified to suit American needs in the thirteen original colonies and the states that later joined them. The history

8. "The Boston Historical Society and Museum," http://www.bostonhistory.org/old_state_hs_hist.php (accessed January 25, 2008).

9. A highly readable overview of this nationalist enterprise, as well as other developments in the discipline of history, appears in Appleby, Hunt, and Jacob, *Telling the Truth about History.*

of the continent only became the history of the country when individual territories and states became part of the political entity that is the United States. From that perspective, a course on early American history might gloss over the French in Canada or Louisiana, the Spanish in California or New Mexico, or both in Missouri, where they played significant roles, and skim over Native Americans' experiences prior to Europeans' arrival. What was important in 1776 in this eastern, British-origins model of U.S. history is what happened in Philadelphia, Boston, New York, or Charleston, not in New Orleans, Santa Fe, St. Augustine, or St. Louis. As will become clear, such oversight of other parts of the continent not only neglects the history of those regions but distorts our understanding of the webs of connections linking east, west, and Midwest.

When I began to study the colonial period of St. Louis in earnest, in the 1990s, I was amazed, both my own appalling ignorance and by the continued lack of attention the era received in St. Louisans' education. As a teenager, I had attended a fine girls' school, Rosati-Kain High School, where the committed and talented nuns and lay teachers taught us the history of the United States; early St. Louis was not, at least then, part of the curriculum. To see if the same approach still prevailed, I asked my then twelve-year-old niece Meghan, a very bright girl at an excellent public school in west St. Louis County, if she knew that a battle of the American Revolutionary War had been fought in St. Louis. "What? No, that's weird," was her inimitable preteen response to the 1780 Battle of San Luis, in which joint English and Indian forces attacked the poorly defended village, and dozens lost their lives or were captured.[10] In a sense, her reaction mirrored my own: surprise, questioning, and a sense that there was something odd about the story.

What that peculiarity was became ever clearer to me: eighteenth-century St. Louis belonged to a continental colonial history, marked by cooperation and conflict between indigenous Americans and colonizers interacting and moving along the great waterways of the interior, the Mississippi and Missouri Rivers. The even broader context of global competition among European powers—expressed in part through the movement of goods and peoples across oceans—was key as well. In short, the history of early St. Louis could not be easily categorized or summarized. No single nation, people, or state was in full control; challenges to those who claimed authority were constant and varied. In the forty years of its colonial incarnation, St. Louis was part of a complicated, untidy narrative of eighteenth- and

10. McDermott, "The Battle of Colonial St. Louis," 131–51.

early nineteenth-century developments, where diverse peoples converged and where borders were ill defined, in flux, and hotly contested.

In recent years, historians of early American history, which used to comprise primarily the thirteen mainland colonies of Great Britain, have been expanding their geographic sphere of interest. The works of earlier scholars interested in the history of the west and a growing number of contemporary historians have inspired renewed interest in eighteenth-century Louisiana, Illinois, and Missouri.[11] With a global economy and the rapid, incessant movement of goods, information, and people seeming to define our world, those who write about the past pay greater heed to the earlier expressions of these phenomena. Nation-state boundaries no longer suffice as the focus or category of historical analysis. The picture is too complicated, peopled by too many characters who migrated long distances and jostled against unfamiliar systems and neighbors, to allow for that narrow approach to continue. For me, living in a metropolis like Los Angeles, founded by Spain in 1781 as El Pueblo de Nuesta Señora la Reina de los Ángeles de Porciúncula, and working at California State University, Long Beach, where the student body reflects the diversity of the urban area, I am very aware of how far from Britain's colonial ventures my students are and how much I need to think about continental and global contexts as I teach. In short, residence in California helped spur my interest in a colonial history broader than the one I had studied. When I planned to research the early environmental history of St. Louis, little did I imagine the riches I would encounter in the archives when I began to study my hometown's past.[12]

As I explored the colonial era in St. Louis, guided by the work of Foley and others, I became fascinated by the complexity of its colonial administration, population, and shifting social relations. Reviewing census and trade records, I discovered a degree of diversity in the earliest years that has perhaps only begun to be matched again in recent years, with influxes of immigrants from Latin America and Asia. In the 1700s, St. Louis was home to French-speaking newcomers from Canada, Illinois, Louisiana, and France; a temporary place of residence for Spanish soldiers, traders, and government officials; and a stopping point for scores of native Americans from dozens of tribes, notably the Missouri, Osage, and Peoria Indians, the latter of whom who built their own settlement close to the colonial village, on what colonists termed the *Prairie des Sauvages*. Enslaved Africans who spoke French or English; enslaved Indians, many

11. See, for example, the work of Usner, *Indians, Settlers, and Slaves in a Frontier Exchange Economy.*
12. See Hurley, ed., *Common Fields.*

of them held in bondage in defiance of the law; and enslaved mixed-race women, men, and children were also part of the society. Some free Africans, Indians, and mixed-race individuals made St. Louis their home as well. British visitors and, after the Revolution, American traders and farmers were all part of this multilingual, multiethnic mix. Clearly, St. Louis was a complicated place, founded by a Frenchman interested in the fur trade, administered by Spain for almost all of its colonial period, and distant from any major concentrations of population or elaborate administrative structures.

Regardless of which European nation had putative authority over the settlement, its inhabitants were most assuredly innovators in social, economic, and religious arrangements, creative because the new situations in which they found themselves demanded they be so. Though shaped by whatever cultural baggage they brought with them, they were, in effect, making up new rituals and rules as they went along. The more I studied them, the more I was intrigued by their remarkable stories. I learned that the first families had their share of philandering fathers, wandering mothers, and founding bastards. I found that the villagers spent a good bit of their time fighting—verbally as well as physically—for all sorts of reasons: over smelly fish and food supplies, personal reputation, seating arrangements in church, alcohol consumption, trading practices, and government authority. I spied them socializing, procreating, doing business, and putting their noses into each other's affairs as they jockeyed for position, influence, and affluence. In the process, those who came to St. Louis for a time, or made it their home, lived among people who were strange to them. Without shared backgrounds, they nonetheless, for reasons of mutual survival and self-interest, had to cooperate and collaborate with each other. Trade, as well as other activities, required men and women to cross linguistic, racial, and religious borders, to find a way to deal peaceably with individuals with whom they might otherwise be at odds.

Some no doubt evinced what historian Margaret Jacob characterizes as the traits of the cosmopolitan individual: enjoying people different from oneself, living next to them comfortably, or socializing and trading with them respectfully.[13] In the eighteenth century, such cosmopolitan values could come into play at a distance from the centers of urban sophistication with which we tend to associate them today, as individuals possessed the skills and knowledge to interact with ease cross-culturally. Colonists in St. Louis were neither indifferent to nor unaware of contemporary cultural concerns or literary achievements; McDermott's study of

13. Jacob, *Strangers Nowhere in the World*, 1.

the contents of creole libraries in early St. Louis demonstrates quite the reverse.[14] Describing the emergence of cosmopolitanism in early modern Europe, Jacob notes that "even amid wars and national rivalries, select places existed where another, more benign experience became occasionally possible." She argues that in Europe, "Small enclaves flourished where social, religious, and national boundaries were routinely crossed and seeds of an expansive social experience took root."[15] In colonial St. Louis, such an enclave developed, not one where tolerance and peace governed all social relations, but one where diversity and trade dictated openness and a degree of accommodation of difference. Far removed from the seats of empire, on the periphery of British, Spanish, and American spheres of control, the people of colonial St. Louis were innovators and individualists, some of them hard-working entrepreneurs on one hand and exploiters of slave labor on the other, overextended administrators and undersupplied soldiers, lawmakers and lawbreakers, farmers and fur traders, enslaved and free men and women of many backgrounds trying to make their way interacting with new people in a new situation. In the view of one critical government official, the residents of the village failed to triumph over the challenges they faced in this new setting and succumbed too readily to the temptations of "the world, the flesh, and the devil."[16] At the center of a confluence region of major rivers, major cultures, and major powers, St. Louis and its environs witnessed fascinating experimentation in the realms of commercial, social, civic, spiritual, and sexual activities.[17] That history—entirely unknown to me as a child, largely ignored by my profession, and consistently sidelined in large-scale narratives of United States history—is the subject of this book. This is my attempt to reconstruct who and what existed, how they lived and loved, in the early years when people from around the world made colonial St. Louis a going concern. Long before the celebrated duo of Lewis and Clark set out to explore the Missouri River and the west and even longer before the World's Fair that celebrated the Louisiana Purchase that led to their journey, St. Louis was a global village, a place where peoples, cultures, and histories converged, and where their collisions gave rise to something new, right here, as Judy Garland noted with wonder, in our own backyard.

14. McDermott, *Private Libraries in Creole Saint Louis.*

15. Jacob, *Strangers Nowhere in the World,* 11.

16. Fernando de Leyba to Bernardo de Galvez, July 13, 1779, in Lawrence Kinnaird, ed. and trans., *Spain in the Mississippi Valley, 1765–1794,* part 1, *The Revolutionary Period, 1765–1781* (hereafter *SMV*), 346.

17. See Aron, *American Confluence.*

Chapter 1

From France to the Frontier

On June 7, 1755, Pierre de Laclède Liguest left France aboard the *Concorde*, a ship bound for America. Twenty-five years old, he parted from his family, not knowing whether this would be a final good-bye. With the energy of youth and a spirit of adventure, he had his ambitions focused beyond the horizon, on the French empire that stretched from the Atlantic Ocean and the Great Lakes to the Mississippi River Valley and the Gulf of Mexico. What prompted him to leave his homeland was the beacon of opportunity that North America offered the younger sons of French families. Whether Laclède spent the voyage languishing in his cabin, missing his absent friends and family, or delighting in the thrill of crossing the Atlantic and planning his future, he faced the hardships that all travelers did: unpredictable weather, with storms that could toss a ship to nauseating effect; food and drink that were seldom fresh or plentiful; and cramped quarters.

When trans-Atlantic voyagers rounded the tip of Florida, sailed into the Gulf of Mexico, and approached the mouth of the Mississippi River, relief at having survived the longest part of the journey across open ocean would have been tempered by the prospect of traveling upriver. Reaching the colonial outposts of French Louisiana required navigating up miles of twisting river from the Gulf while plagued by sand bars, fast-moving tree limbs, and uncooperative winds.[1] For some, the last leg of the journey proved especially taxing, punctuated by exposure to the elements and environment.[2] Mosquitoes swarmed travelers after sunset, joined by other biting insects, sometimes in such numbers "that one could cut them with

1. Ingersoll, *Mammon and Manon in Early New Orleans*, 26.
2. Emily Clark, ed., *Voices from an Early American Convent*, 68.

a knife."[3] But signs of settlement provided reassurance that the journey's end was at hand. By the 1760s, from the mouth of the river up to New Orleans, "plantations and well-built houses on each side [of] the river afford[ed] a very pleasing and agreeable prospect."[4]

After a comparatively quick journey, Laclède arrived in mid-July at the port of New Orleans, France's imperial outpost on the lower Mississippi.[5] The ship pulled up to the raised bank, the Levée, and discharged its passengers. Walking the streets of his new home, Laclède might have pondered how far he had come and how small the settlement he found seemed in comparison to the bigger communities he had known: the ancient university town of Toulouse, where he had been a student, and the thriving port of Bordeaux, where grand and gleaming new buildings proclaimed the inhabitants' sense of their commercial significance. Through both settlements flowed the Garonne River, an important waterway in southwestern France. In contrast to these cities, New Orleans was a small town, laid out on a grid of perfectly straight streets and tucked into a bend of the Mississippi that earned it the nickname of the Crescent City. Founded in 1718, the town had nothing of the antiquity that characterized the French countryside Laclède knew as a boy, where Roman ruins, medieval churches, and grand chateaus stood as constant reminders of the powerful players of the past. Despite the lack of such structures in New Orleans, the same kind of military, political, and religious energies that fueled France's earlier conquerors inspired the French empire of Laclède's day. Around New Orleans' central square, the *Place d'Armes*—which abutted the river—stood a few government quarters, some merchants' homes, a prison, a guardhouse, and the church. Together, these places represented the sources of power on both sides of the Atlantic: trade, the state, and the church. Erecting new structures in the colonies and meeting in these places, ambitious private individuals and official representatives of European governments attempted to impose their control on this environment, to make whatever and whomever they encountered in North America into what they desired: the stuff of profitable and competitive ventures. Laclède was coming to Louisiana, like many of his compatriots, in search of fortune, leaving behind his family home in Bedous, in the French Pyrenees, to take his chances in a different clime.

When Laclède came to America in the mid-1750s, yet another of the era's many conflicts between France and England was underway, a conflict

3. Clark, ed., *Voices from an Early American Convent*, 68.
4. Pittman, *The Present Satte of the European Settlements*, 9.
5. Coleman, *Gilbert Antoine de St. Maxent*, 23.

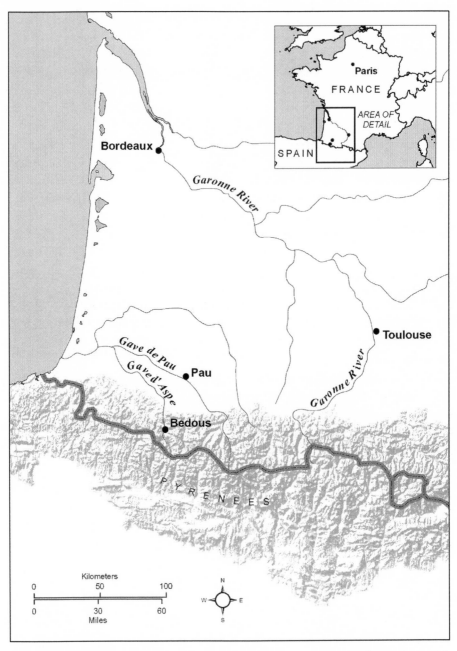

Southwestern France (John Speargas, Department of Geography, California State University, Long Beach)

that began on American soil in 1754 and assumed trans-Atlantic dimensions in 1756. How the hostilities affected Laclède's decision to migrate is not known. Several years before, at the age of eighteen, he had graduated from a military academy in Toulouse. It seems possible that when he journeyed to New Orleans, he may have come in a military capacity, or, as William Foley and David Rice suggest, he might have moved into mercantile endeavors very early.[6] What is clear, however, is that he was leaving one region with a history of conflict to come to another similarly marked.[7]

The province of Béarn, where Bedous was located, had a distinctive and complex history. Among the most notable historical figures in Laclède's part of the country was Henry IV, king of Navarre, the first Bourbon king of France. Known for his role in the sixteenth century's Wars of Religion, Henry IV was born not far from Bedous in nearby Pau. A sovereign principality in the Middle Ages, Béarn had a history and economy that were profoundly shaped by the key topographical feature of the area, the Pyrenees.[8] Topped with forests, the Pyrenees shaped the climate of Bedous, where harsh winters were followed by cool springs and hotter, drier summers.[9] Raising livestock was an important part of the local economy, shaping land use practices significantly.[10] Snow-covered peaks, rushing streams, hillsides covered with vines, and fertile plains gave the area a varied and dramatic beauty it retains today.[11]

These mountains acted at once as formidable barriers and conduits, with the rivers and perpendicular valleys that descended from their heights creating "privileged axes of communication" to Spain. Bedous, in the Aspe Valley, was only a short distance from the frontier, and through the nearby Port d'Aspe, at the Spanish border, large quantities of Spanish wool, grains, and oil entered France, and textiles, cured meats, cattle, and salt were transported into Spain.[12] As a young man, Laclède might have learned Spanish; his personal library in St. Louis included twenty-four volumes in Spanish, more than 10 percent of his collection.[13] He may also have gained

6. Foley and C. David Rice, *The First Chouteaus,* 3. In contrast, Frederick A. Hodes, *Beyond the Frontier,* 69.

7. Hugon, "La Frontière Pyrénéenne pendant l'Ancien Régime," 122.

8. Christian Desplat, *Pau et le Béarn au XVIIIe siècle: Deux Cent Mille Provinciaux au Siècle des Lumières,* 1: 26.

9. Desplat, "The Climate of Eighteenth-Century Béarn," 31.

10. Vivier, "Les Biens Communaux de Béarn et Pays Basque," 57–70.

11. Desplat, *Pau et le Béarn au 18ᵉ siècle,* 1: 21.

12. Desplat, *Pau et le Béarn au 18ᵉ siècle,* 1: 20–25, 26, 36. The Aspe Pass through the Pyrenees enabled travelers to cross the French-Spanish border. A Roman road, the Via Tolosana, once marked the path, and pilgrims on *El Camino Santiago,* the St. James pilgrimage route, used it for centuries.

13. McDermott, *Private Libraries in Creole Saint Louis,* 26–27.

Laclède family home in Bedous, France, photograph by
the author

familiarity with the cultural exchanges of borderlands regions.[14] How well
this environment and education prepared Laclède for what he encountered
in America is difficult to say. What one can imagine is how strange New
Orleans and its environs would have appeared to Laclède after his youth in
the French Pyrenees.

Laclède's family was prominent in the Aspe Valley. His ancestors had been
landowners since the fourteenth century and held positions of responsibility
as public servants, holding a variety of government offices repeatedly. His
father was a lawyer, his grandfather acted as a notary and high-ranking official, and his brother Jean practiced law. Pierre's elder brother by a year, Jean

14. Particularly notable for shaping the discussion of early American borderlands are White, *The
Middle Ground;* and Adelman and Aron, "From Borderlands to Borders," 814–41.

de Laclède remained in Bedous and acquired some fame and reputation, becoming head of the water and forestry service in Béarn and implementing a variety of agricultural experiments, most notably the distribution of mulberry trees.[15] An uncle authored a history of Portugal, and Jean de Laclède wrote papers on agriculture.[16] As befit the Laclèdes' status, the family residence in Bedous was a grand three-story turreted home, one of the largest buildings in the village. Over the course of the eighteenth century, however, as the economy of Béarn suffered an irreversible shrinkage in its functions and influence, the merits of seeking one's fortune abroad grew.[17]

When Laclède reached New Orleans, the buildings and streets of Bedous and nearby communities must have seemed a world away. Instead of villages full of stone buildings perched on steep hillsides and vistas of snow-covered mountains, he saw flat land with one-story houses, raised several feet above the ground and surrounded by wide galleries for protection from the weather. (A notable exception was the Ursuline convent completed two decades before, an imposing building of three stories topped by a mansard roof, an impressive monument to the priority placed on religious education as well as the dedication and resources of the nuns who inhabited it.) Rather than being situated in the midst of mountains, cliffs, and waterfalls, New Orleans was located on some of the flattest, lowest-lying land in North America, the Mississippi delta, where the river ran barely below the surface of the soil, a vast expanse of water spreading its fingers through salty marshland, its path changing slowly over time as sediment accumulated and shifted.[18] Where in France he had been surrounded by icy streams—the Aspe sometimes a torrential river—and snowy ridges, Laclède now experienced bayous where enormous alligators swam and sunned themselves. The flora was different, too. In the cypress swamps that blanketed the Mississippi delta, huge trees reaching as much as 120 feet rose straight out of the water, their trunks bulging with root-like shoots reaching down to the surface. Hanging from their branches like giant furry spider webs was Spanish moss. When earlier French explorers encountered the plant, they learned that the Indians called it "tree hair." The Spanish and French both named it after each other: "French beard" or "Spanish beard" respectively. Regardless of nomenclature, the air-feeding plant had many uses—as

15. Desplat, *Pau et le Béarn au XVIIIe siècle*, 1: 84–93; John Francis McDermott, "Myths and Realities Concerning the Founding of St. Louis," in McDermott, ed., *The French in the Mississippi Valley*, 11.

16. McDermott, "Myths and Realities Concerning the Founding of St. Louis," 11.

17. Desplat, *Pau et le Béarn au XVIIIe siècle*, 1: 42.

18. The Maison Laclède, the family home that is now a B and B, is still operated by Laclède family descendants.

kindling, as stuffing for mattresses, and as building material when mixed with mud—and imbued the landscape with an air of mystery.[19]

The foods, smells, and tastes of New Orleans were different, too. There was no sparkling mountain stream water. Rather, drinking water came directly from the muddy Mississippi; inhabitants kept it in jars to allow the sediment to settle out.[20] While some French foods were available, the diet also reflected the influence of indigenous foodways. By the 1730s, local French farmers were producing rice, maize, pumpkin, beans, and peas, an international mixing of plants and expertise, with rice cultivation likely informed by the technological know-how of Africans from the rice-growing coast of that continent. Maize, pumpkin, and beans were the all-important cornerstones of Indian cuisine, with peas the sole item likely of European origin.[21] Back in France, only livestock consumed American corn, but here, Laclède would have seen other Europeans eat it regularly and with relish. Even maize beer and maize brandy graced the tables of New Orleans diners and drinkers. Bread, the staff of life, had a new world spin as well. In place of wheat flour, bakers often used a blend of rice and maize flours. The labor and tools were mixed as well, with enslaved Africans pounding grains that were soaked overnight and then sifting them in baskets made by Indian women. Wheat flour, known as "French flour," was highly prized and added when available. On the serving platters in New Orleans homes, Laclède might have seen salted or smoked buffalo, opossum that some claimed tasted like suckling pig; alligator, catfish, or rattlesnake; or stews made with corn, buffalo, and bear fat roux, all to be washed down with maize beer. Indigenous foodstuffs were widely available and consumed, yet archaeological evidence indicates that the food available in inns was more "French" and less "wild," suggesting that visitors sought the comfort of familiar foods when frequenting such establishments.[22]

While the fantastical flora, fauna, and food of the New World could provoke interest, delight, or alarm in the newcomer, even the less dramatic features of the area made an impression. The humid air of the Gulf and the rising miasmas of the swamps kept clothes perpetually damp. Oppressive heat slowed movements to a lethargic crawl on summer afternoons, while thriving populations of mosquitoes turned the nights into a misery of

---

19. Pittman, *The Present State of the European Settlements,* liii, 39.

20. Ibid., 5.

21. Dawdy, "First you make a roux . . . ," 8 n. 11; Peter H. Wood, *Black Majority,* 35–62.

22. The details about food in this paragraph are drawn from Dawdy, "First you make a roux . . . ," 8–9 n. 12, 9 n. 13, 16 n. 30, 18 n. 35, 28, 29.

biting and buzzing. A French nun described becoming acquainted with "Monsieurs Mosquitoes" as a distressing process. "They cause blisters and violent itching," she told her father. "They take away the skin, and then ulcers come when one scratches." Although like gnats in France in some ways, she thought, the mosquitoes of Louisiana possessed a bite "more poisonous and more painful."[23]

Everything Laclède would have seen in New Orleans was affected by the presence of water. Houses, raised on sills several feet high, did not have cellars, as they would have filled with water. Near the town, flooding made it impossible to keep the dead buried. Initially interring corpses in the natural levees of the Mississippi that lay on the outskirts of town, colonists soon discovered the error in their funerary practices: annual floods freed caskets from their resting places to drift into the town.[24] St. Peter's Cemetery, founded in the 1720s, was the first attempt at a permanent solution. Located outside the village, the cemetery was situated so that if floods did disgorge caskets, the remains would not float into New Orleans.[25]

In this unfamiliar and occasionally unpleasant environment, French immigrants like Laclède attempted to make their fortunes by carving out their own pieces of France's North American empire. In some ways, Laclède's timing could not have been worse. In 1754, the year before Laclède sailed, Virginia colonists under the command of a young officer, George Washington, had crossed the Appalachians to counteract what they saw as French encroachment in the region west of the mountains. At that point, the interior of the continent was a scene of military maneuvers and challenges. France had moved troops south from Canada and had constructed forts in the Ohio River Valley, making its military presence more visible and more worrying to both the British government and the predominantly Anglo-American colonists settled along the Atlantic. Feeling crowded along the eastern seaboard, many colonists had begun to think about moving west, some forming land speculation ventures like the Ohio Company, others picking up and squatting wherever they saw fit. Such land grabs did not go unnoticed either by the French who claimed the territory or by the many Indian peoples who had inhabited the area for millennia.

23. Clark, *Voices from an Early American Convent,* 56. Also a problem was the *frappe d'abord,* or deer fly, which cuts a cross into the flesh and then sucks blood, resulting in a painful bite. Steve Fleck, CSULB, e-mail communications, May 14 and May 19, 2008.

24. Hortard, "Bombarding the City of the Dead," 20; Florence, *New Orleans Cemeteries,* 3; see also Florence, *City of the Dead.*

25. Hortard, "Bombarding the City of the Dead," 21; Xavier Cronin, introduction to Keister, ed., *Going Out in Style,* 16. Another method of disposing of human remains had to be found, and the first above-ground cemetery, the New St. Louis cemetery, was founded in 1789.

When Washington's party encountered a French patrol about fifty miles southeast of contemporary Pittsburgh, in 1754, bloodshed resulted, and a prominent French officer, Joseph Coulon de Villiers, Sieur de Jumonville, died. Washington had been attempting to interrogate the wounded officer when Tanaghrisson, known as the Half King, a Seneca leader and member of Washington's party, interrupted the questioning by striking and killing the Frenchman (who had relatives serving in French Illinois) with his tomahawk. This initial skirmish provoked the French and Indian War (1754–1763), which expanded into a trans-Atlantic conflict, the Seven Years' War (1756–1763). For decades, Great Britain and France had fought each other in wars with both European and American theaters of action, enlisting indigenous allies and colonial subjects in bloody battles that never resolved decisively the issues of imperial dominance that lay behind the conflicts. Historic antagonisms between the two European nations, coupled with mercantilist theories that dictated the importance of colonial possessions to economic success, fueled their military and political agendas. Always in the picture were the many Indian nations of the East Coast, the Great Lakes, and the Ohio, Mississippi, and Missouri River Valleys, whose rights to occupy their traditional homelands were treated as inconsequential by European governments.

At stake was control over North America. After Great Britain decided to throw its military, naval, and financial might at France in the 1750s, French defeat was practically guaranteed, particularly after the fall of Quebec in 1759. The logistics of waging war thousands of miles from the center of the government, with only a small colonial populace in place, derailed French ambitions. Putting its resources into the campaign, Britain vanquished France, in the process generating a sizeable wartime debt. Efforts to defray some of the costs of the war through revenue-raising measures in the colonies soured the mother country's relations with its colonists over the course of the 1760s and early 1770s. Along the eastern seaboard, colonists engaged in protests, boycotts, and rebellion. In 1775, the conflict assumed a military complexion, and the infant United States eventually defeated the mother country in 1783, just twenty years after Great Britain had triumphed over France.

With the treaty that concluded the French and Indian (or Seven Years') War in 1763, France lost its empire, and nearly 160 years of French colonial presence in North America ended with "the scratch of a pen."[26] France ceded Canada and all territory east of the Mississippi to Britain, and tens of thousands of French Catholics suddenly became subjects of an English,

26. Calloway, *The Scratch of a Pen.*

Protestant king. (Its territory west of the Mississippi was gone as well, ceded to Spain under a secret treaty in 1762 as compensation for the loss of Florida). Whether former French subjects in what is today Illinois would decide to stay in newly British territory was unclear. At the same time, extensive trading networks of fur traders and merchants east of the Mississippi were threatened. Thus, Laclède arrived at a moment of uncertainty, with his nation at war, on the eve of the demise of France's dreams of a North American empire. He came to the colonies when trans-Atlantic conflict was about to sweep away France's imperial ambitions and throw allegiances, national identities, and colonial economic endeavors into a state of flux.

As France's southern imperial base—the counterpart to Québec and Montréal, both a century older—New Orleans in the 1750s was a bustling, thriving port town, French in some regards and altogether not in others. Its wooden buildings with peaked roofs were modeled on French architectural styles, with occasional modifications for the local climate. An early song compared the beauty of its streets to Paris, and one newcomer praised its whitewashed, paneled, and sunlit houses.[27] Yet its diverse population, distinguished by a black majority, marked it as very different from any town in France. In addition to native-born colonists—the French creoles—and new arrivals from the mother country, there were also ethnically French residents from Canada and the Illinois country, the *pays des Illinois*, to the north. Indigenous Americans of many nations, some of whom were enslaved and others of whom came freely into town to trade, added to the polyglot diversity and cultural mix of the community. Most numerous were enslaved Africans and their creole offspring, whom the colonizers put to work on the surrounding plantations. With a slave society marked by a black majority from its earliest days, New Orleans was home to Africans from many different regions, a majority of them Senegalese, Guineas, Bambaras, and Ibos.[28] Large-scale transportation of enslaved Africans had begun in 1719, the year after the town was established, when ships carrying five hundred Guinean men and women arrived.[29] From the beginning of settlement, free blacks were also present, some involved in the founding, others freed within the next decade for providing military assistance in campaigns against members of the Chickasaw and Natchez

27. Clark, *Voices from an Early American Convent,* 77.
28. Ingersoll, *Mammon and Manon in Early New Orleans,* 67, 69.
29. Hanger, *Bounded Lives, Bounded Places,* 10. Later in the colonial period, a significant free black population developed as well, growing from 3.1 percent of the total population in 1771 to 17.1 percent in 1791; Hanger, 18.

Indian nations. In the mid-1740s, a decade before Laclède arrived in New Orleans, the population of the town's approximately 4,500 residents was roughly two-thirds black and one-third white.[30]

Plantation agriculture and access to all of the goods and trade that flowed down the Mississippi River and its tributaries made New Orleans an important economic center, one coveted by imperial powers and sought out by men, and some women, in search of opportunity. It also developed a reputation for an unhealthy climate and a licentious society. Forced emigration of French criminals in 1719 and 1720 added to that stigma. One remarkable observer and resident, a young novitiate in the Ursuline order, Marie Madeleine Hachard, described New Orleans in the late 1720s as a vice-ridden place, asserting that "the devil has a great empire here."[31] In characterizing her new home this way, Hachard underlined the scandalous behavior, vanity, and lack of social controls that made her mission of bringing religious education to the populace seem all the more imperative. More compelling to European immigrants over the next several decades, however, were the commercial and financial rewards the region promised, whether through large-scale agriculture or trade.

While there is some suggestion that Laclède entered into an early plantation enterprise and failed at it, it is clear that he quickly made business and private connections and choices that determined his future in St. Louis.[32] Although his movements upon his arrival in New Orleans are unknown, within a few years, Laclède formed the critical professional and personal relationships that shaped the rest of his life, the former with merchant and French immigrant Gilbert Antoine de St. Maxent and the latter with the Louisiana-born Marie Thérèse Bourgeois Chouteau, a French creole woman in her early twenties who had a young son. Maxent, Madame Chouteau, and her son Auguste all shaped the history of early St. Louis. Maxent and Chouteau were neighbors as well, living twelve houses away from each other in the same street in New Orleans.[33]

When Pierre Laclède first encountered Marie Thérèse Bourgeois Chouteau, she was a married woman, likely living in a less than ideal situation. Born in 1733, she was married on September 20, 1748, at the age of fifteen to a twenty-five-year-old French immigrant, René Chouteau; marriages between very young brides and older grooms were not uncommon.[34] On September

---

30. Ingersoll, *Mammon and Manon in Early New Orleans,* 77–79, 17.

31. Clark, *Voices from an Early American Convent,* 78; Dawdy, *Building the Devil's Empire.*

32. Coleman, *Gilbert Antoine de St. Maxent,* 24.

33. Fausz, "Founding St. Louis," 15.

34. Bardet, "Early Marriage in Pre-Modern France," 354.

9 of the following year, Marie Thérèse and René appeared before a priest of New Orleans' St. Louis Cathedral, presenting their two-day-old son for baptism. Whether they were happy for a time we cannot know. Indeed, the records are even confusing as to whether they had another son, and if so, what happened to him. (Years later, René's will made mention of a second child, but no baptismal record or other evidence of him exists.) Before many years had passed, something had clearly gone wrong for the couple. Sometime after 1752, René walked out of his young wife's life. Leaving behind his occupation as an innkeeper and tavernkeeper and his responsibilities to Marie Thérèse and their young son, he sailed back to France and remained there until 1767.[35] In whatever manner Marie Thérèse managed to support herself (and whether her neighbors pitied, scorned, or helped her), her predicament was not unique. After the desertion, she styled herself "Widow Chouteau," claiming a respectable title in her abandonment. The one surviving portrait of her, painted many years later in St. Louis, reveals light blue eyes, arched brows, and a steady and direct gaze, suggestive of a certain force of character. Although there is no visual record of Laclède—a portrait long assumed to be of him was eventually determined to be from a later period—one can imagine that a man of his background and education had a cultivated air, polished manners, and an erect, military bearing.[36] He was, as an English officer wrote, "sensible, clever" and "very well educated."[37] In short, he may have cut a dashing figure. Whatever the case, the two were quickly drawn to each other.

In their twenties when they met, the "Widow" Chouteau and Pierre Laclède became intimately involved. For a married woman like Marie Thérèse, entering into an illicit relationship was a risk, an act that could expose her to censure and criticism. She and Pierre, however, flouted custom and law, managing to form a long-lasting union and raise a family.[38] Over the course of the next decade, they had four children, the first, Jean Pierre, born three years after Laclède's arrival, in 1758. Carrying the names of his father and his father's elder brother, Jean Pierre was known as Pierre

35. This discussion draws on McDermott, "Laclède and the Chouteaus" (unpublished manuscript in the John Francis McDermott Mississippi Valley Research Collection, Lovejoy Library, Southern Illinois University at Edwardsville; hereafter JFM), 47–51; Foley, "The Laclède-Chouteau Puzzle," 18–24.

36. Anne Woodhouse, art curator at the Missouri Historical Museum, e-mail communication, April 21, 2010; Ravenswaay, "Director's Notebook," 275.

37. Harry Gordon, "Journal of Captain Harry Gordon 1766," in Alvord and Carter, eds., *The New Regime, 1765–1767*, 299–300.

38. Francini, "Divorce and Separations in Eighteenth-Century France"; Hayhoe, "Illegitimacy, Inter-generational Conflict, and Legal Practice," 673–84.

Chouteau. The three other Chouteau-Laclède children, all girls—Marie Pélagie, Marie Louise, and Victoire—followed in 1760, 1762, and 1764.

Throughout these years, the lovers maintained the legal fiction of legitimate paternity. Each of Marie Thérèse's four younger children—born during her self-declared "widowhood"—was given the surname Chouteau, and each was acknowledged in New Orleans baptismal records as the legitimate child of the absent René. Such rituals enabled the couple to assume the guise of legitimacy—to perform respectability—even when they could not legally claim it, and indeed, they had no other option at the time, with divorce not available to Catholics. (Interestingly, some descendants of the Chouteau-Laclède family attempted to deny the fact that Marie Thérèse gave birth to their ancestors out of wedlock, one even penning an outraged defense in 1921, entitled "Madame Chouteau Vindicated," in which the peeved author argued that "alleged historians" should do research instead of giving the "world barefaced falsehoods" and besmirching the "character of an honorable, respectable, and unordinarily gifted woman.")[39] In contravening the truth with baptisms naming René Chouteau as the children's father, Pierre and Marie Thérèse were assisted by friends who presumably recognized the social importance of not rearing bastards. Those who attended the baptisms, serving as witnesses and godparents, were mercantile associates of Laclède's; their presence and willingness to act as spiritual sponsors suggests the degree to which the Laclède-Chouteau union met with acceptance among the men of his business circle.[40] From such slender hints, one can infer that the relationship involved ongoing cohabitation and recognition from the pair's friends.

At the same time that Laclède was busy starting a family, he was also deeply involved in business, trying to establish himself as a player among the merchants who traded in the Crescent City. Prominent among them was Maxent, two years Laclède's senior and like him, a French-born immigrant who came to America with military training and mercantile aspirations. Maxent migrated to New Orleans a decade earlier than Laclède had, enlisted in the military, and gradually rose in rank. His fortunes improved significantly on his 1749 marriage to a wealthy young widow, Elizabeth La Roche. Aided by her income, he bought a building on Conti Street, right in the center of the action in New Orleans, with the goal of establishing

---

39. Alexander N. DeMenil, St. Louis, October 13, 1921, from the *St. Louis Globe-Democrat*, October 16, 1921, "Dr. A. N. DeMenil Writes on History of Early St. Louisans." A pamphlet version is titled "Madame Chouteau Vindicated" (St. Louis: William Harvey Miner, 1921), JFM, Lovejoy Library.

40. McDermott, "Laclède and the Chouteaus"; Foley and C. David Rice, *The First Chouteaus*, 1–2.

himself in the fur trade.[41] A few years later, he assumed the rank of colonel in the Louisiana regiment and participated in the defense of Louisiana during the French and Indian War. While engaged in military exercises, Maxent also pursued his mercantile dreams and discovered that the two spheres of endeavor had carryover benefits.

On July 6, 1763, in recognition for service against the British and the Chickasaw Indians, Maxent received an exclusive trading patent from the French government of Louisiana, the first man to obtain sole rights to trade with the Indian tribes of the Missouri River and the Mississippi River, from the Illinois Country to the mouth of the St. Peters, or Minnesota, River. Maxent invited Laclède to join him in business, and together, the two formed the firm of Maxent, Laclède, and Company, in which Laclède, the junior partner in age, resources, and experience, held 25 percent ownership.[42] United by ambition, the French traders embarked on a vast commercial enterprise. Their partnership, in concert with geopolitical events beyond either man's control, lay the basis for the founding of St. Louis. In granting Maxent a monopoly over the Indian trade on the Missouri, France's newly appointed director-general of Louisiana, Jean-Jacques-Blaise D'Abbadie, who arrived in June 1763 to serve as interim director, was making a strategic move to bolster the financial situation of the colony.[43] Previously, trade had flowed through local commandants, military men who sometimes interfered with traders and enriched themselves to the detriment of the crown's coffers. By removing governmental oversight from commercial enterprises, D'Abbadie was following the example of predecessors who had granted exclusive trading rights elsewhere. In a recent essay, J. Frederick Fausz argued that the "real mastermind" behind St. Louis's founding was not D'Abbadie but Louis Billouart, comte de Kerlérec, the man who preceded him as governor-general in Louisiana, serving in that post from 1753-1763; Kerlérec made an initial grant to Maxent, which D'Abbadie reconfirmed formally on taking office.[44] D'Abbadie also made tentative grants in a number of districts, including Arkansas and the *pays des Illinois*, in hopes that awarding traders with "an exclusive privilege for the Commerce and Trade of the Savages" would stimulate the overall economy.[45] Such monopolies proved

41. Coleman, *Gilbert Antoine de St. Maxent*, 16–17.

42. Coleman, *Gilbert Antoine de St. Maxent*; Foley, *A History of Missouri*, 1: 16.

43. McDermott, "The Exclusive Trade Privilege of Maxent, Laclède, and Company," 274; Nasatir, *Before Lewis and Clark* (hereafter *BLC*), 1: 60.

44. Fausz, "Founding St. Louis," 10–13.

45. Duc de Choiseul to D'Abbadie, January 18, 1765, quoted in McDermott, "The Exclusive Trade Privilege of Maxent, Laclède, and Company," 274.

far from popular, with merchants in New Orleans later denouncing both D'Abbadie's administration and his method of according exclusive trading rights when there was supposed to be free trade.[46]

Given that the company had unparalleled authority to trade with the Indian nations of the Missouri River basin, locating a trading post in closer proximity to them was the first order of business. Accordingly, after Maxent and Laclède had assembled goods to send upriver, Laclède set off to seek better access to the indigenous peoples who would produce and trade furs in the continent's interior. With Maxent in place in New Orleans, Laclède journeyed northward at the head of a sizeable contingent of men and material. Parting company from Marie Thérèse and the children must have been difficult. The journey was dangerous, the outcome unpredictable, and the separation would last for months at least. At the time, the couple's three children were quite young; their eldest, Pierre, was not yet six.[47] As Laclède planned the trip, Marie Thérèse became pregnant again. Taking this young family and a pregnant partner made no sense on his first journey upriver. However, one of Marie Thérèse's children did accompany Laclède. Just in his teens, Auguste Chouteau became his de facto stepfather's trusted aide and companion.

More than Laclède's sidekick, Chouteau proved to be future generations' most important source of information about Laclède's journey and the establishment of St. Louis. What Laclède may have thought and said comes to us from the founding narrative of St. Louis written by Auguste Chouteau, and still the key source for reconstructing what happened in 1763 and 1764. This document, penned long after the events it describes, is only a fragment of a longer memoir recorded by Chouteau. Sadly, the fuller text—apparently a more complete early history of the city—was destroyed in a fire.[48] Another tantalizing and no-longer-extant source is from Laclède, who kept a journal that has since been lost.[49] While we are fortunate to have even Chouteau's partial narrative of the founding, using it presents the historian

---

46. Twenty-two merchants signed a June 6, 1764, statement critical of D'Abbadie. *BLC,* 1: 60–61.

47. Cunningham and Blythe, *The Founding Family of St. Louis,* 59.

48. "Chouteau's Journal of the Founding of St. Louis," 336; Auguste Chouteau, "Narrative of the Settlement of St. Louis." An updated translation of the narrative appears in Gregory Ames, ed., *Auguste Chouteau's Journal: Memory, Mythmaking and History in the Heritage of New France* (forthcoming). The latter will be cited when the translation seems more apt than that offered in earlier versions.

49. Charles E. Peterson, *Colonial St. Louis;* Hunt's Minutes, April 18, 1825 (typescript, Missouri History Museum Archives, hereafter MHMA), Chouteau, "Narrative of the Settlement of St. Louis"; Hunt's Minutes, November 16, 1825, 4 (St. Louis, 1911), 349–66; McDermott, "The Exclusive Trade Privilege of Maxent, Laclède and Company."

with challenges. The recollections of a fourteen-year-old boy, written down much later, undoubtedly have gaps and distortions. The tone and direct quotations ascribed to Laclède and other actors, particularly the Missouri Indians, are difficult to accept at face value. Nonetheless, a careful reading of what Chouteau recalled, placed in the context of other contemporary sources, allows for some reconstruction of what transpired as well as some understanding of how the French founders wished to portray their own actions and conduct.[50] In St. Louis, as in so many other places, framing the story to clarify moments of historical importance has been a practice since the community's earliest days. Clearly, the journey upriver to found a new trading post, begun in the sweltering heat of summer, was one such drama.

Together, in early August 1763, Laclède and Chouteau left New Orleans to undertake the arduous 700-mile journey up the Mississippi River, carrying with them provisions and goods for the Indian trade. Traveling on narrow vessels forty-five to seventy-five feet long, they could have transported an enormous amount of goods.[51] John Francis McDermott, an important historian of early St. Louis, speculated that Laclède's boat might have been the one he owned at the time of his death: fifty feet long, ten feet wide, capable of carrying thirty to fifty tons of cargo, and requiring a crew of at least twenty to operate; there is no record of him owning another.[52] Although the keelboats were pointed at both ends and had shallow drafts that made them maneuverable, moving such encumbered vessels upstream could be terribly difficult.[53] Rowers formed an important part of the crew. Besides rowing, the means of propulsion included poling, wherein the crew pulled a vessel upstream by standing near the front of the boat, sinking a pole into the river's muddy bottom, walking to the rear of the boat, and then repeating the action; they might also have inched a vessel northward by cordelling, or towing, it from the shore with ropes.[54] Given that the boat's advance depended literally on manpower when the winds were unfavorable for sails, it is not surprising that progress was measured in painfully small increments of several miles per day. Added to the current—six to seven miles per hour during the spring—the river's twisting

50. An excellent example of foregrounding the indigenous perspective is DuVal's *The Native Ground.*

51. Coleman, *Gilbert Antoine de St. Maxent,* 25.

52. McDermott, "Myths and Realities Concerning the Founding of St. Louis," 9.

53. F. Terry Norris, "Where Did the Villages Go?: Steamboats, Deforestation, and Archaeological Loss in the Mississippi Valley," in Hurley, ed., *Common Fields,* 76–77; William J. Peterson, *Steamboating on the Upper Mississippi,* 50–52.

54. A harrowing description of keelboat travel appears in Denny, "Running the Lower Missouri River Gauntlet," 283–313.

course could make navigation a nightmare. Although traveling was easier for one reason in late summer, when the annual floodwaters had dropped and the current slowed, it was more difficult in another sense. Islands, sandbanks, and shoals, some miles around, appeared as the river level fell and made "the voyage more dangerous, longer, and less expeditious."[55] Exposed on the slow-moving vessels, the passengers had plenty of time to think about their vulnerability.

Different species of mammals and fish added to the unfamiliarity and sense of danger. An early explorer and missionary on the Mississippi in the 1670s, Father Jacques Marquette, described how "from time to time [they] came upon monstrous fish, one of which struck [their] canoe with such violence that [he] Thought that it was a great tree, about to break the Canoe into pieces." Marquette's description of a water "monster with the head of a tiger, a sharp nose Like That of a wildcat, with whiskers and straight, Erect ears" sounds like a catfish.[56] (In 2005, an Illinois man caught a 58-inch long, 124-pound catfish just north of St. Louis).[57] Laclède probably saw other strange creatures of the region: charcoal-eyed raccoons with distinctive ringed tails, pungent skunk, rodent-like possum, alligator garfish with razor sharp teeth, venomous water moccasins, and bison.

The Mississippi River, the dominant waterway of the Louisiana colony, shaped the land and the journey. In many places, the Mississippi was lined with long grasses, canes, and reeds, which trapped the wood, leaves, and "vast quantities of slimy mud" carried by the annual floods. As a result, the riverbanks were built up higher than the interior landscape and prevented floodwaters from easily returning to the main channel. Below the confluence with the Missouri River, the "gentle and clear" Mississippi became brown with silt. One traveler measured how "remarkably muddy" the river was by filling "a half-pint tumbler with it." After it settled, the water contained "a sediment of two inches of slime." Nonetheless, he reported, the water was both wholesome and tasty, cool even in the hottest weather, so refreshing that the rowers "drink of it when they are in the strongest perspiration, and never received any bad effects from it." Working their way north in August, Laclède, Chouteau, and their fellow travelers must have appreciated the cold, thirst-quenching river as they

---

55. Pittman, *The Present State of the European Settlements*, 7.

56. Jacques Marquette, "Voyages du P. Jacques Marquette, 1673–1675," in Thwaites, ed., *The Jesuit Relations and Allied Documents*, vol. 59, *Lower Canada, Illinois, Ottwas, 1667–1669*, 107.

57. "DOA catfish swimming with the fishes," http://www.msnbc.msn.com/id/7978360/ (accessed June 4, 2008). A 646-pound Mekong River catfish was caught a few weeks later in Thailand http://www.msnbc.msn.com/id/8404622/ (accessed June 4, 2008).

endured the excessive heat and violent thunderstorms that typified late summer along the river. As the journey continued into the fall, Laclède and his party no doubt faced their share of foul weather.[58]

As they moved slowly up the Mississippi, the travelers occasionally glimpsed signs of human habitation. About one-fourth of the way into their journey, they passed Natchez, a hilltop fort at a distance from the river, with meadows, hills, and fruit trees surrounding the village. Some of the bloodiest conflicts between Europeans and the Natchez Indians who had inhabited the region for centuries took place in the area in the late 1720s and early 1730s. When low, the river at this point still measured over 1,800 feet wide. Far to the north, roughly halfway through their journey, they passed near the Arkansas Post, several miles upstream on the Arkansas River, close to its confluence with the Mississippi. If they stopped, they would have seen the post's distinctive appearance. For protection against the river's floodwaters, the fort and other buildings were all raised six feet off the ground. Going in and out of these structures, no one could have remained unaware of the river's force and destructive powers. Outside of the fort stood fewer than ten homes, occupied by families who subsisted more by hunting than by farming. Again, the river was key; sandy soil and the dangers of flooding made tilling the soil impractical. Nearby, hundreds of warriors of the Arkansas tribe lived, divided into three villages, their presence a strong reminder to newcomers that they were encroaching on lands long settled.[59]

Farther to the north, Laclède, Chouteau, and the rest of their party reached the Illinois Country settlements of the Mississippi's eastern shore, villages inhabited by French farmers and traders and Jesuit missionaries. Kaskaskia was the next settlement in their course, a well-situated village notable for the Jesuit mission there, with cultivated lands, cattle, and a brewery, as well as a church, a house for the missionaries, a small chapel, and other stone dwellings. A large wooden fort stood on the summit of a high rock opposite to the village.[60] Fortifications served multiple purposes, enabling the French to patrol the river and control access to indigenous trade and markets. Close to Kaskaskia on the west bank of the river was Ste. Genevieve, the only major French settlement on that shore in Upper Louisiana. Established sometime in the mid-eighteenth century—there is no evidence of its exact date of founding—the village was a small,

58. Pittman, *The Present State of the European Settlements*, 3–5, 51.
59. Ibid., 37–38, liv.
60. Ibid., 42–43.

French-speaking outpost of the empire, its inhabitants drawn from France, Canada, and the other side of the Mississippi.[61] The site possessed several appealing attributes: proximity to a salt spring used for both personal consumption and trade, fertile soil for farming, and a lead mine. A water mill, for processing both corn and wood planks, belonged to the village's leading resident, François Vallé.[62]

When he arrived in Ste. Genevieve, many weeks into his journey, Laclède found nothing that satisfied his commercial needs. The village did not offer a single building large enough to store the trade goods he had brought with him. Worse, because he certainly could have constructed a sizeable warehouse, the location of the village was ill-suited to his needs. Distant from the mouth of the Missouri, Ste. Genevieve was situated on low-lying lands along the Mississippi River's edge. One French visitor described the site in unflattering terms, suggesting it would have been healthier and more agreeable if the villagers, instead of building at the foot of the hill, had built "on the hill itself."[63] "Unhealthy" was Laclède and Chouteau's pronouncement.[64] (These concerns about Ste. Genevieve's position proved prescient; in 1785, the year of the floods—*l'année des grandes eaux*—the village was inundated and damaged so severely that residents relocated the entire settlement to higher ground.) During his brief stay in Ste. Genevieve, Laclède likely sought out Vallé, the de facto head of the community, or other residents for information about what lay upstream. (Although Vallé was known for both his hospitality and his authority, there is no evidence that the two met at this time; later, however, they knew each other well enough for Vallé to ask Laclède to witness his will.)[65]

Above all, Laclède wanted to identify and secure a location that would suit a trading post. His choices were not unlimited, however. He sought proximity to the Missouri River—still distant at Ste. Genevieve—and all the potential indigenous consumers that lived in its vast basin. He also hoped to preclude British interference; with the British destined to take over the east bank of the river with the 1763 peace treaty, the closer Laclède could be to the Missouri's mouth, the better. In the meantime, learning of Laclède's storage problems, the commandment of Fort Chartres, the French outpost on the eastern bank of the Mississippi a few miles to the north, sent an officer to tell Laclède that he had space to accommodate the

61. See Ekberg's masterful study, *Colonial Ste. Genevieve.*
62. Pittman, *The Present State of the European Settlements,* 50.
63. Perrin du Lac, *Voyage dans les Deux Louisianes,* 167.
64. Chouteau, "Narrative of the Settlement of St. Louis," 48.
65. On Vallé's leadership role in Ste. Genevieve, see Ekberg, *François Vallé and His World.*

goods at the fort. "Necessity," wrote his stepson Auguste, made Laclède accept the "generous offer."[66]

Continuing northward, Laclède and his party traveled on to St. Anne de Fort Chartres, arriving there on November 3, three months since their departure from New Orleans. (The reverse journey, traveling with the river's current, could take as little as three weeks.)[67] As the seat of French authority—both military and civil—in the Illinois Country, Fort Chartres was an important installation. An irregular quadrangle built of stone, it included two barracks, the commandant's and commissary's houses, a prison, a bakery, a powder magazine, a storehouse, and a guardhouse. It was, according to one visitor, "generally allowed that this is the most commodious and best built fort in North America." Like many of the structures in the region, Fort Chartres stood close to the Mississippi River, indeed too close, some feared. Although constructed some distance from the river's banks, the fort, due to shifts in the river's course, was soon near the water's edge; the original fort of the late 1710s was reconstructed farther from the river in the 1720s, and a third fort was built in the 1750s. The Mississippi was a constant threat. "The bank of the Mississippi, next the fort," wrote a visitor, "is continually falling in, being worn away by the current." When new construction began in 1756, the fort was a half-mile from the river's edge; within a decade, that distance had dwindled to "but eighty paces."[68]

Comfortably settled in the village at Fort Chartres, Laclède quickly got down to business. Only three days after arriving, Laclède joined other villagers after Sunday mass to attend an auction of the property of the Jesuits, who were being forced to decamp. After decades as missionaries in the Illinois Country, they found themselves targeted by a decree issued in July 1763 that accused them of self-interest, declared their constitution "hostile to royal authority," forbade members to wear their traditional garb, and further dictated that all their property was to be seized and sold at auction.[69] The decree of banishment arrived at Fort Chartres on September 23.[70] Stationed in Kaskaskia for many years, the Jesuits left the Illinois country in late November 1763, heading for New Orleans with forty slaves.[71] Coming nearly at the moment the order's seized property was put

66. Chouteau, "Narrative of the Settlement of St. Louis," 47.

67. Coleman, *Gilbert Antoine de St. Maxent*, 26.

68. Pittman, *The Present State of the European Settlements*, 45–46.

69. "Banishment of the Jesuits," July 9, 1763, in Alvord and Carter, eds., *The Critical Period, 1763–1765*, 67–69.

70. Lahey, "The Catholic Church on the Frontier of Spanish Illinois," 16; Alvord, *The Illinois Country*, 268.

71. Hodes, *Beyond the Frontier*, 71.

up for sale, Laclède bid on a house and other items but did not make the final purchase.[72] He did, however, invest in land and buildings for his firm later that month, purchasing a house and barn as well as livestock from a French private, Jean Gerardin. That house and its outbuildings were situated in the main street of the village, close to the church.[73] The property included a two-room house, a shed, a barn, and a pigeon house, all encircled by a cedar post fence. Seventeen cattle, twenty hogs, 150 fowls, and a large amount of tobacco rounded out the property.[74]

With the east bank of the Mississippi destined for eventual transfer to the British, Laclède's setup at Fort Chartres was only a temporary solution. During the fall and winter of 1763, the situation in Upper Louisiana was far from settled. It was clear to everyone that with the end of the French and Indian War, France had lost control of its North American empire. French Canada and all lands east of the Mississippi were now claimed by the British. Wasting no time, Laclède set out "to seek a more advantageous site," leaving with Auguste Chouteau in December to explore the territory on the west bank of the great river.[75] Weather at that time of year could vary widely, with beautifully clear, bright days alternating with freezing rain, sleet, and snow, with temperatures typically averaging in the low 30s but sometimes much colder. In the depths of winter, ice could choke the Mississippi and make navigation difficult, dangerous, or altogether impossible until the spring thaw.

As Laclède was making his plans for the future, investigating different locations on the western banks of the Mississippi, across the river at Fort Chartres, the military commander, Captain Pierre-Joseph Noyen de Villiers, was making his own preparations for leaving the area; he knew that French withdrawal from the region was imminent. The French residents of the area were ambivalent, many disinclined to remain and become subjects of a British, Protestant king, but equally unwilling to abandon a region they had called home for most or all of their lives. Some packed up and sailed for New Orleans, while others bided their time, undecided as to the next step. Further complicating matters but unbeknownst to Laclède

---

72. Alvord and Carter, *The Critical Period, 1763–1767,* 126–31.

73. September 8, 1766, deed of sale from Thomas Smallman to Edward Code, regarding a house "late in the Occupation of Monsr La Cled, with the Outhouses, Land, and all the appurtenances thereunto belonging, as they now stand, for and in consideration of the Sum of Six hundred Dollars." In Alvord and Carter, eds., *The New Regime, 1765–1767,* 372; Mazrim, "The Ghost Horse Site"; e-mail communication May 20, 2010; excerpt from Mazrim, *At Home in the Illinois Country* (courtesy of the author).

74. Laclède purchase, November 19, 1763, in Peterson, *Colonial St. Louis,* preface; Brown and Dean, eds., *The Village of Chartres in Colonial Illinois,* 788–90.

75. Chouteau, "Narrative of the Settlement of St. Louis," 48.

when he began his trek north, lands west of the Mississippi were no longer French possessions either.

Secret negotiations in Europe between France and its ally Spain had profoundly altered the status of Louisiana. To avoid all of its North American territory falling into British hands and to urge its ally Spain to agree to peace, the French had decided to cede lands west of the Mississippi to Spain. Under the terms of the Treaty of Fontainebleau, a secret pact of 1762, New Orleans and the rest of France's Louisiana territory fell under the authority of Spain's King Carlos III, a Catholic monarch and Bourbon cousin of Louis XV, whose losses elsewhere during the war, namely Florida, were thus somewhat recompensed.[76] As a result, the francophone residents of both Lower and Upper Louisiana became subjects of a foreign prince, and the transition proved far from easy for the inhabitants of *le pays des Illinois*. France's decision to cede vast territories to Spain at the war's end, rather than risk losing them to Great Britain, its ancient and bitter enemy, left its colonists in a political twilight zone, uncertain as to where their loyalties, identities, and economic opportunities lay in both the immediate and long-term future. Ultimately, the situation sparked a rebellion in New Orleans against the Spanish, a short-lived and ultimately unsuccessful attempt to stave off Spanish occupation. Several colonists were executed for treason.

With these international political currents in the background, Laclède concentrated on the task at hand, exploring the area and closely examining the west bank south of the confluence of the Missouri and Mississippi rivers, from Fort Chartres to the Missouri. Given his trading ambitions, he was willing to move his business and his family to an uninhabited spot if it met his requirements; settled institutions, cultural comforts, and neighbors all were secondary considerations. He sought, above all, to form "an establishment suitable for his commerce," a site with the greatest potential for reaching the peoples accessible via the Missouri, a river whose extent was as yet not fully known by Europeans.[77]

Ten miles south of the rivers' confluence and sixty miles north of Fort Chartres, Laclède saw what he wanted. According to Chouteau's version, Laclède "was delighted to see the situation" and "did not hesitate a moment" to propose building there, persuaded by "the beauty of the site" and "all the advantages" conducive to settlement that it seemed to possess. Located well above the river's flow, the spot Laclède selected occupied one of the most beautiful and healthy positions along the banks of the Mississippi, in the view

76. See Foley, *History of Missouri,* 1: 16.
77. Chouteau, "Narrative of the Settlement of St. Louis," 48.

of one later visitor.[78] An early historian of the city wrote in similarly glowing terms about the advantages of elevation and a limestone shore: "Such situations are very rare, as the Mississippi is almost universally bounded either by high perpendicular rocks or loose alluvial soil, the latter of which is in continual danger of being washed away by the annual floods."[79] Limestone outcroppings, heavily timbered land, and a plateau uninterrupted by ravines promised the ideal combination of elevation, abundant building materials, and flat land needed to construct a new trading post.[80]

Laclède marked some trees with an ax and gave his companion some instructions. As his young lieutenant Auguste recalled in later years, Laclède delivered his orders authoritatively: "'Chouteau, come here as soon as navigation opens. Have this place cleared to make our settlement, after the plan I shall give you." After making this pronouncement, Laclède hurried back to Fort Chartres, Chouteau in tow, where "with some enthusiasm" he reputedly described to the officers the location "where he was going to establish a settlement," declaring it might become "one of the finest cities in America" because of the many advantages of the site.[81] If Chouteau's recollections are accurate, Laclède may have enlarged his ambitions as he gauged the situation in the Illinois Country. No longer intent just on establishing a post for the fur trade under the auspices of Maxent, Laclède, and Company, he had begun to think about something bigger, a new community surrounding the post, with a population of farmers from across the river joining the traders to build a prosperous settlement.

With this propitious site selected, Laclède spent the rest of the winter procuring "everything necessary for the settlement—many men, provisions, tools," and making other necessary arrangements. Of these, men to provide the labor for constructing the new post were perhaps the most important. Accordingly, Laclède made arrangements to hire Illinois residents, many of them with crucial skills for a new settlement. Three carpenters—François Dellin, Joseph Mainville, and Antoine Pichet—were among the initial group of thirty men enlisted by Laclède to begin work on the site. Eight farmers, three millers, five traders, a gunsmith, a blacksmith, and a choir chorister rounded out the work party; several men with no noted occupations signed up to work on the new post as well.[82]

78. Perrin du Lac, *Voyage dans les Deux Louisianes*, 188.

79. John Paxton, "Notes on St. Louis," May 26, 1821, in McDermott, ed., *Early Histories*, 63.

80. Peterson, *Colonial St. Louis*, 3; Peterson also cites Hunt's Minutes, July 29, 1825, testimony of Baptiste Riviere.

81. *Auguste Chouteau's Journal*, 4.

82. Ibid.; Frederic L. Billon, *Annals of St. Louis*, 17–18.

When the river became navigable in early February, Laclède had a boat fitted out and sent Chouteau and thirty men back to the spot he had selected in the fall. Once again, his directions were clear. According to Chouteau's recollections, Laclède told him to land where they had marked the trees, clear the land, and "build a large shed to store the provisions and the tools, and some small cabins to lodge the men." After completing their sixty-mile journey, Chouteau and the others arrived at the site on February 15 and began to clear the land for the new settlement on February 16. The shed and cabins went up quickly, with a temporary storehouse for goods one of the first buildings constructed.[83]

Only after clearing for the new settlement had begun did Laclède request formal permission to establish the post. In March, Fort Chartres' commandant reported to Governor D'Abbadie that Laclède had presented to him "a request asking for permission to form a settlement on the other side of the river." According to Neyon de Villiers' account, Laclède indicated that he had already obtained the governor's "verbal agreement to do so at the place he deems most suitable." With that authorization, Laclède had "already decided upon a site, and consequently he has started clearing the area." At this point, the commandant could have disappointed Laclède by rejecting his petition. Instead, he wrote, "I merely told him that he could continue."[84] In turn, the officer informed Louisiana's governor of the newcomer's plans.

Several weeks later, in early April, Laclède rejoined Chouteau and the work crew and dubbed the new settlement St. Louis, in honor of the king, Louis XV, "whose subject he expected to remain, for a long time," and more precisely for the king's patron saint, Louis IX. As Chouteau recalled, Laclède "never imagined he was a subject of the King of Spain." Clearing and building continued throughout the spring, with storage sheds and cabins already completed by the time Laclède arrived. Busying himself with plans for the future, Laclède "fixed the place where he wished to build his house" and "laid a plan of the village which he wished to found," ordering Chouteau "to follow the plan exactly" in his absence. Although he likely wished to remain to supervise the construction himself, he had to return to Fort Chartres "to remove the goods that he had in the fort, before the arrival

83. Chouteau, "Narrative of the Settlement of St. Louis," 48–49. Quotation to *Auguste Chouteau's Journal,* 5 (unpublished manuscript). Ames notes that the controversy over Chouteau's arrival date stemmed from misreadings of Chouteau's penmanship and conflicting accounts, *Auguste Chouteau's Journal,* 26 (unpublished manuscript).

84. Pierre-Joseph Neyon de Villiers to Jean-Jacques Blaise D'Abbadie, March 13, 1764, Favrot Collection, Tulane University Library, New Orleans, LOUISiana Digital Library website, http://louisdl.louislibraries.org/ (accessed May 1, 2008).

of the English, who were expected every day to take possession of it." [85] Soon, French colonists from Illinois began to join the infant village. Rather than live under English rule, they were willing to abandon the farms they had improved to live on the western side of the Mississippi, unaware that the territory Laclède was promoting for their relocation had passed into Spanish hands.

While the French presence in St. Louis grew, that across the river declined rapidly. Receiving his orders to vacate the garrison at Fort Chartres in April 1764, Neyon de Villiers sailed for New Orleans several weeks later, on June 15, taking with him six officers and sixty-three of the soldiers under his command. Assuming control of the fort, Captain Louis St. Ange de Bellerive, formerly the commander at Post Vincennes, remained behind with a reduced force of twenty officers and soldiers to deal with the British when they arrived to take charge of their new possession.[86] Neyon de Villiers' convoy descending the river must have been an impressive sight, including twenty-one bateaux and seven large dugout canoes, known as pirogues; they arrived in New Orleans on July 2.[87] Several dozen French colonists decided to join the exodus south, unwilling to remain under British rule and uninterested in Laclède's new trading post.[88]

Back at Fort Chartres, Laclède had tried to dissuade departing colonists from leaving, doing "everything possible to keep them from going down." Presenting himself as acting without self-interest, he claimed he was motivated only by "humanity." Laclède told the colonists that the English government was "not so terrible" as portrayed and that indeed he had a favorable opinion of it. If, due to "false prejudices," they did not wish to stay to be ruled by the British, he urged them to consider going to his new settlement. According to Chouteau, Laclède promised to facilitate the journey of those who joined him and to assist with the transportation of their personal effects. With the trip only nineteen leagues "by a good road," he thought conducting livestock would be quite easy. While some colonists remained unmoved, others thought the new settlement offered them the best chance for the future. Families who accepted Laclède's offer and promises, numbering dozens of people, quickly sought out wagons for their journeys. Some partly demolished their homes to make building new ones easier, taking "floors, the windows and door

85. Chouteau, "Narrative of the Settlement of St. Louis," 49.
86. Billon, *Annals of St. Louis*, 15; Foley and C. David Rice, *The First Chouteaus*, 6.
87. Journal of Governor D'Abbadie, in Alvord and Carter, *The Critical Period, 1763–1767*, 189.
88. Foley, *History of Missouri*, 1: 18.

frames, and everything else they could carry to the places where they believed they could settle."[89]

As the village of Fort Chartres was becoming "totally deserted" except for the garrison and a few government employees, St. Louis was being rapidly peopled by a ready-made, conveniently close supply of French farmers and craftsmen. Already possessed of knowledge and experience of the local environment, they knew the climate, the soils, and the crops that thrived; such knowledge held the promise of self-sufficiency. Perhaps even more important for a future trading center, the settlers knew the indigenous inhabitants of the area and had experience interacting with them. In short, the French colonists from Illinois were the kind of people useful to a new settlement far removed from sources of supplies and large population centers. St. Louis, it seemed likely, had a very good chance of becoming a going concern very rapidly. But before anyone could pronounce it a success, the foundations of the new village were rocked, not by the repercussions of international political intrigue and European warfare, but by a threat closer to home.

89. Chouteau, "Narrative of the Settlement of St. Louis," 53–54; *Auguste Chouteau's Journal,* 13, 14, 16 (unpublished manuscript).

Chapter 2

Settling "Paincourt"

INDIANS, THE FUR TRADE, AND FARMS

With French colonists from Illinois rapidly populating the post in the spring and summer of 1764, St. Louis was off to a good start. But its future success was far from determined. Over the course of the next few years, it became clear that international political conflicts would keep British, French, and Spanish colonists and officials at odds. Throughout the region, competition for indigenous allies and trading partners complicated diplomacy and created tensions. Adding to the unsettled state of affairs, Pontiac's War, an Indian uprising, broke out in 1763. Fueled by anti-English sentiment, Pontiac's Rebellion, as it was also known, raised the prospect of a pan-Indian alliance of many tribes united against colonizers and occupiers. East of the Mississippi—in the Great Lakes region, the Ohio River Valley, and just across the river in Illinois—Pontiac was an alarming presence for European colonists.[1] In the absence of tensions with allied tribes, what sort of a future St. Louis would have was unclear: would it grow into a center of the fur trade dominated by merchants and roving trappers, or would it develop into an agricultural community populated by sedentary tillers of the soil? Before the village was firmly established, an incident took place that upset the new French inhabitants of St. Louis and nearly derailed the settlement. The encounter, involving Missouri Indians, Chouteau, and Laclède, exposed the weakness of European authority along the Mississippi

---

1. See Dowd, *War under Heaven;* Carl A. Brasseaux and Michael J. Leblanc, "Franco-Indian Diplomacy in the Mississippi Valley 1754–1763: Prelude to Pontiac's Uprising?" in Conrad, ed., *The French Experience in Louisiana,* 333–44.

River and underscored the dependence of the colonizers on the actions and decisions of the region's native inhabitants.

In the nineteenth century, St. Louisans confined themselves both physically and psychologically to a city of limited size by separating permanently from surrounding St. Louis County. In the earlier colonial period, however, St. Louis must be considered as either a place without borders or with multiple and overlapping cultural, political, and geographic borders. Tied to a vast territory as a center of commercial exchange, it was a global village. St. Louisans were at once isolated—distant from European seats of power—and part of vast continental and trans-Atlantic networks of trade and migration. As a British observer asserted, the region's numerous and intersecting rivers, lakes, and creeks lay the basis for the greatest means of interior communication and foreign intercourse "yet discover'd in the known World."[2] The village's inhabitants resided in Upper Louisiana, the name used to distinguish the area from Lower Louisiana; New Orleans was the capital of all of Louisiana, the seat of the colony's government. St. Louisans lived upon the banks of the mighty Mississippi, situated at the shifting crossroads of European empires, in a region fully inhabited by indigenous peoples, primarily the Missouri, Osage, and Kansas on the western side of the river and the Kaskaskia, Michigamea, Cahokia, and Peoria on the eastern side. Many of the traits that made the area appealing to Indians over previous millennia were the same ones that attracted Europeans in the eighteenth century.

The immediate vicinity of St. Louis was the ancient home of the Mississippian Indians. Long before the French arrived, those whom archaeologists refer to as the Mound Builders had practiced intensive agriculture and developed vast urban centers. Around Cahokia, just across the Mississippi River from St. Louis, had stood the largest pre-contact indigenous community north of Mexico City, with ten to twenty thousand inhabitants at its height. The many rivers in the region, as well as climatic and glacial changes that took place over millennia, had created a well-watered, fertile terrain, suitable to large-scale agricultural endeavors, in particular maize cultivation. For hundreds of years, Indians around Cahokia used fire to clear the land, put increasing amounts of acreage under tillage, and built over a hundred massive earthen mounds. The largest of these, Monks

2. Lord Shelburne, September 11, 1767, in Alvord and Carter, eds., *Trade and Politics,* 20–21.

Mound, still stands and contains over 22 million cubic feet of dirt that the Mound Builders moved to construct it. Well before the French arrived in the territory, these agrarian people had largely abandoned Cahokia and shifted away from their primary emphasis on farming. For reasons not entirely clear, but which may have included the cultivation of different crops such as new varieties of corn and beans or the movement of game that they hunted for food—bison had migrated further east—the large population of the area had dispersed.[3]

Traces of this much older indigenous occupation of the region were also apparent on the western banks of the Mississippi River, where twenty-six earthen mounds, constructed between 800 and 1200 A.D., dotted the landscape in the area that became St. Louis. Their presence earned St. Louis one of its nicknames: "Mound City."[4] Although Chouteau makes no mention in his founding narrative of this indigenous imprint on the site, early French residents noted and named some of the mounds, including a huge one called *La Grange de Terre*, the earth barn, just beyond the northern outskirts of the village.[5] Over the course of the nineteenth century, despite some efforts to enclose and preserve several of the mounds as a city park, these monumental reminders of the former inhabitants were razed, the earth carted away by railroad companies for landfill.[6] St. Louisians in that period seemed to have equal disregard for preserving either the colonial or the ancient past. One of the few surviving structures, named Sugar Loaf Mound by eighteenth-century residents for its shape, lies just off Highway 55, near a freeway ramp close to the Mississippi River.[7]

In addition to the massive footprint of earthen construction left by the Mound Builders on the landscape, early European descriptions of the area suggest that the indigenous population had in the more recent past used fire as a tool to manipulate the physical environment. Indians burned away

3. Details in this paragraph are drawn from William R. Iseminger, "Culture and Environment in the American Bottom: The Rise and Fall of Cahokia Mounds," in Hurley, *Common Fields*, 38–57.

4. Walter Schroeder, "Environmental Setting of St. Louis," 27; Iseminger, "Rise and Fall of Cahokia Mounds," 47, 57; both in Hurley, *Common Fields*.

5. Schroeder, "Environmental Setting of St. Louis," 27; Primm, *Lion of the Valley*, 1. See also Peterson, *Colonial St. Louis*, 19, who cites Hunt's Minutes, July 10, 1825, testimony of Baptiste Riviere, and notes that *La Grange de Terre* was also sometimes referred to as *la butte* or *la monticule*, or "mound." See also Kelly, "The Preservation of the East St. Louis Mound Group"; Sailor, "Thomas Easterly's Big Mound Daguerreotypes"; Smit, "Old Broadway, a Forgotten Street, and Its Park of Mounds."

6. Kilgo, *Likeness and Landscape*, 201–8, 224–27.

7. Sugar Loaf Mound, with a platform 141' x 109', is at Ohio Avenue near the 4500 South Broadway exit. See Fox, *Where We Live*, 29. In 2009, the Osage tribe of Oklahoma completed purchase of the site, with plans to tear down the house and build an interpretive center. See *St. Louis Post-Dispatch*, August 3, 2009.

"La Grange de Terre." Big Mound. Watercolor and ink on paper by Anna Maria Von Phul, 1818, Missouri History Museum, St. Louis.

dense undergrowth, increasing the grasses sought by grazing animals, thereby contributing both to the proliferation of large animals and the ease of their hunting. Although the extent to which Indians engaged in this practice is difficult to measure, it is clear that Europeans registered the results. One early history of St. Louis noted that the site "presented the aspect of a beautiful prairie, but already giving the promise of a renewed luxurious vegetation." Since the arrival of Europeans, wrote author Joseph Nicollet, "the annual fires [had been] kept out of the country." Nicollet's precise description supports the idea that Indian peoples in the area had used burning techniques to create a landscape conducive to particular plants and animals, a park-like setting suitable for game.[8] Indians' roles as custodians and creators of particular environments were not always acknowledged by French colonists. Long after the founding of St. Louis, Auguste Chouteau

8. Joseph Nicollet, "Sketch of the Early History of St. Louis," in McDermott, ed., *Early Histories,* 135–36. On the indigenous use of fire as an environmental tool, see Cronon, *Changes in the Land.*

inaccurately described the Indians of North America as "always [having] lived in a state of nature deriving their subsistence from the wild animals of the forest."[9] Chouteau's remark casts Indian peoples as both "uncivilized" and as part of nature, rather than as shapers of it; he did not recognize either the Indians' farming history in the region nor their intentional manipulation of the landscape. What Chouteau always acknowledged, with no awareness of the Indians' role in creating it, was the beauty of the landscape.

The key environmental factors that sustained the early, sedentary indigenous population at Cahokia—fertile soil and plentiful water—also drew Europeans. Even more, the changes in Indian agricultural and hunting practices that had contributed to the decline of Cahokia as a population center also made the region more attractive to European settlers. Coming with their own plans to exploit the natural resources and the human inhabitants of the region, colonists sought Indians who hunted and produced hides rather than Indian neighbors who exclusively farmed. The former were necessary to a flourishing fur trade, while the latter would have been an obstacle to colonists' ambitions. In the eyes of many European visitors, the most notable features of the Mississippi River valley were the fertility of the land, the mineral deposits, and the abundance of game, all of which promised wealth to those willing to work to secure it.

Over the course of the seventeenth and eighteenth centuries, decades of trading together had laid the basis for alliances, business endeavors, and friendships between various Indian nations and the French in the continent's interior, from the St. Lawrence River to the Great Lakes and the Ohio and Mississippi River valleys. Early in the eighteenth century, French newcomers and Missouri Indians had lived in proximity and harmony. The countryside of the Missouri Indians was, according to one visitor, the most beautiful in the world and full of wild animals.[10] In the 1720s, the French constructed a fort close to the Missouri village near the confluence of the Grand and Missouri Rivers in north central Missouri, in order to gain an advantage over Spanish competitors in the Indian trade.[11] (Spanish outposts in the southwest, the northernmost points of their American empire, were an ongoing source of concern for other European powers.) Although that

9. Auguste Chouteau, "Notes of Auguste Chouteau on the Boundaries of Various Indian Nations," 122.

10. Étienne Veniard de Bourgmont, "Exacte description de la Louisiane, de ses ports, terres, et rivières, et noms des nations sauvage qui l'occupent et des commerce et avantages que l'on peut tirer dans l'établissement d'une colonie," in Villiers du Terrage, La Découverte du Missouri, 60–61.

11. Chapman, "The Little Osage and Missouri Indian Village Sites"; Norall, Bourgmont; "Instructions donnés au sieur Bourgmont," 17 Janvier 1722, in Margry, Découvertes et Etablissements des Français, 6: 390.

venture was not a lasting one, subsequent decades had witnessed the development of webs of contact between various Indian tribes and the French
in the region. Missionary villages, forts, religious conversions, and inter-
marriages, along with the thriving fur trade, deepened the personal and
cultural ties between the peoples.[12]

The European presence, while a source of useful trade goods sought
after by Indians, signaled the onset of profound changes and disruption
for indigenous communities. As Indian peoples incorporated European
weapons into intertribal warfare, hostilities became deadlier. Exposure to
smallpox proved an ongoing nightmare, and the disease's devastation swept
across the continent.[13] As European colonists and then Americans grasped
ever more territory and moved relentlessly and violently westward, they
encroached on the indigenous inhabitants' lands, leading to vast migrations
of Indian peoples and new pressures on traditional territories and hunting
grounds. By the end of the eighteenth century, some Indian tribes had suffered such losses that their few remaining members had to unite with other
tribes to survive, and their nations ceased to exist independently. Thus,
for example, the survivors of a 1752 attack on a Cahokia and Michigamea
village in Illinois ultimately dispersed, joining the Peoria and Kaskaskia
Indians.[14] Other tribes faced both internal and external pressures.[15]

Decades before the Missouris faced the question of which other tribes
to join in order to survive, they played a critical role in the founding of
St. Louis. The first act of the drama took place on the eastern shores of the
river. In July 1764, Missouri Indians sought the aid of the French captain
Louis St. Ange de Bellerive, who had been left in charge of Fort Chartres
to await the arrival of the British after the commandant, Neyon de Villiers,
descended to New Orleans. "With their wives, children, arms, and baggage," the Missouris came to St. Ange's post, after having visited Cahokia,
seeking refuge from the Big Osages, the most powerful and feared people
in the region, with whom they were at war.[16] The Missouri Indians also

12. Ekberg and Pregaldin, "Marie Rouensa-8cate8a and the Foundations of French Illinois,"
146–60.

13. On the continental spread of the disease, see Fenn, *Pox Americana.*

14. Hauser, "The Fox Raid," 220, 224.

15. Similarly, in the 1790s, the greatly reduced Missouris joined with other Indians, notably the
Little Osage, who had been their allies, as well as the Kansas and the Oto; Foley, *History of Missouri,*
1: 5. A useful book on the role of the Osage is Din and Nasatir, *The Imperial Osages.*

16. After the Osage tribe split in the early eighteenth century into two groups, the Little Osages

requested that St. Ange endeavor to negotiate peace for them with their enemies. Unreceptive to their pleas, or perhaps unable to imagine how he—with his skeleton crew and limited resources—might achieve any kind of an agreement, St. Ange instead eventually "persuaded them to return to their villages in order to avoid a greater expense and to give peace to [the] inhabitants."[17] The Missouri had been at Fort Chartres almost a month, and St. Ange wanted them to move on. He was wrong, however, in assuming that they journeyed home. They headed north, but instead of returning directly to their village up the Missouri River, they stopped at the construction site of the new trading post at St. Louis.[18]

Barely in his mid-teens, Auguste Chouteau found his small group at the construction site overwhelmed by these unwelcome visitors. "There arrived among us," he recalled, ". . . all the Missouri nation—men, women and children." According to his memoir, which provides the only description of this episode, at least 150 warriors showed up, accompanied by their families. Although there is no other evidence to corroborate the words and actions that Chouteau attributed to the actors in this drama, the historian can tease out from his narrative the dynamics of the encounter from the European perspective and speculate cautiously about the Missouris' agenda, values, and influence. The Missouri Indians, it was clear to Chouteau, did not harbor "any evil intentions" toward the French work party, but were, in his eyes, problematic. Despite the fact that they "did not appear to have anything hostile in mind," he declared their presence a burden. According to his report, they made "constant demands for provisions," and he claimed that they stole tools.[19] The Missouris' requests for supplies were not at all extraordinary, given the long history of gift giving and reciprocity in trade in the area; gifts were expected and deployed to open and ease diplomatic and commercial negotiations. In 1764 St. Louis, however, Chouteau was simply neither prepared nor equipped to deal with Indian visitors or their demands.

These issues aside, Chouteau soon made an alarming discovery: the Missouris intended to reside permanently on the site he was overseeing. With

---

settled on the Missouri River near the Missouri Indians, while the Big Osages remained on the Osage River; Din and Nasatir, *The Imperial Osages,* 14.

17. St. Ange to D'Abbadie, August 12, 1764, in Alvord and Carter, *The Critical Period,* 292–93.

18. J. N. Nicollect reported that the Missouri Indians had arrived in St. Louis on October 10, 1764; see Nicollet, "Sketch of the Early History of St. Louis," in McDermott, ed., *Early Histories,* 138. An October arrival date, repeated by other scholars, is problematic, as Chouteau's narrative makes clear that he had to request that Laclède come from Fort Chartres, while Laclède was in residence as of September, when his family arrived.

19. Chouteau, "Narrative of the Settlement of St. Louis," 49–50; *Auguste Chouteau's Journal,* 6 (unpublished manuscript).

fewer than three dozen men under his supervision and a large party of Missouri Indians declaring their intentions to stop and settle there, the situation was challenging, to say the least. "They told us repeatedly," wrote Chouteau, "they wanted to form a village around the house we intended to build and that it would be the center." It is not surprising that "all this talk troubled" Chouteau "greatly." At this moment, when the colonizers found themselves colonized—or rather occupied by those who possessed the indisputable historic claim to the territory—many of the French who had recently moved from Illinois to St. Louis decided to leave. Crossing the river in the first place because they preferred not to live under British rule, these Illinois colonists had even less desire to live in a community where they would be vastly outnumbered by Missouri Indians. Decamping, they recrossed the Mississippi. The combination of the arrival of the Missouris and the departure of the French newcomers—and the latter especially—determined Chouteau to send for Laclède, then still at Fort Chartres, where he was concluding his business.[20]

While waiting for Laclède to arrive, Chouteau tried to make the best of the situation. He claimed that he employed the Indians in his construction effort, enlisting the women and children to help dig a basement for the main storehouse. During their stay, they dug most of the cellar "and carried the soil in wooden platters and baskets, which they bore upon their heads." Thus, indigenous labor—and perhaps Indian technology in the form of baskets and wooden implements—literally helped build St. Louis. For their exertions, Chouteau paid the Missouris with highly prized goods: pigments—vermilion for red and verdigris, used to make vibrant greens—and metal awls, which could be used for many purposes such as punching holes in leather.[21]

Laclède's return to St. Louis triggered a confrontation. Immediately, according to Chouteau, "the chiefs of the Missouri came to see him to hold a council."[22] Presumably, they gathered near the trading post site, today part of the park where the Arch stands, overlooking the river below. A face-to-face conversation between powerful men made sense from the perspective of both cultures. As Kathleen DuVal points out with regard to the superficial similarities between French and Indian diplomacy, "men were responsible for greeting outsiders, and a particular man usually had the primary authority to speak during ceremonies of contact."[23] In the ensuing

20. *Auguste Chouteau's Journal,* 6 (unpublished manuscript).
21. Ibid., 10; Chouteau, "Narrative of the Settlement of St. Louis," 52.
22. *Auguste Chouteau's Journal,* 7 (unpublished manuscript).
23. DuVal, *The Native Ground,* 72.

discussion between the Missouri leaders and the French merchant, the Indians declared that the Missouri wished to settle permanently at the new village. According to Chouteau's approximation of what transpired, the Missouris described themselves as "worthy of pity" and "like the ducks and the geese who sought open water" in which to rest and live with ease.[24] The Missouris' explanation highlights a worldview firmly grounded in the natural order and in the connections between human beings and other living creatures. As environmental historian Carolyn Merchant has demonstrated for New England's indigenous inhabitants, nature and culture were not separated, and human beings and their animal neighbors were closely linked equals participating symbiotically in life's many processes.[25] Likening themselves to other semisedentary denizens of the river valley— water fowl—the Missouri leaders' words evoked the idea of a return to favored nesting grounds and seasonal migration as resources dictated.

Just as Laclède had, the Missouris found the site of St. Louis appealing: "they did not find any place more favorable than where they were." Although the conversation continued at length, the theme remained the same: the Missouris "desired to settle where they were."[26] By choosing to establish their homes in proximity to a French trading post, the Missouris acted as had other tribes in the Illinois Country, seeking both ready access to imported goods and the possibilities of alliances and mutual aid with French authorities. The issue of ownership of or rights to the land did not come up in Chouteau's account. The Missouris made it quite clear on another occasion that they considered the lands they inhabited to be theirs. Addressing French officials, they declared, "These belong to us. We inherit them from our ancestors. They found them by dint of wandering. They established themselves there and they [the lands] are ours; no one can contest them."[27]

In the face of the Indians' insistent declaration about settling at the trading post site and no doubt weighing his options, Laclède postponed his response until the following day.[28] Then, gathered near the great river's banks, he and the Missouri chiefs faced each other once again. When the council resumed, the opening did not promise much. There was a great deal

24. *Auguste Chouteau's Journal,* 7 (unpublished manuscript).

25. Merchant, *Ecological Revolutions,* 44–48.

26. Chouteau, "Narrative of the Settlement of St. Louis," 50; *Auguste Chouteau's Journal,* 7 (unpublished manuscript).

27. In this speech, the Missouri and Osage also declared they only wanted "to have the French" among them, not the English. "Another speech by the chiefs of the Osage and Missouri," enclosed in letter of M. Aubry, May 16, 1765, in Alvord and Carter, *The Critical Period,* 480.

28. Chouteau, "Narrative of the Settlement of St. Louis," 50.

of vague, preliminary talk. Unfortunately, because Chouteau did not either recall or care to record what constituted that vague talk, even speculating as to what transpired is risky; nor do we know who served as translator. In other conversations between the Missouris and the French in this period that were recorded by French officials, the Missouri and other nations often opened their remarks with statements summing up their understanding of the historic relationship between the two peoples: the friendships, trade, and promises that had linked them. Whether a Missouri chief made a similar speech on this occasion, we cannot know. But it is nonetheless useful to note that such comments often served to shape the terms of the cultural exchanges that followed.

When Laclède spoke, he employed, according to his stepson, "his usual firmness." He began by summing up his understanding of the previous day's meeting: "You told me, yesterday, that you were like the ducks and the geese, who traveled until they found a fine country, where there was beautiful, open water." Seizing on the analogy, Laclède said that the Missouris traveled like the fowl "to find a place to settle" and had not found any spot "more suitable than that where [they were] at present." Not surprisingly, Laclède did not draw the parallel with his own wanderings and search for an ideal location. "You wished to form a village around my house, where we should live together in the greatest friendship," he concluded.[29] An alliance with trading benefits and cohabitation was at the top of the Missouri agenda, as far as Laclède understood it. Wrapping up his summary of the Missouri chiefs' position, Laclède responded bluntly. "I will reply to your speeches in a few words," he stated. "I will say that if you followed the examples of the ducks and the geese in settling yourselves, you followed bad guides, who have no foresight." Pursuing the comparison the Indians had made, Laclède urged them not to follow such poor examples. If they had good sense, ducks and geese "would not alight on open water" where eagles and other birds of prey might discover them. Clearly, the Missouris would "not be eaten by eagles."[30] A potentially worse fate awaited them. Envisioning their future, Laclède predicted an attack by the Big Osages, who had previously sent a party of three hundred warriors against them.[31] "Those who have waged war against you for a long time [and] are in great numbers against you, who are

29. Ibid.

30. *Auguste Chouteau's Journal,* 8 (unpublished manuscript). The language of being consumed by enemies appeared in the aftermath of an attack in 1752: the Wabash tribe said that the French bore some responsibility for causing the Illinois Indians "to be eaten by the tribes." Macarty to Vaudreuil, in Pease and Jenison, eds., *Illinois on the Eve of the Seven Years' War,* 672, 669; Hauser, "The Fox Raid," 220.

31. Din and Nasatir, *The Imperial Osages,* 54.

few," Laclède purportedly said, "will kill your warriors, because they will want to defend themselves." With the warriors dead, the women and children would become slaves. Directing his rhetoric at the Missouri women, Laclède pushed his point further: "You women present here, listening to me: go, caress your children tenderly," embrace your "old folk,'" and "take them all tightly in your arms." The women should, he advised, "show them all the signs of the tenderest affection until the fatal moment which shall separate you from them." That moment, he warned, was "not far distant" if the men "persist[ed] in wanting to settle here."[32]

Characterizing himself as "a good Father," Laclède advised his audience that six or seven hundred warriors were currently massed at Fort Chartres, there "to make war against the English." These warriors were focused on the south, "whence they expect[ed] the English" to come to take possession of former French forts in Illinois. If, however, these warriors learned of the Missouris' presence at Laclède's post, there was no doubt that they would hurry there to destroy them. Better to leave "rather than remain to be massacred," he counseled. If they stayed, the outcome would be certain: their "wives and children [would be] torn to pieces, and their limbs thrown to dogs and to birds of prey."[33]

Such a disastrous encounter was not unprecedented in the area. Only a dozen years before, in 1752, between four and five hundred warriors from the Sauk and Fox nations traveled downriver in sixty canoes to a village just north of Fort Chartres, inhabited by two sub-tribes of the Illinois Indians, the Cahokia and Michigamea. Using muskets acquired from Europeans to attack the village of roughly 400 men, women, and children, the war party killed numbers of Cahokia and Michigamea men, captured and enslaved women and children, and wrought havoc on the settlement. They left behind over two dozen dead, and took with them thirty scalps and forty prisoners, some of whom they put to death over the next few days. Proximity to a French fort and village had not saved the Illinois Indians. Indeed, information that emerged in the aftermath of the attack also raised the possibility that a French officer was implicated in allowing or encouraging it. These suspicions, based on circumstantial evidence, seemed plausible and did damage to French-Indian relations in the area.[34]

Whether Laclède was intentionally hearkening back to the 1752 attack or not, it is clear that his grisly prediction of a similar outcome was a not

32. Chouteau, "Narrative of the Settlement of St. Louis," 50–51; *Auguste Chouteau's Journal,* 8 (unpublished manuscript).

33. Chouteau, "Narrative of the Settlement of St. Louis," 50–51.

34. Hauser, "The Fox Raid," 210, 211, 217–18, 222.

particularly subtle attempt to undermine the will of the Missouris to remain. The situation was precarious. He clearly could not force them to leave, nor did he want to alienate them. He was not in a position to offer protection to them himself, nor did he have troops at his disposal. With a fort, munitions, and men at his command, St. Ange had turned away the Missouris, and now Laclède was trying to do the same. He finished his statement to his would-be neighbors by urging them to think carefully about what he had told them and give him their answer that evening. He could wait no longer, for he had to return to Fort Chartres.[35]

That evening, all of the Missouris—"the whole nation—men, women and children"—approached Laclède to deliver their response.[36] If Chouteau's representation of this movement is accurate, what he and Laclède were witnessing was the political participation of the larger community, both men and women.[37] As Laclède had urged, "they had listened very carefully to his speech." The Missouris had deliberated, come to a decision, and developed a set of demands, framed in Chouteau's account as petitions for aid. According to Chouteau, the Missouris agreed to follow Laclède's advice in every regard, at the same time pleading with him to give them some provisions, pity their plight, and furnish them with ammunition to hunt while traveling up the Missouri and to defend themselves if attacked. From the Europeans' perspective, it seemed that Laclède's words, with their combination of advising and threatening, had proved effective, and he answered "that he would have pity" on them. It is also clear that the Missouris were making a counteroffer of the terms Laclède would have to meet in order to secure their departure. Once the parties had agreed to conditions, Laclède had to obtain additional stores to fulfill his part of the bargain. He stalled the Missouris until the next day, in the meantime sending to Cahokia for more corn to be ferried across the river. Once the food had arrived, all of the supplies were distributed. The following day, after fifteen days in the village, the Missouris left, carrying with them "a large quantity" of corn, knives, cloth, and ammunition. Whether obtaining foodstuffs, imported goods, and ammunition was part or perhaps even all of their initial agenda when they came to St. Louis, the Missouris left the settlement with a variety of much-valued items. As Chouteau recalled,

35. Chouteau, "Narrative of the Settlement of St. Louis," 51.

36. *Auguste Chouteau's Journal,* 10 (unpublished manuscript).

37. DuVal noted that among the Quapaw Indians in Arkansas, "representatives of the clans came together to make political decisions for the whole." DuVal, *The Native Ground,* 73. Ames suggests Laclède addressed the women as well because they were present in greater numbers than the men. *Auguste Chouteau's Journal,* 28 (unpublished manuscript).

"All the Missouris went away, to go up the Missouri and return to their ancient village" in north central Missouri.[38]

Undoubtedly breathing a sigh of relief at having prevented the settlement of hundreds of Missouri Indians at their village site, Laclède, Chouteau, and the men under their command resumed their labors. Clearly, while Laclède needed the cooperation and assistance of Indians to accomplish his fur-trading ambitions, he did not want them populating his new post at the outset. For these French colonists, establishing control over the contours of St. Louis, both physically and demographically, was crucial. A few days after the Missouri Indians left, Laclède did as well, heading back to Fort Chartres to ready his stock and property there for transfer to St. Louis before the British arrived. The successful conclusion to the conflict over who would occupy the settlement soon worked its magic on the other side of the river. In a further sign that the situation had calmed, "those persons who had fled to Caos [Cahokia] on the coming of the savages, returned as soon as they knew that they had gone away, and commenced building."[39] With the colonists from Illinois back in St. Louis and dozens of men hard at work on constructing houses and enclosing their lots, in accordance with Laclède's plan, the village began to assume a more substantial appearance. St. Louis would survive not as an Indian settlement built up around a lone trading post but as a community designed to serve European and colonial economic aspirations.

By September, work on the company headquarters was completed.[40] More colonists from Illinois arrived, in addition to a key party originally from New Orleans, to add to the burgeoning population. Of particular importance to Laclède and to the future of St. Louis, among the new colonists crossing the river were Madame Chouteau and their four children, including the infant Victoire. Her name, meaning victory, was perhaps an expression of her parents' optimism regarding their personal dreams. Leaving New Orleans, Marie Thérèse Bourgeois Chouteau had brought her children upriver to join their brother and father. (Foley and Rice speculate that the five passengers whom Louisiana governor D'Abbadie noted as leaving New Orleans on June 12 on three royal barges sent by traders of the Illinois and Missouri were likely

38. Chouteau, "Narrative of the Settlement of St. Louis," 51; Foley, *A History of Missouri,* 4.
39. Chouteau, "Narrative of the Settlement of St. Louis," 52.
40. Coleman, *Gilbert Antoine de St. Maxent,* 27.

Madame Chouteau and her four children.[41]) Like all of her elder brothers and sisters, Victoire too had been baptized in New Orleans as the legitimate child of René Chouteau, by this time in France for several years. Although there is no record of the journey that the young Chouteau family made upriver, one can imagine the extra challenges facing a mother—presumably the only woman making the trip—traveling with an infant and three other very young children. In September, after a brief stay at Laclède's property near Fort Chartres, the family came by cart to Cahokia, escorted by Antoine Rivière Senior, nicknamed Baccane, and then crossed the river to St. Louis.[42] There, they moved into the largest building in the village, the stone company headquarters of Laclède, situated at the center of the planned village. If anyone voiced any criticism of the unmarried pair and their children setting up housekeeping together, such censure has not survived.

At around the same time that Madame Chouteau came to the village, the arrival of additional French colonists from Fort Chartres "commenced to give some permanence to St. Louis."[43] The presence of these French settlers was crucial. One missionary even described the new village as "formed out of the ruins of St. Philippe and Fort de Chartres."[44] From Chouteau's account, it seems clear that Laclède considered himself both a good advisor and a source of important aid to these newcomers. Some were settlers who had descended in 1764 to New Orleans with Fort Chartres' former commander Neyon de Villiers and then decided to return to Illinois. Having lost all they had in the journey downriver, they were utterly without resources and therefore altogether dependent on Laclède's help. As Chouteau recalled, Laclède "observed to them, that if they had been willing to follow his advice, as others had done" and not followed Neyon de Villiers to Lower Louisiana, "they would not now be in the unpleasant situation in which they found themselves."[45] If Laclède did make this ungracious comment, those who turned to him would have been in an awkward position to make any response; in effect, he was putting them on notice as to where their debts and allegiances lay.

41. Foley and C. David Rice, *The First Chouteaus*, 11 n. 35; D'Abbadie's journal, in Alvord and Carter, *The Critical Period*, 188, notes a convoy of seventy-seven persons, three commanders of bateaux, four patrons, sixty-five rowers, and five passengers.

42. Foley and C. David Rice, *The First Chouteaus*, 6–7; Houck, *A History of Missouri*, 1: 9 n. 23 (hereafter *HM*). Houck relied on Pierre Chouteau's testimony for this chronology, from Hunt's Minutes, book 3: 100, 282, 283, Commissioner's Minutes.

43. Chouteau, "Narrative of the Settlement of St. Louis," 54.

44. Sebastian Louis Meurin to Bishop Briand, March 23, 1767, in Alvord and Carter, eds., *The New Regime*, 523.

45. Chouteau, "Narrative of the Settlement of St. Louis," 53.

From the perspective of the colonists and traders who settled St. Louis, this outcome—a village of French colonists from Illinois without any Indian neighbors living next door—was the desired one, for the moment at least. They wanted to establish a francophone settlement, populated by French colonists and immigrants, not a community with a majority indigenous population. The ironies in their position abound. In the first place, the fur trade, the raison d'être of St. Louis, required those who engaged in it to work closely with Indians as partners, whether as producers of hides or consumers of imported goods. In obvious contrast to the semisedentary Missouri Indians, who hunted in the winter and spent part of the year settled, the French had no historic claim to the territory, and their new settlement was yet another invasion by largely unwelcome outsiders.[46] The Indians were willing to countenance the settlers' presence only to the extent that the French met their trading and military needs.

In St. Louis, Laclède's early effort to prevent Indians from settling nearby appears to have been a temporary expedient, rather than an expression of any deep-seated hostility to Indian neighbors. Within two years, a group of Peoria Indians, fleeing enemies in Illinois, sought refuge at Kaskaskia, just to the south of Ste. Genevieve but on the eastern bank of the Mississippi, and then crossed the river, requesting and receiving permission from authorities to build a village two miles below St. Louis. Led by Chief Little Turkey, they founded a settlement, called the *Prairie du Village Sauvage* by the French, which was considered by outside observers as linked to Laclède.[47] According to a British officer, Captain Harry Gordon, Laclède was "readily served by the Indians he has planted within 2 miles of him."[48] Even before the Peorias settled nearby, Indians of various tribes had already begun to make regular visits to the village, bringing in furs to exchange for European manufactures and turning St. Louis into what its founder had hoped: an important trading center. Clearly, Indians were crucial to Laclède's recipe for success. Proximity to them fueled the entire venture and inspired much of the colonial enterprise for the French, Spanish, and the British colonists and governments in the region.

Indeed, many French colonists saw trade with the Indians of the Missouri River and Illinois Country as a quick path toward great wealth, so

---

46. "Voyage fait par M. du Tisné en 1719, chez les Missouri pour aller aux Panioussas. Extrait de la Rélation de Bernard de La Harpe," in Margry, *Découvertes et Etablissements des Français.*

47. Hodes, *Beyond the Frontier,* 89.

48. "Journal of Captain Harry Gordon 1766," in Alvord and Carter, *The New Regime,* 299–301; Matson, *Pioneers of Illinois,* 192. Auguste Chouteau offered an earlier date for the settlement. See Auguste Chouteau, "Testimony before the Recorder of Land Titles, St. Louis, 1825," in McDermott, ed., *Early Histories,* 94.

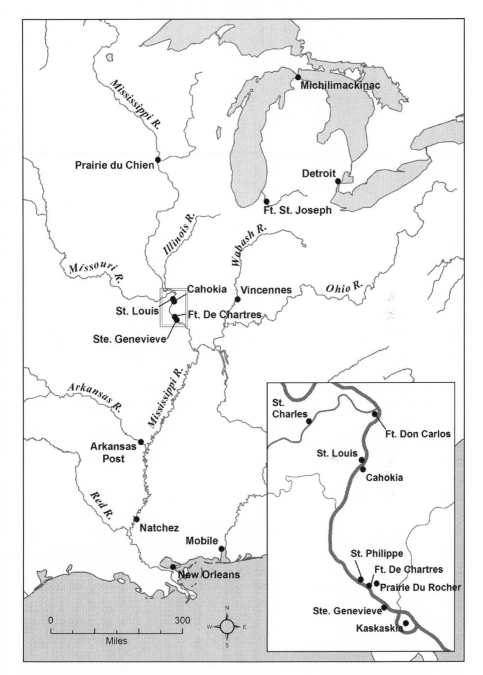

Colonial Settlements (John Speargas, Department of Geography, California State University, Long Beach)

appealing that villagers neglected farming, despite the fertility of the soil and the proven abundance of crop yields in Upper Louisiana. The desire for fur trade riches created a host of problems in early St. Louis, as the less spectacular returns generated by farming led to a shortage of men willing to pursue their livelihoods in the fields. Within a few years, Laclède's village had acquired the insulting nickname of *Paincourt,* French for "short of bread." (Its neighbor to the south, Ste. Genevieve, gained an equally unflattering moniker, *Misère,* or misery.) St. Louis was rapidly becoming infamous for its lack of foodstuffs and for the disinclination of many of its residents to pick up a plow.[49]

Like all colonial settlers, the villagers on the bluffs above the Mississippi faced the problem of feeding themselves from the moment they broke ground. Unlike others engaged in colonial enterprises along the Atlantic seaboard, however, such as the Puritans and Pilgrims in Massachusetts Bay, many of the French colonists in St. Louis possessed a pronounced preference for roaming the land to hunt and trade, rather than tilling it to eat. Their understanding of nature and approach to exploiting its resources are more reminiscent of the get-rich-quick mentality that typified Jamestown, Virginia, in its first decades. In St. Louis, grain had to be imported early on. There were, of course, those who wished to farm, and they recognized the fertility of the soil in the area, as well as the potential profit to be made from selling their surpluses. Demand for foodstuffs from Lower Louisiana was a reliable constant, and indeed, officials in New Orleans monitored reports on harvests carefully. But farming took a distinct second place to the fur trade.

For French colonists and adventurers, like Laclède, Chouteau, and the men who took their chances on fur trading or farming in the region in the 1760s, nature was understood as a source of commodities to be extracted or produced. One French promoter imagined a proposed settlement just to the south of St. Louis, along the Meramec River, as a place "where riches abound," offering "an infinity of resources and innumerable provisions." Neatly capturing the money-making mentality of many colonists, he envisioned "lands of an ever-renewing fertility" where some would grow wealthy through farming, "while others with their sharp pickaxes would tear without expense from the entrails of the earth the vast lead mines that it encloses."[50] Coming from a European background where land and

---

49. John Francis McDermott objected to the linking of the derogatory French nickname and poverty among village inhabitants, seeing "Paincourt" as a more neutral term that reflected the need of the commercially oriented residents to import flour. McDermott, "Paincourt and Poverty," 210–12.

50. Jacques Clamorgan to Zenon Trudeau, April 1, 1793, in Nasatir, *BLC,* 1: 170.

forests were scarce and belonged to the crown or to the extremely wealthy, and hunting was the purview of aristocrats, colonial immigrants and their American-born descendants saw their new home as a wild place of unfathomable natural abundance, ready for the taking. For colonists, it was understood—even a religious mandate—that human domination of nature should translate into an organized, enriching landscape, ideally through agricultural endeavor.

An ordered landscape was certainly at the forefront of Laclède's mind when he set out the plan for St. Louis in the spring of 1764. With ambitions to establish the dominant trading center in the region and a sizeable colonial settlement, he thought big, orienting the village toward the all-important Mississippi River and developing a design similar to that of New Orleans. Stretching nearly two miles along the bluffs that ran along the river, the village he envisioned contained elements of both French and Spanish land use patterns. Key to his plan was a central residential area organized on a grid and anchored by a public plaza.[51] This degree of urban planning and predetermined street design distinguished St. Louis from other contemporary French villages on either side of the river.[52] As a first step, Laclède laid out and named three principal roads that ran roughly parallel to the Mississippi: the *Rue Royale, Rue de l'Eglise* (Church Street), and *Rue des Granges* (the Street of the Barns). As historian Eric Sandweiss nicely sums up the early village plan, these names "reflected the perceived unity and mutual dependence of crown, church, and husbandman at the edge of a pagan and uncultivated wilderness."[53] A small outpost in the wilderness needed the protection of the king as well as the spiritual and physical sustenance provided by clergyman and farmer. Intersecting these three symbolic anchors of the community were short streets set at perpendicular angles. Despite the fact that street naming was more haphazard and less documented early on, the design of the village overall was much more intentional than that of any other settlement in the region; it was the result of Laclède's early planning—likely shaped by his years in New Orleans—and his desire to exert control over the post's contours.

At the center of the village, Laclède placed its most important spaces and buildings. Closest to the river was the *Place d'Armes,* also known as the *Place Publique,* the public square or meeting place. Laclède had seen such a design in New Orleans, with its grid and orientation toward the

51. Peterson, *Colonial St. Louis,* 3, 5. See also Sandweiss, "Construction and Community in South St. Louis," 9–14, and *St. Louis.*

52. Ekberg, *French Roots in the Illinois Country,* esp. 72, 96–101.

53. Sandweiss, *St. Louis,* 29.

river. As historian Carl Ekberg notes, "Laclède planned St. Louis in much the same fashion, and the plan of Upper Lousiana's capital was in fact a smaller version of Lower Louisiana's capital."[54] At the center of both communities was a multipurpose space, a square that served for the public market, large gatherings, and militia training. Like the other two central blocks leading away from the river beyond it, St. Louis's *Place d'Armes* was 300 feet square. By positioning this important space at the head of a path that descended down to the riverbank at the most convenient spot for landing boats, Laclède insured that visitors would be channeled into his village, where they would see its most impressive structure, his home, at its center.[55]

Set back a block further from the Mississippi and occupying a full block between *Rue Royale* and *Rue de l'Eglise* stood Laclède's company headquarters, which also served as home for him and Madame Chouteau and their children, and, for a time, as the seat of government as well. Built of stone hewn from the limestone bluffs along the river, it was the most substantial structure in the village, twenty-three by sixty feet, with a high basement— dug by the Missouris during their brief stay in the summer of 1764—that gave it the appearance of a two-story building. Wide galleries, or porches, encircled it and offered protection from the elements; a thick stone wall ultimately enclosed the property.[56] Any first-time visitor to St. Louis, particularly one walking up the path from the river, would likely infer from its size that this building was the most important one in the community and head there directly for business or an introduction.

The last main central square in Laclède's design was the church block, set aside at the beginning for the religious structure that would one day fill it. Religious services, held in a chapel in a tent, and a cemetery occupied the space, today the site of the Old Cathedral, well before the construction of a church or a rectory for a priest. During the first several years of St. Louis's existence, infrequent pastoral care came from priests in Illinois, who crossed the river sometimes under cover of night. Obtaining regular spiritual guidance and sacraments was an ongoing preoccupation of early villagers, and civil leaders were anxious to promote the church.

---

54. Ekberg, *French Roots in the Illinois Country,* 100.

55. Peterson, *Colonial St. Louis,* 7, 8.

56. Years later, after Auguste Chouteau had purchased and remodeled the building, a visitor described it as an "elegant domicile" occupying a full block, "enclosed by a solid stone wall two feet thick and ten feet high, with port holes about every ten feet apart," in case of Indian attack. The galleries were fourteen feet wide. Stevens, *St. Louis,* 1: 116; Peterson, *Colonial St. Louis,* 25 n. 5. The house, demolished in 1841, stood in what is part of the riverfront park dominated by the Arch.

The rest of the village blocks were typically subdivided into anywhere from two to six smaller house lots, each with some space for gardens and some with sufficient room for substantial outbuildings. In the largest lots, there was typically a courtyard area for livestock and carts and a garden with a variety of vegetables under cultivation; fruit orchards were planted very early, with apples and peaches soon supplementing the local diet.[57]

Combining the architectural styles of French Canada and Lower Louisiana, the residents of the new village built houses that were typically one story, with steep roofs, generous porches, and whitewashed plaster walls. There was initially abundant timber for construction, and the houses were built with *poteaux en terre,* large pieces of lumber placed vertically into the soil to form the walls. By building in proximity to neighbors and adding palisade-like fences around the house lots, St. Louisans constructed their village in a way that augmented the possibilities for mutual self-defense. Using the abundant wood in the area, some added tall enclosures made of mulberry, cedar, or oak, giving their individual properties stockade-like appearances. Spanish regulations for a 1767 settlement at the mouth of the Missouri specified the details of such enclosures, emphasizing their defensive purposes and dictating that each householder construct at his own expense "an encircling pointed fence . . . in order to prevent the savages from making any sudden rush at night and surprising them."[58]

Most distinctive, and perhaps most important to the subsistence of population, were the common fields for farming and the commons for pasturage. Key features of French medieval villages, the common fields and commons represented a pattern of land use distinctive among French colonists in North America. There was a separation between village structures and farmlands, and the line between the two blurred along the *Rue des Granges.* There, large animals, like horses and cattle, were housed in barns built in between the village proper and the village commons, the land designated for grazing and timber; this location made it easier to drive the animals to pasture and to store hay and grain harvested from the fields. So many barns dotted the rise in the terrain there that the spot became known as early as 1768 as the *coteau des granges,* or hill of barns; they typically stood on lots of sixty by eighty feet and were surrounded by high fences.[59]

57. Peterson, *Colonial St. Louis,* 11.

58. Peterson, *Colonial St. Louis,* 11; Ulloa's 1767 "Instructions for the expedition to the district of the Ylinneses," in Houck, *The Spanish Regime in Missouri,* 1: 16 (hereafter *SRM*). An example appears in Jean-François Benjamin Dumont de Montigny, *Mémoires historique sur la Louisiane,* 1753, reproduced in Ekberg, *French Roots in the Illinois Country,* 53.

59. Peterson, *Colonial St. Louis,* 11.

Sociability, security, and the positive value St. Louisans placed on living close to their neighbors dictated not only that they live within sight of each other, but also that they conduct a significant portion of their agricultural activities at a remove from their homes. By making village lots suitable for homes and not big enough for fields, Laclède insured that early villagers lived within sight and shouting distance of each of other. From their village homes, they walked to the fields beyond the tidy grid of planned streets. French agricultural practices of open-field farming reflected their communal ethos as well as their medieval heritage.[60] Residents received grants for land both within the village and in the common fields outside its bounds; the fields corresponded to village lots, with farmers receiving acreage in relation to the size of their house lots.[61] Thus, beyond the streets lay the common fields, long, narrow lots of thirty or sixty acres, in widths of 180 or 360 feet, which were assigned to individuals and which resembled the land-grant patterns of other French communities in Upper Louisiana. As in the village, the allotments reinforced community; farmers moving along their long, narrow fields could easily work within earshot of their neighbors. The first set of common fields began just beyond the village to the west, in what was known as the St. Louis Prairie. When those fields had all been assigned, new sets of farm lots were surveyed to the south and the northwest, the Petite Prairie and Grande Prairie fields respectively; three others sets of common fields were added over time.[62] The road that ran across the Grande Prairie was known as the *Chemin du Roi,* the King's road or public road, with the adjacent lands named *Prairie de la Grange,* after the Indian mound *La Grange de Terre* nearby.[63]

In addition to the common fields was the commons, two thousand acres of communal land set aside when the village was mapped out. The commons, to the southwest of the village between two sets of farm lots, represented continuity with the past, both in terms of European agricultural practices and in regard to French Canada and the Illinois Country. Surrounded by a fence, which the inhabitants had the collective responsibility to maintain, the commons provided a safe grazing area for livestock. Each spring, villagers gathered to perform repairs near grain planting time, April 15.[64] If the fence fell into disrepair, animals could enter the fields and leave a swath of destroyed crops in their wake. Hogs, cows, and horses ran loose on the commons, eating what and where they could. A visiting English botanist,

60. Ekberg, *French Roots in the Illinois Country,* 111–13.

61. Peterson, *Colonial St. Louis,* 9.

62. Sandweiss, *St. Louis,* 29.

63. Peterson, *Colonial St. Louis,* 19; Peterson also cites Hunt's Minutes, July 10, 1825, testimony of Baptiste Riviere.

64. Peterson, *Colonial St. Louis,* 14; Sandweiss, *St. Louis,* 30–31.

John Bradbury, noted that hogs feasted on strawberries, nuts, and roots.[65] Ultimately, the tradition of the commons was a casualty of the new world setting, where abundant land and the commercial incentive and comparison with Americans prompted colonists to disperse. By the end of the colonial period, the commons' fence had fallen into disrepair and the commons had begun to lose their role as a communal economic institution. Gradually, as St. Louis expanded, the commons disappeared beneath new buildings. The only bit of the original commons that remains open is Lafayette Park.[66]

As they arrived in St. Louis to begin their new lives, colonists turned to Laclède for permission to build and land to till. Without any formal government authority in place, Laclède assumed the responsibilities of administration and acted as a de facto land granting officer, assigning village lots and fields verbally to the French colonists he had persuaded to join his venture. Before the end of 1765, he had acquired many neighbors and had granted most of the village lots to men who built as quickly as they could. Those who had helped to construct the settlement in 1764 were among the first to receive land grants. Subsequent newcomers from Illinois acquired land quickly as well. On the northern edge of the village, Louis Tesson Honoré, a trader from Kaskaskia, received a full block closest to the river. Jean B. Cardinal, a farmer from St. Philippe, and Louis Deshêtres, formerly of Cahokia, occupied most of the next block inland. Other Cahokia residents were closer to the center of the village, with wheelwright Jean B. Provenchère two blocks away from Laclède's headquarters.[67] The new residents set about building homes—most of them quite modest and comprised of only two or three rooms—fencing their lots, planting gardens, and preparing to cultivate the fields.

Gradually, the village assumed a look of permanence. With timber being cleared from the site and construction on multiple buildings underway, Laclède's settlement grew rapidly. The first child to increase the population was born in September 1765. Meanwhile, the Illinois villages of Fort Chartres and St. Phillippe were gradually depopulated as their inhabitants crossed the river. Nearby Kaskaskia, Cahokia, and Prairie du Rocher also decreased in size due to the same out-migration pattern.[68] As the months passed, on the gentle rise on the western banks of the Mississippi River, a village of wood and stone buildings emerged.[69]

65. Bradbury, 260–61, cited in Peterson, *Colonial St. Louis,* 14.
66. Fox, *Where We Live,* 67.
67. Billon, *Annals of Early St. Louis,* 20; Hodes, *Beyond the Frontier,* 85–87.
68. Billon, *Annals of Early St. Louis,* 79, 76.
69. By the end of 1766, there were seventy-five structures. Within six years, one hundred wood

While St. Louis's future seemed promising, much else in the region was in a state of confusion and upheaval. Ongoing movements of Indian peoples, shifts in the fur trade, and international politics brought further change to the area as imperial powers attempted to govern their new possessions. After the 1763 treaty that dictated France's loss of lands east of the Mississippi to the United Kingdom, the British government had been slow to send its representatives to Illinois. Because Britain made no provisions for civil government, military leaders had responsibility for administering the area.[70] In the 1760s, their efforts to establish authority proved problematic, to say the least. With Pontiac's forces gathering to oppose British possession of the territory, French settlers fleeing in droves across the Mississippi, and a growing St. Louis challenging any likelihood for developing a successful trading center in Illinois, the British were flummoxed. The political, military, and economic situations were unstable in ways that hampered the British imperial agenda and helped St. Louis to grow.

Unlike the French who preceded them in the continent's interior, the British did not initially approach the Indians as either allies or equal trading partners, but as conquered peoples in the aftermath of the French and Indian War. Neither interested in nor prepared to engage in the gift-giving practices and diplomatic overtures that the French had pursued, the British antagonized the Indians. Opposed to the British presence, warriors from a number of Indian nations joined together to fight the newcomers. Led by Pontiac, an Ottawa chief, they engaged in hostilities throughout the Ohio River valley and won numerous victories over British forces. Several forts were captured, hundreds of British colonists died, and British officers employed smallpox as a military tactic in one of the first known instances of biological warfare, distributing contaminated blankets to Indians visiting Fort Pitt.

In Illinois, large numbers of Indians massed to pledge their aid to the French in resisting the British takeover. For a time, they succeeded in turning back British forces sent to occupy the territory. One officer, Major Loftus, reported that his men simply could not proceed to their intended destination: Illinois. "The Savages having been Determined to Oppose Us, Posted themselves at an Advantageous Place," he wrote. Trying to proceed cautiously upriver from New Orleans, he discovered the Indians "were possessed of both Sides of the River" and that "it was in Vain" to go farther and so returned to New Orleans.[71] Although Neyon de Villiers had, he believed,

---

and fifteen stone buildings had been constructed. Billon, *Annals of Early St. Louis,* "Plat of St. Louis in 1770," inserted after 74, 75–76.

70. Alvord and Carter, *The New Regime,* xvi–xvii.

71. Loftus to Thomas Gage, April 9, 1764, in Alvord and Carter, *The Critical Period,* 237–39.

initially persuaded the Illinois tribes to accept the British, Pontiac's arrival in April 1764 changed the game. Writing to Major Loftus that month, Neyon de Villiers declared that Pontiac's arrival had "destroyed in one night what [he] had accomplished in eight months," and that the Illinois nation were "as bitterly determined" to oppose a British takeover there "as all the Indians of the continent are united in not suffering the English."[72]

At Fort Chartres, where French troops waited for the British to arrive to take possession of the fort, commanding officer St. Ange reported daily arrivals of Indians who both drew upon his food stores and declared their opposition to the British.[73] Many Indians believed it unlikely that the French were willingly going to turn over their forts and possessions to their historic enemies, the British, and so promised their assistance to renew the fight against them. On June 26, 1764, chiefs of the Miami, Kickapoo, Mascoutens, Wea, and Piankashaw came to Fort Chartres to discuss their loyalties and wishes with St. Ange. He reported that they assured him "of their fidelity and of their attachment to the French nation." They also asked him for aid, declaring themselves destitute and requiring necessities for their wives and children to survive.[74]

As far as the British military was concerned, the French in Illinois had been doing all they could since the conclusion of the war both to turn the Indian population against the British and to destroy the military and commercial foundations of the posts they planned to take control of east of the Mississippi. Indeed, General Thomas Gage reported that the French had given Pontiac a letter telling him that they were not crushed, "as the English would make the Indians believe" and that they mentioned "a large Fleet coming into the Mississippi."[75] On another occasion, Gage accused the French commanders of Louisiana posts of treating the cession of the territory to the British "as a vulgar Report only."[76]

Pontiac's occasional presence in Fort Chartres helped to foment and concentrate anti-British sentiment. In November 1764, St. Ange complained that Pontiac sent out signal belts to other tribes to communicate his anger at the prospect of having to negotiate with the British. With the belts, he invited other nations to join him, and, noted St. Ange, pictured "the English as the most cruel enemies around," men not to be trusted. As a result of Pontiac's message, Indian peoples from the surrounding territory

72. Neyon de Villiers to M. Loftus, April 20, 1764, in ibid., 244–45.
73. Middleton, *Pontiac's War,* 184.
74. St. Ange to D'Abbadie, July 15, 1764, in Alvord and Carter, *The Critical Period,* 289.
75. Thomas Gage to Johnson, October 26, 1764, in ibid., 349–50.
76. Thomas Gage to Earl of Halifax, November 9, 1764, in ibid., 351.

flocked to Fort Chartres, where St. Ange could do little to assuage them: "I am unable to make them speak of peace that is all; nothing can content them less." Also troubling St. Ange was the difficulty he had in meeting these angry visitors' basic needs, noting that "every day there are here fifty red men whom it is necessary to nourish."[77] He had neither the authority nor the supplies to continue to do so. Over the next several months, Indians who visited Fort Chartres confirmed that there remained considerable anti-British sentiment afoot. Some demanded munitions for making war against the English, leaving St. Ange to repeat that with the peace, the English had become their brothers and were no longer enemies. Such statements did not persuade the Indians, who, according to officials, declared themselves free and uninterested in having "any other father except the French."[78]

In April 1765, while the fort was still under French authority, Lieutenant John Ross, a British officer, traveled there to talk with St. Ange about the upcoming transfer and indigenous opposition to it. Together, the two military men met with principal chiefs of the Osage, Missouri, Peoria, Cahokia, Michigamea, and Kaskaskia tribes, trying to present the upcoming occupation by the British as both peaceful and beneficial to the Indians in the area. Addressing the assembled indigenous leaders, St. Ange told them to accept Ross and his government. Employing paternalistic language, he said, "Once more, my dear children, lay down your arms and be disposed to receive the English here. It is for your good and for the good of all your brothers, the French, who are here."[79] Unmoved, Tamarois, a Kaskaskia chief, declared that he was speaking "in the name of all [his] nation," and announced that his people did "not wish the English to come on their lands." The English officer, said Tamarois, should give his chief a message: "Tell him that these lands are ours and no one claims them, not even other red men."[80] Tamarois concluded by urging Ross to leave and giving him his hand. The Osage and Missouri chiefs agreed with Tamarois. St. Ange summed up the Kaskaskia position and that of the other tribes as being "all unanimously agreed to continue the war" against the British. The hostility of the Indians toward the British was so pronounced that St. Ange "trembled" for Ross's safety.[81]

According to the British officer, Indian hostility toward his presence created a potentially explosive situation, and he barely escaped with his life.

77. St. Ange to D'Abbadie, November 9, 1764, in ibid., 356, 358.

78. Aubry to the Minister [M. Dubuq], February 12, 1765, in ibid., 434.

79. St. Ange speech, April 4, 1765, in ibid., 475.

80. Speech of Tamarois, April 4, 1765, in ibid., 476–78.

81. St. Ange to D'Abbadie, April 7, 1765, in ibid., 469, 470.

After days of meetings when conversations ended with Indians singing war songs and declaring their intentions to show Ross how they felt, an Osage chief attempted to put the threats against Ross into action. Coming to the fort to see St. Ange, the Osage leader "threw himself in a Rage" (according to Ross) when he encountered the British emissary and attempted to give him "a Stroke with his Hatchet." Only St. Ange's timely "interference" saved Ross's life. Interpreters on the scene tried to appease the chief, who, in Ross's account, "kept Singing the War Song and Hollooed out" that he would "sacrifice" Ross if he could; with only one warrior accompanying him, however, "he could not at present Satisfy his Desire." Unable to carry out his threat to kill Ross, the Osage chief told the assembled audience that he had "promised Pondiac [*sic*] to Strike at all Englishmen" and that he would "stay there until his arrival to have his Satisfaction."[82] Ross might not have fully understood the chief's actions and words; his account does, however, convey clearly the British fear of Indian resistance and force, as well as the visible, vocal presence of indigenous actors on the scene.

When another British officer, Lieutenant Alexander Fraser, arrived, charged by General Gage with seeking Indian permission for occupying the lands—a real shift in British strategy as well as a clear indication of their tenuous hold on the territory in the wake of defeats at Indian hands—he encountered a similarly volatile situation. While Fraser was dining with St. Ange, Pontiac and eight of his men interrupted the meal to seize the British officer. Again, St. Ange acted to save the British guest's life. Declaring that Pontiac would have to kill him first, St. Ange demanded Fraser's release. Pontiac agreed to do so and also to hear Fraser speak at a council of Indians gathered at Fort Chartres. With St. Ange's clear support, Fraser tried to persuade Pontiac of the peaceful intentions of the British. The Ottowa leader adopted a new approach of accepting and promoting the change in regime.

On more than one occasion, Pontiac personally intervened to preserve a British officer's life. In May 1765, Fraser recorded a terrifying encounter: after hearing news of a joint English-Cherokee party killing and scalping fourteen Indians, some Indians near Fraser laid hands on him and his men, threatening to kill them. Pontiac and some of his men rushed in and ordered the prisoners released.[83] Prevailing on Pontiac to stay for a while, Fraser acknowledged that the Ottawa chief seemed the most "inclined to peace" of any of the Indians. "It is much to be wished that He may be prevail'd on to make a Peace, as it will probably be of a longer duration

---

82. Ross to Farmar, May 25, 1765, in ibid., 482.
83. Alexander Fraser to Thomas Gage, May 15, 1765, in ibid., 492.

than any made without him," wrote Fraser. "He is in a manner Ador'd by all the Nations hereabouts, and He is more remarkable for His integrity and humanity than either French Man or Indian in the Colony."[84] The successful efforts of these three men—the French commandant St. Ange, the British officer Fraser, and most importantly, the Ottowa leader Pontiac—ushered in a new phase in Indian-British relations. Pontiac endeavored to calm the hostilities by urging the trading benefits of the British presence, and his skillfulness in doing so before he left the Illinois Country helped to bring about peace.[85]

Although Pontiac succeeded in diffusing some of the conflict he had earlier urged in Illinois, relations between the British and Indian peoples remained tense, as representatives of various tribes communicated to the British how negatively they viewed the situation. Importantly, they reminded the newcomers that while the French might have been defeated by the British, the Indians had never had been conquered by anyone and indeed had allowed the French to remain on their lands insofar as doing so benefited their own interests. Only if the British could meet Indian needs would they be tolerated. In August 1765, British officer Colonel George Croghan met with chiefs of several nations, who informed him that they welcomed "a general peace" and the prospect of British "possession of the Posts in their Country," particularly as they looked forward to an increase in trade. If the promised augmentation in imported goods did not happen with alacrity, they would resort to trading with "their old Fathers the French."[86]

After clarifying their expectations, the chiefs declared their sovereignty and rights. "We have been informed," they began, "that the English where ever they settle, make the Country their own, & you tell us, that when you Conquered the French, they gave you this Country." Just to insure that any misconceptions would not mar future, peaceful exchanges, the Indian chiefs continued, "That no difference may happen hereafter, we tell you now that the French never conquered [us] neither did they purchase a foot of our Country, nor have [they a right] to give it to you."[87] While the Indians had given the French "liberty to settle" on their lands, the French had paid for the privilege. "They always rewarded us & treated us with great Civility," noted the chiefs. If the British expected to keep possession of the posts they had taken over, they had better understand the terms. "We will expect," the

84. Fraser to Gage, May 18, 1765, in ibid., 495.
85. Middleton, *Pontiac's War*, 188–97.
86. Ibid., 197; Croghan's journal, August 30, 1765, in Alvord and Carter, *The New Regime*, 47.
87. Ibid.

chiefs informed Croghan, "to have proper returns from you."[88] Reinforcing what the British had come to appreciate over the previous months, the Indian leaders reminded the newcomers that their presence was provisional and contingent on Indians' good will and permission; it was most definitely not permanent, legally authorized, or militarily guaranteed. The Indians would allow the British to stay, as they had the French, if and only for as long as it served their own interests.

The fact that the French had not altogether left the region but had moved to the new settlement of St. Louis and shifted their commercial enterprises there fueled ongoing British distrust of their former European enemies. Croghan complained in his reports that the Indians were being chiefly supplied by the French and urged that British trading posts be established very quickly in the Illinois Country. Otherwise, "the French will carry the best part of the Trade over the *Misisipi,* which they are determined to do if they can."[89] If they succeeded in doing so, they would "engross all the Traffic" with the "numerous Nations" to the west as well, and thereby "deprive" the British "of *the present use* of [their] Canada Conquest."[90] St. Louis was clearly a significant part of the problem. Rumor had it that the establishment of the post was part of a plan to keep the Illinois trade in French hands. Croghan denounced the French to his superiors, claiming that they had the previous summer "in a private manner Transported 26 pieces of small Cannon up the River for that purpose."[91]

If the officer was right—that the French had secretly moved weapons from Fort Chartres to St. Louis in the summer of 1765—that would explain some of the difficulties the British faced when they finally arrived to take possession in October. Under the command of Captain Thomas Stirling, a detachment of the Forty-second Royal Highland Regiment of Scotland, also known as the Black Watch, left Fort Pitt for Fort Chartres on August 24, sailing down the Ohio River and then ascending the Mississippi to arrive on October 9.[92] Arriving on eight barges carrying a hundred men and three officers, Stirling's force would have made an impressive sight in

88. Croghan's journal, August 30, 1765, in Alvord and Carter, *The New Regime,* 47–48.
89. Col. George Croghan to Johnson, November 1765, in ibid., 55.
90. Col. George Croghan to Benjamin Franklin, December 12, 1765, in ibid., 63.
91. Croghan to Johnson, November 1765, in ibid., 55.
92. Alvord, *The Illinois Country,* 264; Calloway, *White People, Indians, and Highlanders,* 104–7.

contrast to the small French garrison, but the Indians in the area report-edly "could not believe that so small a party dared to have ventured 1500 Miles into a country full of enemies."[93] Fort Chartres did not make an altogether good impression on its new occupants. Although one officer described it as "one of the Prettyest Stone Forts I ever Saw," he added that that was all he could say, for there was neither ammunition nor any other of the other supplies and equipment usually found in a fort.[94] The documents of the next day's formal cession from the French to the British, including a detailed physical description of the fort and its contents, reveal the less-than-stellar condition in which Stirling and his men found their new home, with numerous items described as "bad" or "damaged."[95] The fort and barracks were both "very dirty," and "very long weeds several feet high were growing all over the Square and round the wall."[96]

Although he found the French commander St. Ange agreeable—another officer described him as "a very Gentlemanly looking old man"—Stirling thought the fort ill supplied and his own situation almost untenable, something he blamed on the machinations of the not-altogether-trust-worthy French.[97] Had he been privy to official correspondence, Stirling would have had his suspicions of the French and Croghan's earlier asser-tions of weapon movements confirmed. In a report to a French minis-ter, acting Louisiana governor Charles-Philippe Aubry noted that the English at Fort Chartres were having some difficulties because they were insisting they had the authority to take possession not only of forts but of all cannon and other property. Stirling took possession of the seven small pieces of cannon the French left at Fort Chartres—four of them ruined—and 250 pounds of powder, but little else of value. Of the full complement of cannon the fort once possessed, Aubry wrote reassuringly, "We had taken precaution to send the others to the other bank," no doubt meaning St. Louis.[98]

93. Daubry to M. Dubuq, January 27, 1766, in Alvord and Carter, *The New Regime,* 139; Captain Stirling, "General account of the fighting with the Indians," Black Watch Regimental Archives, Balhousie Castle, Perth, cited in Calloway, *White People, Indians, and Highlanders,* 106.

94. Eddingstone to unknown, in Alvord and Carter, *The New Regime,* 105.

95. Cession of Fort de Chartres, October 10, 1765, in ibid., 105.

96. "Official journal" [kept by Lt. Eddington or the surgeon], October 9, 1765, in Caroon, ed., *Broadswords and Bayonets,* 84.

97. "Official journal" [kept by Lt. Eddington or the surgeon], October 10, 1765, in ibid., 83.

98. Charles-Philippe Aubry to M. Dubuq, January 27, 1766, in Alvord and Carter, *The New Regime,* 139. An inventory taken of the goods in the king's warehouse in St. Louis, in possession of Judge Lefebre Desbruisseau in April 1767, contained items that seemed likely to have been in the stores at Fort Chartres, such as 844 pounds of balls and 1,500 gun flints. Although possibly destined for the Indian trade, such goods had clear military application. See Billon, *Annals of St. Louis,* 47–49.

The moment of transfer in the fall of 1765 was an emotional and distressing one for the French garrison at least, and likely for the French residents of the area as well. St. Ange refused to lower the French flag, saying he would never do so and insisting that a member of the British detachment perform that task instead.[99] In the opinion of one of the British participants in this drama, the French troops assembled for the transfer ceremony were "old Men looking like Invalids without any sort of uniform." They wore jackets of different colors and slouched hats, and they sported weapons that "seem'd to be old and in very indifferent order." When the French colors were pulled down, the "Honest Old Veterans" who comprised the French garrison "were greatly Chagrind." Venting their indignation, they cried out that when they had fought, "no such dishonour was then ever seen. In fact, all Europe trembled at the French name."[100] The scene was full of pathos, as men who had given their lives to serve France witnessed the dying moments of an imperial dream.

In the aftermath of the transfer, the British had to deal with a diminished French population, a hostile indigenous one, a poorly stocked fort, and a bustling new settlement, St. Louis, across the river, all factors which could only bode ill for their aspirations for their new territory. Within two weeks of reaching Fort Chartres, Stirling was already embarrassed in his interactions with the Indians. He had no agent or interpreter to facilitate communication, making diplomacy and trade nearly impossible.[101] Numbers of Indians came to the fort to receive presents, as had been their custom with the French, but Stirling could offer little but "small things, and Promises of more in the Spring." The visitors' demands that the British continue French practices forced Stirling to plead with his superiors. He urged them to send large quantities of goods and additional troops, in order to keep the Indians "in awe." While St. Ange assisted Stirling "in quieting the Indians," he did not provide his British successor with adequate military supplies. There was very little ammunition and few weapons on hand, and Stirling was forced to apply to the merchants in the vicinity for what he needed. With many having already moved their stock over to St. Louis, the merchants held all the cards. "They put it out of my Power of laying my Hands upon it," he complained regarding the ammunition, "as they Transported it to the other Side."[102] They insisted,

99. Thomas Stirling, "General Account of British Attempts to Occupy the Illinois Country," in Caroon, *Broadswords and Bayonets,* 45.

100. "Official journal" [kept by Lt. Eddington or the surgeon], October 10, 1765, in ibid., 83.

101. Thomas Stirling to Thomas Gage, October 18, 1765, in Alvord and Carter, *The New Regime,* 109.

102. Stirling to Gage, October 18, 1765, in ibid., 107.

and Stirling had no option but to agree, that he buy other goods from them as well.

In Stirling's view, the diminished French military presence in the region since the end of the war had contributed both to the growth of St. Louis and to the restiveness of the indigenous population. The fort at Kaskaskia had been abandoned, Fort Chartres was undermanned and undersupplied, and his own troops far too few to make an impressive show. "Indeed my party is so small and the Indians so Numerous, so easily assembled, and so insolent," he reported, that his ability to act was limited. Even worse, he believed that the Indians had grown unaccustomed to having "troops among them since the Peace" and as a result "have been quite Masters here, and treated the Inhabitants as they thought proper, which has drove several of them to the other Side of the River." Repeatedly, despite the agreements seemingly worked out between Pontiac, his allies, and the British, Stirling's reports underlined the weakness of his position, the forcefulness of the Illinois Indians, and the importance of the growing settlement at St. Louis as a destabilizing factor in diplomatic and commercial realms. St. Louis, he noted, already counted forty families, and had been "esstablished [sic] since the Cession of this Country to the English, by those who either did not like our Government, or were frightned [sic] for the Indians."[103] In addition to those who had already crossed the river, more planned to leave, wanting permission only to stay long enough in Illinois to sell their property to English merchants whom they anticipated would arrive in the next year.[104] When the French settlers of British Illinois asked to be allowed nine months to make up their minds about their place of residence before being required to take a loyalty oath to Great Britain, they were initially flatly refused by Stirling. Realizing that most would go over to St. Louis immediately, Stirling soon reconsidered, allowing the colonists half the time they requested, but insisting they pledge their allegiance to the crown. They all agreed and pledged fidelity to the British king, for the time being.[105]

After Stirling assumed command over Fort Chartres, an exodus of French colonists to St. Louis followed. Nothing Stirling did or said could dissuade them from leaving. He hoped that many would stay and thought he had persuaded them to do so but soon learned his assumptions had been ill-founded. He considered himself fooled by their remarks when "many of them drove off their Cattle in the night and carried off their Effects and grain." Without sufficient troops, Stirling could not monitor the ferrying

103. Ibid.
104. "Memorial of the Illinois French to Gage," in ibid., 112.
105. Stirling to Gage, October 18, 1765, in ibid., 109.

spots at either Cahokia or Kaskaskia. Without any real enticements to offer, he worried that he would lose the rest of the colonists "if the gentlest methods are not used."[106] Evading the British authorities, some colonists even crossed the Mississippi river at night with building materials in hand, carrying with them parts of their homes—"the board, the windows and door frames"—to their new lives in St. Louis.[107] One can imagine these French creole men and women disassembling their homes, packing up whatever they could, and moving under the cover of darkness. Clearly, St. Louis was thriving, to the delight, no doubt, of Laclède and much to the chagrin of the British. According to Stirling, all of the local Indians—almost five hundred Kaskaskia, Metchis, Peoria, and Cahos—informed him and St. Ange in a council that they intended "all going to the other side to live."[108]

With St. Ange's removal from Fort Chartres to St. Louis, the population drain from the newly British territory on the eastern banks of the river continued. A British officer sent to survey the territory noted the importance of the French military presence in St. Louis. "For the further security of this settlement," reported Captain Philip Pittman, "the French Staff of officers were order'd to remove to it on the rend'ring Fort Chartres to the English." Now, the added weight of a French garrison in St. Louis had the effect of drawing "the greatest part of the Inhabitants of the Village of Ste Anne de Fort de Chartres" to the new post.[109] As Louisiana's French governor summed up the situation, "The majority of the inhabitants who lived there on the English side have already sent their cattle across to our shore both because the English commandants have given them only four months to decide [their future place of residence] and because they are not pleased at all to remain under the English yoke."[110]

With a long history of deep-seated antagonisms between France and England, cultural differences in language and religion, and a fear of the unknown, many of the French residents of Britain's new Illinois territory concluded that their best chances for living as they wished lay elsewhere. (Those crossing the Mississippi in the 1760s were continuing a pattern of migration begun in the 1750s, when settlers seeking more productive

106. Stirling to Gage, December 15, 1765, in ibid., 125.
107. Chouteau, "Narrative of the Settlement of St. Louis," 54.
108. Stirling to Gage, December 15, 1765, in Carter and Alvord, The New Regime, 126. In a letter written the next day, Fraser reported that the Indians had gone over to the Spanish side; Fraser to Gage, December 16, 1765, in ibid., 130–31.
109. Pittman, The Present State of the European Settlements, lx.
110. Charles-Philippe Aubry to M. Dubuq, January 27, 1766, in Alvord and Carter, The New Regime, 139; "Memorial of the inhabitants of Kaskaskia in Illinois to Major General Gage," January 1766, in ibid., 111–14.

farmland established Ste. Genevieve.)[111] As military movements and the occupation of Fort Chartres made clear, British authority on the eastern bank of the Mississippi was unmistakable and unavoidable. The resulting shift of people from one side of the river to the other benefited St. Louis, and its residents reconfigured their lives, evading the rule of one foreign prince only to be disappointed in their hopes of living under a French monarch in St. Louis. That dream died before it was fully born, ended by news that the territory had been ceded to Spain before the first tree was cleared. Yet Spain's rule remained an abstraction for St. Louisans in the settlement's first few years. Busy with their own affairs, the inhabitants of the new village could easily ignore an absent government.

.

111. Ekberg, *Colonial Ste. Genevieve*, 22, 31, 35, 37.

Chapter 3

"A Strange Mixture"

RULERS, MISRULE, AND UNRULY INHABITANTS IN THE 1760S

In the fall of 1768, General Thomas Gage, the commander of British forces in North America, sent his superiors in England a curious report about the state of affairs in St. Louis and its environs. His informants in Illinois had told him of "a Strange Mixture of French and Spanish government on the opposite Side" of the river. While the French commandant, Louis St. Ange, exercised authority on the Spanish side of the Mississippi River, a Spanish officer held sway a few miles away, over the mouth of the Missouri River, and the two were said to operate entirely independently. Indeed, Gage's informants suggested that the two officials were even prohibited from consulting with each other. In the British general's view, this peculiar situation meant that there was "no knowing to whom the Country belongs." He had heard that only a short time after Spain had begun to occupy this territory, the confused state of affairs was already having a negative affect on trade and settlement. He further reported that a newly constructed Spanish fort at the confluence of the Mississippi and Missouri rivers had been destroyed almost immediately by floodwaters. "The French Inhabitants appear to be much disgusted," noted Gage, adding "that it was expected many of them would become British subjects."[1] Gage's accounts of a confused government and a disgruntled French population would have been very welcome in England. Despite Gage's optimistic dream of a return migration of French colonists to British Illinois, such an exodus never came to pass. Much of Gage's assessment amounted to little more than wishful thinking. The British clearly wanted settlers to populate the countryside

1. Gage to Hillsborough, October 9, 1768, in Alvord and Carter, *Trade and Politics,* 414–16.

around their new Illinois posts, and they viewed the French and Spanish across the Mississippi suspiciously, as rivals for trade and empire.

However wrong in some regards, Gage's report did get one thing right: there was a "strange mixture" of French and Spanish government in place in Spanish Illinois, as the territory of Upper Louisiana was often called. An unusual mixture of people was present as well, with French colonists from Canada, France, Illinois, and New Orleans interacting with Spanish soldiers and officers, while a constantly changing population of Indians from many different nations came to St. Louis for temporary sojourns and longer stays. With incompetent rulers on one hand and an unruly assortment of colonists, soldiers, and Indians on the other—all of them attempting to achieve often-conflicting personal goals and agendas—St. Louis in the late 1760s was an unsettled, chaotic place. As a result, and perhaps predictably, the village was a site of uncertain governance, shifting sources of authority, and social, economic, and political instability.

From their vantage point on the eastern side of the Mississippi River, the British were deeply interested in St. Louis from the moment of its founding in 1764. Once they had established a general peace with the indigenous inhabitants of the region in August and September of 1766—agreeing to peace terms with over a thousand Indian men representing twenty-five tribes—they were even more interested in the west bank and its French residents.[2] Peace with the Indians opened the possibility of profitable trade, but obstacles remained. Since the moment the British had taken possession of Fort Chartres, their commercial efforts had been undercut by the French as surely as the fort's site had been eaten away by the river. One British officer, George Croghan, complained that the biggest traders of Kaskaskia, Fort Chartres, and Cahokia had all "removed" to the opposite side of the Mississippi, where they settled in St. Louis. Sending men and goods up the Mississippi and Illinois Rivers, these rogue traders were carrying on a "most profitable," albeit illicit, trade. "I am Convinced," wrote Croghan, "it will be very difficult, if not impossible, except at a vast Annual expense in Presents, to retain the Indians in our Interest."[3]

Eyeing their neighbors, the British sized up St. Louis and Pierre Laclède as key barriers to their ambitions. The existence of the village clearly had undermined British attempts to build up a colonial population in Illinois, and Laclède's activities had prevented British traders from obtaining a

2. George Croghan reported the successful councils at Fort Chartres; Alvord and Carter, *The New Regime*, 373; Alvord, *The Illinois Country*, 273.

3. Croghan to Gage, January 16, 1767, in Alvord and Carter, *The New Regime*, 491.

sizeable share of the lucrative fur trade of the Missouri River basin. St. Louis was situated advantageously, "pleasantly situated on a high Ground which forms the W. Bank of the Mississippi," noted Captain Harry Gordon, a British officer assigned to survey the territory in 1766. By his calculations, the new settlement already had fifty families, primarily former residents of Cahokia. The village, he noted, "seems to flourish very quick." The promising start to St. Louis could be attributed in part at least to Laclède. "At This Place Mr. LeClef [Laclède] the principal Indian Trader resides," Gordon informed his superiors, "who takes so good Measures, that the whole Trade of the Missouri, That of the Mississippi Northwards, and that of the Nations near la Baye, Lake Michigan, and St Josephs, by the Illinois River, is entirely brought to him." [4] Such success was not a matter of luck. According to Gordon, Laclède was an astute and well-educated man. (Gordon's assessment was accurate, for not only had Laclède been well educated in France, attending school in both Pau and Toulouse, he built one of the largest libraries in colonial St. Louis.[5]) Moreover, so established were the French merchant's relations with the Indians, in Gordon's view, that no one could easily compete with him. In sum, the officer declared, Laclède "is very active, and will give us some Trouble before we get the Parts of this Trade that belong to us out of His Hands."[6] To the "active" nature Gordon ascribed Laclède, one could easily add ambitious, daring, and enterprising.

From the time of its establishment in 1764, St. Louis had an important leader in Laclède. As founder, partner in a firm that possessed exclusive rights to trade on the Missouri, and head of the trading post at the heart of the community, Laclède held great sway over his neighbors and their pursuits. He had verbally assigned village lots to many of the families that migrated from the eastern bank of the Mississippi and acted as creditor to many of the new arrivals. Laclède also often assisted the government officials appointed to exercise authority in St. Louis. After he moved into a newly constructed home in 1768, he began to rent out his former storehouse to Spanish officials, with the lieutenant governor and his family occupying the top floor and the soldiers garrisoned in part of the lower level. At the same time, Laclède sold necessities to the Spanish, providing gunpowder among other items, and stored supplies for the government at his own house.[7]

4. "Journal of Captain Harry Gordon 1766," in ibid., 299–300.

5. McDermott, *Private Libraries in Creole St. Louis.*

6. "Journal of Captain Harry Gordon 1766," in Carter and Alvord, *The New Regime,* 299–300.

7. Billon, *Annals of St. Louis,* 47–49, 150; Francisco Ríu to Antonio de Ulloa, May 2, 1768, AGI-PC 109-1116, MHMA microfilm. (See Anna L. Price, translator and compiler of Archivo General de Indias-Papeles Procedentes de Cuba, "Archaeology of the Saline Creek Valley, Missouri," Saline

When called upon, Laclède assumed leadership roles in civic affairs, as well as taking it upon himself to spearhead a range of initiatives and economic developments.[8]

Laclède's influence was such that when he saw someone act in a way that went against his own interests, he did not hesitate to intervene, as in the case of two Ste. Genevieve merchants, John Datchurut and Louis Viviat. In April 1765, Laclède ordered a boat belonging to the two, which was loaded with items for trading with Indians along the Missouri, to be brought to St. Louis and its goods seized and inventoried. Laclède considered the merchants to be violating his exclusive trading patent. Little did he know that the days of his monopoly were numbered. With a new Spanish governor having decided to cancel all exclusive trade grants, Laclède was in the wrong, and Datchurut and Viviat won the suit they brought against him.[9]

Joining Laclède as a source of authority in early St. Louis was the French commandant St. Ange, who left Fort Chartres in the hands of the British in the fall of 1765. Up to this point, he had spent some forty years in the military, serving France both in Canada, where he was born, and in the Illinois Country, where he assumed his final post at Fort Chartres when its commander, Neyon de Villiers, left for New Orleans.[10] About sixty at the time of the fort's transfer, St. Ange appears to have been a man both flexible and tolerant. He seemed to interact well with people from different backgrounds and enjoyed a reputation for good relations with the Indians. (Although St. Ange never married, the records leave hints that he may have had a family in St. Louis with an Indian woman, Charlotte. In his will, he made Charlotte his niece's slave for life, but her two children, Angelique, nine, and Antoine, sixteen months, were to be freed at the age of twenty. When Antoine was baptized, his godmother was Victoire Chouteau, the founder's youngest child.)[11] Above all, it seemed that St. Ange possessed the personal traits that led people to seek him out when they needed assistance in working out compromises.

Creek Valley Project, University of Missouri–Columbia, 1988, MHMA, hereafter Price compilation, MHMA, for an invaluable finding aid to the microfilm holdings.)

8. Billon, *Annals of St. Louis,* 144.

9. Ibid., 50–51; McDermott, "The Exclusive Trade Privileges of Maxent, Laclède, and Company," 278.

10. Billon, *Annals of St. Louis,* 29.

11. St. Ange's will, December 26, 1774, in Billon, *Annals of St. Louis,* 125–27. *Register of Baptisms of the St. Louis Cathedral, 1766–August 6, 1779,* transcribed by Oscar W. Collet, Missouri History Museum Library (hereafter MHML). There were also reports that St. Ange had a long-term liaison with an enslaved Indian woman named Angelique; Ravenswaay, *Saint Louis,* 27.

While the British officers who took over command of Fort Chartres were busy dealing with myriad problems in Illinois, St. Ange, with his move to St. Louis, inaugurated the era of the village's official governance. There he assumed civil and military authority, becoming the highest-ranking colonial administrator west of the Mississippi, standing in for the Spanish government until its leaders could send their own representative to assume those responsibilities, a task they seemed in no hurry to complete.[12] Traveling with St. Ange were the officers and troops under his command, the first military men to arrive in St. Louis. Fifteen of the thirty-five men St. Ange had with him had to be sent to New Orleans because of food shortages in St. Louis; the English had kept the flour supplies of Fort Chartres, which they renamed Fort Cavendish, for their own use.[13] Among the French troops who remained were Lieutenant Pierre François DeVolsey, a man whose marriage and extramarital liaisons became a scandal in the 1770s, and Sergeant Pierre Montardy, whose wife also became involved in public discussions over sexual impropriety. Several other officers and soldiers completed the party. Like the French colonists from Illinois who preceded them, many of these men received land grants for building homes in the village in 1765 and 1766.[14]

For the next two years, St. Ange held the position of chief administrator in St. Louis. In the dual system of governance in place, he, a French officer, dutifully sent reports to New Orleans, first to other French officials and then to Spanish ones, apprising his superiors of the challenges facing St. Louis and soliciting aid for the struggling outpost. In describing the community's needs, he noted that the inhabitants had very little, were scarcely settled in houses, and had no black laborers to enable them to produce all the supplies needed. Labor shortages and food shortages were chronic problems in early St. Louis, giving truth to its nickname of *Paincourt*. In addition to these issues, St. Ange drew attention to difficulties with Indians. On one occasion, a party of Osages came to the village and stole some horses. When one of the group was taken captive by some Illinois Indians, St. Ange had the offender put in irons and informed the Osages that their companion would not be released until they compensated villagers for their horses.[15] In another instance, St. Ange reported the disruptive effects of alcohol in St. Louis.[16] Such communication from St. Ange, including pleas

12. Foley, *A History of Missouri*, 18–19.

13. Charles-Philippe Aubry to M. Dubuq, January 27, 1766, in Carter and Alvord, *The New Regime*, 139.

14. Billon, *Annals of St. Louis*, 69–70.

15. St. Ange to [Ulloa], August 4, 1766, AGI-PC 2357-22 (Price compilation, MHMA).

16. St. Ange to Ulloa, June 16, 1766, AGI-PC 2357-14 and AGI-PC 2357-18 (Price compilation, MHMA).

for some troops and presents to help in dealings with the Indians, seemed unlikely to be met, given Spain's desultory response to administration in the area.

St. Ange was aided in his governing duties by two men who had held similar positions in Illinois: Joseph Lefebvre Desbruisseau, a French immigrant who had served as judge, attorney general, and keeper of the king's stores; and Joseph Labuscière, a Canadian who had acted as clerk and notary. The two accompanied St. Ange and his men to St. Louis and there set immediately to work.[17] One of the first orders of business was putting into writing the oral land grants that Laclède had made. Accordingly, on April 27, 1766, Labuscière, former resident of St. Phillippe, in the Illinois Country, began to document the land transactions of St. Louis, the capital of Upper Louisiana, noting the concession to himself of block thirteen.[18] The *Livres Terriens,* or land books, begun in April 1766, constitute some of the oldest documents for St. Louis's history.

As the ranking official in St. Louis, St. Ange continued to interact with French residents in Illinois, as well as the British garrison. To inhabitants remaining in English territory who had sent their goods to Spanish territory, he sent word that they had to decide their permanent place of residence within eight months. Some, he expected, would choose to resettle in St. Louis.[19] On one occasion, St. Ange hosted some official British visitors for a few days, including an assistant engineer at Fort Chartres.[20] In doing so, he was fulfilling the Spanish government's goal of maintaining the "greatest harmony" possible "with the English of the vicinity who occupy the opposite bank." Unofficial guests, on the other hand, especially those who sought to engage in trade with the Indians or private citizens, were entirely unwelcome.[21]

With St. Ange in charge and Laclède continuing to exercise authority, the French residents of St. Louis might have been forgiven if they did not expect the Spanish ever to show up to take possession of the village. Many

17. Alvord and Carter, *The New Regime,* xx; Houck, *HM,* 2: 18; Billon, *Annals of St. Louis,* 46–50.

18. McDermott, ed., *Early Histories,* 34; Billon, *Annals of St. Louis,* 25–26, 28–29, 79. The documentary evidence of official government in St. Louis began with the sale of a house and plot of ground in January 1766. The first concession of land recorded in the *livre terrien* followed in April, and the first baptism was recorded in May.

19. St. Ange to [Ulloa], August 4, 1766, AGI-PC 2357-22 (Price compilation, MHMA).

20. St. Ange to [Ulloa], August 4, 1766, AGI-PC 2357-22 (Price compilation, MHMA). Two of the visitors, Lt. Philip Pittman and Captain Harry Gordon, recorded their observations: Gordon's journal, in Alvord and Carter, *The New Regime,* 299–302; and Pittman, *The Present State of the European Settlements.*

21. Ulloa, "Instruction for the expedition to the district of the Ylinneses," March 14, 1767, in Houck, *SRM,* 1: 12, 13.

in the new settlement found themselves living near former neighbors and doing business with the same people they had dealt with for years. Under the command of a French military man that many already knew from their time in Illinois, they had no reason to anticipate a different regime or style of government. Moreover, and perhaps most importantly, news of the 1762 cession of the territory to Spain did not reach Lower Louisiana until October 1764, and Upper Louisiana until some time later, in either November or December 1765.[22]

Even slower than England about taking over its new North American possessions, the Spanish government allowed three and a half years to pass before sending its first governor, Don Antonio de Ulloa y de la Torre-Guiral, to New Orleans. Born in 1716 in Seville, Spain, Ulloa had a substantial if not altogether positive record of government service in the colonies prior to his appointment to Louisiana.[23] His most celebrated achievements lay in the realm of astronomy as part of a joint French-Spanish delegation engaged in taking measurements of the earth at the equator; the resulting publication he authored was well regarded and widely translated.[24] A student of natural history, Ulloa possessed scientific skills that made him a logical choice for another assignment in a Peruvian province, where a new governor was needed to oversee mining operations. However, during his stint there in the late 1750s and early 1760s, Ulloa managed to alienate the resident aristocracy completely; there were even rumors that he had to leave home each night for fear colonists would torch his quarters.[25] Resistance to his efforts to reform the Peruvian mining system turned to outright opposition, and he resigned his post in 1764.[26] A history of antagonistic relationships with the local elite was not a good precedent for the work Ulloa was assigned to do in New Orleans, where French colonists were loath to accept Spanish rule.

In March, 1766, Ulloa landed in New Orleans with a small escort of two companies, a total of ninety men, twenty of whom deserted soon thereafter.[27] He was ill equipped to meet the vast challenges of the position or to address the problems of either the northern or southern parts of the vast colony. As Carl A. Brasseaux summed up the situation, "Between 1763 and 1766, Louisiana, suffering from fiscal instability and official bickering,

22. Foley, *History of Missouri*, 1: 18.
23. Houck, *History of Missouri*, 1: 288.
24. Moore, *Revolt in Louisiana*, 4–5.
25. Brasseaux, *Denis-Nicolas Foucault*, 50–51.
26. Moore, *Revolt in Louisiana*, 7–8.
27. Aubry to Minister, March 12, 1766, in Alvord and Carter, *The New Regime*, 181–87; Brasseaux, *Denis-Nicolas Foucault*, 51.

became an isolated, highly unstable entity, a powder-keg waiting for a spark."[28] In New Orleans, French residents bitter over the transfer of the territory to Spain greeted the new governor unenthusiastically, their attitudes a forewarning of a restive and troublesome rule.[29] Although Ulloa spoke French, he had few other skills or resources suited to the demands of his new post. Nor did his personality promise much. The leading French official, Captain Aubry, observed that unlike most of his countrymen, Ulloa did "not listen enough to what people had to tell him."[30]

By hesitating to take formal possession of the colony because of his small forces, Ulloa exposed at the start the weakness of Spain. Moreover, the lengthy delay in sending officials led some colonists to doubt the validity of the cession.[31] Aubry, who had been acting governor and commandant of French troops since the death of the previous French governor, D'Abbadie, the year before, continued to maintain his military role.[32] Soon, the hostility of New Orleans' French residents toward Ulloa led him to reconsider his location. Rather than forcing the inhabitants of the Crescent City to accept Spanish rule, Ulloa decided to govern at a distance, and in late summer 1766, relocated his troops to a French settlement near the mouth of the Mississippi at La Balize, almost 100 miles from New Orleans, remaining there for several months.[33] Clearly feeling unable to take charge of the situation, Ulloa entreated Aubry to take control of the government until more Spanish troops arrived. Surprised and embarrassed by the request, Aubry attempted to dissuade Ulloa from the plan but ultimately agreed to it.[34] Thus, in January 1767, Ulloa and Aubry signed an agreement for joint governance of the colony, until such time as sufficient Spanish troops arrived to guarantee Ulloa's position. Under its terms, Ulloa formally requested that Aubry continue to exercise military and civil authority in New Orleans and its outposts while he would do so at the Balize post. Only at Balize was the Spanish flag displayed; the French colors continued to fly in the capital and elsewhere.[35]

Despite this peculiar dual governmental structure, Ulloa nonetheless acted to further Spain's interests and to address what he considered one

28. Brasseaux, *Denis-Nicolas Foucault,* 35.

29. On the Louisiana revolt, see also Chandler, "Ulloa's Account of the 1768 Revolt"; Leumas, "Ties that Bind"; Pierre H. Boulle, "French Reactions to the Louisiana Revolution of 1768," in McDermott, *The French in the Mississippi Valley.*

30. Aubry, March 30, 1767, in Gayarré, *Histoire de la Louisiane,* 2: 157.

31. Brasseaux, *Denis-Nicolas Foucault,* 91.

32. Leumas, "Ties that Bind," 184.

33. Din, "Captain Francisco Ríu y Morales," 125.

34. Aubry, March 30, 1767, in Gayarré, *Historire de la Louisiane,* 2: 159.

35. Moore, *Revolt in Louisiana,* 49.

Louisiana governor Antonio de Ulloa, Collections of the Louisiana State Museum

of the most pressing problems of the Spanish empire in North America: staving off the British threat to Upper Louisiana. Indeed, it was the prospect of British competition for the Indian trade, combined with the fact of British military occupation of lands east of the Mississippi, that ultimately prompted the Spanish to take possession of their new territory upriver. Despite having limited manpower and money, Ulloa outlined an ambitious defense program, with plans for new forts in several locations along the region's waterways, including directly across the Mississippi from a British fort at Natchez and on both banks of the Missouri at its confluence with the Mississippi, just to the north of St. Louis.[36] With many tribes settled along the tributaries of its vast basin, the Missouri River seemed to promise immense wealth to those who controlled access to it, and the British

36. Din, "Captain Francisco Ríu y Morales," 125.

cast a covetous gaze in its direction. Anxious to thwart Britain's commercial ambitions for the region, Ulloa decided to send Captain Francisco Ríu and a number of soldiers to Spain's Illinois post, as St. Louis was known, in the first official act designed to formalize Spanish possession of Upper Louisiana. To underline the meaning of their mission, the Spanish were ordered to fly their banners and pennants when they passed English forts as they traveled upriver, a blunt visual reminder that they were finally coming to claim what they had gained by treaty in 1762: the lands of western Illinois and the trade of the vast Missouri River basin.[37]

Before sending officers and troops to occupy the area and build new fortifications near St. Louis, Ulloa prepared sets of instructions that collectively outlined Spanish hopes for the social, economic, and diplomatic future of Upper Louisiana, as well as the means to achieve them.[38] The central goals were straightforward: the preservation of the royal domains belonging to the king and the maintenance of the same good relations with the Indians that the French had enjoyed. To accomplish these aims, those in authority needed to be possessed "of great prudence, of great reflection, and of great tolerance" in their interactions, "not only with the savage, but also with the soldiers, and with the other employees who may go." The command could not be purely military, and troops had "to be asked civilly, courteously, and affably" to fulfill their tasks. Toward the nonmilitary workers, lonely men far from their homes in "strange and distant lands," the commandant needed to be especially accommodating. If they found "but little kindness, harsh treatment, and a lack of affability in their superiors" or if they were treated like soldiers, these laborers would "grow weary of and desist from the undertaking." Highlighting the importance of personal style, Ulloa averred that "the government of those districts depends more on politeness and urbanity, than on the civil and military departments."[39] Indian relations in Upper Louisiana required even more care. Declaring the indigenous peoples to be "like brute beasts in their customs and manners" and liable to commit "the most ferocious barbarities," Ulloa employed racist stereotypes freely in his instructions. Whoever dealt with them must understand that Indians wished to "be regarded with distinction and respect"; officers must remember that the Indians saw the decision to allow Europeans to enter their lands as an expression of their wishes, not as recognition that the newcomers had any

37. Ulloa, "Instruction for the expedition to the district of the Ylinneses, which is in charge of Captain Don Francisco Rui [sic]," March 14, 1767, in Houck, SRM, 1: 3.

38. Ibid., 1: 1–19; "Secret instruction of Ulloa to Captain Ríu," January 7, 1767, in ibid., 1: 20–28.

39. Ulloa, "Instruction for the expedition to the district of the Ylinneses," March 14, 1767, in ibid., 1: 4, 5.

right to do so. Always, the Indians should be "treated as brothers" and not offered "the slightest affront, jest, or mockery." No one should "offend them through their women" because they considered it "an injury, even more serious than do the most cultured nations."[40] In short, in Ulloa's view, only a socially adept and careful administrator would be able to interact with the Indians successfully and thereby compete with the British for indigenous trade. As Ulloa reminded his officers, the two chief ends behind the founding of the settlement were "to keep the savages in friendship and alliance with the colony" and "to prevent the neighboring English from entering the territories and domains of his Majesty." Maintaining harmonious exchanges with the Indians would be especially tricky given that the Spanish wanted to modify practices the French had used successfully. In particular, the Spanish sought to lessen the quantities of goods designated for presents for the Indians in order to cut costs significantly.

The man Ulloa picked to handle the difficult and delicate role of head of the expedition was Captain Francisco Ríu, an experienced officer who proved an unfortunately inept leader. Recently assigned to Louisiana, Ríu was saddled with a less than desirable group of officers and troops, most of them newly arrived as well. (Historian Gilbert Din notes that Ríu lacked support from Ulloa regarding troop discipline and also suffered from Ulloa's decision to reduce Spanish troops' pay to match that of French soldiers. Disobedience and desertion plagued the expedition from the outset, with fairly disastrous consequences.)[41] In early 1767, Ríu began preparing for the journey following Ulloa's lengthy and detailed instructions for the expedition, which dictated the composition of the expedition party as well as its members' conduct. Of seventy-four soldiers available, Ríu would take forty, as well as four officers, including a second lieutenant, Fernando Gómez (a man who proved highly problematic), two sergeants, and four corporals.[42] Two French officers would accompany the Spanish troops. Several other skilled, nonmilitary men of French, Spanish, and African backgrounds—a carpenter, a bricklayer, a stonecutter, an interpreter, a chaplain, a smith, and a surgeon—also joined the expedition.[43] In this group, one sees signs of social and political flexibility, with French officers receiving permission from their government to serve under Spanish commanders, and a racially

40. Ibid., 1: 10–11.

41. Din, "Captain Francisco Ríu y Morales," 122–25. Ulloa, "Instruction for the expedition to the district of the Ylinneses," March 14, 1767, in Houck, *SRM,* 1: 1–19.

42. *Estado* given by José de Loyola, January 16, 1767, AGI-PC 109, in Moore, *Revolt in Louisiana,* 76.

43. Ulloa, "Instruction for the expedition to the district of the Ylinneses," March 14, 1767, in Houck, *SRM,* 1: 2; Billon, *Annals of St. Louis,* 58–62.

mixed group forming part of Spain's first formal mission to their territory in Upper Louisiana.

As commander of this diverse crew, Ríu would be called upon to exercise tight control en route. On Sundays and holy days, everyone would be required to attend mass. At night, the rosary was to be recited, and each day's work was to commence at dawn. The soldiers had to keep their weapons loaded and ready, and sentinels posted around each night's camp would guard against surprise attack. Of the many regulations Ríu had to enforce on the journey, the one that generated the most conflict was the prohibition of alcohol. Declaring his intention "to reform abuses" and asserting that giving soldiers and sailors rations of brandy led to "intoxication and disorder," Ulloa made the singularly unpopular decision not to include alcohol as part of the men's daily rations. He did, however, allow those "in the habit of drinking" to take some for their own consumption, but even they would not be allowed to drink "to excess."[44]

In Ulloa's vision, once the Spanish arrived in Illinois, they would construct a fort and a new permanent settlement populated by married families. This new community would be the Missouri Post, with its own commandant, to distinguish it from Spanish Illinois, with its headquarters a few miles away in St. Louis, the post headed by St. Ange.[45] "Inasmuch as the garrison is Spanish," Ulloa declared, "the settlement shall be so also, and that its government, customs, and manners shall be those of that nation."[46] To promote a settled population, Ulloa urged the inclusion of married men and their families in the expedition. Although the troops celebrated his decision and wanted to take advantage of it in the weeks before their departure, they faced two problems: a shortage of women and a lack of funds. One corporal became engaged to a fourteen-year-old convent-educated girl, but there seemed to be no other marriageable young women within its walls. Ríu hoped that others could be brought to New Orleans from Havana.[47] To encourage the men to marry, Ulloa ordered that the soldiers be provided with dowries and promised that they could live with their wives in the homes they built, so long as they fulfilled their military duties. Once the fort was finished, married families would receive lands around it. Those who traveled upriver without spouses were encouraged to marry

44. Ulloa, "Instruction for the expedition to the district of the Ylinneses," March 14, 1767, in Houck, *SRM,* 1: 3.

45. Houck, *HM,* 1: 288–89.

46. Ulloa, "Instruction for the expedition to the district of the Ylinneses," March 14, 1767, in Houck, *SRM,* 1: 8.

47. Ríu to Ulloa, February 6, 1767, AGI-PC 109-851; February 12, 1767, AGI-PC 109-860; petitions for permission to marry, February 21, 1767, AGI-PC 109-867, MHMA microfilm.

when their enlistments expired, and those of the troops who acquired trading licenses could settle after they received a land allotment only on the condition that they married within a year; otherwise, they had to leave. If men who wanted to marry encountered a shortage of marriageable women, the government would be informed, "so that arrangements can be made for orphan girls of the colony, or some of the Florida orphan girls who shall go from Havana where they are destitute." Such girls had traits that made them particularly appealing in Ulloa's eyes: "The latter are a light complexioned race and of good morals." [48] Complexion did matter to the Spanish, but it was not as important as factors such as shared Catholicism or the support of the institution of marriage.

Planning for the new settlement, Ulloa insisted that practices that undermined marriage—such as illicit, interracial sex—and those that fostered sin—such as alcohol consumption—should be prohibited. "Those who are married," he wrote, "even though of humble rank and mixed blood, must be regarded with especial distinction and esteemed highly." Those who avoided marriage must be monitored. Thus, any trader who built a house or store in the planned settlement would be subject to its laws and not allowed to "introduce the detestable crime of concubinage with the negro and mulatto slave women." Any man in commerce, no matter how small his business, would be required to marry within two years or leave the settlement permanently. "This regulation is most important," insisted Ulloa, "in order to uproot the vice which is generally reigning in the colony." Not surprisingly, prohibitions about illicit sex were accompanied by regulations regarding liquor, as the consumption of the latter was believed to contribute to the former. To protect the proposed new settlement from the "very common vice" of intemperance rife in the colony, Ulloa forbid disorderly taverns and limited the availability of alcohol. Liquor would be tightly controlled, with "the introduction of brandy, not only to the savage tribes, but also to the settlement" entirely prohibited. If some individuals claimed they "must absolutely have it for necessary use," they would need to procure "a special license for it." Anyone who exceeded the amount allowed would have his liquor stores confiscated, with the surplus to "be emptied into the river itself in the presence of the storekeeper, the subaltern officer, the surgeon and the offender, and a certificate of it shall be sent to the government." Other violators would be fined, with the penalties to be awarded in equal parts to a fund for orphans and hospitals and to the commandant.[49]

48. Ulloa, "Instruction for the expedition to the district of the Ylinneses," March 14, 1767, in Houck, *SRM*, 1: 18, 9, 16.
49. Ibid., 1: 9, 16, 9, 15.

Weighed down with Ulloa's lengthy rules for the conduct of the voyage to Upper Louisiana and his prescriptions for the fort and settlement, Ríu and his men set out for St. Louis in April 1767. Traveling in a large convoy, the expeditionary forces left Lower Louisiana in seven boats laden with goods, passengers, troops, and officers; three boats were destined for Spanish Illinois and four for two other locations closer to New Orleans.[50] Each boat carried a pilot, master, and ten oarsmen in addition to the troops.[51] A second lieutenant, two sergeants, six corporals, one drummer, and thirty-five soldiers completed the military party. Each boat would thus have had thirty-one men able to row, and at least five able to rest, making continuous rowing possible.[52] All of that manpower was necessary to travel up the Mississippi, a daunting waterway for those who braved it. At some points, when the water was low, falling mud banks, traces of floods, and dense canes along the edge made finding firm footing on shore nearly impossible. Elsewhere, "Streams of Water interspersed with a thousand Logs" and great pieces of clay "tumbling into the Torrent" made navigation a nightmare. "It may be thought next to impossible to navigate against this Stream," noted one observer, "yet such is the Force of Oars, that large Boats of 20 Tons Are brought by them to the Illinois in 70 odd Days" from New Orleans.[53]

Barely had the journey begun when Ríu's problems with his men commenced. Complaints and desertions abounded, as sailors and soldiers alike pronounced the food inadequate and the liquor situation unacceptable. In mid-May 1767, as the convoy reached Spanish Natchez, the men unanimously declared themselves unwilling to proceed on the expedition unless they were allotted an increase in food and daily rations of rum. Many deserted. Only when six barrels of rum arrived at the post several weeks later were the men persuaded to continue. In July, at the Arkansas post, troubles continued, with more desertions and more protests about too little food. Throughout the journey, Ríu's officers lent him little or no support, and one in particular, Fernando Gómez, was routinely insubordinate. Finally, on August 30, the travelers reached Ste. Genevieve, where they received a cordial welcome from the residents, who arranged themselves in two lines from the landing to the house of the leading citizen of the community, François Vallé. Ríu and his men disembarked to a salute of musket

50. Din, "Captain Francisco Ríu y Morales," 127.

51. Ulloa's commissary of war Loyola called for nine sailors for each boat. *Estado* given by José de Loyola, January 16, 1767, AGI-PC 109, in Moore, *Revolt in Louisiana*, 76.

52. Houck, *HM*, 1: 288–90.

53. Captain Harry Gordon's Journal, May 8, 1766–December 6, 1766, in Alvord and Carter, *The New Regime*, 301–2.

fire from the local militia.[54] Vallé and the post's military commandant, Philippe Rastel de Rocheblave, tried to assist the Spanish as much as possible, Vallé providing them food on credit and Rocheblave acting as Ríu's personal guide for the remainder of the journey.[55]

After a brief respite in Ste. Genevieve, Ríu and his party reached St. Louis on September 9, there to establish Spanish authority on the west bank of the Mississippi.[56] Although the journey had taken almost five months, the actual travel time was under three months.[57] Any relief Ríu may have experienced at arriving must have quickly dissipated. To celebrate the end of the journey and St. Louisans' enthusiastic reception, Ríu had ordered new clothing to be distributed to those under his command. As soon as his men received this apparel, however, many of them sold it and failed to appear when he called them for inspection.[58] This initial act of misconduct was echoed and amplified soon thereafter. Hearing rumors that more soldiers planned to desert and knowing they were at a dance, Ríu ordered his men to come back to camp for roll call. On their return, they behaved outrageously, so much so that an incensed Ríu struck one sailor with his sword. The soldiers who saw the blow chanted, "Long live the king of Spain and death to bad government." Clearly, the situation was out of Ríu's control. At Lieutenant Gómez's urgings, the men quieted down, but the next day they refused to go to their proposed destination at the mouth of the Missouri in Ríu's company. They would only go, they insisted, if Gómez went with them as their commanding officer. Agreeing to this plan, sprung on him by disobedient and disorderly soldiers and supported by his insubordinate second-in-command, the unfortunate Ríu stayed behind in St. Louis, thereby cementing his inability to rule his own men.[59]

Regardless of whether Ríu was on hand to supervise the construction of the fort, he was responsible for it, and he proceeded at an initial meeting held in St. Louis in early October 1767 to discuss difficulties facing

54. Din, "Captain Francisco Ríu y Morales," 127; Ríu to Ulloa, November 12, 1767, AGI-PC 109-981, MHMA microfilm. Details of the complaints regarding food and alcohol, as well as discussion of the desertions, appear in numerous letters penned by Ríu during the journey, in AGI-PC 109, MHMA mirofilm.

55. Ekberg, *Colonial Ste. Genevieve,* 54.

56. St. Ange, "Certificate of the Manner in which Captain Ríu Discharged His Duties as Commandant on the Missouri," March 2, 1769, in Houck, *SRM,* 1: 39.

57. Ríu to Ulloa, No. 2, St. Louis, November 12, 1767, AGI-PC 109, quoted in Din, "Captain Francisco Ríu y Morales," 127.

58. Ríu to Ulloa, nos. 3 and 5, St. Louis, November 12, 1767, quoted in ibid., 109.

59. Ríu to Ulloa, November 12, 1767; Barrera to Ríu, September 23, 1767; Ríu to Barrera, September 23, 1767, all in AGI-PC 109, cited by Din, "Captain Francisco Ríu y Morales," 130.

the project with engineer Guy Dufossat and second lieutenant Gómez.[60] The spot that Ulloa had dictated for the fort on the northern bank at the mouth of the Missouri was submerged under eight or nine feet of water during annual floods. The officers agreed that Ulloa's plan could not be implemented at the exact site and sent a report to inform him that they would construct only a small blockhouse on the north shore, with a larger fort to be built on the south side. Thus, access to the Missouri would still be fully monitored and the fortifications would be safe from the yearly inundations. When the expeditionary forces—sailors, troops, and workers, but not Ríu—traveled to the location a few days later, they took formal possession of both banks of the Missouri in the name of King Carlos III, firing artillery to mark the moment.[61]

That seemingly auspicious moment of ceremony aside, the mission at the Missouri confluence continued to be plagued by problems with supplies and conduct. Within a few weeks, Ríu had to send two boats with his storekeeper, Barrera, to Ste. Genevieve for food, as the presence of the expedition forces, about 100 people in total, had created shortages in St. Louis.[62] While off on that official business for nine days, Barrera misbehaved. He sold liquor while en route, got soldiers and workers into debt, failed to keep Ríu informed of his success in obtaining supplies, and violated Ríu's direct orders by purchasing a milk cow and meat (which turned out to be spoiled) on the English side.[63] In Ste. Genevieve, the foraging party got into more trouble, with Ríu's men "trying to get Indian men drunk in order to sleep with their woman," a practice Ríu said they were also guilty of with regard to the black population of the posts. Alcohol abuse and interracial sex were both potentially significant problems from Ríu's perspective.[64] Despite Barrera's less than satisfactory performance while away from the camp, he did procure some welcome victuals: two barrels of salted beef and a month's supply of flour and vegetables. Unfortunately, the bread situation was bad as well, due to a lack of bakers and ovens.[65] Hungry and isolated, the soldiers, sailors, and craftsmen complained of poor and insufficient food—on one occasion

---

60. Council of war held at St. Louis, October 2, 1767, in Houck, *SRM,* 1: 29.

61. Din, "Captain Francisco Ríu y Morales," 131, citing Ríu to Ulloa, November 12, 1767; Gómez to Ríu, October 11, 1767, Barrera to Ríu, October 11, 1767; representation of troops to Gómez, October 11, 1767; all in AGI-PC 109.

62. Din, "Captain Francisco Ríu y Morales," 133, citing Ríu to Ulloa, November 12, 1767, AGI-PC 109.

63. Ibid.; Ekberg, *Colonial Ste. Genevieve,* 127–28; Ríu to Ulloa, November 12, 1767, AGI-PC 109-991, AGI-PC 109-995, MHMA microfilm.

64. Ríu to Ulloa, November 12, 1767, AGI-PC 109-1031, MHMA microfilm.

65. Ríu to Ulloa, November 12, 1767, AGI-PC 109-991, MHMA microfilm.

objecting to going twenty-four hours without eating—as well as harsh treatment.[66]

Rebellious men and outrageous behavior aggravated Ríu in St. Louis and slowed the pace of work at the Missouri construction sites. The troops were more or less in open revolt, and workers refused to do their assigned tasks. One crossed the Mississippi to spend the day in Cahokia, failing to seek permission to do so, and returned by way of a lie. Standing on the bank at nine o'clock in the evening, Miguel de Trilles yelled that he had come from Ste. Genevieve with correspondence from New Orleans. On hearing that report, St. Ange sent a boat across to carry him over, but Trilles was arrested when his subterfuge was discovered. By mid-November 1767, Ríu had had his fill of disorderly conduct and had filed his first appeal to Ulloa to relieve him of his commission, a request he repeated several times thereafter.[67]

Meanwhile, with living and working conditions at the mouth of the Missouri dire, some workers sought help in St. Louis. In November 1767, a master stonemason, Joseph Balboa, the sole member of the expedition identified as having African ancestry, had had enough. Hoping to get permission to leave, Balboa asked the surgeon, Juan Bautista Valleaux, for a certificate declaring him too ill to work. He promised to pay the doctor forty *piastres* to diagnose an illness, which he would then feign, a ruse that would enable him to reach New Orleans and then go on to Havana. Far from complying with this request, Valleaux took the opposite step, swearing in writing that the man was quite well and exposing his attempt to solicit false testimony.[68] After Valleaux refused to aid the mason, Balboa sought other means of leaving, going to St. Louis to secure secret passage, or, if need be, to buy a boat.[69] As a Spanish speaker, he first needed to locate someone to translate for him with the francophone villagers and found a willing liaison in Jean Cambas, whom he hired to help him get men, supplies, and a pirogue. Cambas at his side, Balboa went to the Denoyer home to seek assistance in obtaining a boat and crew. Although Madame Denoyer told Balboa she did not want to get involved, she did promise, at his request, to sell him twenty-five pounds of bread and twenty pounds

---

66. Ríu to Ulloa, November 18, 1767, AGI-PC 109-1066, MHMA microfilm.

67. Ríu to Ulloa, November 12, 1767, AGI-PC 109-1046, MHMA microfilm. Later requests were made on January 4, 1768, June 25, 1768, cited in Din, "Captain Francisco Ríu y Morales," 137.

68. Juan Bautista Valleaux to Ríu, November 12, 1767, AGI-PC 109-1044, MHMA microfilm.

69. Ríu to Ulloa, November 18, 1767, AGI-PC 109-1056, MHMA microfilm and Price compilation; Joseph Balboa testimony November 18, 1767, AGI-PC 109-1061, MHMA microfilm and Price compilation.

of meat. Another villager, Ignace Mayhon, agreed to sell him a boat. The two fixed terms, and Balboa paid Mayhon for the boat and for the wages of two men whom he hired to help Balboa reach his destination.[70] For some reason, after involving themselves in Balboa's plans, both Denoyer and Mayhon shared suspicions about his conduct with Ríu, and the commandant ordered Balboa to be placed under arrest.

Balboa's own testimony of his flight and interactions with St. Louisans suggests a village setting where individual contacts may have had more influence than rules and where outsiders were tolerated, if not altogether accepted. In explaining his actions, Balboa admitted that he had come to St. Louis without a license from any superior to do so. His goal was to reach New Orleans, see Governor Ulloa, and inform him about the bad treatment that workers and soldiers were receiving at the hands of Lt. Gómez, the officer in command at the fort site. Gómez had purportedly refused to allow Balboa to leave, and both the engineer, Dufossat, and another officer asserted their belief that Ríu would deny the mason's petition as well. According to Balboa's statement, Madame Denoyer was more active than she had admitted in her deposition; he said she decided to help him when she learned of his circumstances.[71] To punish Balboa for acting without permission, Ríu had him returned to the fort as a prisoner and ordered him to work for his upkeep. (Despite Ulloa's order that Ríu send Balboa to New Orleans as soon as possible, Ríu failed to do so until the following July.[72])

Back at the fort, the situation continued to deteriorate, with the disorderly soldiers and laborers creating havoc throughout the region. When Ríu ordered the storekeeper to take the last of the three expedition boats remaining in Upper Louisiana, the *San Antonio,* to Ste. Genevieve for more supplies, the twelve men he sent behaved badly.[73] Instead of sticking to the business at hand, they pursued pleasure, seeking dances, women, and wine. The storekeeper, Barrera, hosted a dance at which he presented a bouquet bedecked with a doubloon to his queen of the ball; large quantities of wine and other spirits were consumed as well.[74] As fall turned to winter, bitter weather added to the problems.[75] With ice blocking the Mississippi

70. Declarations made to Joseph Labuscière, November 18, 1767, AGI-PC 109-1058, MHMA microfilm and Price compilation.

71. Joseph Balboa testimony, November 18, 1767, AGI-PC 109-1061; see also AGI-PC 109-1063, 109-1065, MHMA microfilm and Price compilation.

72. Din, "Captain Francisco Ríu y Morales," 135.

73. Ibid., 136. See Houck, *HM,* 1: 209; Ríu to Ulloa, December 10, 1767, AGI-PC 109-1077, MHMA microfilm.

74. Ríu to Ulloa, November 30, 1767, AGI-PC 109-1075, MHMA microfilm.

75. J. N. Nicollet, "Sketch of the Early History of St. Louis," in McDermott, ed., *Early Histories,* 152 n. 1.

in Upper Louisiana, the boat sent to Ste. Genevieve for supplies could not reach the fort, and food rations had to be reduced.[76]

Gómez was at the center of several troubling incidents. Livestock sparked one conflict between Gómez and the inhabitants of St. Louis after the Spanish began holding horse races with the villagers' animals. A St. Louis *habitant,* or farmer, Renaud, had taken his horses to the vicinity of the fort to pasture them and was displeased when he learned what the Spanish had been doing. When he sent his son and another man, Chancelier, to hobble his horses and bring them back to St. Louis, Gómez prevented them from doing so, reputedly saying he wanted to ride them. Objecting that the horses did not belong to him, the Frenchmen were outraged by Gómez's reply that he would keep the animals regardless. When Renaud told Gómez that he would complain to Ríu, Gómez was unimpressed. He declared that while Ríu might be in command at St. Louis, he was in charge at the fort, and he did not care what the Frenchman said. Faced with such brazen contempt and perhaps puzzled as to how best to proceed, Renaud turned to his countryman, St. Ange, to intervene. St. Ange took up the man's cause, describing the incident to Ríu as "scandalous" and "contrary to all law and rights of men," and urging the Spanish commandant to do something to resolve the matter for the sake of "the peace and well-being" of the people.[77] Gómez was accused of abusiveness repeatedly. In August 1768, Labuscière went to the fort from St. Louis to interview twenty-three witnesses about Gómez' conduct toward his engineer, Joseph Barelas. Uniformly, they testified that Gómez routinely applied offensive epithets toward Barelas, whom they all described as faithful and trustworthy in discharge of his duties.[78]

As the winter of 1767 turned to the spring of 1768 and the construction project neared completion, troubles did not abate. The workers, including soldiers and sailors, protested the excessively high prices they were charged for alcohol—a bottle costing more than a day's wages—and sent a delegation to Ríu to enlist his support. Their gesture seems ironic, to say the least, given how often they had thwarted him. Lodged in St. Louis, he met with them and urged them to put their complaint into writing. Ill himself, Ríu was not faring well, as his request to Gómez to send the doctor to attend him had elicited a blunt refusal. Back at the fort, Gómez had troubles of his own, with Indians having briefly seized and held the blockhouse built on the north shore, across from the main fort on the south bank. Particularly

---

76. Din, "Captain Francisco Ríu y Morales," 137, citing Ríu to Ulloa, December 13, 1767, and Ulloa to Ríu, February 3, 1768, both in AGI-PC 109.

77. St. Ange to Ríu, March 1, 1768, AGI-PC 109-1104, MHMA microfilm.

78. Billon, *Annals of St. Louis,* 54, 57.

problematic was the state of the fort's defensive stores; the too-small fort had no place for gunpowder, so it was kept in a rented warehouse several miles away in St. Louis, minimizing its usefulness.[79] Ongoing desertions were matched by official requests for leave. Petitioning for release from his duties at the fort, the surgeon, Valleaux, asserted that he could not endure any more abuse, threats, or insults. Ríu had done nothing about his complaints, but the surgeon did not blame the commandant, adding that he heard it said publicly that the rebellious men planned to kill Ríu.[80] Valleaux, who had acquired a house lot in St. Louis, had his own problems and had fallen seriously ill by late spring 1768. Attributing his sickness to spending the previous frigid winter in a miserable cabin with no chimney, Valleaux had developed a lung ailment and was coughing up blood. He died that November at the Denoyer home in St. Louis.[81]

Conflict over food and drink at the fort erupted regularly. In June 1768, Spanish mason Miguel Trilles got into a fracas over a piece of fish. When a soldier complained that the fish the mason had lying on the ground smelled bad and should be thrown out, Trilles protested that "it smelt no worse than the salt meat issued to them in their rations." A heated exchange followed, during which another soldier tried to knock Trilles down with his musket, and Gómez, who came upon the brawl, had the mason clapped in irons and sent to St. Louis as a prisoner. As it turned out, the bone of contention was not just the smelly fish. Gómez had another problem with Trilles, who regularly brought brandy to the fort for his own consumption and generously shared it with coworkers and soldiers. In doing so, he interfered with Gómez's financial interests as purveyor for the troops. When Trilles gave away alcohol, he cut directly into the profits Gómez stood to make from liquor sales.[82] Despite repeated direct orders forbidding the sale of alcohol, Gómez and a few others at the fort sold liquor to the rest of the men.[83] On another occasion, bad meat was fed to the troops and workers, making some ill. As the odor from the spoiled meat worsened, the men could no longer eat it, and Gómez ordered it thrown in the river. The stench of five barrels of rotten meat floating down the Mississippi, reported Ríu, was "sufficient enough to infest a republic."[84]

79. Din, "Captain Francisco Ríu y Morales," 137–39, citing Ríu to Ulloa, April 15, 1768, with enclosure from Gómez to Ríu, February 13, 1768, both AGI-PC 109.

80. Valleaux to Ríu, November 12, 1767, AGI-PC 109-1045, MHMA microfilm.

81. Billon, *Annals of St. Louis,* 59–60.

82. The incident also exposed the difficulties of communication. When Joseph Labuscière went to the fort to take depositions in the matter, interpreters helped him to question several workmen but then refused to interpret for the soldiers. Billon, *Annals of St. Louis,* 55–56.

83. Ríu to Ulloa, June 25, 1768, AGI-PC 109-1182, MHMA microfilm.

84. Ríu to Ulloa, June 25, 1768, AGI-PC 109-1191, MHMA microfilm.

During the fall of 1767 and the spring of 1768, while Ríu's forces were busy making a great deal of trouble in the area but very little progress on the new defenses, Ríu was in St. Louis pursuing the other main goal of the expedition: establishing relations on behalf of Spain with the region's indigenous population. Governor Ulloa had instructed Ríu to seek the advice of the French, the long-time residents of the region, in dealing with the Indians. In particular, Ríu was to follow the lead of St. Ange, an "elderly man" who was "very well known among the tribes" because he had fought with them against the English. Such a reputation was very valuable, and the Spanish were dependent on St. Ange's experience; it would be some time before their own officers had learned all they needed to about the "management of the Indians."[85] Accordingly, when a group of Indians had come to see him during his brief stay in Ste. Genevieve, Ríu put them off, telling them to go ahead to St. Louis, where he would speak to them and give them presents.[86] On reaching St. Louis, Ríu sought St. Ange's counsel, and the two worked closely together, living as "true brothers" and participating jointly in all councils with Indians.[87] Even before Ríu's arrival, St. Ange had extended a warm welcome to the Spaniard, telling Ríu he eagerly awaited his arrival and looked forward to informing him about the character of the inhabitants, the dispositions of the different nations, and the maneuvers of their neighbors across the Mississippi: *Messieurs les anglais.*[88]

Willing to follow the French officer's guidance regarding Indian relations, Ríu found his job a difficult one, complicated by indigenous hostilities and slow communication. In the fall of 1767, not long after he came to St. Louis, Ríu was visited by two Peoria chiefs, la Babiche and el Canar de Francia, who came to see him and inform him and St. Ange of unrest among the Missouri Indians. The principal Missouri chief's daughter had died of some sickness, and to assuage his grief, the chief had reportedly urged his warriors to shed others' blood, specifically, to journey to St. Louis to murder St. Ange and his people. En route to St. Louis, the Missouris had allegedly killed a French trader and a Kaskaskia Indian in Ste. Genevieve. Seeking "satisfaction" for the Kaskaskia man's death, the Peoria chiefs discussed the matter with St. Ange and Ríu. The two commandants said they would apprise the governor in Louisiana of the situation, and in the meantime, asked the Peorias to convey a message to the Missouri chief to come to

85. Ulloa to Grimaldi, August 4, 1768 (AGI, Aud. SD, 86-6-6), in Kinnaird, ed., *Spain in the Mississippi Valley,* 1: 59 (hereafter *SMV*).

86. Ríu to Ulloa, St. Louis, November 12, 1767, AGI-PC 109-981, MHMA microfilm

87. St. Ange, "Certificate of the manner in which Captain Rui [*sic*] discharged his duties as commandant on the Missouri," March 2, 1769, in Houck, *SRM,* 1: 39.

88. St. Ange to Ríu, June 27, 1767, AGI-PC 187A-391, MHMA microfilm.

St. Louis to give them his own report. In a postscript, Ríu reported that the French trader, whom the Peorias said had been murdered, also turned up in St. Louis. Although safe himself, he confirmed the death of the Kaskaskia Indian with whom he had been traveling while trading with the Big Osage. The Kaskaskia man had been guarding their canoe and its contents alone at one point, and when the French trader returned, he found his companion beheaded and all the merchandise gone.[89]

At the same time that Ríu was becoming acquainted with the intricacies of intertribal alliances and hostilities, he was also facing the complexities of building relationships for Spain that would be initiated and cemented through the giving of presents. In the fall of 1767, Ríu accepted St. Louis as a distribution center for presents, with St. Ange as his partner in overseeing their allocation.[90] By the time St. Louis was established, traditions of gift-giving had long underpinned relations between European governments and the indigenous peoples whose lands and custom they sought. Presents constituted an important form of cultural exchange and could denote many different ideas and actions, ranging from a mark of distinction, a sign of thanks or friendship, to a request or expression of tribute.[91] Before Ríu's arrival, St. Ange had anticipated Ríu's assistance with the great number of nations that frequently visited him; providing for them had impoverished him. St. Ange maintained that he had worked to keep the peace prior to Ríu's arrival.[92] The refrain of Indian visitors and colonial officials alike was "presents." Indians who came to St. Louis expected them, demanded them, and required them in order to open and maintain trade and communication. Their colonial hosts resented them, rationed them, and gave them to comply. Fraught with the potential for cultural misunderstanding, the entire process was marked by mutual miscommunication, recriminations, clashing expectations, and dissatisfaction.

Ríu complained repeatedly of the demands visiting Indian nations made for presents. On the first occasion he presented gifts to a delegation, not long after coming to St. Louis, he failed to fulfill Indian expectations. Distributing the goods in St. Ange's presence, and with the French officer's input, Ríu quickly learned that his visitors were neither uncritical nor passive recipients of royal largesse. When they complained, St. Ange spoke up, assuring the Indian visitors that the French and Spanish were as one

89. Ríu to Ulloa, St. Louis, November 12, 1767, AGI-PC, 109-1039, MHMA microfilm.

90. St. Ange to Ulloa, St. Louis, November 19, 1767, AGI-PC 107, cited in Din and Nasatir, *Imperial Osages,* 62.

91. Jacobs, *Indian Diplomacy and Indian Gifts,* 17; White, *Middle Ground,* 179–83, 403–4.

92. St. Ange to Ríu, June 27, 1767, AGI-PC 187A-391, MHMA microfilm.

and that they could expect the same gifts from the newcomers. The Peoria Indians who had come to the village pronounced the presents Ríu passed out insufficient and ungenerous. A Peoria Indian chief, reported Ríu, proclaimed English presents to be far superior. Indeed, the chief purportedly claimed that the English generosity was such that they gave his people more presents than they asked for, including liquor anytime they wanted it, night and day.[93] Whether or not his assertion of English generosity was true, the Peoria chief was skillfully playing on Spanish fears of British competition for the fur trade. Across the river in Illinois, the English shared such anxieties. Unaware of indigenous criticism directed at the Spanish newcomers' stinginess, the English worried that Spain would spare no expense in ingratiating its representatives "into the favour of Savages."[94]

As the fall of 1767 progressed, St. Ange, more experienced in dealing with Indian trading partners and allies, advised Ríu to prepare himself for his first big test the following spring. Then, after completing their own spring planting, Indians from many different nations would come to see the Spanish official for the first time. The Osage, for example, typically returned from the winter hunt to their villages in March for the women to prepare the fields and then left their villages at the end of the planting season.[95] As St. Ange had predicted, the spring of 1768 brought a large influx of tribes to St. Louis, with 240 Indian men from as many as seven different nations, including the Kickapoo, Potawotami, Chippewa, Ottawa, Sac, and Fox in the village at the same time in early May.[96] The official reports of the tribes receiving presents of alcohol, gunpowder, clothes, and other items between September 1767 and May 1768 listed fifteen different tribes and twenty-one chiefs, with some nations such as the Missouri sending multiple delegations under different chiefs, and at least one group of Peoria Indians crossing the Mississippi from the English side to receive goods in St. Louis.[97] They expected significant quantities of merchandise, and St. Ange told Ríu to be prepared to deliver large initial presents, which could be followed on subsequent visits by smaller gifts. St. Ange also urged the Spanish government to consider giving medals to

93. Ríu to Ulloa, St. Louis, November 12, 1767, AGI-PC, 109-989, MHMA microfilm.

94. Edward Cole to Croghan, October 25, 1767, in Alvord and Carter, *Trade and Politics,* 98–100.

95. Foley, *The Genesis of Missouri,* 10–11.

96. The numbers appear in Ríu to Ulloa, May 2, 1768, AGI-PC 109-1145, MHMA microfilm. Tribal affiliations appear in the journal of Jennings, May 5, 1768, Fort Chartres, in Alvord and Carter, *Trade and Politics,* 275–78, and in Ríu to Ulloa, May 12, 1768, AGI-PC 109-1147, MHMA microfilm.

97. Ríu, lists of Indians receiving presents at St. Louis (various dates, Fall 1767–Spring 1768), AGI-PC 109-1117 to 109-1124, MHMA microfilm.

particular chiefs; no Osage leader had received a medal and Ulloa ought, in St. Ange's opinion, to distinguish an Osage chief by rewarding him with one.[98]

Acting in consultation with St. Ange, Ríu gave a variety of imported goods to his Indian visitors, employing Louis Deshêtres, who belonged to a family of interpreters, to conduct the presentations.[99] In addition to the food he provided as host to his indigenous guests—the cost of which, he grumbled, posed an excessive burden—Ríu turned to the king's store-houses for a whole range of practical, decorative, and ceremonial items.[100] Dry goods, blankets, women's chemises, children's shirts, feathered hats, and mirrors were distributed to the delegations. Other objects, destined for use in hunting, defense, daily tasks, and diplomacy, included powder, gunflints, shot, guns, tomahawks, knives, vermillion, and calumets, the long-stemmed pipes used for smoking tobacco in councils and other cere-monies.[101] Perhaps the most controversial item Ríu furnished to his visitors was one they demanded and suffered from consuming: alcohol.[102]

Highly sought after by many Indians, alcohol generated a range of problems for indigenous communities in the long term and immediate problems for Ríu and the French inhabitants of St. Louis in the spring of 1768. Prohibited from distributing it by his superiors and also ordered to maintain peaceful relations, Ríu felt he had to violate one of his orders. The choices were clear: dispense liquor or face a breakdown of Indian alli-ances. Good relations with the Indians and the abuses that attended alco-hol seemed preferable to him to sobriety and open hostilities. St. Ange backed the newcomer, urging Ríu, as did others in the village, to give the Indians what they wanted—rum, brandy, spirits—in order to avoid trouble when such visitors, with tomahawks and knives in hand, insisted on alcohol. Satisfying the Indians who came to the village was no easy task, Ríu insisted.[103] Part of the problem was that St. Louis residents plied Indian men with intoxicating beverages in order to secure the furs they offered. Alcohol was an infamous element of trade, demanded by Indians and exploited by Europeans.

98. St. Ange to Ulloa, St. Louis, November 19, 1767, AGI-PC 107, cited in Din and Nasatir, *Imperial Osages,* 62.

99. Houck, *HM,* 2: 67.

100. Ríu, lists of Indians receiving presents at St. Louis (various dates, Fall 1767–Spring 1768), AGI-PC 109-1117 to 109-1124, MHMA microfilm.

101. Thorne, *The Many Hands of My Relations,* 30–40.

102. Ríu, lists of Indians receiving presents at St. Louis (various dates, Fall 1767–Spring 1768), AGI-PC 109-1117 to 109-1124, MHMA microfilm.

103. Ríu to Ulloa, May 2, 1768, AGI-PC 109-1145, MHMA microfilm.

In late April and early May 1768, alcohol-fueled chaos erupted in St. Louis. The large numbers of Indian visitors in the village received liquor from both Ríu and local merchants, but the supplies did not satisfy demand. One night, at the end of April, a group of Indians pounded on St. Ange's door at one o'clock in the morning. According to Ríu's agitated report, St. Ange opened a window to find out what was going on, and, on seeing the group gathered there, called for an interpreter to discover what prompted this nighttime visit. The interpreter learned why the Indians had awakened St. Ange: they wanted brandy.[104] Ríu complained that "in all the country there was only one capable of interpreting for the nations of the Missouri" and that he agreed to come and assist only if paid; the challenges of cross-cultural communication put Ríu at a distinct disadvantage.[105] Midnight disturbances were not the only problem, and reports of threats of Indian violence and thefts of village livestock followed. For St. Ange, Ríu, and the rest of the village's inhabitants, such news was undoubtedly a disturbing reminder of their vulnerability and dependence on the region's original inhabitants' good will.

The large numbers of Indians in St. Louis, and all that their presence entailed, unnerved Ríu, who found the situation exhausting and unmanageable. In early May 1768, he wrote to Ulloa to disabuse the governor of his notions regarding the state of Indian affairs in Upper Louisiana. While Ulloa was under the impression, Ríu believed, that representatives of various tribes came to St. Louis once a year to receive presents from the government on behalf of their nations, the practice was very different. Some tribes visited frequently, others came to see him constantly, and the Kaskaskia kept returning to get more presents.[106] A Kaskaskia chief with fifteen or twenty of his tribe came to St. Louis for presents, followed almost immediately by another contingent coming in to receive a share of the king's bounty. For his part, Ríu wanted to stop this custom. He complained that the Indians were taking up so much of his time—not leaving him alone for an instant—that it was difficult for him to attend to any other business. Even his sleep was disturbed, as during one evening when seven Cahokia Indians entered his rooms near midnight.[107] In reporting his interactions with Indians, Ríu insisted that using kind words made no impression if he refused to give them the brandy they demanded; rather, they insulted him repeatedly. Ríu declared himself not to blame for the mess: all of the Indian peoples coming

104. Ibid.
105. Ríu to Ulloa, May 2, 1768, AGI-PC 109-1138, MHMA microfilm.
106. Ríu to Ulloa, May 2, 1768, AGI-PC 109-1145, MHMA mirofilm.
107. Ríu to Ulloa, May 26, 1768, AGI-PC 109-1164 (Price compilation, MHMA).

in to St. Louis appeared to believe firmly that the Spanish had come to give them treasures, and for that reason, came frequently to see him.[108] The Spanish seemed unable to recognize that the "presents" they distributed amounted to a form of tribute to the Indian peoples who were willing to tolerate Europeans only to the extent that such trespassers met their needs.

The disturbances of late April and early May 1768 prompted the first collective community action on the part of St. Louisans, a May 8 petition in which residents begged the government for an ordinance to prohibit the sale of alcohol to Indians. Notably, the villagers addressed St. Ange as captain and commandant of the post and Labuscière as the acting judge and attorney, rather than writing to the Spanish commander, Ríu. In their opening remarks, the distressed villagers declared it impossible for the government to defend the trade in brandy, so contrary was it to commerce, peace, religion, and the preservation of their own and their children's lives. They insisted that those who traded liquor with the Indians must be stopped in order to prevent further depredations. In their opinion, brandy had already inspired criminal actions among the Indians, with the result that villagers were exposed to looting and robbery, with animals being stolen and slaughtered. Alcohol made its indigenous consumers "victims" and "slaves" to "disordered desires," and introduced the villagers and their children to the dangerous misbehavior it engendered. According to the petitioners, if not prevented, continual exposure to Indians' dissolute conduct would damage the morals of young St. Louisans, who would turn deaf ears to their parents and lose sight of their religion. Public tranquility would suffer as well, and all sorts of negative effects would inevitably follow if the trade were not stopped, and stopped immediately.[109]

Knowing that St. Ange lacked the troops to enforce any prohibitions on the distribution of alcohol, the petitioners volunteered themselves to act as an extralegal body of law enforcers, an offer that underlined the weakness of governmental authority in Upper Louisiana. Willing to take matters into their own hands, they pledged to name and stop anyone they spotted giving liquor to the Indians, thereby making it possible for the violators to be punished as fully as any regulations would allow. The ninety men who signed the petition, most of them with the "X" of the illiterate rather than signatures, included village founder, Pierre Laclède, and numerous other prominent merchants. Together, these petitioners likely constituted the overwhelming majority of the adult male French population.[110] Given the

---

108. Ríu to Ulloa, May 2, 1768, AGI-PC 109-1145, MHMA microfilm.
109. Petition, May 8, 1768, St. Louis History Collection, box 1, folder 1, MHMA.
110. Ibid. A census for 1766 showed St. Louis with a population of 332, which included 75

numbers of indigenous visitors to St. Louis that spring, these colonial men were likely outnumbered by Indian men.[111] Just as in the opening months of the village's history, when a group of Missouri Indians planned to settle at the site, St. Louis may have seemed briefly an indigenous community to a greater extent than its predominantly ethnically European inhabitants desired. Once again, the complications of the fur trade exposed both the contradictions implicit in it and the limitations Indians placed on European power. Merchants and governments seeking to gain wealth from trading with Indians needed their presence, their cooperation, and their custom. Repeatedly, Indians insisted on trading on their own terms and reminded the newcomers of their strength and command in the region. Encountering repeated manifestations of Indian forcefulness and presence, as they did in the spring of 1768, St. Louis inhabitants banded together to try to shift the balance of power by controlling the distribution of and access to alcohol.

Faced with such a clear statement of community fears and likely sharing his neighbors' concerns, St. Ange granted the villagers their request by issuing a decree about alcohol that same day. Its provisions were clear and the penalties it outlined severe. Calling the villagers' request just and acknowledging the mayhem that the liquor trade had caused in St. Louis and elsewhere, St. Ange declared it necessary to use "all the remedies and force" in his power to prevent future disorders. He forbid the sale of all intoxicating beverages by everyone, instituting a 500-pound fine and ordering confiscation of the liquor; the fees so gathered would go toward support of the church. Repeat violators would receive more serious punishment. Admitting the inadequacy of his forces to implement such a policy, St. Ange accepted the villagers' offer of aid, calling on them to stop and denounce all whom they saw providing alcohol to the Indians. One exception was allowed: only the liquor designated as presents from the king could be distributed. To insure that everyone knew of the new regulation and to enlist community compliance with its provisions, St. Ange ordered that the ordinance be read out loud to the public that day, Sunday, and then delivered to the king's attorney.[112] (In early St. Louis,

---

slaves, at least 50 of them Indians; Ekberg, *Stealing Indian Women,* 53. An official census for St. Louis, recorded nearly four years later in December 1772, showed 176 white males over the age of fourteen, many of whom were likely too young or not yet resident in the village when the 1768 petition was drafted. Houck, 1772 census, *SRM,* 1: 53–54.

111. Three years later, the 1771 census of Louisiana listed a total of 497 inhabitants of St. Louis: 251 white boys and men, 122 white girls and women, 74 enslaved African boys and men, and 50 enslaved African girls and women. Kinnaird, "Census of Louisiana," in *SMV,* 1: 196.

112. St. Ange, ordinance, May 8, 1768, St. Louis History Collection, box 1, folder 1, MHMA.

Sundays held an important place in the conduct of community business. Later, when a church had been constructed, announcements were routinely read at the church door after mass. With everyone gathered for weekly services, a variety of activities, such as auctions, could be conducted with ease.)

The shift in community attitudes toward the sale of alcohol was duly noted by Ríu and conveyed to Ulloa. Ríu acknowledged that to compete for Indian furs, traders had to supply their customers with liquor, a commodity they demanded. The English, just across the Mississippi River, apparently gave the Indians all the alcohol they could drink, and their traders were well supplied; St. Louis villagers' efforts to keep up with the English in that regard had had disastrous results. What was clear to Ríu was that the conflicts with the Indians, over alcohol and over trade, required a military presence and a coordinated response on the part of the government. In order to defend the colonial populace from hostile Indians and to enforce new regulations on commerce, troops needed to be on hand, he believed, particularly because Indian visitors did not take the reduction in the availability of alcohol lightly. Three groups of Indians and their chiefs, dissatisfied with their reception in St. Louis, killed chickens and pigs in the village, and seized an Englishman and demanded to know who he was, threatening him with raised knives. An interpreter who saw the confrontation sprang into action, declared that the man was a Spaniard, and so secured his freedom. The Indians left the village singing war songs and went to visit the fortifications recently constructed at the mouth of the Missouri to ask for brandy. When refused, they threatened to attack.[113] As May 1768 progressed, other tribal delegations coming to St. Louis for gifts objected to the inadequacy of Ríu's presents. Expressing their displeasure at not being given rum, one group of Iowa Indians said they would kill any livestock they encountered as they left St. Louis. St. Ange assured Ríu they were capable of carrying out these threats.[114]

Meanwhile, trying to control commercial and other exchanges with the Indians, Ríu provoked the ire of both St. Louis merchants and the Indians with whom they traded. Acting on Ulloa's orders, Ríu banned traders from going to Indian villages along the Missouri and its tributaries, insisting that they first travel to New Orleans to seek trading licenses.[115] The merchants responded immediately by refusing to supply the Spanish and

---

113. Ríu to Ulloa, May 12, 1768, AGI-PC 109-1147, MHMA microfilm.
114. Ríu to Ulloa, May 26, 1768, AGI-PC 109-1161, MHMA microfilm.
115. Foley, *Genesis of Missouri*, 33; Ríu's Trade Regulations, [June 1768], in Houck, *SRM*, 1: 35–36.

assembling to protest Ríu's actions.[116] As they had before, they turned to their champion and fellow Frenchman, St. Ange, gathering at his home to deliberate on how to present their "humble addresses" in order to persuade the Spanish commander to grant them permission to trade.[117] They griped that they could not afford to go to New Orleans to seek licenses, and they worried that Indians would object violently to the trade interruption.[118]

In mid-June 1768, when representatives of several tribes, including the Panis, Otos, Kansas, and Big and Little Osages visited St. Louis and learned of the trade ban, the Indians made their displeasure abundantly evident in a council meeting with Ríu and St. Ange. In a typical first meeting, a council was held immediately upon the arrival of Indian tribes visiting St. Louis. After listening to what the visitors had to say, the interpreter at hand, Ríu would employ the typically paternalistic and patronizing language of Europeans toward Indians and state that he was "very glad that his children [had] taken the trouble to come see him." Then, a time would be set for Ríu's answer to their remarks, at which point he would "have ready the present which is to be given to them. The present shall be placed before them, and they shall receive an answer to as many matters as they discussed in the previous council." (Ríu concluded these instructions by urging that every important Indian council be recorded and signed by the French and Spanish present "so that it may be a lasting record.")[119]

On the day the chiefs arrived, they presented two requests to Ríu and St. Ange, neither of which the officials were willing to satisfy. The chiefs asked that their villages be sent traders and that they be provided with water transportation back home; on a previous trip, several had died, purportedly from the heat, while returning overland. Following the custom of such exchanges, Ríu met with the visiting delegations again the following day, gave them presents, and delivered his answer: he could not comply with their wishes, nor could the king afford to send them by boat. In reporting the Indian response, Ríu quoted at length the Kansas chief's reply, which began with a recollection of his people's history with the French. According to Ríu's account, the chief declared that four years earlier, the French had provided the Kansas with everything they needed. The French had also told the Kansas that when the Spanish father arrived, they would be well treated. Now, on coming to see the Spanish, ready to accept them

116. St. Ange to unknown, AGI-PC 187A-397 (Price compilation, MHMA).
117. Petition of merchants of St. Louis to Ríu, January 15, 1769, in Houck, *SRM*, 1: 37.
118. St. Ange to Ulloa, May 27, 1768, AGI-PC 2357-14 (Price compilation, MHMA).
119. Ríu, "Instructions for holding councils with the Indians," March 9, 1769, in Houck, *SRM*, 1: 46, 48.

and expecting great presents, the Kansas were already learning how clearly the Spanish were falling short of their predecessors. If they traveled home by land, their enemies would fall upon them, and Ríu's unwillingness to oblige them with transportation would cause deaths; it was as though Ríu had received them with tomahawk in hand, ready to kill them, especially an old man such as himself, the chief purportedly said.[120]

Before Ríu could offer a rejoinder to these statements, the Kansas chief withdrew from the council, leaving the presents at his feet lying on the ground. The rest of his people immediately followed him. The principal Oto chief then expressed his opinion that no matter what present Ríu offered, it could not compare to what they had been promised. Trying to gain some control of the moment, Ríu felt obliged to urge the remaining Indians to come back to see him the next day, that he "would increase their presents and make them happy." This appeal had no effect. Indeed, the rest of the tribal chiefs walked out of the council. Sending the interpreter as an envoy to request the return of the head Kansas chief accomplished nothing. Everything took place in public, with witnesses. Ríu soon learned that members of one tribe had stated they would not admit the Spanish without great presents and that others had discussed destroying the Spanish fort if Ríu failed to send them home with the traders and merchandize they stipulated.[121] Spanish prospects in the region did not look good.

Such incidents likely confirmed St. Louis traders' underlying concern: if frustration at Spanish government policies led to hostilities among Indian tribes and actions against the French, the country would become uninhabitable.[122] Fear of Indian attacks had already begun to affect the daily activities of St. Louis' residents, with farmers and traders alike hunkering down in the village. They complained that they were compelled to abandon their labors and the cultivation of their fields "in order to shut [themselves] up," as well as "destitute of all fortification and with no hope of relief." To the dismay of St. Louis's apprehensive inhabitants, there were reports that the English in Illinois had begun to rejoice on observing the villagers' behavior; the English imagined gaining new allies among the Indians, "since some of the villages have already accepted their banner." English jubilation across the river was reportedly matched by Indian resentment closer to home. Accustomed to acquiring merchandise from St. Louis but now deprived of it, many tribes were "on the point of

120. Ríu to Ulloa, June 23, 1768, AGI-PC 109-1184, MHMA microfilm; Din and Nasatir, *Imperial Osages,* 62–63.

121. Ibid.

122. St. Ange to Ulloa, May 27, 1768, AGI-PC 2357-14 (Price compilation, MHMA).

executing their threats" and attacking those who failed to bring the trade goods to their villages.

Displaying a tactical awareness that Spanish authority in the region required support from the French colonists as well as, and perhaps more importantly, recognition that some Indians were prepared to take action against Spanish military installations and posts, Ríu revoked the trade ban. The merchants, who had claimed that "it was absolutely necessary to send traders for the tranquility of the tribes" believed that their "repeated petitions" made Ríu listen to reason, "notwithstanding the orders" of Governor Ulloa. They were relieved that their pleas and protests had not fallen on deaf ears, a fact they attributed to Ríu's willingness to conform to "the conduct of Monsieur St. Ange in this matter."[123] Given the delicate role St. Ange played in negotiating such crises, it is not surprising that the Spanish government in New Orleans formalized his role as commandant of St. Louis. In Ulloa's view, there were compelling reasons to keep the French officer as the head administrator of Spain's new territory, "not only on account of his conduct but also because of the credit and reputation which he has among the Indians."[124]

No doubt at St. Ange's advice, Ríu canceled the requirement that all traders journey to New Orleans. Instead, all who traded on the Missouri were ordered to appear before him in St. Louis sometime before the end of June 1769. Every trader among Indians throughout the Missouri basin who had received his license from St. Ange or any other French commandant would retain the right to trade in his designated area. If any traders from English territory were discovered among the tribes of the Missouri, they would be forced to cease trading, leave their posts, and return to English lands; those who failed to comply would be seized and have their goods confiscated.[125] On a final note, Ríu charged all those involved with the Missouri trade to preserve good relations with Indian peoples, reminding them that "the tranquility of the colony depends upon it." Anyone who behaved tyrannically toward the Indians or did not treat them with the consideration required would be punished and permanently lose the right to trade. Once Ríu made the decision to open the Missouri, he soon issued licenses, and traders began to set out from St. Louis. In mid-June 1768, six French colonists left the village to journey up to trade with various branches of the Pani, Kansas, and Oto nations. Traders heading to the Big

123. Petition of merchants of St. Louis to Ríu, January 15, 1769, in Houck, *SRM*, 1: 37–38.
124. Ulloa to Grimaldi, August 4, 1768, in Kinnaird, *SMV*, 1: 59.
125. Regulations made by Captain Rui [*sic*] to govern the traders on the Missouri, [1769], in Houck, *SRM*, 1: 35.

Osage, the Missouri, and the Petizo planned to depart for their destinations in July.[126]

Ríu justified his disobedience to Ulloa's orders on the grounds of preserving peace with the Indians and keeping the post functioning. As with the prohibition on alcohol, Ulloa had charged Ríu with two tasks entirely at odds with each other: not sending traders out of St. Louis and maintaining peaceful relations. If Ríu wanted to accomplish the latter objective, he would have to violate the former. Clearly hoping to cast a positive light on his failure to fulfill all of his instructions, Ríu suggested that perhaps his decision would be useful to the king, since the traders heading upriver could carry the five disgruntled chiefs back to their villages at no charge. He insisted that no one could have acted differently and still have managed to avoid a war. Equally important, he had kept the residents of the village happy. St. Louis's traders had told him and St. Ange that if they were not allowed licenses, they intended to go to the English side in order to avoid having their goods taken by Indians.[127] Forestalling this movement of people and merchandise was no mean feat.

Changing his stance on the Missouri trade did little to restore Ríu's woefully bad reputation among Indian peoples or instill confidence that his actions were having their desired effects. He acknowledged that he sent away Big Osage Indians "disgusted" at his refusal to provide them with traders immediately. Soon thereafter, he had a scare when a trader who had been traveling on the Illinois River arrived in St. Louis, breathless with reports of Indian complaints about Ríu's treatment. Encountering members of three nations who had just seen Ríu in St. Louis, the trader said he had heard them say they were very disgusted with the small presents they had received and the complete lack of tobacco. These disgruntled Indians said they planned to fight against the Spanish, "not their true Father," if the French asked them to do so. Clearly alarmed, Ríu took the trader to St. Ange's house and had the man repeat his tale. Although this account of Indian dissatisfaction and willingness to fight the Spanish was contradicted by a number of traders who arrived later, it is clear that Ríu found the first trader's version altogether plausible.[128] Besieged, bothered, and beleaguered, Ríu appears to have been struggling to hold on to any semblance of control in the summer of 1768. He pleaded with the governor to send him tobacco to distribute as presents, insisting it was essential as the only sign of peace the Indians accepted and used in all councils; every single

---

126. List of traders, June 17, 1768, AGI-PC 109-1188, MHMA microfilm.
127. Ríu to Ulloa, June 23, 1768, AGI-PC 109-1184, MHMA microfilm.
128. Ibid.

Indian who visited him requested it.[129] Trying to keep costs down, Ríu did not seek to make generous gifts or attract new nations to trade; rather, he declared, he tried to do the minimum required to maintain peace with the Indians and harmony with the traders.[130]

Downriver in New Orleans, Ulloa was unimpressed by Ríu's handling of Indian trade, diplomacy, and command. In the governor's view, the problems stemmed from the practice of giving presents to the Indians. "To continue giving them everything, as was formerly done," opined Ulloa, "is to keep them addicted to this bad practice." Efforts to reduce the "extraordinary Indian expenses" and to persuade the commandants "that the Indians cannot be despotic in their demands" seemed to be having little impact. As a solution, Ulloa proposed sending out "a better class of traders" who would be required to persuade Indian peoples not to come in to St. Louis except at set times and to supply them better so that they would not need "extra presents." Confidently, and with some ignorance of how matters stood on the ground in Upper Louisiana, Ulloa predicted that his plan would make the Indians "less burdensome" and that the "vicious custom" of giving presents would be abolished.[131] As difficult as Ríu's situation in St. Louis appeared to be and as unsatisfactory as his conduct of Indian trade was from Ulloa's perspective, Ríu was an even bigger failure with his troops. Throughout the fall of 1767 and spring of 1768, as Ríu remained in St. Louis while the rest of his expedition was at the mouth of the Missouri to construct new defensive works, his troops behaved badly.

By August of 1768, Ríu's resounding failures finally led Governor Ulloa to remove him from his command. While Ulloa acknowledged it was difficult to determine who exactly was most culpable for the disobedience and disorders in Upper Louisiana, he believed Ríu bore a great deal of the responsibility. From the beginning, his manners had made the troops and workmen very angry, so much so that they had refused to permit him to go to the fort or to take charge of the project there. Under Ríu's incompetent command, little had been achieved in Upper Louisiana. The fort was unsatisfactory, the troops had deserted, and the commercial control Ulloa sought had failed to materialize. Indian visits and the costs for their presents and maintenance remained problematic from the perspective of the Spanish administration. If Spain were to accomplish any of its goals in St. Louis and its environs, a change would have to be made.

129. Ríu to Ulloa, June 25, 1768, AGI-PC 109-1173, MHMA microfilm.
130. Nasatir, *BLC,* 1: 66.
131. Ulloa to Grimaldi, August 4, 1768, in Kinnaird, *SMV,* 1: 61–62.

Chapter 4

Power Dynamics and the
Indian Presence in St. Louis

When Governor Ulloa decided to remove Captain Ríu from his post in August 1768, he had no idea of how tenuous his own position was. Anxious to establish a firm foothold for crown and country in Spanish Illinois, Ulloa searched for a replacement for Ríu, someone with the skills to make Spain's imperial dreams a reality. Little did Ulloa imagine that within a few months, an uprising of French colonists in New Orleans would bring about his own removal from office. In the meantime, hoping to stamp out the pattern of bitterness that distinguished Ríu's interactions with the garrison in Upper Louisiana, Ulloa replaced the captain with Pedro Piernas, a man as celebrated for his ability to get along with others as Ríu was infamous for his capacity to inspire hostility and insubordination. Piernas was so well liked that the troops formerly under his command bewailed his absence and praised his "methods, jovial spirits, and good treatment."[1] In a spirit of cooperation, Piernas pledged to work with St. Ange, whom Ulloa reconfirmed as commandant in St. Louis on the grounds of his service, conduct, and reputation.[2] Shared governance seemed the best way to go, with the existing leadership in the village possessing the knowledge and experience needed to deal with both the residents and the large numbers of Indian peoples who regularly visited and traded there. Ready to lead Spain's second

1. Houck, *HM,* 1: 296; Ulloa to Marquis of Grimaldi, August 4, 1768, in Houck, *SRM,* 1: 33–34.
2. Pedro Piernas to Ulloa, September 3, 1768, AGI-PC 2357-136, September 4, 1768, AGI-PC 2357-140 (both Price compilation, MHMA); Ulloa to Marquis of Grimaldi, August 4, 1768, in Kinnaird, *SMV,* 1: 59.

attempt to establish control in Upper Louisiana, Piernas sailed for St. Louis on September 4, 1768. Forces beyond his control derailed his mission, and Spain had to make a third attempt before its hold over the region achieved anything like an air of permanence. Although control of the trade and population of the territory continued to elude officials in the short term, the Spanish government ultimately achieved success in establishing a firm foothold in Upper Louisiana.

Where Ríu's expedition had been plagued by desertions and disobedience during the journey upriver, Piernas's trip up the Mississippi in the fall of 1768 was beset by sickness and terrible weather. As they traveled north, most of his men fell ill. When the temperatures dropped suddenly, their boat became trapped in ice ninety miles south of Ste. Genevieve. After a week with no sign of a thaw, Piernas marched half of his troops overland to that village, where they recovered from their bitterly cold trek and awaited the arrival of their companions by water. When the boat did reach Ste. Genevieve, it needed repairs, further delaying the party's progress. Finally, after what must have felt like an epic journey, Piernas and his men arrived in St. Louis at the end of February 1769.[3] Shortly thereafter, on March 6, he reached his final destination on the south bank of the Missouri, Fort San Carlos El Principe, and on March 10, formally took possession of it from Ríu.[4] That smooth moment of transition aside, Piernas's mission in Upper Louisiana proved an abortive one.

Piernas could not have known that while he was en route to St. Louis, the French residents of Lower Louisiana had staged a rebellion against Spanish rule. By the end of October 1768, New Orleans was in the midst of an uprising. Two years before, Ulloa's failure to take formal possession of the colony on his arrival had contributed to a belief among French colonists that Spain lacked authority over the area. During his tenure, economic difficulties facing local merchants had increased, compounded by restrictive trade regulations, a scarcity of specie, and government indebtedness; conflicts among officials also contributed to the revolt.[5] On October 28, when a large number of rebellious New Orleans residents assembled in the capital, joined by 500 German immigrants and recently transplanted

3. Houck, *HM,* 1: 296; Pedro Piernas to Alexander O'Reilly, October 31, 1769, in Houck, *SRM,* 1: 66–67.

4. Houck, *HM,* 1: 296–97; Piernas to O'Reilly, October 31, 1769, in Houck, *SRM,* 1: 66–67.

5. Brasseaux, "Confusion, Conflict, and Currency," 161–69; Moore, *Revolt in Louisiana,* 124–25; Leumas, "Ties that Bind," 183–202.

Acadians, Ulloa calculated that he could do little by way of response. With only 100 soldiers (roughly ninety of them aged French veterans and the rest Spaniards), he had no real military option. On October 29, when the New Orleans Superior Council adopted a memorial declaring the commercial classes' grievances and demanding the governor's ouster, Ulloa was forced to comply, leaving the city on November 1 and reaching Havana on December 3.[6] Ulloa remained dismissive of the rebels' grievances, noting that some residents protested that new commercial regulations would cut off their supply of Bordeaux wine and force them to drink Catalonian. His Majesty, Ulloa declared, did not want subjects who only behaved well for the sake of their preferred intoxicating beverage.[7]

News of the rebellion traveled faster than Piernas had, reaching him almost immediately after he arrived in St. Louis. Thus, no sooner had Piernas begun to execute his duties than he learned that Spanish authority had been overturned and his assignment abruptly brought to an end. Ulloa ordered Piernas to vacate the premises and head south as soon as possible. In acknowledgment of the change in regime, Piernas delivered the fort on the Missouri and its contents to St. Ange, with all the ceremonies such an occasion required, only a day after he had taken it over.[8] It took a couple of weeks for him to complete the inventories he needed to prepare before leaving the fort permanently. Once he had done so, he evacuated, taking the troops comprising the garrison, the workmen, and the other employees to St. Louis.

While Piernas was no doubt briefed about the poor state of the fort and lack of discipline and order among the troops prior to his expedition north, he was perhaps surprised by what he observed over the next weeks in St. Louis, in particular in the conduct and character of its leaders. In reporting on St. Ange and the other members of the village council, as well as some of the merchants and other inhabitants, Piernas assigned them less-than-admirable qualities. Indeed, Piernas pulled no punches in sketching a negative portrait. In his view, St. Ange was a "good-for-nothing" judge, the head of a village council who enacted whatever his fellow counselors, a bunch of self-interested men, determined. Singularly unimpressed by the men who sat on this council, Piernas declared that it was comprised of four "useless habitants" and an attorney, Labuscière, who was "a notorious drunkard."[9]

6. Moore, *Revolt in Louisiana,* 153, 155–61, 164.
7. Ulloa to Grimaldi, October 26, 1768, in Kinnaird, *SMV,* 1: 80.
8. Piernas to O'Reilly, October 31, 1769, in Houck, *SRM,* 1: 67–68.
9. Piernas to O'Reilly, October 31, 1769, in ibid., 1: 73.

Equally problematic, some of the village merchants were grasping and greedy to the point that they advocated illegal acts for private gain. Apparently, a number of St. Louis traders had persuaded the village council, which was in charge of overseeing military and civil affairs, to seize the king's goods, a "novelty" as Piernas described it. They wanted the stores to be sold to satisfy debts contracted by a Spanish storekeeper who had fled. After Ríu, ineffectual as ever, had appeared before the council to protest its action and the council members had ignored his objections, proceeding to decree an embargo, Piernas intervened. Addressing St. Ange as the head of the village council, he reminded the French officer of his duties to the Spanish crown, which most certainly included protecting the king's stores. Swayed by his words, St. Ange suspended the recommendation and Piernas prevailed. Perhaps more useful than St. Ange's reversal in placating the dissatisfied merchants was Piernas's offer to pay all of the villagers who were creditors for foodstuffs or other supplies used to sustain the Spanish at the fort. In short, he managed to preserve good will among merchants in the community, but he thought them unreasonable. Clearly, they were invested in protecting their own interests, not in serving the king. Despite his critical comments about the merchants and council members, Piernas did have a few words of praise for other St. Louisans. He remarked approvingly that the inhabitants generally expressed satisfaction with the Spanish and sorrow that they were leaving. Even more significant, the "humble habitants" declared their submission to Spanish rule and desire not to follow "the example of the mob" in New Orleans.[10]

With the crown's business in Upper Louisiana concluded, Piernas left St. Louis on April 24, 1769, with Ríu, as the senior officer, in command of the departing Spanish party. Ríu was probably relieved to be leaving the scene of so much turmoil, though equally likely to be concerned about his future and anxious to exonerate himself. (Subsequently, Ríu accused several of his men of insubordination. Two were found guilty and sentenced to six years of hard labor. One of the exonerated, Sergeant Cobos, then accused Ríu of misconduct, sparking an investigation that began in Louisiana, carried over to Havana, and may have concluded in Spain. The records, unfortunately, do not indicate what ultimately happened to Ríu.)[11] For Piernas's part, although he expressed no regret at leaving St. Louis and its residents after his brief time among them, he did acknowledge that the inhabitants preserved "their spirit of subordination" until his departure.[12] Such sentiments

10. Ibid., 1: 68–69.
11. Din, "Captain Francisco Ríu y Morales," 143–44.
12. Piernas to O'Reilly, October 31, 1769, in Houck, *SRM,* 1: 68–69.

in mind, Piernas left St. Louis with his fellow Spaniards and made swift progress downriver, reaching New Orleans in less than three weeks, a more palatable time than the nearly six months he had spent traveling the other direction.[13] Two months later, he and Ríu were en route to Havana. When he left St. Louis in the spring of 1769, Piernas likely assumed he was leaving the village and Louisiana for good.[14]

Since the previous fall, however, when the fires of rebellion had burned bright, the mood and situation in New Orleans had changed. Although they still controlled the city in late spring and early summer 1769, most of the rebels had begun to repent their actions and had grown increasingly anxious when accounts they sent to France justifying the uprising received no response.[15] Then, suddenly, in late July 1769, word arrived that Alejandro O'Reilly, an Irish-born general of the Spanish army, was already at the mouth of the Mississippi with more than 2,000 men and at least twenty ships.[16] With the full support of the French crown, the Spanish government had authorized O'Reilly to do whatever he deemed necessary to take possession of Louisiana, restore order, and punish the traitors. On learning of O'Reilly's superior force, the French residents of New Orleans realized that resistance would be futile and awaited their fate. When the acting commandant Aubry addressed an assembly of inhabitants to inform them of O'Reilly's imminent arrival, they listened in "profound silence, looking at one another," deeply conscious of "the danger they were in."[17] Taking formal possession of the colony on August 18, 1769, O'Reilly wasted no time, requesting a list of the rebellion's leaders from Aubry the next day.[18] Although six of the leading conspirators were eventually sentenced to death for their crimes, the rest of the inhabitants received a general pardon.[19]

Trying simultaneously to preserve goodwill among the French populace and rebuild the colony's economy, O'Reilly made a number of strategic

13. They arrived in New Orleans on May 12; Piernas to O'Reilly, October 31, 1769, in Houck, *SRM,* 1: 69.

14. If their ship had delayed only a few days, they would have met Governor Alejandro O'Reilly's convoy on its way to Louisiana. Din, "Captain Francisco Ríu y Morales," 142.

15. For French responses, see Pierre H. Boulle, "French Reactions to the Louisiana Revolution of 1768," in McDermott, *The French in the Mississippi Valley,* 143–57.

16. Moore, *Revolt in Louisiana,* 194; Brasseaux, *Denis-Nicolas Foucault,* 84. For debate about the number of ships, see R. E. Chandler, "O'Reilly's Voyage from Havana to the Balize," 199–200.

17. Francisco Bouligny to Alejandro O'Reilly, in Chandler, "O'Reilly's Voyage from Havana to the Balize," 206–7.

18. Brasseaux, *Denis-Nicolas Foucault,* 85.

19. Moore, *Revolt in Louisiana,* 199–209. One pivotal figure, Denis-Nicolas Foucault, who served as the colony's commissary from 1762 to 1769, avoided prosecution in Louisiana, was briefly imprisoned in France, and ultimately regained his position in France's colonial service. Brasseaux, *Denis-Nicolas Foucault,* 5.

Louisiana governor Alejandro O'Reilly, State Historical
Society of Missouri, Columbia

decisions to strengthen Spanish authority, such as abandoning lesser military installations to concentrate forces. The three subdivisions of Spanish
Illinois—Ste. Genevieve, St. Louis, and the fort on the Missouri—were all
retained as necessary for the defense of Upper Louisiana.[20] With O'Reilly's
arrival in New Orleans, backed by a significant military force, Spain established control of Louisiana on firmer ground, and its authority was never
seriously challenged again by French colonists. Legal and administrative
reorganization followed as well, with O'Reilly abolishing the Superior
Council of Louisiana in November 1769 and issuing his own decrees.

Far to the north in St. Louis, in the wake of the revolt, villagers were
called on to declare their loyalty to the Spanish crown. The submissive
spirit they had shown to Piernas seemed to be on full display when the
requirement was made known. On November 19, 1769, St. Louis habitants
dutifully took the oath of allegiance before St. Ange, who administered it

20. Moore, *Revolt in Louisiana,* 221, 222.

on behalf of Spain. Delivered in French, the oath of allegiance dictated the terms of continued residence in St. Louis: "all subjects of this colony who wish to remain here under the domination of His said Majesty" must promise to be faithful to the king, to obey his laws, and if need be, "to sacrifice their lives for his service." Among the St. Louis men who swore to be loyal were thirty-one literate individuals and forty who signed "under ordinary marks."[21] Although this moment signaled future change, little was different for the present. Spain's first attempt to establish fortifications and a strong presence at St. Louis had failed, and the aged French military commander St. Ange remained in charge, with Laclède the leading merchant. As 1769 drew to a close, St. Louisans might well have agreed with a British visitor at Fort Chartres, who pronounced that the Spanish made "but an indifferent appearance" in the region.[22]

By the time St. Louisans signed the loyalty oath to the Spanish crown in late 1769, Pedro Piernas was making preparations to return to Upper Louisiana and resume the mission he had pursued so briefly earlier that year. Whether he, as Spanish commander, would be an improvement over Ríu remained to be seen. Returning to Louisiana from Havana in early October, Piernas set about writing a detailed report, based on his experiences, for O'Reilly.[23] At the governor's request, Piernas prepared "an exact and authorized description of the country," its products, settlements, population, "their manner of living and trade," as well as "its tribes of wild Indians, their customs and trade, and all the other things" necessary to understand the district of Spanish Illinois, or Ylinoeses, as the Spanish alternately termed it. Piernas's report, based on "as much information" as he was able to acquire in his "short time" in that country, captured his sense of the potential of the territory, his ambivalence about its French inhabitants, and his wariness regarding its indigenous ones.

Singled out for praise in Piernas's account was the land. "The country of Ylinoeses is, in general," he pronounced, "healthy and fertile, its climate delightful, and suitable for all sorts of plants, fruits, and grains." Mountainous in some places and flat in others, it held "vast prairies fit for

21. "The Oath of Allegiance to Spain," 205–7.

22. George Butricke to Barnsley, February 12, 1769, in Alvord and Carter, *Trade and Politics, 1767–1769,* 498. Butricke offered a bleak assessment of Ríu's expedition, asserting that only seventeen men survived out of the hundred who started.

23. Din, "Captain Francisco Ríu y Morales," 143.

the pasturage of cattle, and cleared level plains for farming." His criterion for assessing the country was clear: did it have the potential to be profitable? The answer was a resounding yes. "With but little cultivation," the fields produced copious harvests of wheat, maize, cotton, and vegetables. The quality of the soil was not necessarily matched, however, by that of the men who tilled it. In Ste. Genevieve, Piernas noted, the primary crop, wheat, "could be obtained in greater quantity if there were more farmers and its habitants applied themselves." Although some raised cattle, hogs, and horses, too few pursued agriculture. In St. Louis, the situation was similar, with excellent, vast fields capable of producing large wheat harvests. Unlike some observers, Piernas seemed to think St. Louis's farmers more diligent than Ste. Genevieve's. Though they had "not yet acquired the means to have slaves," he noted, the habitants applied themselves "industriously to the cultivation of the fields." Indeed, he anticipated that if they continued "with the energy" they had thus far exhibited, St. Louis's farmers would soon make their settlement "one of the most populous, extensive, well managed, and respectable."[24]

Piernas remarked that many colonists, having discovered that farming was not the only path to wealth, pursued hunting and the fur trade instead. By his reckoning, many men spent four to six months roaming the countryside to engage in hunting, with the backing of merchants. The territory abounded "in game of all kinds, and hunting is the chief occupation of the inhabitants." The pursuit of wild animals satisfied most of the inhabitants' needs: "from the flesh they obtain their food, and from the skins their profits." But these restless, unsettled men were wanderers, inclined to waste whatever wealth they gained "in reveling and scandalous chambering," forever in pursuit of a life of idleness. Through their "evil example," they did nothing so much as "corrupt the native youth." The fur business, "the sole and universal trade," involved more than just individual colonists hunting on their own, however. "In order to establish it," Piernas pointed out, "they enter with the permission of the commandant-general of the colony among the savage tribes." In short, they had to obtain government approval to enter the lands of the Indian peoples with whom they traded, "giving those tribes merchandise in exchange for the skins, by which they receive very great profit."[25]

---

24. Piernas to O'Reilly, October 31, 1769, in Houck, *SRM,* 1: 69, 70, 73. In an anonymous tract from 1772, the author celebrated the fertility of the area, urging greater industry and the cultivation of tobacco, which could make Illinois the most flourishing colony in the world; "Un Habitant des Kaskaskias," *Invitation Serieuse aux Habitants des Illinois,* 13.

25. Piernas to O'Reilly, October 31, 1769, in Houck, *SRM,* 1: 69–71.

In Piernas's view, trade with the Indians served only to enrich individual colonists and impoverish the Spanish crown. During his brief stay in St. Louis the previous spring, he had met members of the Osage, Iowa, Kickapoo, Ottawa, and other tribes who had come to the post to see him as the new commandant and to receive the presents that custom dictated on such occasions. Typically, the greatest gathering of Indians in St. Louis was in May and June, when "they descend[ed] the rivers in numerous parties with their traders to declare the furs." Providing themselves with meat while in the village, the Indians were furnished with bread and corn from the king's stores. Although the inhabitants of St. Louis benefited from "the goods and products of the hunt," it was the king who bore all "the expense of the Indians' maintenance during their time in the village, and he makes no profit from it." In addition to criticizing the financial burden created by provisioning Indians during their visits to St. Louis, Piernas complained that the commandant of the post had to listen to the visitors patiently and attentively, and "sometimes make rulings and mediate in their peaces, with persuasions, sometimes with firmness, and most always with presents."[26]

Clearly, Piernas thought that St. Louis and its environs, the colonists, their economic activities, and the Indian fur trade all had great potential but needed improvement. Whether he, in his new role as commander, would be able to shepherd through the changes he saw as necessary was uncertain, but he declared himself willing to try to fulfill the duties of his post. St. Louis might yet prove an important center for Spanish control in the region. Planted on a "high and pleasant" spot well above the risk of floods, St. Louis had a large plain behind it, which dominated the river and village and was ideally suited for the construction of a fort. The troops being sent to the area under Piernas's command could, if lodged there, easily defend themselves and "have the village and its territory under shelter." Envisioning the future, he posited that "the garrison could be supported from the products of the territory without any need of other aid." Such a self-sufficient fort would bolster Spanish authority and increase chances for victory in any war.[27]

Just as the fortifications could use some improvement, so too, did the governance of St. Louis leave much to be desired. In addition to assigning a poor character to the men who sat on the village council, Piernas doubted the virtue and efficacy of their administration. "Although the common welfare ought to be the concern of all, they only look after their own individual interests," he opined. Nor did they exercise much authority. "That council

26. Ibid., 1: 74–75.
27. Ibid., 1: 75, 72.

is not recognized by anyone, its orders and provisions are not obeyed in the country, for each person lives as he pleases, and does whatever he pre-meditates," he declared.[28] While such laxity might gratify individuals who sought to live in a state of independence or self-sufficiency, it held no appeal whatsoever for law enforcers and officials like Piernas. The Spanish govern-ment wanted to insure that justice was administered "promptly, impar-tially, and according to the laws."[29] Thus, when Piernas came back to St. Louis, he did so prepared to take charge.

On the eve of his return, Piernas held mixed views of the people of St. Louis. While he saw St. Ange and his fellow counselors as inept at best and corrupt drunkards at worst, he approved of both the submissive spirit of the villagers and the industry of the farmers. Piety and morality, how-ever, were another matter altogether. During his previous stay, Piernas had been appalled by the state of the church in Upper Louisiana. "Religion is given but scant respect," he reported, "or to speak more correctly, is totally neglected." With regard to the inhabitants of Ste. Genevieve, he wondered whether the problem lay in "the lack of a spiritual minister to correct, instruct, and withdraw them from the license in which they are living." There, the villagers formed "a small rabble, which is in no wise different from the very savages." (In this case as in others, officials used terms they applied to the Indians to describe colonists in negative ways. By likening colonists with undesirable traits to "savages," they simultaneously criti-cized both peoples, labeling them "uncivilized" and "immoral.") The same distasteful behavior was true of St. Louis as well, Piernas believed, where the distinguishing traits of the population were "looseness of conduct" and "dissoluteness and license."[30] Clearly, getting the church established on firmer ground would be important.

As had his predecessor, Piernas traveled to St. Louis with a set of instruc-tions from the governor. No doubt informed by Piernas's report and echo-ing many of the ideas that had appeared in Ulloa's orders for Ríu, O'Reilly's guidelines covered the subjects of trade regulations, Indian relations, and English competition. "The great distance from this capital to the Ylinneses," O'Reilly began, "demands so much greater prudence in the discharge of its command." In appointing Piernas, O'Reilly clearly hoped he had selected a man capable of successfully negotiating relations with the British, whose presence across the Mississippi River and involvement in Indian trade

28. Ibid., 1: 70.
29. "General Instructions of O'Reilly to the Lieutenant-Governor of the Villages of St. Louis, San Genevieve, Etc.," February 17, 1770, in ibid., 1: 76.
30. Piernas to O'Reilly, October 31, 1769, in ibid., 1: 70–71, 73.

remained ongoing sources of concern. Piernas's task was a delicate one, and every relationship was fraught with the potential for misunderstanding and conflict. For example, while punishing traders who did business with the English, Piernas needed to work to preserve the "greatest harmony with the English."[31] In dealing with traders, Piernas was charged with only allowing those with a reputation for good conduct to go to Indian villages.[32] Such traders were required to report in detail on the tribes they visited.

Ensuring tranquil relations with the Indians was a main goal of Piernas's mission. Choosing to approach the indigenous nations of the area neither as pagans to be converted by missionaries nor as hostile peoples to be conquered through military force, Spain had to rely on diplomacy.[33] O'Reilly ordered Piernas to accord good treatment and a just price for furs to the Indians who came to St. Louis while encouraging them to keep their visits short, as doing so would lower the king's expenses. In Piernas's conduct and distribution of annual presents, the Indians would ideally see "the greatness, clemency, and generosity of the King."[34] If possible, Piernas should enlist their assistance in capturing fugitives by promising rewards to those who did so. Furthermore, Piernas should also do his best to persuade the Indian peoples living in Spanish territory not to "cause any trouble to" the English who navigated the Mississippi nor to cross the river to offend British subjects.

Most notable of all of O'Reilly's pronouncements relating to Indians were his declarations regarding slavery. In December 1769, he issued a decree outlawing the slave trade: "All subjects of His Majesty, and even all transients, are expressly forbidden to acquire, purchase, or take over any Indian slave."[35] (It is important to note that O'Reilly's proclamation did not outlaw Indian slavery itself, only the trade in Indian slaves, a fact which contributed to the ongoing, if illegal, Indian slave trade and ambiguous status of the enslaved for the remainder of the colonial period.)[36] To demonstrate the truth of Spain's "magnanimous, pious and just" reputation, Piernas received additional directives to "show the order of the King, to the effect that no Indian slave shall be allowed in his states—not even those of hostile tribes."[37] O'Reilly added a reminder, which Piernas may

---

31. "General Instructions of O'Reilly," February 17, 1770, in ibid., 1: 76.

32. Ibid., 1: 77.

33. Kathleen DuVal, "The Education of Fernando de Leyba: Quapaws and Spaniards on the Border of Empires," 4.

34. "General Instructions of O'Reilly," February 17, 1770, in Houck, *SRM*, 1: 78.

35. O'Reilly decree, December 7, 1769, in Kinnaird, *SMV*, 1: 125–26.

36. Ekberg, *Stealing Indian Women*, 54.

37. "General Instructions of O'Reilly," February 17, 1770, in Houck, *SRM*, 1: 78; Ekberg, *Stealing Indian Women*.

have found galling, about how to deal with the Indians. With regard to St. Ange, whom Piernas had described as "good-for-nothing" in his report to the governor, O'Reilly ordered that Piernas should work to "preserve the best of relations" with him, as the French officer's "practical knowledge of the Indians will be very useful." Perhaps suspecting that his simple directive might be insufficient, O'Reilly outlined exactly how Piernas should conduct himself with St. Ange: "He [Piernas] shall do whatever he can to gain his [St. Ange's] friendship and confidence, shall listen to his opinion attentively on all matters, and shall condescend to him so far as possible without prejudice to the service."[38] In other words, Piernas had better defer to the aged Frenchmen as much as he could tolerate doing so.

With his appointment, Piernas became the first to occupy a new administrative position created by O'Reilly: lieutenant governor. Responsible for the villages of St. Louis and St. Genevieve and "the whole district of the Misuri River and the part of the Ylinneses" claimed by Spain, the lieutenant governor became the highest-ranking official in Upper Louisiana, reporting directly to the governor in New Orleans.[39] On reaching St. Louis in mid-May 1770, Piernas set to work immediately, taking formal possession of the territory from St. Ange, whom he promptly hired as an adviser.[40] As new commandant, he received a catalogue of documents written by Joseph Labuscière, covering the business of St. Louis and its inhabitants from April 1766 until May 20, 1770, including sixty-one land and lot deeds, sixteen marriage contracts, three estate inventories, two emancipations of slaves, one will, and various other legal records. For his first official act, Piernas appointed Martin Milony Duralde, a Spanish member of his company, to survey village lots that had been granted by his predecessors.[41] These earlier land grants were a matter of significant concern to villagers facing a new administration.

Acting with alacrity, Piernas sat down to do business with village founder Pierre Laclède. One can imagine that their meeting had some strong undercurrents, with each sizing up the other and weighing the authority of their respective positions and reputations. Whether their paths had crossed the previous spring is unknown, but it is very likely that they had met and taken each other's measure then. On this occasion, they probably met in the

38. "General Instructions of O'Reilly," February 17, 1770, in Houck, *SRM*, 1: 83.

39. "Office of Lieutenant-Governor for St. Louis, Ste. Genevieve, the District of Missouri and the Ylinnesses established by O'Reilly in 1770 and his order approved by royal cedula in 1772," August 17, 1772, in ibid., 1: 108–9. O'Reilly wrote to the king on March 1, 1770, to inform him of Piernas's appointment; in ibid., 1: 110.

40. Foley, *Genesis of Missouri*, 36.

41. Billon, *Annals of St. Louis*, 94–95, 100, 447.

government house, Laclède's two-level warehouse and former home, a building that could not help but remind those within its walls of the founder's
role and influence in the village. One of the first items on Piernas's agenda
with Laclède was to arrange for the housing for his troops. Backing him
and residing in St. Louis were seventeen soldiers, including a drummer, a
number of sergeants, and corporals.[42] Since 1768, Laclède had rented his
first home out to the government, and the governor considered the rent he
received for it "very high."[43] Now, on his first day in charge, Piernas reconfirmed that arrangement and pledged to pay Laclède an annual rent of 300
pesos for the building, to be used partly as barracks for the troops.[44] The
two signed a second contract, this one for provisions for the Indians, with
Laclède agreeing to provide the lieutenant governor with the bread needed
during their visits.[45] With these concrete agreements, the relationship
between the two men got off to a mutually beneficial start, with Laclède
retaining his position at the nexus of power. Over the next several years,
Piernas entered into legal agreements with Laclède repeatedly, contracting
with the merchant to furnish all the flour needed by his troops in St. Louis,
hiring him to build a jail, choosing him to command an expedition up the
Missouri, and continuing to rent his house for the government seat.[46]

A few weeks later, Piernas was still busy organizing matters in St.
Louis, turning his attention to forming militias for both St. Louis and Ste.
Genevieve. All men "from the age of 15 to 50" were required to join.[47]
In instituting militia companies, Piernas was following the governor's
explicit instructions, which not only called for the creation of such bodies
but named the officers as well. In St. Louis, those officers were to be Juan
Baptista Martinez, Juan Luis Lambez, and Eugenio Pane. Once men had
enlisted, Piernas was to send his superiors "the muster of each company,
which shall give the name, age, nationality, height, and trade of each one."
Drawing on the local French population for purposes of defense required

---

42. Twenty-five soldiers were supposed to comprise his contingent; "General Instructions of
O'Reilly," in Houck, *SRM*, 1: 81. Nine soldiers were posted at Ste. Genevieve and seven at Fort Don
Carlos; Foley, *Genesis of Missouri*, 36.

43. "General Instructions of O'Reilly," February 17, 1770, in Houck, *SRM:* 80.

44. Piernas to Unzaga, July 6, 1770, in Kinnaird, *SMV,* 1: 190–91; Houck, *SRM,* 1: 128.

45. Houck, *SRM,* 1: 128.

46. Pierre Laclède contract with Piernas, May 2, 1771, AGI-PC 81-362, MHMA microfilm;
Billon, *Annals of St. Louis,* 124; Account of expenses for jail construction, February 20, 1775 (St.
Louis History Collection, MHMA, box 1, folder 1). One of O'Reilly's instructions to Piernas called
for the establishment of a prison and the appointment of a jailer to look after the prisoners; "General
Instructions of O'Reilly," in Houck, *SRM,* 1: 82.

47. "General Instructions of O'Reilly," February 17, 1770, in Houck, *SRM,* 1: 81; Piernas to
Unzaga, June 14, 1770, AGI-PC 81-325, MHMA microfilm.

Spanish authorities to proceed with care. They needed to treat the men with discipline "so mild" that villagers would be "greatly satisfied with the new formation," and they should make sure that service was not at all "burdensome" or a hindrance to the members' livelihoods. Practice would be held "on Sundays when the weather permits," during which the men would be drilled and trained in firing, all the while being careful not to waste the king's powder.[48] The tasks Piernas took on seemed endless, and a month into his tenure, he could not rest. Daily, he found himself annoyed by the disputes of St. Louisans. Creditors and debtors pestered him continually, and he complained he was utterly occupied with resolving their petty affairs with a spirit of firmness, fairness, and justice. The challenge left him personally agitated. Everything was tranquil, he reported, with the exception of his mind.[49]

Communication posed real problems as well, not least because several Indian interpreters died in quick succession. First to die was Louis Deshêtres, soon followed by his replacement Gabriel Decarry, a skilled interpreter whose loss Piernas regretted. The official next nominated Pedro Denaux Detally for the position.[50] By the time Piernas received word of official approval of Detally's appointment, the man had already died. On hearing the news of Detally's death, Piernas went to the interpreter's house to investigate, accompanied by two witnesses, Labuscière and René Kiersereau, where they met an Indian woman, whom Piernas noted was "his wife legally married."[51] As Detally's replacement, Piernas proposed Antonio Deshêtres, brother of Louis, the first interpreter he had employed.[52] Piernas turned to others for assistance with writing and translating French.[53]

Dealing with merchants and trade also absorbed Piernas's attention. In July 1770, he granted passports to a number of local men to send boats laden with the commodities of Upper Louisiana to New Orleans. A few examples of their freight suggest both the range of wares produced and their quantities: Laclède sent a vessel with sixty-nine packs of pelts; another boat with a crew of ten carried several passengers, lots of furs, and 27,800 *livres* of flour; and a third, with a cargo of flour, had a planned stop at Ste.

48. "General Instructions of O'Reilly," February 17, 1770, in Houck, *SRM,* 1: 81.
49. Piernas to Unzaga, June 27, 1770, AGI-PC 81-328, MHMA microfilm.
50. See Piernas to Unzaga, March 13, 1771, AGI-PC 81-352; June 18, 1771, AGI-PC 81-379; June 26, 1771, AGI-PC 81-384, all MHMA microfilm; Inventory of Detailly estate, October 25, 1771, in Billon, *Annals of St. Louis,* 108.
51. Inventory of Detailly estate, October 25, 1771, in Billon, *Annals of St. Louis,* 108.
52. Piernas to Unzaga, November 2, 1771, AGI-PC 81-397, MHMA microfilm.
53. Piernas turned to "Martin de Uralde" for assistance with French correspondence, as well as for tutoring his son. Piernas to Unzaga, 24 September 1773, AGI-PC 81-488, MHMA microfilm.

Genevieve to collect beaver, deer, and otter skins as well as more flour.[54] In 1771, St. Louis farmers produced more flour than the villagers consumed, a fact of interest to authorities.[55] For Spanish plans for the territory, charting the growth of St. Louis, both of its population and its products, was critical. Accordingly, O'Reilly ordered an annual census of the population, as well as an annual report that listed the amount of flour and quantities of furs brought to New Orleans. The goal was to "know exactly whether that trade results in benefit to the vassals in proportion to the expense which the King has in protecting them."[56] In short, was it worth Spain's while to support and defend settlements like St. Louis?

While some aspects of commerce seemed to be off to a good start under Piernas's tenure, traders coming into St. Louis in July 1770 carried a troubling cargo: Indian slaves. Their arrival posed a real dilemma for Piernas. As they had left St. Louis before O'Reilly had made any pronouncements regarding Indian slavery, the traders could not know they were violating the ordinance by bring fourteen Indian captives to the village. The question that Piernas had to decide was whether or not the Indians should be considered free.[57] Given how many colonists held Indian as slaves, the traders no doubt imagined a ready market, and various inhabitants "had even advanced money" to buy slaves, despite knowing of the prohibition. In other words, the deals were done, and a collective thwarting of the law had taken place. In this case, O'Reilly's replacement, new governor Luis de Unzaga Y Amezaga, ruled against the Indians: "The fourteen Indians bought by the inhabitants of St. Louis, even after the publication of the ordinance, may be kept by their owners as slaves, but not sold pending the decision of His Majesty." Unzaga told Piernas to instruct the St. Louisans involved in this case, "as well as all others in that jurisdiction, not to buy any Indians henceforth nor subject them to slavery."[58]

Indigenous slavery had an important place in the histories of both French and Spanish Louisiana. While traffic in slaves existed in North America prior to the arrival and participation of Europeans, the trade evolved significantly with their involvement.[59] In Louisiana, not only did Indian slavery

54. Passports for Laclède, July 14, 1770, AGI-PC 188a-4-2; Kennedy, July 23, 1770, AGI-PC 188a-4-10; Perrault, July 28, 1770, AGI-PC 188a-4-3, MHMA microfilm.

55. Piernas to Unzaga, Statistical Report, April 1, 1773, in Houck, *SRM,* 1: 57.

56. "General Instructions of O'Reilly," in ibid., 1: 82, 83.

57. Piernas to Unzaga, July 2, 1770, AGI-PC 81-330, MHMA microfilm.

58. Unzaga to Piernas, [undated], in Kinnaird, *SMV,* 191.

59. Alan Gallay, *The Indian Slave Trade: The Rise of the English Empire in the American South, 1670–1717;* James F. Brooks, *Captives and Cousins: Slavery, Kinship, and Community in the Southwest Borderlands.*

raise legal, religious, and diplomatic issues regarding its justification and implications, it sparked controversies over race mixing, or *métissage,* as intimate relations between colonial men and Indian women invariably accompanied it.[60] Whether sexual encounters took place outside of marriage or within it, they provoked commentary and concern on the part of authorities. As Carl Ekberg noted in *Stealing Indian Women,* "The debate among French administrators and missionaries over the Indian slave trade was never resolved during the colonial era, and Indian slaves from western tribes continued to be brought into the villages of the Illinois country." In the years after its founding, St. Louis "became the eastern terminus for the slave trade."[61] For those of mixed Indian and African ancestry, the prohibition on Indian slavery led to further complications.[62]

As ordered, Piernas set about taking a census of the enslaved Indian population of St. Louis.[63] At the beginning of July 1770, every St. Louis resident with Indian slaves was required to come before Piernas to declare the "name, age, and cost" of each.[64] In a village of roughly 500 total residents, thirty-seven colonists held sixty-nine Indian men, women, and children in bondage.[65] These numbers meant that colonial St. Louis had the largest proportion of Indian slaves, nearly 17 percent of the population, of any European-founded community in North America.[66] Among the sixty-nine Indians were eight men between the ages of fifteen and thirty, six of them baptized; eighteen women between fifteen and forty, sixteen of them baptized; twenty-one boys, ten of them baptized; and twenty-two girls, eight of them baptized.[67] These numbers highlight a demographic fact of life for Indian slaves in St. Louis: few lived in complete family units.[68] At most,

60. On the term *métis,* see John E. Foster, "Some questions and perspectives on the problem of métis roots," in Jacqueline Peterson and Jennifer S. H. Brown, eds., *The New Peoples: Being and Becoming Métis in North American,* 73–91; "Introduction," 3–16.

61. Ekberg, *Stealing Indian Women,* 29.

62. In 1799, an African-Indian St. Louis woman, Marie Scypion, sued for her freedom on the grounds of her Indian lineage. Missouri courts eventually sided with her, but not until 1834, after her death; Lorenzo J. Green, Gary R. Kremer, and Antonio F. Holland. *Missouri's Black Heritage,* 17.

63. Ekberg interprets O'Reilly's requirement for a census of all Indian slaves as an indication of his hopes to see Indian slavery itself ended; Ekberg, *Stealing Indian Women,* 54.

64. Piernas's report of Indian slaves at St. Louis, July 12, 1770, in Kinnaird, *SMV,* 1: 172.

65. Ekberg, *Stealing Indian Women,* 60–62; Piernas's report of Indian slaves at St. Louis, July 12, 1770, in Kinnaird, *SMV,* 1: 172–79.

66. To arrive at this figure, Ekberg added the fourteen Indian slaves who had recently arrived but whose status had not yet been determined by Unzaga; Ekberg, *Stealing Indian Women,* 63.

67. Piernas's report of Indian slaves at St. Louis, July 12, 1770, in Kinnaird, *SMV,* 1: 172–79; Ekberg, Table 3, *Stealing Indian Women,* 61–62.

68. Ekberg noted that only a single married Indian couple was found in the 1770 Spanish Illinois slave list; Pawnee Indians Suzanne and Joseph Canghé lived as slaves in Ste. Genevieve; see Ekberg, *Stealing Indian Women,* 68.

four enslaved adult Indian men lived in households with enslaved adult Indian women. Although all were reported with French names—Angelique, Thérèse, and Charlotte were common—signs of their inclusion in other aspects of the local culture were less common.[69] Most notably, roughly 50 percent of Indian slaves in St. Louis remained unbaptized. In contrast to Ste. Genevieve, where only 10 percent of Indian slaves were unbaptized, St. Louis was a new settlement with a transient population, a place where violations of regulations and customs took place more often and the slave trade, albeit illegal, continued to exist.[70] For most of the enslaved Indians in St. Louis, tribal designation is unknown, but not one Osage Indian appears in the records as a slave, an indication of that nation's indomitability.[71]

One can imagine the scene on July 12, 1770, the day of reporting: a group of French colonists gathering at the government house at the center of the village, waiting their turns to appear before the rule-making and rule-enforcing newcomer Piernas. Did they stand in line, chatting with their neighbors, or approach the exercise with a quiet air of resentment at this imposition of Spanish regulations? As they were ushered in to see Piernas, they may have wondered whether their days of holding Indians in bondage were numbered. What is clear is that they answered the call to acknowledge their bondsmen, women, and children before the crown. The first to appear was Labuscière. Ninth was Marie Chouteau (as she signed herself), consort of the village founder, appearing in a room of the government house that had formerly been her home, there to tell the Spanish commander that she had two baptized Indian girls, Thérèse, sixteen, and Manon, thirteen, as her slaves. (Only two other women came in to declare Indian slaves, and one of them had her son-in-law sign her statement for her.) Twenty other villagers appeared before Madame Chouteau's partner took his turn; Pierre Laclède reported that he held six Indian slaves, all baptized, among whom were two family groups of mothers and children. In total, they cost him 7,350 livres in silver. Immediately following Laclède was St. Ange, who also acknowledged six Indian slaves. The two men held the largest numbers of enslaved Indians; twenty-three St. Louisans reported only one.[72]

Many other prominent members of the community filed into the government headquarters that day, all of them testifying to the human capital and

69. Piernas's report of Indian slaves at St. Louis, July 12, 1770, in Kinnaird, *SMV,* 1: 172–79.

70. Ekberg, *Stealing Indian Women,* 68.

71. The tribal designations for only seventeen Indian slaves in St. Louis can be determined prior to 1785, with six Padouca, two Litanes, three Panis, two Panimahas, one Panis Noire, one Illinois, one Scroto, and one Sioux. See table one, ibid., 48, 49.

72. Piernas's report of Indian slaves at St. Louis, July 12, 1770, in Kinnaird, *SMV,* 1: 172–79.

involuntary servitude that shaped the economy and society of their community and rendered their households studies in diversity and exploitation. Pointing to the fact that there are nine streets in St. Louis today with family names belonging to Indian slave owners in 1770, Ekberg concluded that a nucleus of a powerful and lasting elite emerged quickly in St. Louis. Moreover, he noted, every member of St. Louis's ruling class in the 1770s owned Indian slaves.[73] They were an educated group, with twenty-four of those who enumerated slaves in July 1770 signing their names rather than marking their sworn statements with the cross, or "ordinary mark" of the illiterate.[74] Described as merchants, voyageurs, and residents, these slaveholders were men and women of means.

The July census, in conjunction with other evidence of Indian visits, makes abundantly clear that Indians had a significant presence in colonial St. Louis. Some were in the village as slaves, new and involuntary members of the community; others were there briefly, as visitors and trading partners. One of the most unusual households in the village was that of an "Indian" slave who arrived in the village in 1770, Maria Rosa Villalpando, a native of New Mexico. How she came to St. Louis was a remarkable story. Born into a family with mixed Indian and Spanish heritage, she married a Taos man sometime in the 1750s, and the two began a family, having at least one son. In August 1760, when 3,000 Comanche Indians attacked settlements in the Taos Valley, Villalpando and her family sought refuge in a hacienda that had defensive towers. During the ensuing conflict, the Indians defeated the settlers, killing fourteen men and an unknown number of women and children. Villalpando's husband was among the slain.[75] Along with fifty-four other women and children, Maria Rosa and her son were taken by the Comanche. For the next ten years, she lived in captivity, first among the Comanche and then with the Pawnee, to whom she was traded. By 1767, she had given birth to a *métis* son. Living with him in a Pawnee village, Villalpando met a St. Louis trader, Jean Salé, who was a native of France, and began a new relationship. In November 1768, she and Salé welcomed a son, Lambert.[76] Two years later, the family came to St.

73. Ekberg, *Stealing Indian Women*, 60.

74. Piernas's report of Indian slaves at St. Louis, July 12, 1770, in Kinnaird, *SMV,* 1: 172–79.

75. Jack B. Tykal, "Taos to St. Louis: The Journey of María Rosa Villalpando," 161–74. A missionary's uncorroborated account, suggesting an underlying urge to portray the Indians as brutal, stated that the Comanches killed some of the women "who had fought like men," and then "insolently coupled them with the dead men." Eleanor B. Adams and Fray Angelico Chavez, ed. *The Missions of New Mexico: A Description by Fray Francisco Atanasio Dominguez,* 4, 251.

76. Tykal, "Taos to St. Louis: The Journey of María Rosa Villalpando," 170. See also "Catholic Baptisms, St. Louis Missouri, 1765–1840," 82; Marriage contract of Marie Rose Vidalpane and Jean Salé, July 3, 1770, instrument #2023, St. Louis Archives, MHMA.

Louis and there formalized their union, signing a marriage contract on July 3 and having their son Lambert baptized the next day.[77] Also on July 3, Salé acknowledged his Indian slaves. Salé's declaration before Piernas included two young, unbaptized, Indian slaves, Louis, thirteen, and Jeannette, also thirteen, in addition to his wife Marie Rose, their son Lambert, and Marie's *métis* son Antoine.[78] In its multilingual, multiethnic composition, their home provides a snapshot of the new social arrangements made possible by geographic mobility, war, and commerce.

In a setting where villagers like Salé traveled for long periods and chose to pursue commerce among the Indians of the Missouri basin, there were chronic shortages of labor that contributed to the demand for slaves, both Indian and African. To his chagrin, Piernas discovered that publicizing O'Reilly's ordinance on slavery did not quell the trade. On one occasion, Piernas felt compelled to throw a colonist into prison after he brought Indian children and eight other captive Paducah Indians into St. Louis. Piernas pronounced the Indians free, jailed the lawbreaker as a warning to others in the village, and arranged for the care of the children. One he sent to Antonio de Oro, a merchant and Spanish officer, to maintain, and he also assumed responsibility; the children were to receive religious instruction and support until they were old enough to take care of themselves.[79] Those who ignored the law risked confiscation of their goods and punishment.[80] Despite such penalties, St. Louis became a center of the Indian slave trade in the 1770s.[81]

With residents and traders blatantly violating the prohibitions on Indian slavery, it is perhaps not surprising that Piernas seemed at pains to establish his authority with the inhabitants of St. Louis wherever he could, dealing out severe penalties for their misconduct in his first months in office. In late June 1770, he banished a penniless bachelor, Michel Calas, for slandering Madame Montardy, a seventeen-year-old villager, and threatened the twenty-six-year-old Calas with corporal punishment if he returned to St. Louis before the ten years of his exile had ended. Disorderly speech was clearly unwelcome, serving only to sully the reputations of blameless

77. Baptismal record of Lambert, son of Jean Salle and Marie Rose Ponda, July 4, 1770, Oscar W. Collet, trans., *St. Louis Register of Baptisms of the St. Louis Cathedral, 1766–1799*.

78. Piernas's report of Indian slaves at St. Louis, July 12, 1770, in Kinnaird, *SMV*, 1: 177.

79. Piernas to Unzaga, March 14, 1772, AGI-PC 81, cited in Ekberg, *Stealing Indian Women*, 90; July 23, 1773, AGI-PC 81-388, MHMA microfilm; Houck, *HM*, 1: 347.

80. A later case involving other violations of commercial regulations notes the penalty in place as of June 1771 for those who traded Indian slaves. Labunière v. Beaudoin, February 23, 1779, Litigation Collection, box 1, folder 4, MHMA.

81. Ekberg, *Stealing Indian Women*, 54.

individuals and disrupt village harmony. As Calas listened to his sentence before an impressive company that included French and Spanish figures of authority in the community—St. Ange, the surveyor Duralde, long-time notary and village councilman Labuscière, and militia captain Eugenio Alvarez—he may have pondered why he ever left La Rochelle, France, and wondered where he would go next.[82] By assembling such a group, Piernas was casting himself as the lead actor in a drama of governance, his associates clearly in secondary roles that emphasized both their support for his decision and their subordination to his authority. Performing the spectacle of Spanish justice for francophone villagers at the periphery of empire, Piernas reminded his audience that power lay with him.[83]

A more direct challenge to village harmony and by extension Piernas's rule came on August 15, the Feast of the Assumption, a major Catholic feast day celebrating the Virgin Mary's assumption into Heaven. On that day, Piernas saw the authority of the crown exposed to direct insult and scorn. He had ordered one of St. Louis's militia officers go to the church to publicize new ordinances regarding taxes. At the close of the service, Louis Lambert stood at the door, reading aloud Piernas's decree as commanded. As he read each passage, Lambert heard a voice of ridicule ring out, saying, "Ah! That is fine . . . , that is put into good rhyme . . . , that is pretty . . . ," and other such derisive remarks. The vocal critic was Amable Letourneau, a Canadian native who had called St. Louis home for six years, a bachelor, and a fellow member of the militia. Ordered to cease his mockery, Letourneau ignored the admonition and promptly found himself in jail. His insubordination could not go unpunished.[84] Labuscière joined with Lambert in the complaint against Letourneau.[85] Perhaps in a more sober frame of mind after a few days in jail, Letourneau was brought before Piernas and questioned. Lambert provided testimony as well, swearing with his hand on the cross of his sword, a more dramatic gesture than that asked of witnesses, who typically raised their right hands, made the sign of the cross, and swore to tell the truth.[86] Piernas declared Letourneau guilty of treating the authorities with contempt, of disturbing the peace, and of setting a bad example

82. Michel Calas case, June 23, 1770, St. Louis History Collection, box 1, folder 1, MHMA.

83. Authoritative speech serves to determine action, in this case banishment, only insofar as those who speak and hear it accept its weight. In other words, collectively they participate in, or enact, a performance of legal power. Judith Butler, *Bodies that Matter: On the Discursive Limits of "Sex"*, 11–12.

84. Letourneau case, August 15, 1770, St. Louis History Collection, box 1, folder 1, MHMA.

85. J. Thomas Scharf, *History of Saint Louis City and Country, From the Earliest Periods to the Present Day: Including Biographical Sketches of Representative Men*, 303.

86. See the Litigation Collection, MHMA, for the usual form of swearing. Swearing on the crosses of weapons invoked God as well as the power of the sword.

to the public. As punishment, Letourneau was banished from St. Louis, condemned to absent himself from the province for ten years. If he violated the terms of his sentence and returned, Letourneau risked harsher punishment for his sedition.[87] Another village troublemaker soon felt the sting of Piernas's will. A few weeks after the Letourneau affair, Piernas heard the case of Jeannot, a man whom St. Ange had previously banished from St. Louis. That punishment was clearly ineffectual, for Jeannot had returned to the village, broken a villager's fence and let loose his cattle into his garden, stolen a blanket and two petticoats from an African woman with whom he was involved, and threatened to do other mischief. Unwilling to tolerate the miscreant, Piernas banished him, as he had Letourneau and Calas, for ten years.[88]

While disorderly, disruptive, and vocal French villagers presented one set of problems, the most complex and significant challenges Piernas faced in the early 1770s came from Indian peoples, in particular the Little Osages and Missouris. The two tribes engaged in what the Spanish officials and villagers alike termed irrational, criminal acts: they attacked colonists, stole horses and other property, and forced traders to relinquish trade goods. Allies and neighbors, the two peoples had "at all times given the commandants plenty to do." Piernas's predecessors had made allowances, suffered, and "overlooked their impertinences in the past." In the Spanish commandant's view, such treatment, coupled with the English involvement, explained the current situation. "Long before my arrival," he opined, "the English made efforts to attract them for their commercial ends, rewarding them lavishly, and giving them a flag which they raised over their village. I learned of this from M. St. Ange." If the Spanish tolerated their "haughtiness" and "extortions," the Little Osages and Missouris would continue to believe "that they inspire fear and their insolence would reach even greater heights."[89] The governor no doubt agreed with the general import of Piernas's analysis, having urged him a few months earlier to reproach the Osages for their role in five murders.[90] In a cold-blooded calculation, Piernas noted that the two nations were "the least numerous of all and the easiest to reduce by means of extermination."[91] Not long after Piernas made

87. Letourneau case, August 15, 1770, St. Louis History Collection, box 1, folder 1, MHMA. Letourneau was banished by the end of August.

88. Peter Baron and Jeannot case, September 17, 1770, St. Louis History Collection, box 1, folder 1, MHMA.

89. Piernas to Unzaga, July 4, 1772, in Kinnaird, *SMV,* 1: 205.

90. Din and Nasatir, *Imperial Osages,* 78–79, citing Unzaga to Piernas, March 14, 1772, AGI-PC 81.

91. Piernas to Unzaga, July 4, 1772, in Kinnaird, *SMV,* 1: 205.

these statements, the Little Osage and Missouri Indians fulfilled his predictions of dangerous and disorderly conduct.

Hostilities with the Little Osage and Missouri Indians reached a crescendo in mid-July 1772. Having traveled to Ste. Genevieve on official business, Piernas received word that the two tribes had attacked the Spanish post of Fort San Carlos, on the Missouri River, the day after he left St. Louis, an action he thought inspired by the British. Showing up at the fort with one hundred heavily armed men, a party of Little Osages and Missouris had demanded entrance, but allowing Indians with weapons inside was not the standard practice.[92] Refused admission, the Indians forced their way in; the small number of soldiers at the outpost fled, leaving behind ammunition and food that the intruders seized.[93] Afterward, the Indians headed to St. Louis and made a "disorderly entrance into the town," giving indications of bad intentions and carrying an English flag.[94] In what Piernas deemed a clear insult to the Spanish crown and a threat to the alarmed inhabitants, the raiding party raised the British colors on the riverbank. Spanish troops and villagers quickly armed themselves, in order to "repress their insolence."[95] When pressured to do so, the Indians apologized for their behavior, and remained in the village to await the lieutenant governor's return.

The sincerity of their regret was suspect in Piernas's view, contradicted by their actions. Thirty Missouri men traveled to Ste. Genevieve to seize horses from the residents there and across the river in British territory, transporting them in pirogues taken in St. Louis. Once news of the theft reached St. Louis, "hands were laid on the chief of the party who had remained in this post with six Indians." The chief's protestations of innocence persuaded no one; Piernas believed him an accomplice and indeed the main instigator of misconduct. "It is he who has incited the party, and he is the one who planted the English flag," declared Piernas. "He is the most insolent of them all and, without the knowledge of the principal chief of his nation, he came with his followers to attack us." Piernas appeared to have no hesitation about what to do: "I caused him to be made prisoner, and I have him secured in irons in order to compel the nation to surrender all the horses and pirogues which it has stolen and to conduct itself" peacefully. If those terms were not met, the chief would be sent to New Orleans to be punished with "perpetual banishment" at the governor's orders. Several

92. Piernas to Unzaga, July 15, 1772, AGI-PC 81-433, MHMA microfilm.
93. Ibid.; Foley, *Genesis of Missouri*, 39, n.28; Din and Nasatir, *Imperial Osages*, 81–82; Piernas to Unzaga, July 30, 1772, in Kinnaird, *SMV*, 1: 206–7.
94. Piernas to Unzaga, July 30, 1772, in Kinnaird, *SMV*, 1: 206.
95. Piernas to Unzaga, July 15, 1772, AGI-PC 81-433, MHMA microfilm.

other of the Indians involved in the thefts were captured by inhabitants, beaten, and imprisoned as well.[96]

The day after the horse incident, the Missouris and Little Osages were on the receiving end of an Indian attack at St. Louis. Other Indians, friendly to the Spanish, found the raid on the fort and the conduct in St. Louis objectionable. "To prove their loyalty and good will toward us," wrote Piernas, "they resolved to avenge this daring act the same as though they themselves were at war with them." Carefully, "they carried out their plan by means of a surprise," attacking and killing the Little Osage chief and his second-in-command as they walked outside of St. Louis. Sallying forth "to avenge the death of their two chiefs," the Little Osages and Missouris remaining in St. Louis were "repulsed by the attacking party and forced to take refuge in the town." There, they found safety among the villagers, as the other tribes did not pursue them within the village proper. "After this occurrence," Piernas noted with satisfaction, the Indians left St. Louis quickly, expressing "a desire for Spanish protection since it had succeeded in freeing them from their enemies. They were made to understand that without our friendship they would all have perished, as was in fact the case, for the opposing party was restrained by consideration and respect for us from doing them any more harm than they had already received."[97] Thus, when Piernas hurried back from Ste. Genevieve to hold a council meeting with the Little Osage and Missouri, he discovered that they had already fled the village.

In the weeks and months that followed, Spanish and Indian efforts to regularize Indian relations took place. In August 1772, the chiefs of the Big Osage visited St. Louis, adopting a conciliatory tone regarding the recent conflicts.[98] In October, a party came to St. Louis to request that Indian prisoners be freed, and as a gesture of good will, brought with them some furs to pay for guns they had forcibly taken from a trader who had come to their village. Piernas refused to grant their petition, insisting that first the Little Osage and Missouri chiefs must come in person to discuss reestablishing the harmony that had once existed. The Missouri chief soon came, and Piernas expected that the Little Osage leader would follow in order to plead for clemency.[99] But Indian promises of peace were not sufficient to cancel Piernas's plans to punish them. To convey as clearly as possible how displeased Spain was with their recent conduct, Piernas decided to

96. Piernas to Unzaga, July 30, 1772, in Kinnaird, *SMV,* 1: 207.
97. Ibid., 206.
98. Din and Nasatir, *Imperial Osages,* 82; Piernas to Unzaga, September 1, 1772, AGI-PC 81.
99. Piernas to Unzaga, November 19, 1772, AGI-PC 81-445, MHMA microfilm.

withhold trade from the problematic tribes. He hoped to bring the Indians around without resorting to force.

The difficulty for the Spanish, of course, was that theirs were not the only settlements in the area full of traders who were ready and eager to exchange European merchandise for Indian furs. In the following fall and winter of 1772, after Piernas decided to withhold trade, the Little Osage gave their business to traders from British Illinois, who were eager to attract their custom. In October or November, a Canadian-born trader, Jean Marie Ducharme, crossed the Mississippi from Illinois with two boatloads of goods, slipped past Fort Don Carlos under the cover of darkness, and traveled up the Missouri, where he and his party traded with the Little Osage for nearly four months, in direct violation of Spanish regulations.[100] From the perspective of those in St. Louis, his excursion had the potential to do tremendous damage. "Fatal consequences" would follow Ducharme's delivering "firearms and ammunition" to Indians who were "declaring war upon the settlers of this territory."[101] Ready to seek Spanish aid, the Little Osages and Missouris changed their minds once they had access to Ducharme's goods. "Egged on by his greed and without thinking of the damage he was causing the settlers of these Establishments," Ducharme had ruined the prospects for peace.[102]

Unwilling to see such a direct and dangerous challenge to Spain's territorial integrity go unchallenged, Piernas authorized an expedition to seek out and capture the trader, astutely selecting Laclède to command it. Although Piernas characterized his decision as a logical one, given Laclède's "capacity and judgment" as well as "his zeal and his exact punctuality," the choice of "the principal and first founder of this settlement" to head the expedition has something of a scripted air about it. Drumming up volunteers to leave the village for an extended period in pursuit of an armed lawbreaker might not have been an easy task, and Piernas turned to Laclède to make the effort succeed. One can almost imagine the crowd hanging back, waiting to see who was leading the party. In his selection of Laclède, Piernas hoped "to excite, by his example, the other inhabitants to prefer service and public welfare to their own interests."[103]

---

100. A. P. Nasatir, "Ducharme's Invasion of Missouri, an Incident in the Anglo-Spanish Rivalry for the Indian Trade," 8.

101. Ducharme Inventory, March 29, 1773, in ibid., 427. From an inventory taken of Ducharme's goods, it appears he may have been carrying an item that conveyed the onset of hostilities. One of the items in his possession was an axe, which a sailor said Ducharme had been given by the chief of the Little Osage, to deliver to Piernas, raising the question of whether this object was meant to communicate a message of war, 424.

102. Piernas to Unzaga, April 12, 1773, in ibid., 9.

103. Ibid., 11.

As Piernas had hoped, Laclède's willingness to take command "had the desired effect," for no one felt able to excuse himself, and forty men quickly stepped up. "Indeed," noted Piernas, "all those intended for his command presented themselves voluntarily and with the ready disposition to follow him."[104] Where Laclède led, others followed. Before Laclède set out, Piernas provided him with a set of instructions as to how to command a detachment of militia volunteers and how to capture goods and *contrabandistas* like Ducharme.[105] Trying to limit Spanish expenditures, the lieutenant governor financed the expedition by promising Benito Vasquez and Joseph Motard a share of any furs that Laclède and the men under his command might capture.[106] (A former soldier in the Spanish garrison and native of Spain, Vasquez had managed to become a notable merchant in St. Louis, one of five from the village to travel to New Orleans on business in 1772.)[107]

Laclède and the other men set out in three canoes, "well munitioned, [and] well supplied with provisions for two months," their hearts likely pounding from exertion and adrenalin as they paddled up the Missouri River in search of the recalcitrant Ducharme.[108] On March 11, at 5:30 in the afternoon, they landed near a bend of the river and began to set up camp. Busy building the camp, they noticed four canoes, tied together in pairs, and a fifth rounding the bend close to the opposite shore. When they hopped back into their boats to go meet the strangers, the members of the other party landed and picked up their rifles. Once they reached shouting distance, Laclède and his men asked the identity of the others. When one replied that he was Ducharme, the men from St. Louis responded that they were there on behalf of the king. Uncowed, Ducharme "answered that he would not surrender," and that if they tried to capture him, they "would not seize him until he was dead." At Ducharme's bold declaration, the new arrivals sought "to avoid going to such extremes" and so "admonished the crew . . . not to attempt any defense on his behalf." Trying to separate Ducharme from his men, Laclède and his companions reminded them of "the risk they were running if they made use of arms," promising that "if they remained peaceful," they would be pardoned for "binding

104. Ibid.

105. Piernas to Laclède, February 18, 1773, AGI-PC 2357, cited in Din and Nasatir, *Imperial Osages*, 84–85.

106. Foley, *History of Missouri*, 1: 25.

107. Janet Lecompte, "Don Benito Vasquez in Early St. Louis," 286.

108. Piernas to Unzaga, April 12, 1773, in Nasatir, "Ducharme's Invasion of the Missouri," 11. The canoes belonged to Labrosse, Larche, and Choret. See the proceedings signed by Laclède and others, March 12, 1773, AGI-PC 2357, translated and reprinted in Nasatir, "Ducharme's Invasion of Missouri."

themselves to a man who was engaged in trade on a forbidden side (of the Mississippi)."[109] Leaving Ducharme to harangue his men, Laclède and his crew returned to their camp "so as to give them time to reflect" during the night. They kept close watch through the darkness, alert to any hostile movements from the other shore.

At eight the next morning, as the St. Louisans readied themselves to attack Ducharme and his party, they spotted Ducharme, standing with his rifle, on the shore opposite their camp. "Why are you waiting to decide what we have to do?" he called out. In return, they asked why he was waiting to decide to surrender himself. When Ducharme again declared himself determined to die rather than surrender, they fired a volley in his direction. He responded in kind, and in the exchange of gunfire that followed, he was wounded. Meanwhile, one of Ducharme's sailors, Pedro Bissonet, came and told Laclède's party that he and the other sailors wanted to surrender but were afraid because Ducharme was watching them and would shoot them if he suspected their plan. Persuaded of a pardon and urged to leave Ducharme, Bissonet and eleven other sailors joined the men of the St. Louis expedition. Ducharme and an Iroquois Indian companion fled into the woods, leaving only one Little Osage Indian, Lagueuletorse, in the camp. Laclède sent a detachment of twenty men to seize Ducharme's boats and goods. Although they had not captured the rogue trader, they had succeeding in seizing a sizeable cargo from which they stood to gain financially. The furs on board included dozens of bundles of deer skins and bear skins, two bundles of beaver skins, buffalo skins, and ferret skin sacks containing deer tongues and beaver tails.[110]

As they traveled back to St. Louis, Laclède and his fellow volunteers were likely pleased, if not altogether satisfied, with their expedition. They had cause for seeing themselves as defenders of their community and their livelihood. Although they had failed to capture the man behind the mischief, they had survived the encounter unharmed while he was wounded, they had seized his goods and canoes, and they had triumphantly taken all of his non-Indian companions. (Ultimately Ducharme reached Canada.) On their return to the village, the men reported to Piernas, who ordered a complete inventory of Ducharme's possessions. Listing the goods took the better part of three days, and the resulting record reveals some of what comprised the Indian trade. At the point when Ducharme's voyage was interrupted, he still had dozens of blankets, fourteen mirrors, dozens of

109. Proceedings, March 12, 1773, in Nasatir, "Ducharme's Invasion of Missouri," 421.
110. Ibid., 422–26.

pairs of scissors, 131 porcelain vessels, copper jars, kettles, a barrel of gun-powder, and six muskets. Among the decorative items he carried for his indigenous trading partners were dozens of silver bracelets, nostril rings, pieces of bone to decorate girdles, and beads.[111] Once the inventory was completed, the goods were divided in half, with part going to the men of the detachment for their work and the "dangers of the undertaking." The other half went to Joseph Motard and Benito Vasquez, who put up the funds for weapons, foods, and all other needs of the expedition. Neither the king nor Laclède benefited. Laclède and his second-in-command, Antonio Berard, "voluntarily yielded the share which belonged to them in favor of the detachment."[112]

Ducharme's incursions into Missouri territory, as well as his pursuit and boat seizure by Laclède and the other men in the expedition, serve as a reminder that the Spanish side of the river was not secure from the threat of English forces nor from the activities of its agents. Europeans fought each other for control of the fur trade, and they did so on an uneasy footing with Indian peoples, who sought the best terms for their furs. With all parties willing to resort to violence to accomplish their aims, a constant threat of hostilities and bloodshed hovered over trade and territory disputes. Maintaining peaceful and profitable relations remained a challenging goal within the larger context of European competition and Indian diplomacy.

April 1773 brought further important developments in Indian affairs, when 130 men and women of the Big Osage came to St. Louis, bringing with them a member of their tribe responsible for a number of thefts and for the murders of five Frenchmen along the Arkansas River in 1772.[113] They delivered the guilty party "weeping as is their custom" and promised to live peacefully.[114] Although Piernas put the principal chief of the nation in prison, he took no further action; some suspected he feared that passing sentence on the chief would inspire revenge. His indecisiveness over the subsequent months provoked official censure. In New Orleans, Governor Unzaga fumed, as Piernas could no longer do what he should have done: deprive the malefactor of life at the hand of his companions. Now such an act would be "done in cold blood" and was therefore impossible to order. To resolve the matter, Unzaga hit upon a solution that likely pleased no one in

111. Ibid., 428–35.

112. Ducharme inventory, March 29, 1773, in Nasatir, "Ducharme's Invasion of Missouri," 436–37.

113. Piernas to Unzaga, April 24, 1773, cited in Din and Nasatir, *Imperial Osages*, 85. The previous year, the governor told Piernas to take them to task for the murders; Unzaga to Piernas, March 14, 1772, AGI-PC 81, in ibid., 78–79.

114. Piernas to Unzaga, April 24, 1773, in ibid., 85.

St. Louis except the man imprisoned there: he decreed "that the criminal be set at liberty."[115]

That summer was one of continual negotiations among Piernas, St. Louisans, and Indian visitors. In June 1773, all of the traders who had been dealing with the Big Osages arrived in St. Louis, reporting good treatment and peace.[116] In August, a council was held where members of the Little Osage, Big Osage, and Missouri tribes and St. Louis's leaders discussed establishing better relations. At Piernas's side were St. Ange, Laclède, and DeVolsey; they agreed to establish peace.[117] For their part, the Indians promised to return stolen horses and to turn in three Indians guilty of murdering Frenchmen.[118] A formal agreement between Spanish authorities and the Indians materialized out of the meeting. Under its terms, the Little Osages and Missouris pledged to deliver any person in their villages who killed "some vassal of His Catholic Majesty" to the commandant of St. Louis. At the conclusion of the council, the Indians received what they wanted as well: Piernas authorized the distribution of presents at the meeting and sent out traders to their villages. Securing reliable access to imported goods and furs was important for both the Indians and the colonial merchants with whom they traded. Before the end of 1773, the Big Osages had agreed to the terms as well.[119] These agreements seemed to bode well for a future that was more peaceful and prosperous, as well as one that was much less frightening for the inhabitants of St. Louis.

The trend toward peace continued the following year, with Piernas sending monthly reports to New Orleans in which he described the tranquility and good order of the posts and peace among the Indian nations.[120] Traders reported receiving no insults from the Indians and declared themselves pleased with their business and the furs the Indians provided. Contented with commerce along the Missouri, the traders had no complaints. Nor did the Indians who visited St. Louis to receive their annual presents, as far as Piernas knew; they only expressed to him a wish for quiet and peace to continue.[121] New,

---

115. Houck, *SRM,* 1: 163.

116. Piernas to Unzaga, July 6, 1773, AGI-PC 81-482 (Price compilation, MHMA).

117. "Consejo formado por Pedro Piernas, Sobre Osages, San Luis," August 21, 1773, AGI-PC 81, cited in Nasatir, "The Anglo-Spanish Frontier in the Illinois Country," 295.

118. Piernas to Unzaga, September 14, 1773, AGI-PC 81, cited in Din and Nasatir, *Imperial Osages,* 90.

119. Piernas to Unzaga, September 14, 1773; December 21, 1773, both in AGI-PC 81, cited in ibid., 91.

120. See, for example, Piernas to Unzaga, April 15, 1774, AGI-PC 81-506; May 8, 1774, AGI-PC 508; July 2, 1774, AGI-PC 81-515; August 4, 1774, AGI-PC 81-523; November 6, 1774, AGI-PC 81-524 (all Price compilation, MHMA).

121. Piernas to Unzaga, July 2, 1774, AGI-PC 81-515 (Price compilation, MHMA).

distant nations living along the Missouri came to St. Louis for the first time, among them the Maha, Pani, and Ricarra; there to request friendship and trade, they too received presents and then left, seemingly content, to return to their villages.[122] As the year drew to a close, Piernas, with an air of satisfaction, informed the governor that the traders reported that all the Indian nations were peaceful that year.[123]

Peace and prosperity prevailed within St. Louis, and its population grew steadily. In 1771, the official census counted 497 people: 251 white men and boys, 122 white women and girls, 74 black men and boys, and 50 black women and girls. No Indian, mulatto, or *métis* slaves were reported.[124] By December 1772, Piernas could report an additional hundred residents, a dramatic increase of 20 percent. The overwhelming majority of the new inhabitants of St. Louis were unfree laborers; of the new villagers, twenty-six were white, and seventy-four were enslaved Africans, an influx that created a population roughly 66 percent white and 33 percent black.[125] These percentages do not take into account the resident indigenous population, as again, not a single mulatto or Indian slave was noted, despite the otherwise documented fact of their presence in the community. A year later, in December 1773, numbers climbed by fifty, with five new enslaved Africans and a more sizeable increase of forty-five among the white population, for a total of 737 people, an overall increase of nearly 50 percent in the village population since 1771.[126]

If he surveyed his first four years in St. Louis, Piernas would have found much to please him. In his charge to establish Spanish authority in St. Louis, he had succeeded. In the realm of Indian relations, after years of turmoil, he could report calm with the Little Osages and the Missouri Indians. Other than the Chickasaw, some of whom had traveled north from the Mobile district and killed Kaskaskia Indians and French colonists, other nations were calm.[127] Interactions with the English on the other side of the Mississippi had achieved a kind of equilibrium, with reciprocal agreements for the return of deserters in place. Harmony reigned between the two banks.[128] The bad condition of the fort on the Missouri, due to floods,

122. Piernas to Unzaga, July 13, 1774, AGI-PC 81-521, MHMA microfilm; Din and Nasatir, *Imperial Osages,* 94–95.

123. Piernas to Unzaga, November 6, 1774, AGI-PC 81-524 (Price compilation, MHMA).

124. Census, September 2, 1771, in Kinnaird, *SMV,* 1: 196.

125. Census, December 31, 1772, Houck, *SRM,* 1: 53–54.

126. Census, December 31, 1773, Houck, *SRM,* 1: 61.

127. Piernas to Unzaga, June 5, 1774, AGI-PC 81-510 (Price compilation, MHMA).

128. Piernas to Unzaga, October 13, 1772, AGI-PC 81-443; copy of letter of English commandant, May 25, 1773, AGI-PC 81-460; Piernas to Unzaba, December 12, 1773, AGI-PC 81-497 (all Price compilation, MHMA).

was perhaps less troubling than it might have been if the situation were less tranquil.[129] Meanwhile, in St. Louis, the population of ethnic Europeans and enslaved Africans (the only groups noted in the census) was growing, both of them necessary, from the Spanish perspective, to a thriving and economically successful settlement.

Working to control St. Louis's traders and other inhabitants, Piernas had pursued various strategies, punishing harshly those who challenged his authority, violated commercial regulations, and disturbed the peace. His much-lauded personal skills, evident in his previous post, worked their magic again in St. Louis. When he finished his term as lieutenant governor, fifty men in the village signed a declaration of appreciation for Piernas's rule. Gathered in the government house, the merchants, *habitants,* tradesmen, hunters, and traders praised his judgment, fairness, and honor. No one had suffered from extortion or poor treatment, including the Indians who came to the post. "In short," they concluded, "we can only speak well of him, and with respect and gratitude."[130] Clearly, Piernas had been a success, bolstering his influence by enlisting the support and aid of the most prominent Frenchmen in the village, men with established reputations and influence such as Laclède and St. Ange. Repeatedly, he involved them in strategic decisions and initiatives. (Often at Piernas's side, St. Ange saw out his final years and his long career of service in North America in St. Louis.)

When the seventy-year-old St. Ange fell dangerously ill in December 1774, Piernas was summoned. Called on December 26 to the home of Madame Chouteau, where St. Ange was a lodger, Piernas, along with Labuscière and Benito Vasquez, entered the sick chamber. There to witness the dying commandant's last will and testament, Piernas learned St. Ange's final wishes. Thinking of the members of the community that had been his home for nearly a decade, St. Ange bequeathed part of his estate "for the construction of the church of this parish," and a sum to his niece Madame DeVolsey. He named "Pierre Laclède Liguest, his friend" to be his executor, "beseeching him to give him this last proof of his friendship." That night, St. Ange died, and he was interred the following day.[131] With the death of the French officer who had spent much of his career in Illinois, overseeing the transfer of Fort Chartres from the French to the British and assuming early command of St. Louis at the behest of the Spanish, an era had come to an end. The last vestiges of France's political and military rule were gone, and Spain had a working government and garrison in place.

---

129. Piernas to Unzaga, April 4, 1773, AGI-PC 81-452 (Price compilation, MHMA).

130. Testimonial to Pedro Piernas, May 19, 1775, in Billon, *Annals of St. Louis,* 129–30.

131. Billon, *Annals of St. Louis,* 125–28.

Chapter 5

Sex, Race, and Empire

THE PEOPLING OF ST. LOUIS

As 1775 opened, Pedro Piernas found himself in an uncomfortable spot. Although he had done well in his position as lieutenant governor of Upper Louisiana, fulfilling the expectations of his superiors, Piernas had received an order which he found very difficult to follow. Governor Unzaga had sent word from Lower Louisiana that a woman in St. Louis, legally married to a man in the capital, had to leave the village as soon as possible to be returned to her rightful husband. Unzaga expected Piernas to see to it that she was on the first boat downriver to New Orleans. Without question, it was the government's role to support a man's claims to his wife's person, labor, and company. "I will not fail to consider the rights of the husband, as your lordship indicates," Piernas assured the governor.[1] While interfering in a married couple's relationship in any capacity might have presented Piernas with an awkward challenge, this situation presented him with a unique nightmare. The woman in question was none other than Marie Thérèse Bourgeois Chouteau, longtime consort of village founder Pierre Laclède and the mother of his four children and their older half-brother, Auguste Chouteau. Forty-two years old, she had lived with Laclède in St. Louis since 1764. Presumably, the last thing the Spanish commandant wanted to do was inform the most influential member of the community, a man with whom he had worked closely and relied upon repeatedly, that it was time to break up the Chouteau-Laclède household. If he had imagined such a conversation, Piernas might have felt that the wintry weather of January had an extra chill, a bitter edge.

1. Piernas to Unzaga, February 26, 1776, AGI-PC 81-534, MHMA microfilm.

How Piernas and other officials handled the unusual union of Madame Chouteau and Monsieur Laclède offers insight into critical issues facing the young colonial outpost of St. Louis. As they struggled to govern and juggled a variety of goals, individuals, and conflicts, Spanish authorities in both Lower and Upper Louisiana devoted considerable thought to populating their territory and settlements. Just as they paid attention to the political and geographic frontiers that defined their colony, they thought about the liaisons that emerged as Indians, Africans, and Europeans interacted, the "intimate frontiers" of sexual relations.[2] Who should inhabit the land and people it? How did marriage and race fit into the calculus of populating new colonies?

In Louisiana, where European men vastly outnumbered European women, interracial liaisons were common. European immigration to North American colonies was typically imbalanced, as young men in search of economic opportunities traveled abroad much more often than did young women. With colonial European men seeking sexual partners among indigenous and African women, mixed-race children resulted, and such miscegenation was sometimes frowned upon and even criminalized. In Lousiana, both Lower and Upper, nonmarital and extramarital sex, bastardy, and slander relating to sexual conduct all preoccupied authorities. As transgressions of cultural norms, these acts highlight women as sources both of social disorder and reproduction. In colonial St. Louis, a transient and diverse population, combined with the tenuousness of imperial control, contributed to the ways in which sexual and marital liaisons were perceived, monitored, legislated, punished, and at times tolerated. Government interest in such matters abounded, with officials deploring unions between white men and black women and scrutinizing carefully those involving others. In this evolving society, a variety of sexual liaisons and familial relations emerged, making the households of colonial St. Louis a patchwork of novel domestic arrangements that transcended legal codes and racial boundaries.

Despite the fact that the Chouteau-Laclède union was a part of St. Louis history from the beginning of the settlement, some descendants denied their progenitors' extramarital liaison until as recently as the 1920s, trying to avoid the stigma of illegitimacy. Alexander DeMenil, who wrote an impassioned if inaccurate defense of his ancestor, saw it as his duty to rescue Madame Chouteau's memory "from the damning stain that has sullied its

2. Hurtado, *Intimate Frontiers*.

purity."[3] He claimed that all of her children were fathered by her legal husband, René Chouteau. DeMenil's evidence for René Chouteau's reproductive role was that Madame Chouteau and her five children inherited from him, not from Pierre Laclède, an argument that missed or misrepesented crucial evidence. Maintaining such claims also required a bit of creative chronology with the birthdates of the children. The paternity issue had been an open secret in St. Louis for decades. In the late 1840s, when a celebration of St. Louis's founding and Pierre Laclède's role in it was held, Pierre Chouteau was an honored guest. A French visitor from Bedous, describing the festivities to a Laclède family member back in the village, wrote, "I believe that all the guests present knew perfectly that he was the son of Mr de Laclede on one side and he must have known too that they were aware of the fact, and nevertheless he did not have the courage to rise and to disclose that the man whose memory they were honoring was his father." Guessing that at least three-quarters of the town's inhabitants knew the secret, Laclède's descendants, all bearing the name Chouteau, continued to "surround all that has the least connection with his name" with mystery.[4]

Despite such moments, public denial and debate about the family tree continued until John Francis McDermott, another Chouteau family descendant and tireless researcher of St. Louis history, pieced together a number of clues and documents to demonstrate definitively that René could not have fathered all of Madame Chouteau's offspring. Indeed, he was thousands of miles away when she conceived the youngest four. McDermott found that after Madame Chouteau's husband, René, had deserted her in New Orleans, he returned to France, leaving no traces in Louisiana records between 1752 and 1767. During that period, she met and formed an attachment to Pierre Laclède, with children arriving every two years from 1758 to 1764. According to William Foley, the fact that Madame Chouteau is listed as *Veuve,* or Widow Chouteau, in the 1763 Louisiana census also indicates that she was claiming for herself the status of head of household after her husband deserted her in New Orleans.[5] Together, she and her four children, the youngest born in March 1764, traveled to St. Louis within months of its founding, reaching Upper Louisiana after the difficult journey upriver, and there joining her son Auguste and her lover Pierre. They set up housekeeping together and were among the first inhabitants of the village, living in the building Laclède had

3. Alexander N. DeMenil, St. Louis, October 13, 1921, from the *St. Louis Globe-Democrat,* October 16, 1921, "Dr. A. N. DeMenil Writes on History of Early St. Louisans." A pamphlet version is entitled: "Madame Chouteau Vindicated," JFM, Lovejoy Library.

4. André Casamayou to Cécile Garnot, translated and reprinted in McDermott, "Pierre de Laclède and the Chouteaus," 282.

5. Foley, "The Laclède-Chouteau Puzzle," 22.

constructed to serve as his store and warehouse. Madame Chouteau, Laclède, their children, and Auguste, Marie's son with René, all shared the "government house," for so it functioned, until 1768, when they moved into a new limestone home Laclède had built one block away.[6]

In 1768, Laclède took an unusual legal step, which amounted to recognition of his parental role, of deeding the new house, several slaves, and some land to all the children, and granting their mother the right to use the property. With regard to Auguste, Laclède expressed his appreciation for the good service the young man had provided as his clerk. He wanted Auguste and the other children to receive the property as "proof" of his "affection for them," declaring the deed voluntary and irrevocable. In crafting the document, Laclède included a statement that glossed over the state of Madame Chouteau's marriage in an intriguing way. He referred to Auguste and his offspring as the children of René Chouteau, "absent from this Post," and Chouteau's wife, Marie Thérèse Bourgeois, "here present, residing in this said Post." Whether those who witnessed the deed felt complicit in the implicit lie is unknown. One can imagine that few would challenge either Laclède's will or authority. On behalf of her children, Madame Chotueau accepted the gift, and she and Laclède each kept a copy of the deed. As part of the process, Madame Chouteau acknowledged that all of the details were agreeable to her and that she knew well and had seen and visited all the property and lands included.[7] Given her force of character, she likely did more than just visit the property; one can easily imagine her walking down the street to the house construction site, a block away, to offer opinions and express her ideas about her new residence.

This act, an expression of Laclède's attachment to his partner and children and sense of responsibility for their well-being, insured that his offspring and their half-brother Auguste would all inherit some of his property, despite the fact that he was not married to their mother. By deeding the property to his biological children and Auguste (whom he appears to have treated as a son and close business confidante), Laclède took advantage of his unmarried state to sidestep the community property risks of Spanish and French legal codes. Under their laws, married women retained much greater property rights within marriage than did women in colonial Anglo-America. Even if he and Madame Chouteau had the chance to marry at a later date, there would be no risk of his debts affecting his children's legacy. Madame Chouteau would enjoy the property during her lifetime, before it passed to her heirs. For over forty-five years, she put it to good use, occupying the home her lover

---

6. Corbett, "Veuve Chouteau," 45.
7. Donation by Laclède, May 12, 1768, Instrument #9B, St. Louis Archives, MHMA.

Marie Thérèse Bourgeois Chouteau, by François Guyol de Guiran,
ca. 1812, Missouri History Museum, St. Louis

deeded to her children until her death. At fifty feet by thirty-four feet, the
house had generous proportions for the village and several rooms suitable
for a large family. Joining the Chouteaus, mother and offspring, were the
enslaved women and children included in the deed: two African women—
Louison and another, unnamed woman—both in their early twenties; the
two-year-old son of one; and two Indian girls, Thérèse and Manon, both
of whom Madame Chouteau reported in the 1770 enumeration of Indian
slaves.[8] In addition, the structure sheltered two important boarders: Laclède
and the high-ranking government official, St. Ange.

8. Ibid.

All might have gone on tranquilly for the Chouteau-Laclède family if not for the return to America of René Chouteau. After an absence of over a decade, he came back to New Orleans, where he set himself up as a baker and quickly made enemies in that trade. In 1771, he antagonzied a rival, Bernardo Shiloc, by alleging that Shiloc sold poisoned pastries. When Shiloc sued, a hearing was held in which several men testified that they were in a billiard hall when Chouteau came in and made his accusations. Governor Unzaga, who heard the case, ordered Chouteau jailed and his property seized. In prison, when prompted to confess, Chouteau described himself as a fifty-year-old married baker, and he blamed a woman he encountered on the levee for the report on Shiloc's pastries. When accused of spreading the rumor to discredit and injure a competitor, Chouteau declared that he had only repeated when the woman had said: that the pastries a black woman sold were made by Shiloc and contained poison. Insisting that he defamed no one, Chouteau refused to acknowledge making slanderous remarks. Unzaga nonetheless found him guilty of slander and ordered him to pay reparations for the injury done to Shiloc's honor, adding that he had shown leniency as this was Chouteau's first offense.[9]

At some point after his return to Louisiana, Chouteau decided that he wanted his wife back and managed to enlist Unzaga's aid in securing her return. Under the law, he was legally entitled to her presence and to sue those who detained her or gave her refuge.[10] As the *Coutume de Paris,* the French legal code, affirmed, *Le Mari est Seigneur,* meaning that the husband was lord to his wife. Why Pierre wanted Marie Thérèse back is unknowable. Perhaps reports of a prosperous family upriver galled him, and he dreamed of gaining access to the property she had acquired; legally, he stood to benefit from wealth she had amassed during the period of their marriage. Or perhaps his male pride was outraged at being a cuckold, despite the fact that he had been the one to leave her. News of his wife's whereabouts and new family would likely have been easy to obtain. St. Louis merchants regularly visited New Orleans, and many in the Crescent City had business interests and contacts up the Mississippi. (If René ever contacted his wife directly, no record survives; any request, command, or pleading on his part would presumably have fallen on deaf ears.) Chouteau may simply have considered himself still the head of a household that should by rights include his legal wife. Regardless of the fact that he had once abandoned her and their young son, René wanted Marie Thérèse, most definitely not

9. "Criminal Suit for Slander, Bernardo Shiloc vs. Chouteau (René) Pastry-cook, 20 April 1771," 324–28.

10. Baker, Simpson, and Allain, *"Le Mari est Seigneur,"* 12.

veuve, back at his side, and he sought the assistance of authorities to achieve that goal. (Whether he physically abused his wife and scarred her face, as family tradition holds, is impossible to verify.)

Although the speed with which he acted and the steps Chouteau took to recover his wife's presence in New Orleans are not clear, what is apparent is that his complaint ultimately reached an official—if not altogether sympathetic—audience. By late 1774, his demand that his wife rejoin him had made it the highest levels of the Spanish colonial administration. In October of that year, Governor Unzaga raised the problem with his second-in-command, upriver in St. Louis. Piernas's response to Unzaga's letter about the Chouteaus indicates the seriousness with which government officials viewed the couple's arrangement, or rather estrangement, and the awkwardness Piernas felt when pursuing René Chouteau's complaint. Over the previous several years, Laclède had been instrumental in assisting the crown on numerous occasions, from providing provisions and housing to leading the expedition against Ducharme. Piernas had developed a deep appreciation for the leadership abilities and other skills of St. Louis's founder, and he depended on Laclède's support.

Addressing Unzaga in an apologetic tone, sounding as though he was trying to justify a delay in acting, Piernas noted that he had just received the governor's letter. In it, Unzaga had advised Piernas to send Madame Chouteau to New Orleans on the first boat possible, so that she might there "enter into the power of her husband." Piernas assured Unzaga that Madame Chouteau would not be on that vessel alone; her children, or at least some of them, would accompany her. With remarkable delicacy, or perhaps ambiguity, Piernas skirted the issue of who had fathered her children, promising the governor that he would see to it that the children belonging to the said husband, that is, Chouteau, would be sent downriver, and those that were not his, would be delivered to their father. If that father, the unnamed Pierre Laclède, chose voluntarily, as an honorable man, to allow his younger children—his three daughters, then ten, twelve, and fourteen—to remain with their mother, Piernas would not interfere.[11]

By this time, the beginning of 1775, *Veuve* Chouteau, as she continued to style herself in St. Louis, had been in the village for over a decade, during which time she had acquired property, purchased slaves, run a household, raised a family, and taken in as boarders two of the most influential members of the community, her partner and St. Ange, who had died just before

---

11. Piernas to Unzaga, January 26, 1775, AGI-PC 81, MHMA microfilm.

the new year. Piernas characterized her as someone who had long main-tained a separate household and possessed her own land and slaves, empha-sizing her status as a head of a household. Piernas went further, underlining the fact that Madame Chouteau had two adult sons, Auguste and Pierre (then in their mid-twenties and late teens respectively) and that these two Chouteau offspring were men of substance themselves, one involved in the Indian trade, the other an active and contributing *habitant.* Not to be trifled with on her own account as a woman of property and substance, Madame Chouteau had additional status, or perhaps immunity to the law, as Laclède's partner, a point on which Piernas maintained silence. Perhaps stalling for time, Piernas promised the governor that he would see to it that she traveled to New Orleans to be delivered to her husband, as instructed by Unzaga, as soon as she had completed settling her affairs.[12]

Whether Piernas ever broached the subject with Laclède or Madame Chouteau is impossible to determine. Even if he did not raise the issue, it seems likely that they would have heard of René Chouteau's demand from some source. What is clear is that the situation remained unchanged nearly a year later, when Piernas's successor as lieutenant governor, Francisco Cruzat, took up the matter. Perhaps the change in leadership in May 1775 delayed a resolution. Or perhaps the adulterous pair simply dragged their feet, with Madame Chouteau soliciting the lieutenant governor's favor in her efforts to preserve her estate and remain in St. Louis. In August 1775, Governor Unzaga wrote to Cruzat, just three months into his tenure as the new lieutenant governor, about the couple. Not responding to that missive until December, Cruzat apprised Unzaga of his progress, noting that he was giving Madame Chouteau the time she needed to conclude her affairs without damaging her finances. His predecessor's promise of sending her south on the first boat seemed forgotten.[13] How complicated enforcing the separation might prove was underlined by another letter Cruzat sent to New Orleans the same day, in which he acknowledged the crucial support of Laclède in producing hemp. "Don Pedro Laclède, who has been been earnestly cultivating hemp for some years, has at length succeeded in pro-ducing a goodly quantity," Cruzat enthused, praising Laclède's "ingenious method" and suggesting the benefit that would likely result; a sample of rope produced with his hemp was on its way to New Orleans. In the same report, Cruzat noted that large quantities of furs were being sent downstream in two pirogues belonging to Auguste Chouteau.[14] In short,

12. Ibid.
13. Cruzat to Unzaga, December 10, 1775, AGI-PC 81-614, MHMA microfilm.
14. Cruzat, statistical report, December 10, 1775, in Houck, *SRM,* 1: 100.

members of the Chouteau-Laclède clan were busy making important contributions to the economy of Upper Louisiana.

Despite the prominence and influence of the family, Cruzat was not turning a blind eye toward the couple's relationship nor countenancing their continued improprieties. He reported that during the time it took Madame Chouteau to settle her affairs, he was forbidding her to have any contact with Laclède. (Presumably, Cruzat had come to St. Louis already aware of the governor's views and orders. Lacking the personal and working relationship that Piernas had developed with Laclède, Cruzat may have been more willing to confront the pair.) Keeping the two apart woud be rather difficult, Cruzat acknowledged, given that they both lived in the village, and in fact, in the same house. Seeking to put an end to that arrangement, Cruzat ordered the two to separate. They agreed to do so, promising Cruzat that one would go live in a dwelling a league outside the village, but there is no evidence that they ever ceased cohabiting. Another half year elapsed before anything happened to alter the situation. When it came, the change was not Madame Chouteau's overdue departure for New Orleans. Rather, René Chouteau fell ill and died. In his will, he claimed his wife again, declaring that he had contracted marriage before the church, the "Holy Mother," with Marie Thérèse Bourgeois, adding that legitimate offspring resulted from the union, and naming his survivors as his heirs.[15] When he died in April 1776, the crisis facing the family came to an abrupt conclusion.[16]

News of her husband's death must have been, at least in part, a relief to Marie Thérèse, Pierre, and their family. Their lives in St. Louis continued without interruption. In July 1776, their fifteen-year-old daughter Pélagie married thirty-nine-year-old Silvetre Labbadie, a merchant from Tarbes, France, not too far from Laclède's birthplace in the Pyrenees.[17] That fall, Laclède went to New Orleans for business.[18] Perhaps the satisfactory resolution of the family's difficulties contributed to a gesture of goodwill Laclède made the following year. In 1777, he sent the governor a gift of produce from Upper Louisiana: hams, pecans, and morels. Laclède acknowledged the governor's known dislike of presents but declared that he wanted to express his affection and share items that he hoped the governor

15. René Chouteau, will, April 10, 1776, copy, Chouteau Collection, MHMA.

16. He died and was buried in New Orleans on April 21, 1776; photostat of St. Louis Cathedral (New Orleans) church register, vol. 2, p. 42, in Chouteau Papers, MHMA. Death certificate, April 21, 1776.

17. Billon, *Annals of St. Louis,* 260–61; Cunningham and Blythe, *The Founding Family of St. Louis,* 145–46.

18. Billon, *Annals of St. Louis,* 144–45.

would enjoy.[19] With the death of René Chouteau, Pierre Laclède and Marie Thérèse Bourgeois Chouteau were finally free to wed, after roughly twenty years together. Yet *Veuve* Chouteau did not remarry, and Monsieur Laclède remained a bachelor. Although their relationship continued until Laclède's death on May 27, 1778, the two never formalized their ties legally. One historian has suggested that a marriage would not have been in Madame Chouteau's interests, as community property laws meant that she would have risked inheriting at least some of Laclède's financial woes; he was heavily in debt to his former business partner in New Orleans, Antoine Maxent, at the time of his death.[20]

What should we make of the Chouteau-Laclède liaison, which provoked official scrutiny? How was it likely perceived by their friends and other villagers? Their relationship, which might have marginalized Madame Chouteau in a more settled, polite society, did not stop her from—and indeed may have assisted her in—becoming one of the most powerful women in the village. Her experience begs the question of what other extramarital or nonmarital relationships were subject to censure in colonial St. Louis. When did they escape condemnation and commentary? Some, such as liaisons between European men and African women, were routinely criticized. Were European women's sexual transgressions treated differently? To answer these questions, it is necessary first to explore other instances in which social relations and sexual liaisons entered the public sphere of debate and action, paying attention above all to the role of race.

Official dismay over the character, moral fiber, habits, and appetites of St. Louisans erupted soon after Spanish authorities assumed control of the outpost. Early on, the villagers developed a reputation for enjoying life's creature comforts. Sundays were not the solemn days of worship to be found in colonial Anglo-American Protestant communities at the time. Rather, after church services had concluded, villagers in St. Louis frequently spent part of the day dancing and gambling. This approach to life extended to what William Foley has characterized as the distinctive pace of life in colonial St. Louis, where residents kept time according to seasonal activities, such as "the month when strawberries ripen"; enjoyed serenading their

19. For his part, the governor hastened to reassure Laclède that he had never considered the possibility of any unsavory intentions on the merchant's part and was very glad of the gift. Laclède letter, June 29, 1777, AGI-PC 190-445, MHMA microfilm.

20. Corbett, "Veuve Chouteau," 45.

neighbors on New Year's Eve while requesting pledges of chickens and pies for the annual Twelfth Night festivities; and spent their leisure hours play-ing billiards.[21] The line between innocent and illicit pastimes was easily blurred, however. As early as 1769, Pedro Piernas had concluded that the villagers were a hopelessly dissipated people, whose "looseness of conduct" and "dissoluteness" could only be deplored.[22] To authorities both civil and clerical, St. Louisans seemed to be people unable to restrain themselves from indulging in all sorts of expensive and immoral habits that led to debt and disorder, all the while revealing deep-seated character flaws.

Officials' perceptions of a morally lax population were reinforced by the apparent lack of interest of colonial European men in marriage on one hand, combined with their enthusiasm for nonmarital sex on the other. In the Louisiana territory, authorities bemoaned the weakness of marriage and worried about interracial unions, particularly those that involved enslaved African women. As a countermeasure—to shore up the beleaguered insti-tution—they sometimes argued that male colonists should be encouraged to enter into legal unions with indigenous women. Typically, such rela-tionships took place within Spanish society, with Indians who had been at least partly assimilated and become members of the colonial church and state.[23] To worried officials, the lack of marriage was a serious and common problem, so much so that Ulloa, when he served as govenor in the late 1760s, had urged that "especial distinction" and high esteem be accorded "those who are married, even though of humble rank and of mixed blood."[24] While such unions with Indians might not be ideal, they were, in Spanish officials' eyes, preferable to relationships between European men and African women.[25] Restrictions prohibiting unmarried men from set-tling permanently in new communities were designed to preclude the too-common practice of concubinage with "negro and mulatto slave women."[26] In St. Louis, the first recorded marriage involved a mixed-race individual. On April 20, 1766, Marie Beaugenou married Toussaint Hunant; both of his parents were one-quarter Indian.[27]

Government officials wanted the population of Upper Louisiana to grow—a desirable and necessary step to maintaining an imperial presence—but

21. William E. Foley, "Galleries, Gumbo, and 'La Guignolée,'" 3.

22. Piernas to O'Reilly, October 31, 1769, reprinted in Houck, SRM, 1: 73.

23. Barr, "From Captives to Slaves," 36.

24. Ulloa's instructions, March 14, 1767, reprinted in Houck, SRM, 1: 9.

25. See Martha Hodes, ed., Sex, Love, Race; Kupperman, Indians and English; Spear, "Colonial Intimacies."

26. Ulloa's instructions, March 14, 1767, in Houck, SRM, 1: 15–16.

27. Thorne, The Many Hands of My Relations, 77.

they were troubled at the prospect of adding mixed-race individuals of African-European ancestry and took steps to limit black-white social intercourse.[28] Such an action reflected widespread views of interracial liaisons. In her research on colonial Mexico, Maria Elena Martinez has found that over time, the Spanish of New Spain increasingly viewed race mixing as negative yet "more frequently and systematically construed [African ancestry] as a stain on a lineage." In St. Louis, in February 1776, less than a year into his term as lieutenant governor and shortly after ordering Madame Chouteau and Laclède to cease cohabiting, Cruzat issued an ordinance forbidding white persons in St. Louis from socializing with slaves. With the Indian slave trade outlawed, the regulation basically targeted enslaved Africans. Perhaps anticipating violations, Cruzat emphasized that the order be "read, published, and posted on the front door on the church." While making announcements after mass on Sunday was the usual practice in this small, oral community, this step underlines the seriousness with which he viewed such potentially disorderly behavior.

Several aspects of interracial socializing bothered Cruzat. In a statement replete with assumptions of racial prejudice, beliefs in innate hierarchies, and notions of profound differences among peoples, Cruzat noted that "while the sole difference in color should be a sufficient reason to keep all whites from getting involved with their slaves, nonetheless, several, without considering the distance which separates them," managed to gain entrance to their meetings. Their intentions were immoral and their actions illicit; white men attended such gatherings to introduce alcohol and thereby to commit with greater impunity "disorders and scandals that dishonor, at the same time, their own persons and debase the conditions of their fellow men." Such excesses had "disastrous consequences" and had to be prevented. Any white person, "of whatever quality, condition, sex, and state," who was discovered "at any assembly of slaves, whether at night or in the daytime," would be punished "with eight days in prison, and a fine" to be put toward the needs of the church.[29] While the transgressors the lieutenant governor was targeting were undoubtedly men, he included both white men and white women in the prohibition. Cruzat's restrictions point to settings seldom illuminated in the records: places where Africans came together day and night to socialize. Where the enslaved gathered for evening companionship in St. Louis is difficult to determine, whether in slave quarters, homes of free blacks, or houses of whites willing to dispense alcohol to all tipplers. Wherever such gatherings happened, the scenes were,

28. Martinez, "The Black Blood of New Spain," 484.
29. Cruzat decree, February 18, 1776, AGI-PC 2358; JFM, Lovejoy Library.

according to the official view, ones where alcohol consumption fueled inter-racial socializing, and sexual contact across racial lines was both possible and initiated by white men. Under the *Code Noir,* the legal code governing slavery, sexual exploitation of enslaved women was forbidden. Clearly, that prohibition required reinforcement.

Cruzat's order highlights important realities of colonial St. Louis: the existence of slavery from the earliest days of the settlement and a notice-able gender imbalance among the adult population. Given the numbers involved, it is not surprising that white men looked beyond the pool of white women for sexual partners. As in other recently settled colonial outposts, an imbalanced sex ratio was the norm, with white men vastly outnumbering white women. The situation was the opposite for Indians in St. Louis, where there were many more adult indigenous women than men in the community, a reflection of their being prized as domestic servants and sexual partners. The ratio of adult African men to women was also skewed, although less so than for either the European or Indian peoples in the village. That disparity was part of St. Louis in the 1760s and continued to be the case for many years. In 1779, in a village of 702 people, the census counted 226 white males and 92 white females between the ages of fourteen and fifty, and 72 enslaved women and 61 men listed as capable of work.[30] A 1787 census lists a total population for St. Louis of 1,182. Altogether, 623 adult men looked for partners among 269 adult women, a ratio of over 2.3 men to every one woman.[31] Of the white St. Louisans, 524 were adult men and 186 were adult women. Among the 253 enslaved individuals were 92 adult men and 81 adult women. Free "colored" people numbered 21, of whom seven were adult men and two adult women.

Within the constraints of a skewed sex ratio and small numbers, some African women and men in St. Louis were nonetheless able to form families. One such woman, Jeanette, also known as Juanita Forchet, seems to have come to the village as a free woman, having been manumitted in Illinois. She received one of the original land grants in St. Louis in 1765, married an African blacksmith, Gregory, and built a French-style colonial post house. By 1770, when Gregory died, they had planted a garden and added a cow and chickens to their possessions. By the time Jeanette remarried in 1773, her property had grown, and she counted seven cows, seven calves, four sows, a dozen hens, and a rooster among her possessions. (The domestic

30. St. Louis census, December 31, 1779, AGI-PC 193a-632, MHMA microfilm.

31. Census, San Luis, December 31, 1787, Francisco Cruzat, Census Collection, MHMA.

scenes suggested in the documents highlight women's roles in making and maintaining homes in new settlements, where their labor, irrespective of race, was critical.[32] Production and reproduction occupied women in colonial St. Louis, as they bore and raised children while tending gardens, keeping households, preserving produce, washing clothes, dairying, and cooking.[33]) Interestingly, her children later adopted her name, Jeanette, as their surname. Other African women also gained significant property holdings to support themselves and their families. Marie LaBastille, for example, owned an entire village block and house, and Elizabeth Datcherut was a homeowner. One scholar has suggested that the government was so anxious to strengthen its presence in Upper Louisiana that it awarded land grants regardless of the recipients' race or sex.[34]

On occasion, French creole colonists acted to protect African American families. In St. Louis, an official blocked a slave sale because of marriage. In 1766, a magistrate stopped the auction from proceeding, declaring that "the negro Mecure is married in the eyes of the Church" and ordering the slaveowner to take care to sell the family together, "not separating any negress from her husband, and no child from its father or mother, unless the girl be twelve years old and the boy fourteen."[35] In Ste. Genevieve, François Vallé tried to follow legal guidelines closely, explaining his unwillingness to separate young children from their parents on the grounds of the French and Spanish sources he had consulted. The colony's French *Code Noir* contained two items that did not help: article 43 mentioned allowing the sale of prepubescent children away from their parents if they all belonged to the same master and article 44 article only addressed slaves between the ages of fourteen and sixty. When he turned to a copy of procedures that Governor O'Reilly had distributed as a guide to administering justice, principles that agreed with the Spanish legal code for the colonies, *la Nueva Recopilacion de Castilla,* he saw in article 27 a reference to the age of competence as fourteen for boys and twelve for girls, presumably the one alluded to in the St. Louis case. As the children

32. Brucken and Scharff, "Home Lands."

33. They raised carrots, parsnips, radishes, turnips, cucumbers, and melons. French, African, and indigenous culinary traditions intersected, with St. Louisans consuming gumbos and locally abundant game, such as bear, deer, squirrel, and catfish. Corn was considered more appropriate food for livestock than for humans, and settlers preferred domesticated animals, such as cattle and pigs, to local game. See Foley, "Galeries, Gumbo, and *'La Guignolée,'*" 8–9, 13.

34. At the death of her second husband in 1790, Jeanette's holdings included a large garden, an orchard of fruit trees, poultry, and agricultural implements, such as a yoke for oxen. Gilbert, "Esther and Her Sisters," 19–20, 23, 16–17.

35. La Frenure to Lefebre and Labuscière, August 6, 1766, St. Louis Archives, MHMA, cited in Foley, "Galeries, Gumbo, and *'La Guignolée,'*" 13.

involved in the case were younger, none of these provisions enabled him to separate the family.[36]

Perhaps most notable among African American women who owned property in St. Louis was Esther, an enslaved woman who experienced both forced separation from a young daughter and an interracial liaison. Esther had come initially to Kaskaskia, on the other side of the Mississippi, with the Camp family of Virginia. In 1784, when Ichabod Camp failed to repay a debt to St. Louis merchant Jacques Clamorgan, the trader took Esther, then around thirty-one, as payment, thus separating her from her eleven-year-old daughter in an act of careless cruelty that could not have predisposed Esther to look kindly on the man who performed it. (It certainly would have underlined Clamorgan's domination and her vulnerability.) Exercising the power of his position, Clamorgan took Esther as his concubine, and she ultimately ran his household and acted as his de facto business manager in his absence. Another merchant noted that she "seemed to have the control within the premises when Clamorgan was absent and very much so when he was at home."[37] The relationship between the two grew more complicated in the 1790s, when Clamorgan, to protect his business interests, freed Esther in order to put his property in her name. Further changing her status and that of her descendants, he sold Esther her daughter, whom he had bought a year after bringing Esther to St. Louis, and freed her grandson. Eventually, Esther had an orchard on a village block, as well as land outside the village granted to her by the government, and raised cattle, known widely as "Esther's cows." When Clamorgan began to pursue affairs with younger mulatto women and beat and verbally abused her, Esther left him, with the deeds to various properties in hand.[38]

Interracial sex, visible and public in colonial St. Louis, lay at the heart of a failed marriage that became a very public scandal in the 1770s. In the legal proceedings that erupted, both husband and wife accused each other of infidelity, and their complaints ultimately reached the ears of the governor in New Orleans. Central to the wife's claim was the charge that her husband had committed adultery with an enslaved black woman. In a lengthy, involved petition, Elizabeth Coulon de Villiers sought the government's protection from her husband, Pierre Françoise de Volsey, a man

---

36. François Vallé to Bernardo de Gálvez, December 12, 1777, AGI-PC 190-475, MHMA microfilm. Vallé referred to the legal texts by name, noting *le Code Noir* and *La Recopilation des lois de Castille.*

37. Gabriel Cerré letter, quoted in Gilbert, "Esther and Her Sisters," 18.

38. The details in this paragraph are drawn from Gilbert, "Esther and Her Sisters," 15, 17–19.

she characterized as immoral, cruel, and greedy. Madame de Volsey was well connected in St. Louis, a wealthy woman in her own right, daughter of one French commandant at Fort Chartres, Neyon de Villiers, and niece to another, St. Ange.[39] Her husband was prominent as well, serving as captain of the French garrisons in Illinois and St. Louis and acting as St. Ange's successor.[40] After years of what sounds like a miserable marriage, Madame de Volsey requested help in securing her estate from her husband. Chief among the improprieties she named was his infidelity. She accused her spouse of having a child with Magdalene, an African slave who had served as nurse to her invalid brother. According to Elizabeth's complaint, everyone knew of the liaison, and her husband acknowledged it by trying to make his mulatto daughter heir to property that rightfully belonged to her, his legitimate wife.

The charge of adultery across racial lines was true. In 1764, after Magdalene died, Pierre purchased her young daughter, Françoise, and took the toddler into his home. A 1768 will named her as sole heir of goods acquired during the de Volseys' marriage. In 1772, the couple manumitted the ten-year-old, an act that often constituted implicit recognition of paternity and interracial sex. Later, in a 1788 will, Pierre acknowledged Françoise as his natural daughter, and she did in fact inherit his property after his death in 1795, including land in the Little Prairie. (Her inheritance, according to one scholar, was sufficient to enable her to leave a bad marriage in St. Louis, take a lover, and flee to the other side of the Mississippi.)[41] To the charge of adultery with an enslaved woman and attempted subversion of spousal property rights, Elizabeth added another, more unusual accusation. She declared that her husband had forced her to accuse his own brother of attempting to rape her while she was dressing. According to her account, Monsieur de Volsey wanted to get rid of his sick younger brother, who lived with them, and so proposed a lie that would justify forcing him out of their household; Pierre threatened his wife with "the cruellest treatment" and she, out of fear, complied. Scandalously expelled from the home on the basis of his sister-in-law's false accusations, the boy went to Ste. Genevieve, where he was taken in by François Vallé and protested his innocence until his early

39. Thwaites, ed., *The Jesuit relations and allied documents,* 70: 318; Billon, *Annals of St. Louis,* 435–36.

40. Certificate of commission for Pedro Francisco de Volsey, June 1, 1777, AGI-PC 190-42 (Price compilation, MHMA).

41. On Françoise's life, see Gilbert, "Esther and Her Sisters," 21. Manumission papers of a girl named Françoise, executed by Pierre François de Volsey and his wife, Elizabeth, June 22, 1772, Slave Papers, MHMA.

death. For her part, Elizabeth deeply regretted the harm her words had done.[42]

Behind her husband's actions, she was sure, was a plan to defraud her of her property. In 1774, while on furlough from his military duties, Pierre decided to go to France and purportedly set about taking with him almost all of their joint property, including substantial funds she had inherited from her mother, grandmother, and uncle, St. Ange. He intended to abandon her, she suspected, but Piernas, still the commandant at that time, had intervened, insisting that de Volsey recognize his wife's property rights. Under Spanish law, women had more property rights than did women in colonial Anglo-America, and so Madame de Volsey retained some power over her property despite being married.[43] French law equally preserved married women's property rights, guaranteeing them both one-half of the couple's community property as an inheritance, as well as other funds identitfied in marriage contracts.[44] Before he left St. Louis, however, Pierre managed to liquidate much of their estate and took the funds with him. When his two-year sojourn in France proved a failure, Elizabeth explained in the divorce petition, he returned to St. Louis to claim the remaining property still in her possession.[45] Her petition, it should be noted, was partly in response to one written by her husband, in which he accused her of adultery.[46] In his complaint, Monsieur de Volsey charged that his wife had been unfaithful with St. Louisan René Kiersereau, the church chorister. When Pierre returned to St. Louis from France, his wife fled the village in Kiersereau's company, and Pierre initiated proceedings for a dissolution of their marriage. She retorted that she was fleeing her husband's abuse, not running away with a lover, and the local priest, Father Bernard, backed her up. (Likely on good terms with the priest, Kiersereau had frequently officiated at religious ceremonies, such as baptisms and internments, when no priest was available.) If he had sex with Madame de Volsey, he was being unfaithful to his wife, Marie Robillard.[47] Interestingly, early St. Louis histories that mention this case attribute much of the scandalous behavior

42. Petition of Elizabeth de Villier to de Leyba and response, September 7, 1779, AGI-PC 193b-657, MHMA microfilm.

43. Married women did have the right to write wills regarding their separate property and their share of community property. On their legal status, see Rosen, "Women and Property across Colonial America," 363–64.

44. Baker, Simpson, and Allain, *"Le Mari est Seigneur,"* 11–12.

45. Petition of Elizabeth de Villier to de Leyba and response, September 7, 1779, AGI-PC 193b-657 (Price compilation, MHMA).

46. Pierre François de Volsey, petition, October 11, 1777, Chouteau-Papin Collection, MHMA.

47. Billon, *Annals of St. Louis,* 423–24.

to Madame de Volsey, and one even characterizes her husband as a kind-hearted man who tolerated her evil ways as long as he could.[48]

Involving himself in the high-profile marital dispute, the village priest turned up unannounced at Monsieur de Volsey's home one day. He came to inform Pierre that Kiersereau, who had fled with de Volsey's "unhappy wife," was coming back to the village, despite an order from the lieutenant govenor forbidding him from doing so. The priest proceeded to upbraid de Volsey about his conduct, including his treatment of his wife. During the interview, de Volsey spoke as softly to the priest as possible, he claimed, but was met with anger and threats, as well as "language ill-suited to his character and injurious to my honor." Supposedly, the priest said he would try to help Madame de Volsey get half of her husband's property. Outraged at the priest's interference, Pierre quickly dashed off a report of the encounter, describing the meeting as a "catastrophe" and himself as having suffered patiently from the terrible conduct of his wife. In response, the governor declared himself too busy to address the matter and bounced it back to the lieutenant governor, on the scene in St. Louis, to handle.[49] As the highest-ranking official in St. Louis, Leyba responded, telling de Volsey to calm down.[50] As the debacle dragged on, Leyba decided the problem was beyond his ability to solve, lacking, he claimed, anyone with whom to confer to reach a judgment.[51]

Establishing sexual misconduct was key to the financial future of both parties. A woman's adultery was treated differently under the law than a man's. Under French legal codes, a woman's conviction led to the loss of all her dower rights and other privileges, and her husband gained the authoirty to order her seclusion in a convent; under Spanish law, a husband could demand his adulterous wife's death.[52] Two years later, Madame de Volsey was sent to New Orleans to live with relatives.[53] Cases such as the de Volseys' might have deepened officials' sense of the need to control interracial and illicit social and sexual contact. In de Volsey's case, the adultery

48. Ibid., 436–37; Houck, *HM,* 2: 13.

49. De Volsey to governor, February 6, 1779, response from governor, AGI-PC 192-1104, MHMA microfilm.

50. De Volsey to governor, July 12, 1779, AGI-PC 192-1106, MHMA microfilm.

51. Petition of Elizabeth de Villiers and de Leyba response, September 16, 1779, AGI-PC 193b-657, MHMA microfilm; Billon, *Annals of St. Louis,* 437.

52. Baker, Simpson, and Allain, *"Le Mari est Seigneur,"* 12; Winstanley Briggs argues that the French in Illinois developed a consensual adaptation of Parisian marriage codes in ways that favored women; "The Enhanced Economic Position of Women in French Colonial Illinois," 63–65; Baker, *"Cherchez les Femmes."*

53. Houck, *HM,* 2: 13; Houck cites Cruzat, February 15, 1781, writing that he was sending her "against her will, because of the occasion of one Malvo."

took place with an enslaved woman in his own household and threatened to derail the legitimate transfer of an estate away from European heirs.[54] Adultery had clear repercussions for the legitimate transmission of property across generations, regardless of the race of those involved.[55]

The experiences of women like Madame Chouteau and Madame de Volsey also suggest the possibility that in thinly settled, struggling new communities like St. Louis, there was a kind of tolerance toward the sexual misconduct of European women involved in illicit relationships with European men. Given the official preoccupation with the cultural and economic dangers of mixed-race unions, perhaps it is not surprising that some white women who strayed within their race received a temporary pass for their behavior. In other words, Madame Chouteau was doubly untouchable. She was not only the consort of the village's leading citizen, but she was a producer of white children. Likewise, perhaps Madame de Volsey could run away with a church worker with seemingly few repercussions because she had done nothing to sully the "purity" of the race. Perhaps some saw her husband's transgression as greater in that it resulted in him fathering a mixed-race daughter.

If the primary concerns of imperial authorities were in promoting population growth and more particularly in promoting that increase among European men and women rather than through mixed-race alliances and liaisons, then they might have turned a blind eye to stable, long-lasting nonmarital unions among European colonists like Chouteau and Laclède or even to the occasional illicit acts suggested by Madame de Volsey's flight or cases of slander. If that theory holds true, perhaps state efforts to support and sustain an ethnically European population trumped the need to maintain religious norms regarding marriage. While European women's intimate behavior became the subject of public interest and debate at times, policy makers had more pressing matters of sexual misconduct to address, such as interracial sex. Civil and clerical authorities were thus perhaps willing to countenance or ignore the illicit conduct of white women. Thus, the potentially disruptive and destructive elements of sexual unions, highlighted by

54. Stoler, "Tense and Tender Ties," 865, 832; Stoler's suggestion that scholars undertake "closer readings of the relationship between racial categories and state intervention in intimate practices" can be usefully expanded to include the sexual conduct of white women, 850.

55. In 1776, for example, St. Louis resident Nicolas Franco Dion, married to Teresa Henrio, wanted his wife to be considered an heir to the estate of her father. But his wife was her father's "natural," that is, illegitimate, daughter; her mother had been married to someone else and had given birth during her husband's absence. Flummoxed by Dion's request for a determination regarding his wife's status, the commandant sought the advice of the governor. Cruzat to Unzaga, February 24, 1776, AGI-PC 81-618 (Price compilation, MHMA).

the Chouteau separation order or by the priest who defended Madame de Volsey from charges of infidelity, were overlooked or downplayed in young communities.

In communities like St. Louis where literacy rates were low, the spoken word held tremendous power. With one's reputation a cherished possession, assaults on it did not go unchallenged. That fact became abundantly clear in the late 1770s, when slander and sexual innuendo made their way into the village court repeatedly. (It should be noted that the archival record for colonial St. Louis is incomplete, with no litigated disputes documented in the first fourteen years after the village was founded and significant gaps for years thereafter.)[56]

A case of mutual insults regarding sexual behavior went from the streets into the courts in 1779, when two women with a history of acrimony brought their complaints to officials. Apparently, the problems began in 1778, when Madame Agnès Denoyer began to make very public and very nasty remarks about twenty-six-year-old Madame Montardy, a woman whose trader husband, Pierre, was often away from St. Louis for long periods. After months of enduring insults, Madame Montardy decided she had endured enough defamation of her character and took her calumniator to court. Writing to the lieutenant governor, Montardy declared herself "grievously offended in her honor and her reputation, which has never been tarnished by any stain." (Montardy had in fact been involved in a slander case years before but had seen the accusations made against her good name refuted.) What prompted the official complaint was seemingly straightforward. Madame Denoyer had left the village and gone to the fort on the Missouri, there to await the return of Monsieur Montardy, then trading on the river. Denoyer intended, according to Madame Montardy's petition, to stain her "with calumnies and pernicious words" in order to destroy the union and harmony of her marriage, by telling her husband that she was the concubine of Diego Blanco, a Spanish soldier.[57] Shortly thereafter, another woman in the village, Marie Dinant, told the aggrieved Madame Montardy that Madame Denoyer had made similar statements

---

56. Banner, "Written Law and Unwritten Norms in Colonial St. Louis," 55–56.

57. Monsieur Montardy purportedly dismissed the charges, "knowing the virtue of his wife," and sent a message to her via Jean-Baptiste Deschamps, to warn her about Madame Denoyer's slanderous speech. Petition of Madame Montardy, September 22, 1779, box 1, folder 8, Litigation Collection, MHMA.

to others, publicly, asserting that she was the whore of Blanco and that he used any pretext to go to her neighborhood to see her.[58] (Blanco often interacted with St. Louisans on official business; a literate member of the Spanish garrison, he was often called upon to witness documents, doing so twenty-nine times in 1776 alone.[59]) Worried that the rumors would affect her husband's spirits, Madame Montardy enlisted the apparatus of the government on her behalf.

Once officials were involved, Madame Denoyer reacted, coming to see Madame Montardy at her home at nine o'clock one evening. In recalling their discussion, Madame Montardy stated that she refused to accept a secret overture and private retraction, asking instead that Denoyer be forced to recant her slander publicly and to pay charges and expenses.[60] A witness, Marie Dinant, reported a different scene taking place that night. While in her front yard, she overheard Madame Denoyer, sitting at her front door, say that she had gone to the Montardy home at the commandant's orders, but instead of begging forgiveness, she had made Madame Montardy cry. Dinant swore that Denoyer said she had reproached Montardy with having another man's child and also with becoming pregnant during her husband's absence and having an abortion. Dinant remembered the charges, she declared, because Denoyer had made numerous remarks about both Madame Montardy and others who did not merit them.[61] The woman to whom Denoyer was speaking, Charlotte Jacinthe, wife of Louis Ride, was a newcomer to the village and so did not know Madame Montardy. She confirmed the general import of Dinant's report, saying that Madame Denoyer called Madame Montardy a lifelong whore. She added that Diego Blanco had passed by while the two women were talking. When Denoyer called out to him, he refused to stop, and Madame Denoyer then predicted he was on his way to see Madame Montardy and that he would pay for it.[62]

When called to court, Madam Denoyer denied the charges against her; her statements were not slanderous because they were true. Denoyer insisted that Montardy had granted forbidden favors to someone other than her husband. Denoyer admitting going to her house, saying she wanted

58. Deposition of Marie Dinant, September 23, 1779, box 1, folder 8, Litigation Collection, MHMA.

59. Dozens of instruments from 1774 to 1784 bear his signature as witness. See, for example, Instruments #195, 197, 210, 267, 281, 1624, 1626, St. Louis Archives, MHMA.

60. Petition of Madame Montardy, September 22, 1779, box 1, folder 8, Litigation Collection, MHMA.

61. Deposition of Marie Dinant, September 23, 1779, box 1, folder 8, Litigation Collection, MHMA.

62. Deposition of Charlotte Jacinthe, September 23, 1779, box 1, folder 8, Litigation Collection, MHMA.

to talk with Montardy to help her avoid exposure. They even discussed throwing Montardy's petition into the fire, she claimed. After the two had come to terms, however, Montardy left her company, avoiding her by taking another road. As a result, Denoyer was being forced to face her sworn enemy in court. "This woman requires the restoration of her honor on my part," Denoyer stated. "She dares much." Denoyer implied that a notorious incident, well known to the public, had recently taken place in the Montardy home.[63]

Faced with the choice of pronouncing guilt or innocence in the case, the lieutenant govenor, by this time Fernando de Leyba, sidestepped the issue. Pointing out that the witnesses' depositions had nothing to do with Madame Montardy's accusations about slanderous remarks made to her husband at the fort, Leyba deemed them irrelevant and threw out the case. With more than a hint of misogynism, he dismissed the matter as nothing more than the old speeches of noisy women.[64] "As a consequence," he pronounced, "we impose silence as much on Madame Montardy as on the Denoyer woman and the others implicated in the present affair." More than just immediate silence was dictated, for Leyba forbid them from making any kind of prejudicial remarks aimed at destroying reputations henceforth. In other words, the resolution of the case was court-mandated silence.[65] A key vehicle for the expression of identity and maintenance of community norms—speech—was thus censored as a source of contention, disorder, and significantly, women's communication and power. Whoever violated the prohibition first would find herself prosecuted to the fullest extent of the law, presumably running the risk of banishment.[66]

Whether either woman was satisfied with Leyba's pronouncement seems unlikely. Madame Montardy in particular had cause for concern. She had been involved in a slander case nine years before, and on that occasion had seen the man who sullied her reputation convicted and banished. Now, she feared that the slander might alienate her husband's affections. She risked

63. Petition of Agnes Denoyer, October 4, 1779, box 1, folder 8, Litigation Collection, MHMA.

64. Leyba, verdict in case of Montardy v. Denoyer, October 7, 1779, box 1, folder 8, Litigation Collection, MHMA. There was another old connection between branches of the Denoyer and Montardy families. In 1769, three men, two of them members of the Denoyer family, sought credit from Pierre Montardy for a trading outfit, and paid off their debt in 1771. Whether the relative financial positions of the families informed the hostility expressed in the women's slander case is impossible to determine. Louis and Bazile Denoier, Instrument #1524, August 17, 1769, St. Louis Archives, MHMA.

65. On legal responses to cases of slander involving women, see Norton,"Gender and Defamation in Seventeenth-Century Maryland."

66. Leyba, verdict in case of Montardy v. Denoyer, October 7, 1779, box 1, folder 8, Litigation Collection, MHMA.

losing his loyalty, protection, and economic support. If not forgiven by a husband, adultery was grounds for a wife to lose her property rights. Thus, the situation combined the key elements required for pursuing justice before the law: damaging someone's honor and injuring a slandered person's ability to make a living were both grounds for action.[67] This case suggests intriguing possibilities about women's position in colonial St. Louis, as well as about community mores.[68] In this instance, two women apparently traded insults for some time, neither feeling compelled to bring the matter to the attention of authorities. Yet Madame Montardy, willing and able to present her grievance to a high-ranking government official, ultimately pursued legal redress. When compared with the results of Madame Montardy's 1770 slander case, in which her husband, given her youth, likely played a significant role, the results in this one suggest the possibility that men might be banished for slander while women were silenced. Indeed, the only individuals exiled from St. Louis during the colonial period were men, and bachelors at that. Perhaps losing the occasional outspoken or disruptive man from a community with a very imbalanced gender ratio would do less damage than applying the same punishment to a vocal and disorderly woman. (That is not to suggest that those administering justice opted for banishment frequently; St. Louis could ill afford to lose men capable of aiding in its economic growth or defense.)

The same year, another case involving charges of a woman bearing a child fathered by someone other than her husband was not so peremptorily dismissed. Just to the south of the main settlement of St. Louis, in an area known as *Vide Poche* (today's Carondelet), alcohol supposedly led a man to impugn the sexual conduct of a neighboring woman.[69] In December 1778, Thérèse Caron, also known by her married name as Madame Petit, charged Jean Baptiste Menard with spreading a false and malicious rumor about her child's parentage. Menard, already convicted once of slander, was found guilty a second time. Although he acknowledged lying, he tried to blame his words not on ill will or a long-standing grudge, but on liquor, under whose effects he had injured an honest woman's honor and reputation. Both sources of disorder, spirits and slander went hand in hand.[70] In

---

67. Moogk, "'Thieving Buggers' and 'Stupid Sluts,'" 536.

68. Insults involving women in French Canada were charges of sexual misconduct. Husbands' responses to their wives' infidelities included violence; Moogk, "'Thieving Buggers' and 'Stupid Sluts,'" 542–43.

69. Also known as Delor's Village and Catalan's Prairie, *Vide Poche* (French for empty pocket), was settled in 1767 by Clement Delor de Treget. McDermott, ed., *Early Histories,* 34; Houck, *HM,* 2: 64.

70. Slander case, December 3, 1778, folio 18–19, St. Louis History Collection, 1762–1843, MHMA.

prison, Menard weighed the options presented to him: prove his accusations, retract his statement publicly, or accept whatever punishment the authorities deemed appropriate. In writing, he declared that he had wickedly and wrongfully calumniated an irreproachable woman's honor and now begged her forgiveness.[71]

Menard's contrite language, however, was worth little if committed only to paper. To punish Menard's crime, the authorities required a public performance. "Considering the gravity of the offence, and that the written recantation is not adequate to the injury done the lady," the lieutenant governor ordered Menard to be conducted to the door of the parish church to disavow his slanderous remarks.[72] In St. Louis, where many people were illiterate, the retraction had to be both visible and oral. Menard was thus ordered to repeat his statement at the church door at the close of high mass the following Sunday. (That punishment differed from the treatment of convicted slanderers in New France, where the guilty had to perform an *amende d'honneur,* in which they appeared in court, head bared, and on their knees begged forgiveness.)[73] Menard was also imprisoned for fifteen days, to serve as a warning to others who spoke unthinkingly; perhaps the court took into account alcohol as a contributing factor when settling on a punishment less severe than banishment.[74] In this case, the church threshhold served as the venue for preserving harmony and order. Secular and spiritual authority united at the church door to cleanse the community of the sin of slander while exposing the dangers of drink. Thus public penitence outdoors complemented the sacred rituals taking place inside.

These slander cases, based on charges that women with long-absent spouses strayed from their marital vows, raise the question of how frequently those traveling husbands pursued sexual liaisons among the Indians with whom they traded. Having Indian wives and families was certainly not uncommon. In their study of the Chouteau family, Foley and Rice assert that it was more than likely that the oldest two Chouteau offspring, Auguste and Pierre Chouteau, both had Indian families in the wilderness.[75] Having spent much of their youth among the Osages, they both

71. Jean Baptiste to Fernando de Leyba, December 4, 1778, reprinted in Billon, *Annals of St. Louis,* 155.

72. De Leyba, sentence of Jean Baptiste Menard, December 4, 1778, in ibid., 155–56.

73. Grievous insults required the further *reparation d'honneur,* which entailed retracting the slander and acknowledging the injured party's honor. Moogk, "'Thieving Buggers' and 'Stupid Sluts,'" 525.

74. Slander case, December 3, 1778, folio 18–19, St. Louis History Collection, 1762–1843, MHMA.

75. Thorne, *The Many Hands of My Relations,* 93–96.

became honorary members of influential clans. "It certainly would not have been unusual, under the circumstances," they argue, "if one or both took an Indian wife away from St. Louis." A *métis* Osage, known both as Paul Loise and Paul Chouteau, was likely the son of one of the Chouteau brothers.[76] Another *métis* man, "Antonio Chouteau," was known as the *hijo naturel,* or natural son, of Auguste Chouteau. Married in Illinois to a French woman, Helena Angelica Docteur, Antonio would have been born before Auguste was twenty.[77]

There appears to be evidence that Auguste Chouteau sought out women of Indian ancestry as partners in St. Louis as well. In 1783, in an unusual legal step, Auguste Chouteau paid the lieutenant governor, Francisco Cruzat, and his wife, Niconora Ramos, a large sum for an unborn child, *en ventre sa mère,* carried by Cruzat's *métisse* slave, Marie. This arrangement suggests strongly that he was the father of the child Marie was carrying. At the moment of the infant's birth, Chouteau's ownership would begin. The sale was followed by the birth of a child who was named Auguste, whose godparents were two of Cruzat's children. Marie's second child, born in 1786, bore the name of one of Auguste's half-sisters, Victoire, and had as her godparents another of Cruzat's children and a Chouteau family grandchild.[78] (The purchase was doubly illegal, violating as it did both O'Reilly's prohibitions on the Indian slave trade and the French *Code Noir,* which forbade the separation of young children from their parents.)[79] Whether longterm relationships with either an Osage woman in her village years before or Marie in St. Louis affected Auguste's marriage plans is unknown. Seven months after the *métis* girl Victoire was baptized, Auguste Chouteau, then thirty-nine, finally married a French member of the community, binding himself to a well-connected sixteen-year-old, Thérèse Cerré; such an age gap and early marriage for women were not uncommon where adult men far outnumbered adult women.[80] At least one other illegitimate *métis* child was fathered by Auguste as well.[81]

76. Foley and C. David Rice, *The First Chouteaus,* citing John J. Matthews, *The Osages,* 285, and Donald Jackson, ed., *Letters of the Lewis and Clark Expedition with Related Documents, 1783–1854,* 305n.

77. FB 1793-03, page 41, #430; November 4, 1796, funeral of Antonio Choutau, native of Illinois, *"hijo naturel,"* aged twenty-eight, Basilica of St. Louis, King of France, New Orleans, Louisiana, in JFM, Lovejoy Library.

78. Ekberg details this remarkable story in *Stealing Indian Women,* 82–86, 210 n. 54.

79. Ibid., 89. Ekberg notes that although it was not clear that the Black Code applied to Indian slaves as it did to black slaves, legal opinion in New Orleans suggested that it did. O'Reilly affirmed that the French Black Code applied to Louisiana in 1769.

80. Foley and C. David Rice, *The First Chouteaus,* 45.

81. Ekberg, *Stealing Indian Women,* 87.

Although the children of European-Indian liaisons most often stayed with their indigenous mothers in Indian villages, some mixed Indian-European families did live in St. Louis. Whether Auguste Chouteau ever cohabited with Marie is unknown, but he clearly took steps to incorporate his offspring with her, three-fourths French and one-fourth Indian, into the Chouteau network, albeit not fully. Unions between indigenous women and European men were often rooted in the exploitive, unequal dynamic of slavery. In 1776, Joseph Thibault married Marianne, "an Indian woman, his former slave." With regard to Maria Rosa Villalpando, the Hispanicized *métis* woman who married Jean Salé, it is impossible to know exactly how their relationship began. She had been a captive of the Pawnee for years before Salé entered the picture; he presumably purchased her at some point. Likewise, in the spring of 1774, Canadian trader Jacques l'Arrivée brought a Sioux woman he had purchased, Angélique, into St. Louis with their two *métis* children, Joseph and Hypolite. Ekberg notes the delicacy with which the village priest euphemistically described these children's origins: they were "born among the tribes, products of the work [*provenants des oeuvres*]" of l'Arrivée. Although it is not clear if Jacques and Angélique ever married, they continued their relationship, having another child the following spring. All three of their offspring became members of the community, receiving sacraments from Father Valentin; the elder two were baptized with their mother in 1774.[82] The circumstances of the family's formation and their existence in St. Louis highlight the cultural and legal ambiguities shaping life, with French names and Catholic baptism side-by-side with maternal enslavement. In the household of Madame Chouteau, miscegenation was also present, with Manon, one of the Indian slaves she claimed in 1770, bearing a *métis* son by an unknown father in 1779; this child was the second *métis* born to the house. The parents of the other boy, born in 1775, are not recorded. With good cause, Ekberg speculates that these two children were Auguste Chouteau's offspring as well, given his likely access to and authority within his mother's house.[83]

For another Indian woman with *métis* children in St. Louis, the process of having a family was fraught. Described in the records as the illegitimate wife of trader André Roy, Angelique Courtemarche, an Iowa Indian, may have first come to Roy's household as a slave. Over the course of several years, she bore four children, all acknowledged as his. At one point, when she returned to her Iowa village with two children, Roy cut her out of his

---

82. Marriages, book 1, and Baptisms, book 1, St. Louis Diocesan Records, Old Cathedral, cited in Ekberg, *Stealing Indian Women*, 75, 78–79.

83. Ekberg, *Stealing Indian Women*, 87–88.

Marriage outfits of Auguste and Thérèse Cerré Chouteau,
September 21, 1786, Missouri History Museum, St. Louis

will; he later changed his mind and left her the family home.[84] Her story
serves as a reminder of the ways in which European and Indian men used
women as social and political capital. As Julianna Barr argues, "Pressed
into service, women became objects for sex, familial reproduction, and
reciprocal trade relations."[85] The fact that Angelique Courtmanche left St.
Louis for a time suggests that, despite the exploitation that likely shaped
the beginning of her relationship with Roy, she was an active agent in
determining her future and that of her children.[86]

84. Deed, Instrument #406; André Roy Will, 1796, Instrument #2251; St. Louis Archives, cited
in Gilbert, "Free Women of Color," 5–6.
85. Barr, "From Captives to Slaves," 46.
86. Spear draws attention to women's participation in *métissage* and their roles as active agents in
relationships. "Colonial Intimacies," 79. In the territorial era, Manuel Lisa, a Spanish trader, had two
children with an Omaha woman, Mitain, daughter of the chief, before marrying a white woman; a
custody battle ensued. Foley, "Galleries, Gumbo, and '*La Guignolée*,'" 15; Oglesby, *Manuel Lisa,* 163,
178n.

Far from unique in St. Louis, interracial marriages, nonmarital unions, and mixed families were visible at the time and left traces in the records. There was, for example, Josette, an Indian woman, who married Jean Baptiste Mayer.[87] A mixed union that made an especially strong impression on villagers was that of Jean Marie Cardinal and Marianne, a Pawnee woman. Cardinal had lived with and traded with the Pawnees for years, forming a family with Marianne and having at least seven children. In 1776, the couple came to St. Louis with their children, all entering the village on horseback, a sight that one resident could recall decades later.[88] There, the couple were married by the priest and had their children baptized. Another villager averred that the children spoke Pawnee when together as they did not speak French well.[89] Following in her parents' footsteps, their twenty-year-old daughter Genevieve Cardinal married French villager Jean Baptiste Vifarenne the following summer, in August 1777.[90] Property records suggest many other ties between Indian women and European men. Joseph Dube, for example, gave a house to an Indian woman, Marguerite Beor, in 1767, for her faithful service as his slave; she was married to rope-maker Louis Beor.[91] Likewise, Daniel Moricio bequeathed a substantial sum to Maria, a Sioux Indian, for many years of service to him.[92]

Although church records in St. Louis and Ste. Genevieve contain no references to marriages between enslaved Indians, baptismal notations make clear that such families did exist. In February 1772, Alexis, son of the "legitimate marriage" of Jacques and Ursule, then in their early thirties and mid-twenties respectively, was baptized in St. Louis. As Ekberg notes, either the couple's owner, *voyageur* Michel Lamy, arranged for the two to be married, or they, as baptized Christians, insisted on it.[93] In late 1783, several baptisms revealed the existence of other enslaved Indian families. Among the Indian slaves of St. Louisan Sieur Joseph were two couples

87. Marriage contract Josette and Jean Baptiste Mayer [or Maillet], Instrument #2126, St. Louis Archives, cited in Gilbert, "Free Women of Color," 12.

88. Testimony of Elizabeth Ortez, November 20, 1847, in Henry W. Williams, *Old Missouri Land Cases,* part 4, *Cutter vs. Waddingham,* 12.

89. Testimony of Mary Thérèse Thibeau, November 22, 1847, in Williams, *Old Missouri Land Cases,* part 4, *Cutter vs. Waddingham,* 18.

90. The two were married by Father Bernard on August 6, 1777, after publishing banns two Sundays and having dispensation for a third; ibid., 8. Marriage contract of Genevieve Cardinal and Jean Baptiste Vifarenne, #2043, St. Louis Archives. After her first husband died in 1782, Genevieve moved to St. Charles and married another French colonist, Jacques Marechal, in 1784; cited in Gilbert, "Free Women of Color," 12.

91. Instrument #36B, St. Louis Archives, cited in ibid., 4.

92. Magnaghi, "The Role of Indian Slavery," 271.

93. Baptisms, book 1, St. Louis Diocesan Records, Old Cathedral, cited in Ekberg, *Stealing Indian Women,* 78, 75–76.

described as legitimately married, Louis and Marianne, and Antoine and Josette. On December 18, 1783, Father Bernard baptized four children belonging to the two couples (and to their master).[94]

Enslaved women and children of mixed African-Indian heritage were also present in St. Louis. In the 1740s, an enslaved black man, Scypion, and Marie (or Mariette), a Natchez Indian woman who became a slave as a captive, had a child, Marie Jean. Born near Fort Chartres, Marie Jean came to St. Louis soon after its founding, in the company of Joseph and Marie Louise Tayon.[95] There, she gave birth to three daughters, Celeste, Catiche, and Marguerite, at least one of whom was identified in the baptismal records as a mulatto, "father unknown," an indication that her offspring may have been multiracial as well as the products of illicit liaisons. Because Marie Jean was also characterized as mulatto, however, one cannot authoritatively state the racial background of her children; it is possible that efforts to conceal the enslavement of Indians led to some blurring of racial categories in the records.[96]

Given the small population and concerns about miscegenation, it is no surprise that officials greeted the prospect of European immigrant families joining the community with enthusiasm. In the spring of 1777, two French Canadian families settled in St. Louis. Their reports of wretched living conditions in Canada encouraged Lieutenant Governor Cruzat to anticipate success in luring more Catholic immigrants to the village. "There will be no difficulty in attracting several families from there," he reported, "provided that some small advances can be made to them of the tools and animals required for farming." Otherwise, they would not survive. "They are so poor that when they arrive in this settlement they come burdened with a family but have not a shirt to wear," he noted. The promise of farming implements should, he expected, be enough to entice them to seek their liberty in Upper Louisiana.[97] New immigrants need not be ethnically French. Any Catholics would do. To encourage relocation, Governor Galvez

94. Baptisms, book 2, St. Louis Diocesan Records, Old Cathedral, in ibid., 76.

95. Deposition of Madame Marie Louise Chauvin, November 26. 1825, and deposition of John B. Riverrie alias Bacan, October 1,1825, both in file 273, Jefferson County Missouri Circuit Court Records, Courthouse, Hillsboro, cited in Foley, "Slave Freedom Suits Before Dred Scott," 2–3.

96. May 29, 1776, baptism of Celeste, "Register of Baptisms of the St. Louis Cathedral, 1766–August 6, 1779," transcribed by Oscar W. Collet, MHML, cited in Foley, "Slave Freedom Suits before Dred Scott," 5.

97. Cruzat to Galvez, December 8, 1777, in Houck, *SRM,* 1: 153–54.

promised provisions to those who immigrated to Upper Louisiana.[98] Secret instructions were sent to St. Louis, ordering the lieutenant governor to do his best to aid any Catholics in English territory to cross the river and thereby increase the population.[99] Such an outcome would be far preferable, in Spanish eyes, to the growth of a mixed-race populace.

Sexual liaisons across racial lines and outside of marriage were clearly of interest to both villagers and officials in colonial St. Louis. Yet what comes through clearly is that there was no completely consistent response to sexual misconduct or interracial liaisons. In their approach to such matters, officials at times attempted to control colonists' behavior and at other times seemed to tolerate, if not altogether approve, actions and relationships that fell outside of law and custom. The French, African, and indigenous inhabitants of the village lived together intimately. On occasion, the ethnically European residents flagrantly violated both legal and religious constraints to find sexual partners, and some had children as a result. With such unions apparently widely countenanced in the community, the government's ability to impose official prescriptions was limited. In exploring the subject of "intimate frontiers" of contact, scholars have paid attention to the development of racial attitudes, particularly among the French, whose comparative reputation for tolerance and openness in the colonial era had been largely unchallenged, until scholars like Guillaume Aubert suggested a much more complicated story, with seventeenth-century assimilationist policies giving way to eighteenth-century efforts to limit interracial unions.[100] Contacts between European men and African women have also been carefully scrutinized.

In looking at the liaisons and conduct of European women in colonial settings, one is reminded that they, too, were an important feature of a sexual landscape. It is important to look at all of the "tense and tender ties of empire and to sex—who with whom, where, and when" in order to assess fully how empires practiced racial politics, managed the intimate lives of their colonists, and participated in the "education of desire."[101] If the misbehavior of white women was either considered not to have taken place, as was perhaps the case with some slanderous speech, or viewed as not fundamentally damaging to the growth and development of the community,

98. Decree of Galvez, February 19, 1778, in ibid., 1: 155–57. Galvez outlined his immigration strategy in a letter to his uncle, Spain's prime minister; Bernardo de Galvez to Joseph de Galvez, June 9, 1778, in ibid., 1: 155.

99. Reprinted in Kinnaird, *SMV,* 1: 259.

100. Aubert, "The Blood of France."

101. Stoler, "Tense and Tender Ties," 832, 865.

then perhaps it could be ignored or minimized. It is possible that as they navigated controversies over sexual behavior, St. Louisans ignored established rules and acted according to their own judgment as to what was best for their community. In sum, a skewed sex ratio among villagers—combined with the long periods colonial men engaged in the fur trade spent among the Indian peoples of the Missouri—contributed to an environment in which illicit sexual unions and concerns about sexual conduct both flourished.[102] The two are obviously connected, and villagers' resistance to the impositions of law and custom was critical.

An important factor in shaping the emerging society of St. Louis was the comparative weakness of institutions that helped insure social control elsewhere, in particular the church and court. In early St. Louis, civil and clerical authorities moved with care, faced as they were with repeated challenges to their power. As Stuart Banner has noted, the legal culture of colonial St. Louis was a typical one to the extent that it allowed for the resolution of disputes, the distribution of property, and the completion of private transactions. Yet Banner has found no evidence that government authorities even possessed copies of Spanish legal codes.[103] The usual legal actions were executed in St. Louis "with little formality, with barely any reference to written law, and with almost no resort to any authority beyond the articulated norms of the community."[104] At times, the metropolitan centers of European empires and even the capital of Louisiana, New Orleans, seemed very far away. Distance attenuated the laws and customs promulgated by authorities, and the women and men of St. Louis socialized, sought sexual companionship, and formed families, intentionally and not, in the process. The result was a multiracial, multicultural society with households shared by people of wildly different backgrounds, who attempted to exercise agency and determine their own fates, even as they confronted forces beyond their control and faced off against the clerical and civil authorities in their midst.

---

102. Thomas C. Holt notes that the links between race and class have a long history and that studies such as Aubert's are informed by Michel Foucault's arguments about the ways in which the state came to see control of biological and social reproduction as a central function. Holt, "Purity of Blood," 437.

103. Banner, "Written Law and Unwritten Norms in Colonial St. Louis," 46. Marriage contracts bore more reference to French rather than Spanish custom. One survey suggested that the goal was exclusion of Spanish marriage law rather than adoption of it, with the overwhelming majority of marriage contracts showing evidence of following French codes and legal practices outlined in the *Coutume de Paris*. In the *Supreme Court of Missouri, March Term, 1856, Norman Cutter, Appellee, vs. Wm. Waddingham & Others, Appellants*, 9, 22.

104. Banner, "Written Law and Unwritten Norms in Colonial St. Louis," 38; Stuart Banner, *Legal Systems in Conflict*.

With each passing year in St. Louis, new people, new institutions, and new practices added to the developing local culture and community. Most St. Louisans were occupied entirely with private matters. Whether engaged in the fur trade or farming, working as artisans, or bearing and rearing children, the French-speaking colonial inhabitants of the village went about their business, even as they recognized their status as subjects of the Spanish crown. Under their control were enslaved Africans and Indians who performed agricultural and domestic labor. Other indigenous peoples and Africans, both free residents and regular visitors, completed the tri-racial society. Far from the capital in New Orleans, and the even more distant seat of empire in Spain, St. Louis possessed a population that presented its leaders with a flurry of challenges in the late 1770s. Military representatives of the crown, civilian authorities, and members of the clergy all endeavored to implement church and state regulations regarding personal conduct and economic activities. In the process, they repeatedly confronted the realities of a population preoccupied with the challenges of building a new society on the frontier, a population willing to circumvent or ignore the law.

$Chapter\ 6$

"The World, the Flesh, and the Devil"

CONFLICTS OVER RELIGION, ALCOHOL, AND AUTHORITY

On the morning of July 19, 1779, around 5:30 a.m., St. Louis resident François Larche made a startling discovery when he found Domingo de Bargas, a thirty-five-year-old Spanish merchant, dead in his bed. Immediately, Larche went to inform the ranking official in the community, Fernando de Leyba, an unpopular man who replaced the previous lieutenant governor, Francisco Cruzat, in the summer of 1778. Accompanied by two witnesses, Leyba hurried to Bargas's house, saw the deceased, and ordered his effects locked up and secured for later appraisal. As the news spread, questions about the manner of Bargas's sudden death arose, put forward by the village priest, Father Bernard de Limpach. When Limpach learned of Bargas's demise, he sought out the lieutenant governor and declared his unwillingness to bury the man in consecrated ground. The priest contended that the Spaniard's death was a *mort ivré*—that he had died from drinking— or from some other cause *non naturelle.*[1] In Limpach's opinion, the dead man had forfeited his right to a place in the church cemetery. The other burial ground, an unsanctified one reserved for infidels and other wastrels, Protestants and Indians, would be better suited to serve as Bargas's resting place.[2] Limpach's assertions, coupled with the need to dispose of a corpse quickly in the middle of a hot St. Louis summer, necessitated that Leyba act promptly. He did so by initiating an inquest.[3]

---

1. Instrument #2356, July 19, 1779, St. Louis Archives, MHMA.
2. The two cemeteries were close to each other, one in the churchyard and the other in unconsecrated ground nearby. Houck, *HM,* 2: 26.
3. Instrument #2356, July 19, 1779, St. Louis Archives, MHMA.

The postmortem investigation of Bargas's death provides a revealing window onto several related aspects of community life and the exercise of authority in St. Louis in the late eighteenth century. Occupying the attention of church and government leaders for a few days, the incident invites speculation regarding personal ties and power dynamics. The relationships among the individuals involved in the inquest, as well as the attitudes each had toward alcohol and religion illuminate contemporary mores. Revolving around inebriating spirits and the performance of spiritual and secular authority, this case reveals the weakness of control in St. Louis, both civil and clerical, in the earliest years of settlement, as well as the significance of community consensus.

To uncover the circumstances surrounding the merchant's death, Leyba sought the advice of scientific authorities and the testimony of village residents. First, he appointed Dr. Bernard Gibkins to examine Bargas's body. It was not the first time he had called upon the physician's assistance in a suspicious case. The previous December, when Leyba ordered the doctor to attend at the sickbed of an enslaved man, Gibkins had discerned clear indications of poisoning in the man's rigid limbs and other symptoms.[4] Now, within a half hour of the discovery of Bargas's body, Gibkins hurried to the merchant's home. "I recognized that he was dead, a sudden death caused by apoplexy," reported the doctor. Bargas's blue face and the bit of blood at his mouth suggested a crippling stroke caused either by a blood clot or the rupture of a blood vessel; the postmortem appearance could have indicated a pulmonary embolism or heart attack.[5] Gibkins discerned no sign of alcohol or any other unnatural cause contributing to the death. After securing this medical opinion, Leyba heard testimony regarding Bargas's actions the day before he died, trying to retrace the man's movements. Before the day was out, three inhabitants of French descent, two men and one woman, appeared before civil authorities to testify about Bargas's last hours.

Although the witnesses could not account for every moment of Bargas's last day, they uniformly maintained that he had not been drinking. Joseph Mainville, who spent several hours with Bargas on the eighteenth, said that the two had spent their time talking with company. Intoxicating beverages had not contributed to the flow of conversation. At 5:30 in the afternoon, Bargas, well and in his right mind, said good-bye to his friend. Bargas's activities and whereabouts for the next few hours, whether at home or elsewhere, alone or in company, abstaining or imbibing, remain obscure; no one

4. Alvord, ed., *Cahokia Records,* 4 n. 3. In June 1779, slaves involved in another poisoning case in nearby Cahokia, across the river from St. Louis, were sentenced to be hanged; ibid., 4–5, 12–21.

5. Instrument #2356, July 20, 1779, St. Louis Archives, MHMA.

reported seeing him. Then, around nine in the evening, a late hour for pay-ing a call, Bargas showed up at the door of his newlywed neighbors, Ignace Laroche and Marie Bequet. According to Monsieur Laroche, who testified for his wife, the merchant arrived at their home near bedtime, wishing to invite them to supper. Madame Laroche, who answered the door, declined the offer, telling Bargas that her husband was already asleep and could not go out; further, she begged her neighbor not to disturb her spouse's slum-ber.[6] Disappointed in his hopes of dinner companions, Bargas prepared to leave. First, however, he gave Madame Laroche a piece of a *torte,* or meat pie, he had made and then left very quietly, apparently perfectly well and sober. In the opinion of Madame Laroche—the last person to admit to seeing Bargas alive—it did not appear he had been drinking. Eight hours later, he was found dead. (Coincidentally, Antoine Bérard, the previous owner of Bargas's home and also a merchant, had not lived in it long, either. After purchasing the property in 1774, he died in 1776 at the age of thirty-six.)[7]

This testimony, coupled with that of the physician, provided ample evidence to undermine Father Limpach's assertions. By insisting that the deceased had not consumed a drop of alcohol, the witnesses implicitly argued for Bargas's burial in sanctified ground. At odds with a man of sci-ence and several members of the community, the priest saw his allegations collapse. The next day, July 20, he proceeded with a religious interment. In the church register, Limpach noted that he had inhumed in the church cemetery the body of Domingo de Bargas, who had "died suddenly at the age of thirty-five." This brief entry differs from others in subtle, inter-esting ways. Limpach almost never offered editorial commentary about deaths, as he did by recording Bargas's "sudden" demise. He also usually listed the sacraments which he administered to the dying and deceased, from the Eucharist, penitence, and extreme unction, to "all the sacraments of our mother the holy church" and interments with *les cérémonies ordinaires.* In the entry for Bargas, the priest left only the briefest of details, his terse account revealing neither the sacramental nor ceremonial aspects of the burial.[8]

Determining why Limpach lost this round in the battle for control of the community's religious life necessitates dissecting the different motivations and social positions of the actors in the inquest, as well as exploring the

6. Marriage contract of Ignace Laroche and Marie Becquet, April 24, 1779, Instrument #2048, St. Louis Archives, MHMA. Although Ignace Laroche testified on his wife's behalf, both signed the account, affirming its veracity with their marks. Instrument #2356, St. Louis Archives, MHMA.

7. Billon, *Annals of St. Louis,* 134–35.

8. July 20, 1779, *Register of Burials of the St. Louis Cathedral, October 4, 1770–May 4, 1781,* transcribed by Oscar W. Collet, MHML.

Church and burial ground, 1770, State Historical Society of Missouri, Columbia

history of conflict between members of the clergy and the community at large. The German-born physician Gibkins, required to conduct the post-mortem exam by civil authorities, had no apparent investment in the outcome of the investigation, although he did soon purchase the dead man's house. The priest, also a German-born newcomer, was attempting to influence the conduct and dictate the final resting place of unruly parishioners. (Whether Limpach's ethnicity informed his parishioners' attitudes toward him does not appear in any records.)

Leyba, the Spanish government official, was undoubtedly interested in preserving order. He also may have been influenced by a desire to preserve harmonious relations with the priest. Leyba's predecessor, Cruzat, had not been on very good terms with Limpach.[9] A series of encounters in 1777 and 1778 involving Cruzat had preyed upon Limpach's peace of mind and had prompted him to complain to the governor. Apparently, Cruzat had demanded a prominent seat in the church and refused to give it up even after the governor had ordered him to do so. He wanted his pew placed above the spot where the priest rested his feet while seated during

9. Limpach to governor, June 30, 1777, AGI-PC 190-449, MHMA microfilm. On sacred and secular elements of ritual celebrations regarding the Spanish monarchy, see Gutierrez, *When Jesus Came*, 316–17.

Lieutenant Governor Francisco Cruzat, State Historical
Society of Missouri, Columbia

the singing of various parts of the mass. Cruzat may have been trying to
extend the symbolic dimensions of royal authority by claiming a sacred
location for his seat. Exasperated by the official's conduct, Limpach opined
that Cruzat would be happy if his pew were placed up against the cel-
ebrant's chair, an outrageous presumption in the priest's view.

After Christmas mass in 1777, Cruzat stunned Limpach by criticizing
the cleric to those assembled. As parishioners were leaving the church,
Cruzat demanded loudly that he wanted to know why the priest was watching him. Limpach quoted him thus: "Did not the priest know that he represented the person of the king, that his pew ought to be placed in the
sanctuary? I will have it put there by my sergeant." Jealous of his position,
the lieutenant governor sent his emissary, a sergeant, to harass the priest. In
contrast to his usual behavior, the sergeant approached Limpach carrying
his sword under his arm, a gesture the priest thought designed to intimi-
date him into providing a place for Cruzat in the sanctuary that the latter

thought suited his position. Limpach was unwilling to comply, as doing so, he thought, would violate protocol, and stalled the sergeant, telling him to convey to Cruzat that he was awaiting a determination on the matter from superiors in New Orleans. Importunings from the priest "to leave things in status quo" did not appease Cruzat. He sent his sergeant to the priest a second time, insisting he would have a superior spot and he would not abandon the issue no matter what the word from the capital. Limpach urged the sergeant to inform Cruzat that it was more glorious to be exalted than humiliated. Far from amused and certainly not placated by the priest's words and refusal, Cruzat insisted that Limpach accommodate his wishes for the present. Unwilling to contribute to any further scandal, Limpach found a compromise. Reminding the governor that all this took place at Christmas, when the church was celebrating the angels announcing to the shepherds the incarnation of the son of God, Limpach ordered the chief church warden to have a special *prie dieu,* or kneeler, constructed and an armchair bought for Cruzat. Placed on the spot in the sanctuary where the priest had previously rested during the Gloria and the creed, the armchair became Cruzat's exalted seat.[10]

Although Limpach wished that Cruzat would reimburse the poor church 44 *livres* for the cost of the *prie dieu* and armchair, he switched his position on the seating issue and urged the governor not to order Cruzat to abandon his request for distinction. Limpach believed that it would be "extremely hard" on Cruzat to comply. More was at stake than the official's potential personal discomfort. People who had grown disgruntled with Cruzat's rule would derive pleasure from seeing him taken down a notch. Exposing the ranking officer of the crown to such ridicule would serve no one's interests, least of all those—whether representatives of the church or the state—who wished for a quiet, compliant populace. Whenever the governor replaced Cruzat, his successor could be given a different church seat without any loss of face. With no official being humiliated publicly, the governor's authority would be sustained and respected.[11]

Cruzat's disdain for following established protocol and chains of command led to his removal from office the following spring. Not only had he embroiled himself in conflict with the village priest, he also decided to send agents across the Mississippi into Illinois to negotiate for the freedom of some captive Missouri and Peoria Indians. Before doing so, he should have obtained orders to that effect or at the very least permission for the

10. Limpach to governor, June 30, 1777, AGI-PC 190-449, MHMA microfilm.
11. Limpach to governor, June 30, 1777, AGI-PC 190-449, MHMA microfilm.

plan.[12] Promptly, the governor sent Leyba to serve as his replacement. After a voyage of ninety-three days, Leyba reached St. Louis on June 10, 1778. Four days later, with appropriate ceremony, Cruzat delivered "command of the post" to his successor. According to Leyba, all the inhabitants of St. Louis received him "with extraordinary signs of rejoicing," which he did not attribute either to his own personal "beauty" nor "to the fact that they were dissatisfied here with [his] predecessor, but only that in the creature they praise the creator."[13]

However Leyba characterized his reception, it seems clear that the people were expressing their will and preference. When problems erupted with Limpach over the Bargas case the following summer, Leyba moved carefully, attempting to sidestep and diffuse any potential conflicts before they grew out of control. While his authority was greater than the priest's, perhaps he felt he could not afford to alienate one of his few allies in positions of authority. And he needed to acknowledge and accommodate—to the extent that it was possible to do so—the concerns and expectations of the villagers.

For Bargas's friends—the French inhabitants who testified—telling the truth may have been their only goal, but there are other possibilities. An unwillingness to speak ill of the dead, especially if doing so prevented a burial in hallowed ground, might have moved them. Perhaps these individuals believed so deeply in the significance of a sanctified burial that their desire to see their friend accorded an appropriate resting place transcended clerical, earthly authority. If he and they had all been drinking, perhaps they declined to mention the fact, considering prohibitions or criticism of alcohol to be irrelevant to generally law-abiding members of the community such as themselves. Without a doubt, their connections to the dead man, as much as their relationships with the priest and lieutenant governor, informed their performance of providing legal testimony.[14]

While it is impossible to know, the idea that members of the community may have cooperated to subvert priestly authority remains a tantalizing one. Given the likelihood that Bargas had been imbibing, regardless of whether doing so contributed to his death, the insistence of the witnesses that he had not done so invites conjecture. It is difficult not to wonder whether the witnesses who testified as to Bargas's last hours perjured themselves (and

12. Houck, *SRM,* 1: xx.

13. Leyba to Bernardo de Galvez, July 11, 1778, in Houck, *SRM,* 1: 161.

14. As the work of Pierre Bourdieu suggests, "The use of language, the manner as much as the substance of discourse, depends on the social position of the speaker, which governs the access he can have to the language of the institution, that is, to the official, orthodox and legitimate speech." Bourdieu, "Authorized Language: The Social Conditions for the Effectiveness of Ritual Discourse," in John B. Thompson, ed., *Language and Symbolic Power,* 109.

thereby committed the sin of bearing false witness). In their eyes, perhaps the priest's refusal to bury Bargas seemed an extreme act requiring a dissembling response. If so, they may have purposefully employed references to space, time, and conversations in order to strengthen the credibility of their testimony.[15] Respect for the law—or concern about committing perjury—may have been less important to them than duty to a friend. Given the alcohol consumption and sociability of early St. Louisans, it is unlikely that Bargas would have passed several hours in company without a glass of spirits; the *habitants* and merchants spent much of their time in this fashion. One can easily imagine a slightly inebriated Bargas knocking in the dark at the Laroche residence, rousing the slumberers and generally disturbing the peace.

From Bargas's inventory, it is clear that alcohol was available, sold, and consumed in his home. On the main floor and in the cellar below, the appraisers found significant quantities of rum. The amounts and containers suggested that Bargas both tippled and traded alcohol; his four-room house had a store and storeroom.[16] A flask half filled with *tafia,* or rum, turned up in a bucket upstairs, while below there were several barrels: a few empty, one containing about forty *potes* of rum, and another six or seven *potes*.[17] He left unpaid bills for purchases of eleven bottles and one pint of rum. With a corkscrew and goblets in his possession, Bargas probably drank as his neighbors did: substantially and regularly. In colonial St. Louis, residents consumed alcohol while they conducted business, dined, and socialized.

Ties of neighborhood, commerce, and friendship linked Bargas to those who testified about his last day. Joseph Mainville, a carpenter, was born in French Canada and lived at the southeast corner of the intersection where Bargas's home stood at the northwest corner.[18] Laroche and Bargas became neighbors in August 1777, when Bargas purchased a four-room post house next to that of Laroche, a twenty-nine-year-old merchant. Purchased from the estate of the previous owner and trader, Antoine Bérard, the house provided ample space for merchandise.[19] These men spent time in each other's

15. The details of the postmortem investigation and inventory appear in Instrument #2356, St. Louis Archives, MHMA. On the significance of spatial references and reported speech, as well as the ethics and performance of legal testimony in colonial Anglo America, see Robert Blair St. George, "Massacred Language: Courtroom Performance in Eighteenth-Century Boston," in St. George, ed., *Possible Pasts,* 337.

16. Billon, *Annals of St. Louis,* 135.

17. A French *pote* was the equivalent of two liters; Jack D. L. Holmes, "Spanish Regulation of Taverns and the Liquor Trade in the Mississippi Valley," in McDermott, ed., *The Spanish in the Mississippi Valley,* 176.

18. Billon, *Annals of St. Louis,* 135, 420–21.

19. Instrument #211, August 10, 1777, St. Louis Archives, MHMA. Laroche's age and trade appear in a list of volunteers in the mounted militia company of St. Louis, December 25, 1779,

company and engaged in business transactions involving both pelts and people. In 1778, the summer before his death, Bargas purchased a six-month-old
mulatto boy named Vitale from Laroche.[20] The boy's mother, Josette, was a
slave belonging to Laroche. (Vitale was baptized on January 11, 1778. Father
Limpach described the infant as a mulatto slave born of Josette, *negresse,* and
belonging to Laroche; he did not, as he sometimes did, list the father as
unknown. Josette may have also had another son baptized nine years before
when Father Meurin noted the baptism of Jean Baptiste, son of a Catholic
slave woman Josette who belonged to Laroche.) Given the extreme youth of
the child and the proximity of Bargas and Laroche's homes, it is reasonable
to assume that Bargas was the father of the child and sought this means of
protecting or claiming his offspring, particularly as the purchase violated
prohibitions against separating enslaved children from their mothers.[21]

Adding further weight to the probability of this relationship was the
fact that the sale of Vitale was noted as taking place with Josette's consent.
Although illiterate, she signed her mark on the bill of sale, in front of
government witnesses Leyba and Benito Vasquez, who was also Bargas's
neighbor, countryman, and devoted supporter of the church. One suspects
those gathered knew of the intimate relationship of Bargas, Josette, and
Vitale. After Bargas's death, Leyba saw the child again. On the second day
of recording the estate inventory, Leyba noted a special item, the presen-
tation of a little mulatto. Who brought the child or where he was living
is unknown. (While Bargas acknowledged receiving Vitale at the time of
sale, he owned no other slaves, and it seems unlikely that he would have
kept the infant on his own.) Soon thereafter, Leyba decided to manumit
the child, purportedly because the arbitrators of the estate informed him
that such had been Bargas's intention, another intimation of deceased merchant's paternity.[22]

Bargas's interactions with his neighbors frequently centered on the
church. Many legal and financial matters were publicized at the door of St.

AGI-PC 193B-665. The proximity of the property appears in Instrument #2356, July 19, 1779, and
Instrument #247, August 8, 1779, St. Louis Archives, MHMA. On Bérard, see Billon, *Annals of St.
Louis,* 135.

20. Sale of slave child Vitale, July 11, 1778, Instrument #239, St. Louis Archives, MHMA.

21. February 7, 1769. *Register of Baptisms of the St. Louis Cathedral, 1766–August 6, 1779*
transcribed by Oscar Collet (MHML). At the time of his death, Bargas had a bill from Laroche for
128 pounds of pelts, dated July 14, 1778; Bargas had purchased Vitale three days earlier for 150
pounds of pelts. Domingo de Bargas estate inventory, Instrument #2356, 1779, St. Louis Archives,
MHMA.

22. Scharf, *History of St. Louis City and County,* 1: 305 n. 1. This manumission is referred to in
"Manumissions executed under the Spanish Government," *General Index, 1766 to 1834, City of St.
Louis,* under the heading 1779 Domingo Bargas to Vitale (Recorder of Deeds, City Hall, St. Louis), 31.

Louis's church. As churchgoers left mass, officials declared pressing items of business. When, for example, an auction of property was to be held, it would be announced on three successive Sundays outside the church. Bargas bought his house and lot in this way, successfully bidding at a Sunday auction. (Later, the doctor who attended his corpse, Gibkins, bought Bargas's home in this fashion, successfully outbidding several other men.)[23] After attending mass another Sunday, Bargas gathered with other men to discuss improving the drainage of village lots. Although not a member of the committee of five men appointed to undertake the task, Bargas was one of sixteen St. Louisans who offered support for the plan.[24] Clearly, Bargas assumed a public role in the life of his adopted community. On numerous occasions, he and Joseph Labuscière, the notary, served as witnesses for Leyba. The year before his death, Bargas participated in a legal matter with Leyba and Labuscière in a way that prefigured the role the men would have after his death; Bargas accompanied the two as a witness for an estate inventory.[25] Ethnicity, as well as proximity and religion, further linked Bargas to other inhabitants. Leyba was Bargas's countryman, Vasquez was his neighbor, and other Spaniards were his friends and business associates. A fellow merchant and native of Madrid, Eugenio Alvarez, who had come to St. Louis as a soldier in 1770, agreed to take responsibility after Bargas's death for his belongings.[26]

The curate saw these men regularly at church services and special sacramental ceremonies. Just a few months before Bargas's death, Father Limpach encountered the merchant, his neighbor Laroche, and the other two witnesses in the inquest at the wedding of Ignace Laroche and Marie Bequet. In April 1779, the priest officiated at their union, listening to the couple state their mutual consent to the match and blessing them before several villagers, including Bargas and Mainville, who had signed the pair's marriage contract in the lieutenant governor's quarters three days before.[27] Of the eight people who attended the nuptials (including the bride and groom), five became involved in the July imbroglio over Bargas's death. A year before, Father Limpach had encountered Bargas in another, more

23. Bargas offered 640 *livres* in deer skins; Instrument #211, August 10, 1777, St. Louis Archives, MHMA. Similarly, after Bargas's death, Gibkins outbid others, making an offer of 1685 *livres* in deer or beaver skins; Instrument #247, August 8, 1779, St. Louis Archives, MHMA.

24. Billon, *Annals of St. Louis,* 140–41; Scharf, *History of Saint Louis City and County,* 1: 184.

25. Instrument #2347, September 3, 1778, St. Louis Archives, MHMA.

26. Billon, *Annals of St. Louis,* 447.

27. April 27, 1779, *Register of Marriages of the St. Louis Cathedral, 1774–August 13, 1781,* transcribed by Oscar W. Collet, MHMA; Instrument #2048, April 24, 1779, marriage contract of Ignace Laroche and Marie Bequet, St. Louis Archives, MHML.

problematic spiritual setting, the baptism of Bargas's illegitimate, mulatto son; two weeks after baptizing Vitale, the priest baptized Dominique Huge, with Bargas acting as godfather.[28] How the priest handled baptizing the off-spring of his parishioner's illicit union followed by Bargas's claim to act as a moral guide and guardian is impossible to determine. Bargas did possess a Spanish catechism and was clearly willing to take on the spiritual responsi-bilities of godparenthood. (In addition to his religious tome, Bargas owned a French/Spanish grammar and a small arithmetic book, two works suited to the commercial needs of life in mercantile St. Louis. A multivolume history of Malta, purchased several months previously at the estate sale of village founder Pierre Laclède, and one part of a three-volume work on the beauties of Italy, rounded out Bargas's small library.)[29]

Part of what is important in this instance, as in many other disputes brought before civil authorities in eighteenth-century St. Louis, is the recourse to members of the community, in this case the dead man's friends, for their opinions and testimony. As Stuart Banner has shown, there is very little reference to written law in early St. Louis records and a much greater reliance upon custom and consensus in making judicial decisions.[30] In other words, unwritten, shared beliefs and norms affected the outcome of litiga-tion more profoundly than did the available codes of law. Few government officials possessed copies of the statutes, either French or Spanish, and those who did appeared to operate more in accord with local precedent than dis-tant legislation. As Banner put it, "Cases were decided according to an intuitive sense of justice shared by the community, or at least by a large enough fraction of the community to make the decision acceptable."[31]

Playing off various constituencies within the community was a deli-cate balancing act for the lieutenant governor. Given that civil and cleri-cal authorities needed to work together to preserve peace, stability, and order in the community, Leyba had to take the priest's charges about

---

28. January 30, 1778, *Register of Baptisms of the St. Louis Cathedral, 1766–August 6, 1779,* transcribed by Oscar W. Collet, MHML.

29. Instrument #2356, Domingo Bargas, estate inventory, St. Louis Archives, MHMA. On the possible provenance and identification of some of Bargas's collection, see McDermott, *Private Libraries in Creole Saint Louis,* 47–49.

30. Banner, *Legal Systems in Conflict,* esp. 51–66. For an analysis of women's influence over legal processes in the Illinois Country and the importance of French legal traditions, see Boyle, "Did She Generally Decide?" 775–89.

31. Banner, *Legal Systems in Conflict,* 52. Describing the legal heritage of colonial St. Louis, Henry Brackenridge noted the governing assumption that "respect should be paid to the usages and customs of the country" and pointed out that "Laws regulating civil contra[c]ts, are so intimately interwoven with the manners of a people, that it is no easy task to separate them." Brackenridge, *Views of Louisiana,* 241.

Bargas seriously and indeed was probably sympathetic to Limpach's concerns about alcohol.[32] Colonial authorities in French and Spanish North America repeatedly expressed concerns about alcohol and tried to regulate it. Only days before Bargas's death, Leyba had decried the arrival of boats from New Orleans: "loaded with rum, sugar, and coffee, which for these people are the world, the flesh, and the devil." Thus invoking the temptations that led men and women to stray, Leyba foresaw little good in the consumption of such substances. Laden with "articles of vice," the boats contained no useful objects for the fur trade.[33] Whether Leyba suspected that this latest shipment might contribute to the likelihood of individuals drinking themselves to death, he had to proceed with care. As a Spanish ruler with a very small garrison of soldiers to back his authority over the primarily French inhabitants, Leyba had to keep in mind the feelings and wishes of the Catholic villagers who were not on especially good terms with their priest.

Only a few years previously, in 1776, the Catholic inhabitants of St. Louis had celebrated the arrival of Father Limpach, a member of the Capuchin order. After more than a decade of irregular clerical care, they had welcomed him as their first full-time pastor. (A branch of the Franciscan Friars Minor, the Capuchins pursued missionary labors in seventeenth-century Maine and Canada and headed such efforts in Louisiana from 1722 to 1750, when Jesuits took on that role. Spanish Capuchins supplanted French missionaries in 1766 and served until 1807.)[34] Formerly stationed in Cuba, Limpach was appointed to join the handful of clerics who served in the Illinois Country.[35] Although he made the long journey upriver from New Orleans to minister to a populace that had sought the presence of clergy, Limpach found his parishioners not altogether appreciative of his efforts. Under his stewardship, the church simultaneously and paradoxically served as a focal point for community cohesion and conflict. For priests like Limpach, who brought institutionalized religion to Upper Louisiana, indifferent reception, shocking behavior, and challenges to authority seemed to be the typical rather than the exceptional experience. Clerics and government officials alike wrestled with problems stemming from the clash

32. Holmes, "Spanish Regulation of Taverns," 149–82; Johnston, "Alcohol Consumption in Eighteenth-Century Louisbourg," 61–76.

33. Leyba to Bernardo de Galvez, July 13, 1779, reprinted in Kinnaird, *SMV,* 1: 346.

34. *Dictionary of American History,* rev. ed. (New York: Charles Scribner's Sons, 1976), 1: 451–52. On the history of Capuchin missionary efforts and conflicts with other religious orders, see O'Neill, *Church and State in French Colonial Louisiana.*

35. Scharf, *History of Saint Louis City and County,* 2: 1639–40. Regarding ecclesiastical jurisdiction over Upper Louisiana, see Rothensteiner, *History of the Archdiocese of St. Louis,* 1: 114 n. 10, 143–44.

between the multiple, complicated, and unwieldy contexts of international imperial politics and distant church struggles with local power and social dynamics.

With the 1762 transfer of Louisiana from France to Spain, both secular and spiritual administration of the vast territory were confused for a time, and St. Louisans were without regular religious services for several years. The paucity of pastoral care was exacerbated by state efforts to control the church. In June 1763, the French government suppressed the Jesuits, the group whose members staffed the wilderness missions, and ordered the expulsion of priests, confiscation of the order's property, and destruction of its buildings; the Spanish likewise ejected the Jesuits for their criticism of royal absolutism. One of the targeted clerics, Father Sebastian Meurin, did not want to abandon his flock and remained to attend to the missions in the Illinois Country, maintaining his residence on the British side of the Mississippi River. Traveling throughout the area in the 1760s, Meurin was the first priest to visit St. Louis, performing a baptism there in a tent in the spring of 1766, and returning several times in 1767 and 1768. After his official banishment, he continued to go to St. Louis.[36] Many of those whom Meurin visited had recently moved from the eastern side of the river, members of his former flock who had chosen to relocate to live under a Catholic monarch rather than a Protestant one.

Despite the clear importance of religious affiliation in settlement choices, the practice of piety in St. Louis was somewhat attenuated. While the predominately francophone inhabitants of St. Louis were Catholics, they did not, in the settlement's earliest years, appear anxious to support the church or to conduct themselves in a godly manner. Spanish authorities criticized residents' halfhearted religious conduct, claiming that all sorts of social diversions and trading activities occupied their energies to the near exclusion of spiritual matters. As Pedro Piernas had reported after his first visit to Upper Louisiana, the populace was immoral and irreligious, displaying a notable lack of piety that he attributed to the absence of a regular priest and the dearth of laws supporting the faith.[37] Some residents seconded his views, describing their situation as "sad" and imploring his intervention with the governor in helping them obtain a priest, so that their children would receive instruction and the ill would not die "without

36. Ekberg, *Colonial Ste. Genevieve*, 382–86; Rothensteiner, *History of the Archdiocese of St. Louis,* 1: 115–26, 361. On the difficulties and complications involved in being a Jesuit in the Illinois Country and his proscription by the Capuchins, see Father Sebastian Louis Meurin to Monsignor Briand, June 11, 1768, in Thwaites, ed., *The Jesuit relations and allied documents,* 71: 32–47; also 70: 310–11.

37. Pedro Piernas to Alexander O'Reilly, October 31, 1769, in Houck, *SRM,* 1: 71, 73.

the consolation" of the holy sacraments.[38] Piernas conveyed their request to his superiors and actively promoted religion in the community; a few months later, Piernas was able to report success: priests were on their way to Upper Louisiana.[39] Indeed, it was at his urging that the villagers built the first house of worship to replace the tent that had sufficed for several years. Although a log church was constructed, the location and presence of the structure apparently did nothing to dampen local enthusiasm for non-religious pastimes on the Sabbath.

Situated on *La Rue de L'Eglise,* one of three streets that ran the length of the village and parallel to the river, the church was a key feature of the initial plan for the settlement, and the church block completed the central core of the village. The church itself was a focal point of the landscape, a perfectly sited spot for exchanging information and goods, discussing community affairs, and making plans for social activities, in addition to, of course, attending religious services. After mass, villagers regularly spent their Sunday afternoons engaged in diversions.[40] Their socializing in a variety of public and private spaces reinforced the bonds of intimacy and community, and visitors noted a pronounced preference among the French for regular social intercourse and village life over isolation on farmsteads.[41] The social geography of the village thus reflected the values of its founder and residents.

In the 1760s, St. Louis, Ste. Genevieve, and the other French settlements in the Illinois Country all experienced a shortage of priests and an absence of regular services. Father Meurin, the missionary priest to the Illinois Country who stayed after the Jesuits had been expelled, crossed the Mississippi to attend to the faithful in Spanish territory. He attempted to meet the spiritual needs of the colonists, but he despaired of the situation. In 1767, when he was sixty-one, he wrote to the bishop to urge that priests be sent to both Ste. Genevieve and St. Louis. He had been in the area for twenty-five years and traveled to serve the whole region, despite his age and infirmities.[42] Increasingly, he was finding it impossible to do the job. In addition to suffering from "decrepitude of body and mind," he had received

---

38. Pedro Piernas to Luis de Unzaga, January 5, 1771, AGI-PC 81-341, MHMA microfilm.

39. Pedro Piernas to Luis de Unzaga, November 2, 1771, AGI-PC 81-397, MHMA microfilm.

40. Foley and C. David Rice, *The First Chouteaus,* 15; for the 1790s, see De Finiels, *An Account of Upper Louisiana,* 120. Two billiard rooms may have been in existence by 1767; Scharf, *History of St. Louis City and County,* 1: 314.

41. See Ekberg, *French Roots in the Illinois Country,* 254–59. On settlement patterns, house and lot proximity, and construction techniques, see Charles Peterson, *Colonial St. Louis.*

42. Father Sebastian Louis Meurin to Bishop Briand, March 23, 1767, in Alvord and Carter, *The New Regime,* 523, 569.

no tithes in the four years he had administered to French colonists in now British Illinois. Debilitated, afflicted with a poor memory, and plagued by conflicts with others, he implored his bishop for release, "prompt deliverance from the too weighty burden."[43] In response to Meurin's pleas, Bishop Briand, in Quebec, appointed him vicar-general and sent him a newly ordained priest from Quebec, Father Pierre Gibault, to assist him.[44] (As he traveled south, Gibault encountered so many *voyageurs* anxious to confess that he spent ten hours one day hearing their confessions, "and that was a short day." He took the men's eagerness to confess sins they had carried with them for as long as ten years as a sign that God had "not been wholly forsaken in these parts.")[45]

Conflicts with the commandant of Ste. Genevieve led to Meurin's flight from the Spanish side.[46] In effect, he lost permission to administer to the devout of Spanish Illinois. "His very ample title of Vicar-General was the reason for his being turned out," averred Gibault. "A Jesuit with so much power is now a suspect in Spain."[47] Spain had expelled the Jesuits in 1767. As Louisiana governor Ulloa reported to his superiors in Spain, St. Louis's acting commandant, St. Ange, advised him that "the old Jesuit who was acting as parish priest in the towns of Ste. Genevieve and Pencur [St. Louis]" had gone over to the English side. Apparently, Meurin had been warned that he would be arrested and brought to New Orleans if he intruded on Spanish territory. As a result, "there remains not a single ecclesiastic in that place," and both villages were "totally without any practice of religion and divine worship." This situation, Ulloa assumed, would be taken seriously and addressed in Spain.[48] From the perspective of the newly arrived Father Gibault, the news was not altogether bad. Although the Spanish had "driven" Father Meurin out of their villages, the English commandant received him well, and he was "delighted" that Meurin was on his side of the Mississippi.[49]

Appointed to serve as curate of Kaskaskia, in British Illinois, Gibault nonetheless crossed the river to St. Louis, conducting services first in a tent, and then in the log church villagers constructed.[50] As he reported to his superiors, he went "to the other bank only to visit the sick and for

43. Meurin to Briand, June 11, 1768, in Alvord and Carter, *Trade and Politics*, 300, 310.
44. Lahey, "The Catholic Church on the Frontier of Spanish Illinois," 21.
45. Gibault to Briand, July 28, 1768, in Alvord and Carter, *Trade and Politics*, 370.
46. Lahey, "The Catholic Church on the Frontier of Spanish Illinois," 21.
47. Gibault to Briand, February 15, 1769, in Alvord and Carter, *Trade and Politics*, 502.
48. Ulloa to Grimaldi, July 20, 1768, in Kinnaird, *SMV,* 1: 56.
49. Gibault to Briand, July 28, 1768, in Alvord and Carter, *Trade and Politics*, 371.
50. Billon, *Annals of St. Louis*, 78.

marriages and baptisms."[51] So, too, did Meurin. Traveling "incognito and during the night," he crossed the river to visit the sick and presumably to offer them sacraments such as last rites. Otherwise, he received St. Louisans in Cahokia, where he celebrated the sacraments of baptism, penance, the Eucharist, and marriage.[52] Together, he and Gibault managed to provide basic pastoral care to St. Louisans who actively sought it. In the fall of 1769, Meurin spent three weeks in Spanish territory, to the apparent satisfaction of officials, whom Gibault declared "greatly pleased" that the elderly priest had gone "to keep souls in peace."[53]

The need for more missionaries in the region was desperate. After years of being "deprived of priests, everything is lax," Gibault pronounced. "Free thinking and irreverence have come in." Adding to the difficulties of serving the people were the dangers presented by Indians. Afraid of being scalped and noting the captures or deaths of twenty-two colonists on one road he frequently traveled, Gibault went about the countryside carrying weapons, accompanied by an armed party of ten to twenty men when possible.[54] In dealing with the faithful, Gibault tried to be less severe than Meurin had been. So disliked was Meurin in Kaskaskia that Gibault found a number of men who had not taken communion in four years, "for the sole reason that they did not want to confess to a Jesuit." Notably, Gibault provided segregated spiritual care to his flock in British Illinois, reading the catechism three times per week for the whites "and once for the blacks or slaves."[55]

While St. Louis in the 1760s witnessed only intermittent pastoral care, the following decade saw the presence of priests on a more regular and ultimately permanent basis. The final expulsion of the Jesuits and the rule of the Capuchin order came to St. Louis in 1772, when a Spanish cleric of that order, Father Valentin, arrived in the capital of Upper Louisiana, assuming the pastoral care of the community, "much to the satisfaction of the inhabitants."[56] Lacking a canonical mission from the Bishop of Quebec, who retained control of the area, Valentin served with permission of Spanish officials, although not as pastor, since the lieutenant governor did not have the authority either to designate a parish or appoint a pastor on his own.

In Upper Louisiana, churchmen were dependent on civil authorities and parishioners for both their presence in particular communities and for financial support. Pastors and civil officials were partners in governance,

51. Gibault to Briand, February 15, 1769, in Alvord and Carter, *Trade and Politics,* 502.
52. Meurin to Briand, June 14, 1769, in ibid., 550.
53. Gibault to Briand, October 1769, in ibid., 609.
54. Ibid., 609, 610, 611.
55. Gibault to Briand, February 15, 1769, in ibid., 503.
56. Pedro Piernas to Luis de Unzaga, July 13, 1772, AGI-PC 81-422, MHMA microfilm.

exercising different kinds of influence and jurisdiction over the same populace. Priests had responsibility to fulfill their duties as both ecclesiastical and governmental authorities dictated, and they needed state permission to form new parishes and build new churches.[57] Thus Valentin, who came to St. Louis with religious credentials, had a government appointment as chaplain to the local garrison. Although not technically the pastor of the village, Valentin nonetheless provided more consistent religious care to the habitants than they had previously enjoyed. During his tenure, he performed 107 baptisms (sixty-five whites, twenty-four blacks, and eighteen Indians) and officiated at four weddings of white inhabitants and seventy-two funerals (forty-two whites, eleven blacks, and nineteen Indians).[58] In exchange for such services, villagers compensated the priest, as in the case of Lambert Vonvarlet, whose executor paid Father Valentin fifty-seven *livres* in furs for a funeral and masses for the dead man.[59]

Welcoming a settled priest, parishioners like merchant Benito Vasquez provided crucial support to the church. In 1772, while in New Orleans, the native Spaniard and soldier set out to acquire a bell to replace the iron mortar and pestle that had been used to summon villagers to the small wooden church. To improve the tone of the bell he ordered, he provided two hundred Spanish silver dollars to be added to the metal. (Probably cast in Europe, the bell, sporting a date of 1772, arrived in St. Louis late in 1774 and was hung first in the wooden church and then in two subsequent structures.)[60] The imported bell likely prompted the villagers to take the plunge and come up with the funds to build a more substantial church, and they met on December 25 to pledge to build a thirty feet by sixty feet structure.[61] The next day, a special ceremony was held to celebrate the bell's arrival and installation at the church. In the presence of Vasquez and other parishioners, the bell was christened "Pierre Joseph Felicité" in honor of lieutenant governor Pedro Piernas and his wife. On the following day, it likely rang at the funeral of St. Ange.[62]

For the few years he served in St. Louis, Valentin ministered to the villagers while complaining to his superiors about both his post and his servants.

---

57. On the interconnectedness of French secular and spiritual goals in the colonies, see O'Neill, *Church and State in French Colonial Louisiana*, 2–11.

58. Rothensteiner, *History of the Archdiocese of St. Louis*, 106–7.

59. Account of debts of Lambert Vonvarlet, May 8, 1775, Instrument #1804, St. Louis Archives, MHMA. The inventory of another deceased villager, a free Indian named Rondo, included debts for the separate costs of internment and the funeral offices of the church. Rondo inventory, May 7, 1777, MHMA.

60. Lecompte, "Don Benito Vasquez in Early St. Louis," 289–90.

61. Billon, *Annals of St. Louis,* 138.

62. Lecompte, "Don Benito Vasquez in Early St. Louis," 292.

In February 1775, he wrote to the governor about his troubles with two of his slaves: an African woman and an Indian man whom he had "raised as [his] own child" since he was less than a year old.[63] Owning an Indian slave may have put Valentin, as well as many other St. Louisans throughout the colonial period, in violation of Spanish decrees prohibiting acquiring Indian slaves; if he had acquired the boy many years before, however, Valentin was in compliance with the law.[64] According to Valentin, the man had turned into a "libertine, drunkard, and thief," running away to New Orleans with the enslaved woman, whom he described as licentious, as well as two slaves belonging to another St. Louisan. Given laws prohibiting the consumption of liquor by Indians and slaves, the man's purported drunkenness highlights the accessibility of alcohol; the priest could plausibly characterize the man as addicted to drink. Valentin asked the governor to use his authority to discover the pair, sell them, and send suitable replacements, a family if possible. If that did not happen, the priest wrote that he would have to abandon his parish before autumn, partly for financial reasons.[65]

The following month, Valentin announced his intention to leave St. Louis later that spring, attributing his decision on this occasion to precarious health rather than domestic difficulties. The cold weather had caused him tremendous pain in his extremities, which the medical care available locally could not cure. In late March, Valentin asserted that to restore his health, he would return to Lower Louisiana; he only needed heat to recover. After he recuperated, he would be willing to settle anywhere the governor instructed him to go except St. Louis.[66] The import of that letter was directly contradicted by one of the village physicians, Dr. Auguste Condé. In May, Condé reported that while Father Valentin had been ill the previous January and February, he had been in good health since then.[67] Such an account could not have aided Valentin in his campaign for release from his post in St. Louis. As May drew to a close, Valentin found himself stuck, lacking permission from both church and civil authorities to leave the village.

63. Valentin to [governor], February 9, 1775, AGI-PC 192-1100, MHMA microfilm.

64. Magnaghi, "The Role of Indian Slavery," 264–72; Ekberg, *Stealing Indian Women;* Pedro Piernas to Luis de Unzaga, July 8, 1770, "Declarations received by Pedro Piernas concerning Indian slaves at St. Louis," July 12, 1770, in Kinnaird, *SMV,* 2: 171–79.

65. Valentin to [governor], February 9, 1775, AGI-PC 192-1100, MHMA microfilm. African slaves were present in the Illinois Country since shortly after the founding of New Orleans in 1718, their status defined by the *Code Noir,* as issued for French Louisiana in 1724. Jesuits were likely the largest slaveholders initially. Ekberg, *French Roots in the Illinois Country,* 2–3, 145–48.

66. Valentin to Unzaga, March 23, 1775, AGI-PC 192-1101, MHMA microfilm, Price compilation.

67. Condé, May 26, 1775, AGI-PC 81, included in Cruzat to Unzaga, May 26, 1775, AGI-PC 81, cited in Lahey, "The Catholic Church on the Frontier of Spanish Illinois," 28.

Perhaps the doctor's assessment of his health prompted Valentin to take matters into his own hands. A few days after Condé declared him healthy, the priest sold an enslaved black woman to a merchant in the village for 700 *livres* in pelts, thereby gaining some liquid assets.[68] The following weekend, he presumably celebrated mass as usual. Then, sometime late Sunday or early Monday, he left St. Louis, "disappearing in the night."[69] He hid in the village and then crossed the Mississippi to the English side with two slaves, "without saying anything or telling anyone" about leaving, "with the intention of never returning" and going to New Orleans. On learning that the priest had "abandoned his house and the church, with all that belongs to it," the lieutenant governor, Cruzat, went to investigate, accompanied by two officers, two church wardens, and two other men, there to serve as witnesses. Valentin's flight exposed important documents belonging to the church, and of interest to the public, to danger.[70]

When the official party reached the priest's abandoned house and the church, they found their entry barred. Although he had deserted his duties, Valentin had not left his possessions and church property accessible to all passersby; he had, at least, locked the door. The man Cruzat ordered to break in managed to do so by a kitchen window, and then opened the door to the lieutenant governor and his companions. There, they found a key and a letter from Father Valentin, containing various instructions. With no understatement, Cruzat described the letter as proof of the misconduct and irregular actions of the priest, a man who had left behind and untended all the registers of baptisms, marriages, and deaths, as well as "all the ornaments and sacred vessels" that ought to be secured in the church. After finding the key to the church hanging on a nail in the house, Cruzat, the officers, wardens, and witnesses entered the church and there inventoried the altar cloths, missals, and other religious artifacts it contained.[71]

When people learned of Valentin's flight and its circumstances, a storm of public criticism swirled. Witnesses who went to the church reported that the sanctuary and the sacred ornaments of the church had been neglected. As the news spread throughout the villages of Upper Louisiana, people were scandalized. According to the lieutenant governor, Valentin's sudden disappearance left people murmuring, in part about the state in which he left the church. Everyone saw his departure as a bad example and

68. Sale of Catherine by Father Valentin to Etienne Barré, May 29, 1775, AGI-PC 81-563, MHMA microfilm.

69. Cruzat to Unzaga, July 12, 1775, AGI-PC 81-559, MHMA microfilm.

70. Inventario de los effectos, July 5, 1775, AGI-PC 81-568, MHMA microfilm.

71. Inventario de los effectos, July 5, 1775, AGI-PC 81-568, MHMA microfilm.

criticized his pastoral commitment, noted Cruzat. By leaving his flock, Valentin revealed a lack of "zeal for the good of souls," an unforgivable deficiency in a cleric whose task it was to inspire love and respect for church doctrine, as well as for the orders of a superior.[72] Having forbidden Valentin to leave St. Louis, Cruzat tried to prevent him from making it to New Orleans. Informed that the priest had made arrangements to travel downriver on a boat belonging to François Vallé, Cruzat sent word to Ste. Genevieve, ordering Vallé not to give Valentin passage on his boat and further demanding that Vallé see to it that the priest not be granted a place on any other vessel, no matter what pretext the cleric might offer for needing to descend to the capital.[73]

During the spring before Valentin's departure, St. Louisans had finalized plans for a new church, thus helping prepare the way for the designation of a parish and a permanent pastor. The proposed church would be a much more impressive and lasting structure. The previous December, villagers had pledged to construct a new church. Seventy-eight householders signed the agreement, an indication of broad community support for the effort.[74] Their commitment likely pleased Lieutenant Governor Piernas, a staunch advocate of the church. In April, members of the parish accompanied Father Valentin to his house after mass one day. There they confirmed the contract for the church.[75] In October, its construction was derailed when the man at work on it died. The following January, parishioners settled on a replacement contractor.[76] Finally, the wooden building, known as the Church of the Palisades, was dedicated in the summer of 1776.[77]

In May 1776, just before the church was finished, a new priest arrived. Father Bernard de Limpach, sent to replace the contentious and scandalous Father Valentin, journeyed to St. Louis and there presented his credentials to Lieutenant Governor Cruzat.[78] According to the February letter of appointment from his religious superior, Father Limpach's selection stemmed from two sources: his "good habits and capacity" and the king's wish to commission missionaries as curates. Limpach's possession of the post, "with all its rights and appendages," was predicated on his "actual

72. Cruzat to Unzaga, July 12, 1775, AGI-PC 81-559, MHMA microfilm.
73. Cruzat to Valle, June 10, 1775, AGI-PC 189b-624, MHMA microfilm.
74. Billon, *Annals of St. Louis,* 128; St. Louis History Collection, box 1, folder 1, MHMA.
75. Adjudicacion de la construccion de la iglesia, April 19, 1775, St. Louis History Collection, box 1, folder 1, MHMA.
76. Billon, *Annals of St. Louis,* 131, 138.
77. Contract for the first church in St. Louis, April 19, 1775, Church papers—Catholic, MHMA. Rothensteiner, *History of the Archdiocese of St. Louis,* 1: 141; see also Peterson, *Colonial St. Louis,* 80–81.
78. Rothensteiner, *History of the Archdiocese,* 1: 142.

personal residence there, and not otherwise."[79] That caveat regarding occupancy was likely informed by the unsatisfactory performance of priests like Valentin and others in the missions.

Quickly welcomed by civil and community leaders, Father Limpach was installed in his new position in a public ceremony that acknowledged the importance of his appointment, the development of the outpost from a mission into a parish, and the closeness of the ties between civil and clerical authorities. Before a church assemblage of "the most distinguished persons of the village," selected by Cruzat and including village founder Laclède, Dr. Condé, merchant and staunch church supporter Vasquez, and Labuscière, Father Limpach took full "legal and formal possession" as curate after performing the appropriate rituals.[80] "I, the said Lieutenant Governor," noted Cruzat, "have caused him to be recognized publicly . . . by all the parishioners" as the new curate. In order that "no obstacle may, at any time hereafter, be interposed to the exercise of his ministry," Cruzat deposited his dispatch regarding Limpach's appointment, the letters from Limpach's superiors, and the act describing the day's proceedings, along with the signatures of those gathered, into the local government archives.[81] Each level of authorization and approval—from the clerical and the civil to the communal—was thus publicly acknowledged and documented, serving collectively to confer legitimacy on Limpach's role. Once the civil performance had come to a conclusion, the priest proceeded to sing high mass for his new flock.[82]

Despite his welcome, the new pastor, like his predecessor, did not find the situation in Upper Louisiana entirely to his liking, either financially or physically. He had expended substantial resources to travel to St. Louis, but cash-poor parishioners could not—or would not—do much to compensate him. Moreover, his quarters left much to be desired. Apparently, the parishioners agreed, for after mass on September 1, 1776, they gathered to discuss a new two-story stone residence to replace the wooden one. Forty-five by twenty-five feet, it would be an impressive addition to the village.[83] Father Limpach's contribution to his new residence was 437 *livres* in pelts, a sum

79. Father Dagobert de Longwy to Father Bernard de Limpach, February 18, 1776, reprinted in Scharf, *History of Saint Louis City and County,* 2: 1639–40; Billon, *Annals of St. Louis,* 139.

80. Cruzat and others, May 19, 1776, St. Louis History Collection, box 1, folder 1, MHMA.

81. Billon, *Annals of St. Louis,* 139.

82. Francisco Cruzat, May 19, 1776, reprinted in Scharf, *History of Saint Louis City and County,* 2: 1640. Limpach officiated in St. Louis from May 1776–November 1789, baptizing 410 whites, 106 blacks, and 92 Indians; performing 115 white marriages; one black marriage, two Indian marriages, and one mixed white and Indian marriage; burying 222 whites, 60 blacks, and 44 Indians.

83. Billon, *Annals of St. Louis,* 140.

largely owed to him for expenses he had incurred in making the journey; in other words, he absolved his parishioners of their debt.[84]

More important than the physical state of his home or his purse, however, were the problems that faced the priest in ministering to the spiritual needs of a neglected and dissolute people. He was, to put it mildly, appalled by what he found in St. Louis. The problems of his parishioners, in turn, contributed to the pastoral and political debacles that marked his ministry. In Father Limpach's view, alcohol was at the center of his difficulties as pastor and a huge hindrance to the development of a prosperous, safe, and harmonious community in St. Louis. The people simply drank too much. Indeed, not long after its founding, the village became known for the tippling of its residents. In March 1767, as Spanish officials made preparations to govern the territory the crown had acquired five years previously, Governor Ulloa compiled a set of instructions for an expedition to the area, noting that intemperance was "a very common vice in the colony," but one that he believed could be "easily restrained" among the Spaniards. To accomplish that end, Ulloa recommended not allowing either "disorderly taverns or vicious gatherings."[85] Two years later, when Piernas offered his own description of the area's inhabitants to the colony's new governor, Alejandro O'Reilly, he declared them to be a dissipated people.[86]

Far from condoning his parishioners' use of spirits and licentious behavior, Father Limpach launched a campaign against inebriating beverages. The curate expressed his disapproval of villagers' drinking habits shortly after his arrival. He found the people in a pathetic state. Many, he informed the governor in 1777, were in such a miserable condition that they lacked funds to clothe themselves adequately and were forced to hide in the woods to conceal their nudity. Descriptions of the European residents of Upper Louisiana as clothing themselves like Indians, naked but for a breech clout, continued until the end of the century.[87] In Limpach's view, the people of *Paincourt* were short of more than just bread; they lacked even the wherewithal to maintain themselves decently.

The cause of their pitiable plight was obvious: alcohol, and in particular, *eau de vie,* or brandy. Every year, according to Limpach, 120 casks of

---

84. Rothensteiner, *History of the Archdiocese of St. Louis,* 1: 145; Peterson, *Colonial St. Louis,* 81–82.

85. Antonio de Ulloa's instructions for expedition to Illinois, March 14, 1767, in Houck, *SRM,* 1: 9.

86. Pedro Piernas to Governor O'Reilly, October 31, 1769, in Houck *SRM,* 1: 73.

87. In 1795, André Michaux, a French agent, described the French of the Kaskaskia village, across the Mississippi from St. Louis, as living "in the manner of the savages," wearing no breeches. Michaux, "Travels into Kentucky, 1793–1796," in Thwaites, ed., *Early Western Travels,* 3: 70.

eau de vie, each roughly sixty gallons, arrived in St. Louis.[88] The priest believed that his parishioners consumed half that quantity themselves. Doing so rendered them impoverished drunkards who spent their funds upon brandy and billiards rather than upon the necessities of life.[89] Over the previous two years, three new *jeux de billiard* had opened, generating 12,000 *livres* per year. No doubt alcohol flowed freely in such establishments. Considering the many occasions on which villagers drank, the priest calculated that his flock expended another 30,000 *livres* annually on alcohol. Together, billiards and beverages cost the population 42,000 *livres,* a veritable fortune that could be much better spent paying one's debts and acquiring basic necessities. From Limpach's perspective, the solution was as clear as the problem: regulation. The Capuchin proposed that the governor prohibit the importation of the dangerous beverage. With the money thus saved, the people would be able to pay their debts and lives more comfortably. Sobriety would lay the basis for prosperity, vitality, and most importantly, piety.[90]

Not too surprisingly, the merchants who exchanged alcohol for furs did not look kindly upon the cleric's suggestion. According to Limpach, these men believed that they would be unable to acquire an adequate number of deerskins to compete successfully in the fur trade; alcohol was a source of direct revenue as well. If royal officials cut off the flow of drink into St. Louis, they would destroy the merchants' business, their whole reason for settling in the wilderness. The possibility of such an outcome did not trouble Limpach in the slightest. Indeed, in promoting his plan to the governor, the priest argued that the future of the post rested not with merchants or *engagés* (European colonists who participated in the fur trade as trappers) but with the *habitants,* if they could be imbued with a desire to practice agriculture. Such solid citizens would remain in the village, supplanting the men of commerce, whom Limpach characterized as largely transient bachelors waiting only for the moment when they had acquired enough capital to leave.[91]

For social and economic reasons, early St. Louisans incorporated alcohol into their lives. In the midst of socializing and engaging in various

---

88. Father Bernard de Limpach to governor, June 30, 1777, AGI-PC, 190-447, MHMA microfilm. On liquid measures, see Holmes, "Spanish Regulation of Taverns," 175.

89. Limpach to governor, June 30, 1777, AGI-PC, 190-447, MHMA microfilm. For details of a billiard hall lease, see Billon, *Annals of St. Louis,* 72–73. Vige agreed to run the table for *"son profit . . . et le render . . . en bon état"* at the end of the lease. Louis Vige and Jean Baptiste Vien, Instrument #2863, February 7, 1770, St. Louis Archives, MHMA.

90. Limpach to governor, June 30, 1777, AGI-PC, 190-447, MHMA microfilm.

91. Ibid.

leisure activities, they drank. While Spanish regulations prohibited the sale of alcohol to Indians, slaves, and military personnel—but did little to curtail it—nothing inhibited the rest of the populace from consuming it. And despite the laws, St. Louis traders employed alcohol in their dealings with the Indians. Not only was liquor a desired article of exchange, it often became part of negotiations, with merchants attempting to make better deals by plying their customers and fur suppliers with drink. In Limpach's view, alcohol was a scourge upon the people's pocketbooks and peace of mind, causing myriad sufferings in the village. He blamed the liquor that came up the Mississippi from New Orleans for cash flowing downstream, empty coffers, sin, and violence.

Evidence of such alcohol-related problems, and an unfortunate connection to unseemly clerical conduct, came to Limpach's attention the following year. In September 1778, he traveled downstream to Ste. Geneviève to clean up the disarray left by the village's former pastor, Father Hilaire. Among other troublesome acts, Hilaire, dissatisfied with the support his flock provided, had apparently directed his slave and a number of others to vandalize church property in exchange for rum. The lumber they gathered from tearing down the fence and stable had been chopped into firewood, stored by Hilaire and claimed as his property. After Hilaire left the village, Limpach inherited the task of bringing order to the church register, and he remained in Ste. Geneviève several weeks to attend to neglected religious matters, including plans for a new church.[92] Hilaire's behavior could have done little to shore up clerical authority and likely only deepened Limpach's animosity toward alcohol.

In championing the regulation and prohibition of spirits, the curate echoed the views of the colony's civil authorities. Throughout the period of Spanish dominion, government officials undertook repeated efforts to control the flow of alcohol but encountered limited success in altering either drinking habits or the use of liquor in trade.[93] The first Europeans in the area, the French, had forbidden the sale of liquor to Indians and slaves, a practice which Spanish authorities continued. Both the French and Spanish attempted to govern consumption of liquor by controlling taverns. In 1769, Governor O'Reilly instituted taxes of twenty pesos on each of New Orleans's six inns, and forty pesos each on the town's six billiard halls and twelve taverns; this income would provide assured support for the city.[94]

92. This incident is discussed in Ekberg, *Colonial Ste. Genevieve*, 391–95.
93. Holmes, "Spanish Regulation of Taverns," 149–82; Holmes, trans. and ed., "O'Reilly's Regulations on Booze, Boarding Houses, and Billiards," 293–300.
94. Alejandro O'Reilly to Julian de Arriaga, December 10, 1769, in Kinnaird, *SMV,* 1: 134.

Granting licenses to operate public houses thus simultaneously served the purposes of raising revenue for the government while enabling officials to control the setting of drinking and curb the disorderly conduct that might arise from unauthorized dispensaries.[95]

Although St. Louisans drank primarily at home and not in taverns (almost all the structures in the early village were residences), alcohol engendered conflict in the area, as it did elsewhere in Spanish Louisiana. As worried as Father Limpach was about the impact of alcohol upon his flock, he was also troubled by its role in fostering violence among the Indians and by the blind eye he thought Lieutenant Governor Cruzat turned to the trade. Evidence of ongoing commerce in alcohol was not difficult to find in this period, as when a rogue trader was caught with large quantities of rum in his canoe.[96] Complaining to the governor, Limpach claimed that the liquor trade with the Indians put the residents of St. Louis at terrible risk, exposing them to sin, crime, and murder.[97] Repeatedly, villagers had complained of visiting Indians becoming inebriated and behaving in disorderly and sometimes violent ways. In December 1778, "Louis Mahas, an Indian" was accused of committing all sorts of crimes, including "debauching slaves with liquor."[98] Alcohol, Indians, and disorder were seen as too often inextricably tied together. Whether or not the situation in the village merited the priest's grim prognostications, it is clear that alcohol consumption fostered disharmony and unhappiness. Such views partly explain Cruzat's decision to sell an enslaved African man, Joseph, when he discovered that he had taken some bottles of liquor, "a petty theft" that led the lieutenant governor to sell him.[99]

In St. Louis, the power of clerics and civil authorities was circumscribed, their influence predicated on the harmony and loyalty—or lack thereof— that they fostered. Thus, when Father Limpach refused to perform his sacramental duties on the grounds that parishioner Bargas had died from abusing alcohol, he was not likely to endear himself to his flock. Over the previous several years, the priest had not proved himself skilled at building his base of support. With seemingly little regard for the rhetorical virtues of persuasion over admonition, he had criticized a lieutenant governor, complained about parishioners, and attacked the drinking and economic habits of villagers. Given that history of acrimony, the possibility that the witnesses in the Bargas inquest collectively acted against the priest's wishes by omitting damning testimony about drink seems plausible.

95. Holmes, "Spanish Regulation of Taverns," 153.
96. Joseph Buteau case, November 1779, Litigation Collection, box 1, folder 10, MHMA.
97. Limpach to governor, June 30, 1777, AGI-PC 190-448 (Price compilation, MHMA).
98. Billon, *Annals of St. Louis,* 156; trial of Louis Mahas, 1779, Litigation Collection, MHMA.
99. Cruzat to François Vallé, March 28, 1778, AGI-PC 191-857, MHMA microfilm.

Not long after Bargas's death, the individuals involved in his inquest all underwent dramatic changes in their lives that altered their status in the community. Before a year had passed, Leyba was dead and buried in the church. The year likewise witnessed Ignace Laroche's death and his widow's remarriage.[100] Six months after buying Bargas's house and land, the physician Gibkins sold the property; he moved downstream to Ste. Geneviève, where he died in 1784.[101] Limpach remained in St. Louis longer, a beleaguered and miserable figure. The year after the Bargas inquest, the priest found himself publicly suspected of unduly influencing Leyba as he lay on his deathbed in order to secure a generous bequest for himself. Occasionally, Limpach had received funds for performing funerals and bequests in wills; in early modern Europe, priestly charges for administering various sacraments were a regular source of conflict.[102] Although St. Louisans could discover none of the details of the lieutenant governor's will, they nonetheless believed he intended to give to the priest 1,000 *livres.* Equally disturbing, according to the discontented villagers, Leyba's reasons for doing so were known only to the priest.[103] As it turned out, the villagers' suspicions were unfounded, for Leyba did not leave anything to Limpach.

For Limpach, the charges must have been yet another galling indication of the lack of respect St. Louisans accorded him and his office. Ultimately, he, like many other missionaries, begged for release from his charge. In 1787, after eleven years in St. Louis, he was a broken man, in ill health and mental anguish, with four villages depending on his services. Population growth, fueled by the emigration of French settlers fleeing the "vexations of the Americans" on the eastern side of the river, left him unable to meet his duties. In envisioning his removal, the priest hoped he would find "somewhere else an alleviation to" physical and mental trouble. "Everything else is of no consideration to me," he wrote. This rather desperate sounding plea did not gain him release until the fall of 1789.[104] Reassigned, he continued to serve as a missionary until his death in 1796.

100. Instrument #302, July 30, 1780, St. Louis Archives, MHMA.

101. Houck, *HM,* 2: 28.

102. Limpach was named as a recipient in the will of Don Luis Perrault, May 9, 1783, Instrument #2222, and received funeral expenses from the estate of Louis Checellier Sr. June 9, 1786, Instrument #1421, St. Louis Archives, MHMA.

103. Describing these secretive transactions to a government official, a concerned St. Louisan signed his missive, *"Virtutis, veritatis que Amicus."* [Anonymous] to unknown government official, June 19, 1780, AGI-PC 193a-644, MHMA microfilm.

104. Thereafter, he became pastor of St. Gabriel, Iberville, in 1790, then of Point Coupee, in 1791, where he died March 27, 1796. Rothensteiner, *History of the Archdiocese of St. Louis,* 1: 155 (original in the Catholic Archives of America, Notre Dame University).

Whether the case of Bargas and Limpach heightened governmental awareness of the problems with drink or led to any successful efforts to control it cannot be determined. In 1780, however, after Leyba's death and the reappointment of Cruzat, the new lieutenant governor issued a series of restrictions upon alcohol. He noted that "notwithstanding the reiterated orders by [his] predecessors and [himself]," which forbid anyone from giving "intoxicating drink" to Indians who came to St. Louis, many villagers not only gave alcohol to the Indians but drank with them. They did so in spite of severe penalties prohibiting their actions, "reckless of public tranquility," and utterly motivated by self-interest with regard to the fur trade. Cruzat believed that St. Louisans hoped, by drinking with the Indians, to obtain "their own private objects."[105]

While the incident and issues that had briefly bound these individuals together quickly faded, what remained was a legacy of attenuated authority and influence distributed among different sectors of the local populace. Nor did problems between clergy and community disappear with time.[106] (On another occasion, Cruzat hesitated to act because he was unsure how far his authority extended over church affairs, in particular over whether priests were required to wear trappings of their office at all times. Cruzat was loathe to get involved in a controversy in Ste. Genevieve over Father Hilaire, who only wore his habit when saying mass and administering sacraments; the priest's failure to dress in clerical attire at other times bothered villagers there.)[107]

Given the frequency with which clerics found themselves embroiled in controversy and suspected of improper behavior, it is clear that their ability to contribute to social stability and order was compromised. State efforts to limit church authority did not help. Efforts to bolster the power of the state at the expense of the church both in Spain and throughout her colonies were evident in both the 1767 expulsion of 2,500 Jesuits from Spanish America and the Royal Pragmatic on Marriage of 1776, which was extended throughout Spanish territories in 1778. Both actions undercut the authority of the clergy in public and private realms by limiting the clergy's role

---

105. Cruzat, Local Ordinances for St. Louis and General Ordinances, October 7, 1780, in Houck SRM, 1: 240.

106. In the late 1780s, a similarly embattled priest, Father Pierre Huet de La Valinière, found himself at war with his flock across the Mississippi River in Kaskaskia. Parishioners' animosity destroyed any demand for Father Valinière's services, leaving him, as he bitterly declared, ample time to write the governor a detailed account of his grievances; a key source of discord was financial. Valinière to governor, May 3, 1788, AGI-PC 191-861; May 12, 1788, AGI-PC 191-863 (Price compilation, MHMA microfilm). On Valinière's career, see Rothensteiner, *History of the Archdiocese of St. Louis,* 1: 161–64.

107. Cruzat to Bernardo de Gálvez, July 2, 1777 (Price compilation, MHMA).

in overseeing colonial settlements and by insisting that the church role in the sacrament of marriage had to be balanced with the civil and contractual components of a union. Given these developments, it is not surprising that clerics, who were regularly challenged by parishioners and not always on good terms with government officials, found their efforts to control behavior and foster piety achieving mixed results at best. Priests found themselves at odds with parishioners over seating arrangements, compensation, and burial rites while government officials could ask for—but had limited means of demanding or coercing—assistance from members of the community. In villages like St. Louis, with a constant stream of newcomers and visitors as well as a changing cast of officials and clerics, the fractured lines of authority, customary legal traditions, and community will regularly generated conflict. When various factions combined to influence the outcome of controversial cases, harmony and consensus could be achieved.

For those who settled in *Paincourt* in its first decades, village life remained distinguished by uncertainty and indeterminacy in politics, religion, and social relations. Weak civil authorities and a scarcity of priests contributed to the laxity of social control. Parishioners who wanted priests to serve them by providing them with sacraments but not guide or reprimand them could more easily assert their independence in the face of fewer clerics and greater distance from spiritual centers. And the behavior that those in positions of power deemed destructive, such as drinking or out-of-wedlock and interracial unions, appears to have been integral to the sustenance, growth, and survival of frontier outposts like St. Louis. Where the reins of civil and clerical authority rested equally lightly, distance from other population and institutional or administrative centers in the empire enabled colonists to innovate in social relations, to escape from church efforts to discipline the laity, and to bring otherwise questionable activities and interactions into familiar spaces. As they wrestled with the problems of building a new community in the 1770s, St. Louisans adapted religious, racial, sexual, and legal norms to suit their needs, embracing a consensus-style governance and tolerance of questionable behavior that made it possible for the community to survive and thrive.

Chapter 7

A Village in Crisis

CONFLICT AND VIOLENCE ON THE BRINK OF WAR

In late 1777, Pierre Laclède undertook preparations for a trip to New Orleans, a journey that proved his last. During his final months in St. Louis, the village that he founded saw moments of celebration amidst a season of suffering. In November, around the time of Laclède's forty-eighth birthday, news of a distant Spanish victory was officially commemorated, with gunfire salutes, illuminations of neighborhoods, and the singing of the Te Deum.[1] Locally, there was bad news in the form of widespread sickness. That fall, some sort of infectious disease swept through the settlement, and doctors were unable to cure it. The fever spread to Indian peoples in the area as well. Unable to work for a time himself, Lieutenant Goveror Cruzat sent a militia officer down to the capital in hopes of securing his health, declaring that the man could not recover in St. Louis.[2] Whether Laclède contracted the ailment is unknown, but the steps he took in December, before making his last voyage, make one wonder if he had been feeling unwell or had some intimations of mortality. Before six months had elapsed, Laclède was gone, and St. Louis was a different place. His death was accompanied by other changes affecting the life of the village, in particular, the onset of a period of conflict and eventually war. The American Revolutionary War, raging since the bloodshed in New England in the spring of 1775, finally reached the Mississippi in 1778, and hostilities among European powers ultimately involved St. Louisans in the Anglo-American quarrel.

---

1. Cruzat to Gálvez, November 29, 1777, AGI-PC 1-226, MHMA microfilm; the celebrations marked the victory of the Spanish at the island of Santa Catalina de los Portugueses.

2. Cruzat to Gálvez, October 18, 1777, AGI-PC 1-209, MHMA microfilm; Cruzat to Gálvez, October 18, 1777, AGI-PC 1-208.

For villagers, the disruption caused by the disappearance of one long-standing source of local authority and influence—Laclède—and the arrival of another—Spanish lieutenant governor Fernando de Leyba—and the proximity of a third—the Americans—contributed to a climate of conflict. Repeatedly, villagers turned on each other in the streets and courts, bringing verbal and physical violence to center stage. Squabbles over trade poisoned relationships between merchants and the new lieuteant governor, and many in the village felt besieged by neighbors and forces beyond their control. As the decade drew to a close, St. Louis was a community on the brink of war, preoccupied by crises within and haunted by the specter of assault from without.

On December 31, 1777, taking quill in hand, Laclède sat down and composed a letter full of instructions, regret, and self-recrimination. Writing to Auguste Chouteau about his forthcoming trip to New Orleans, Laclède explained his business affairs in full. Although he had gone on similar voyages before, this time Laclède expressed his wishes as though he expected never to return to St. Louis. He informed Chouteau that he had left a number of business papers with Madame Chouteau, including the records of the partnership between him and Auguste. Laclède asked the younger man to collect any debts due to them and to act on other matters, if necessary. "If, by the will of God, I die on this voyage," he wrote, "will you have the good will and the kindness to render me this service?" The service Laclède anticipated was the payment of various sums he owed to numerous creditors. And deep in debt he certainly was. If he died on his journey, he wanted Auguste to take his letter of instructions to the ranking official and to give copies of it to his former business partner, Maxent, still very much his creditor, in New Orleans. Confessing his worries to Auguste, who had been his companion, confidant, and business partner for many years, Laclède expressed great regret. "Goodbye, my dear sir," he wrote. "I desire to see you again, and to be able myself to settle my affairs, because it is very hard and painful as I see, to have to die in debt." Saddened by his own circumstances and worried about the potential difficulties he might cause his loved ones, Laclède acknowledged his predicament head-on: "One bequeathes nothing but pain and trouble to friends when one dies poor." His final words were full of pathos, the comments of a man who sounded disappointed and depressed. "Such is my deplorable situation," he wrote, "one must suffer and not murmur." In closing, Laclède used the formal style of the day, tinged with emotion, "Good-bye again," he wrote, "and believe me, entirely yours, your very humble and obedient servant Laclède Liguest."[3]

For Laclède, the journey to New Orleans would have provided time to reflect on the disastrous state of his finances. Once the de facto leader of St. Louis and always a man of influence—someone to be reckoned with—Laclède had seen his fortunes fall. In 1769, when he and Maxent decided to dissolve their partnership, Laclède was already in serious debt to his partner and conveyed the building he had first constructed in St. Louis, which served as his warehouse and then later as the headquarters of the Spanish government, to Maxent. For the assets the company held in St. Louis, which totaled roughly 80,000 *livres* in merchandise, furs, slaves, livestock, buildings, and other items, Laclède agreed to make annual payment of 20,000 *livres,* starting in 1771, but he failed to fulfill his part of the bargain. Fortunately for Madame Chouteau and their children, he had deeded title of their home to them in 1768. Once in New Orleans, Laclède's actions are unknown, but he likely spent time with Maxent, with whom he remained on good terms despite the debt that stood between them. According to his elder brother Jean, back in France, Pierre wrote a last letter to him from New Orleans, telling him that he was ill but planned to make one more voyage, his last commercial journey, back to St. Louis. Jean de Laclède later maintained that his younger sibling had also written that his business in New Orleans had been successful, that he planned to return to France, and that he had bequeathed his fortune to Jean and his offspring.[4] Given the letter Laclède had written to Chouteau a few months before, with its dire assessment of his financial situation and air of doom, one could imagine that Laclède wanted his older brother to think that he had done well. Or perhaps Jean assumed a fortune and fabricated the promise of a bequest. Over the next few years, Jean de Laclède undertook efforts to obtain his brother's estate, unaware of the debt in which he died and insisting to authorities that there was property from the estate due to him.

Soon thereafter, Laclède began the return journey to the village he had founded, but he never laid eyes on it again. His health deteriorated, and he died at the mouth of the Arkansas River on May 27, 1778. When news of his death reached the Arkansas Post, a few miles away, the commandant came to the spot, inspected the body, and declared Laclède's death to be from natural causes. With witnesses in attendance, the officer took an

---

3. Laclède to Chouteau, December 31, 1777, Pierre Laclède Collection, MHMA.

4. Coleman, *Gilbert Antoine de St. Maxent,* 91–94. Coleman alludes to a 1770 letter Laclède supposedly wrote to his brother Jean that stated his intention to return shortly to France, but neither the letter nor any corroborating evidence has been uncovered.

inventory of Laclède's property on board the boat. Apparently, the merchant traveled in some comfort and style, having on his journey feather pillows, as well as a beaver hat and well-worn silk clothing embroidered with gold thread. He had with him items likely purchased in New Orleans for personal use, including some chocolate and mustard and two books, presumably new acquisitions for his substantial library.[5] Both by noted Swiss doctor Samuel Auguste Tissot, *L'Onanisme* (Masturbation) and *Un Avis au Peuple* (Advice to the People) were published in the 1760s and soon considered authoritative.[6] The former, a "dissertation on the diseases produced by masturbation," proved an important and widely reprinted text in the history of sexuality, contributing to views of masturbation as both a manifestation and a cause of mental illness.[7] It is not surprising that Laclède sought out new and well-received works on medicine. At his death, Laclède's library of over 215 volumes held a number of medical treatises.[8] There is some irony in his having Tissot's *Advice to the People* in his possession at his death. In this volume, Tissot directed his attention to "those, who, by their Distance from regular Physicians" lacked adequate medical care and so needed instruction on how to cure themselves.[9] Far from both physicians and all of his loved ones, Laclède was soon buried, at a location that has been lost to time and the river.

With Laclède's death, an era came to an end. News of his passing, which likely reached St. Louis by mid-July, must have been greeted with interest by most villagers and a real sense of grief and sorrow by some, especially his family. As executor, Auguste Chouteau faced the task of settling the estate and authorized the sale of Laclède's belongings to begin to defray the debts he left; the principal creditor was Maxent.[10] As Foley and Rice suggest, the younger man took the lessons of Laclède's financial disaster to heart, adopting more conservative and cautious business strategies than Laclède had employed.[11] Over the course of the next year, Chouteau set about dismantling Laclède's estate, arranging for the sale of his mill and farm in the summer of 1779. Gathering at the public auctions where the property was sold, villagers outside the church looked on as Laclède's intimates made their bids. At bargain prices, two members of the Chouteau family purchased

5. Inventory of Laclède Liguest, May 27, 1778, AGI-PC 191, JFM, Lovejoy Library.

6. Tissot, *L'Onanisme;* Tissot, *Advice to the People in General.*

7. Singy, "Friction of the Genitals and the Secularization of Morality"; Carol, "Les Médecins et la Stigmatisation du Vice Solitaire."

8. McDermott, *Private Libraries in Creole St. Louis,* 27, 29, 38, 42.

9. Tissot, *Advice to the People in General,* title page.

10. Ibid., 94.

11. Foley and C. David Rice, *The First Chouteaus,* 24.

significant pieces of property, with Auguste acquiring a mill, its equipment, and its land for 2,000 *livres* in pelts.[12] Madame Chouteau, now truly René Chouteau's widow and Laclède's survivor, purchased a piece of land adjacent to land she already owned, along with the structures on it: a log house, cabins for slaves, and barns, as well an orchard and garden.[13] When Auguste traveled to New Orleans in 1780 for a final settlement of the estate, he delivered over 41,000 *livres* to Maxent, of which nearly 28,000 were "irrevocable," leaving Laclède's erstwhile partner significantly out of pocket for the 80,000 owed to him.[14] Acknowledging that he could expect no more, Maxent released Chouteau "from any responsibility, he having executed his commission."[15]

Shortly before Laclède's death en route to St. Louis, an important newcomer traveling upstream on the Mississippi River reached the village after a journey of ninety-three days. Arriving in the capital of Upper Louisiana on June 10, the new lieutenant governor, Fernando de Leyba, sent to replace Francisco Cruzat, reported being received by "all the inhabitants with extraordinary signs of rejoicing."[16] Far from heralding the era of harmony and good will that his initial reception suggested, Leyba's arrival, coinciding with the month of Laclède's death, presaged quite the opposite, a period of conflict and crisis in a community on the periphery of war. From the secret instructions Leyba carried with him, one can infer the problems officials anticipated the lieutenant governor would encounter in Upper Louisiana. Leyba was instructed to encourage the cultivation of hemp and flax, no easy task given how disinclined the populace was to farm. In addition, Louisiana governor Gálvez told Leyba he must endeavor to win the good will of Indian tribes in both Spanish and English territory, a herculean labor considering the ample grounds these nations had for animosity toward European intruders. An equally elusive goal lay behind another instruction: Leyba should do his best to encourage Catholic immigration; the Spanish very much wanted to people the thinly settled land with ethnically European colonists. Finally, Leyba was charged with

12. Ibid., 24; Madame Chouteau purchase from Laclède estate, June 20, 1779, Instrument #264, St. Louis Archives, MHMA.

13. Madame Chouteau purchase from Laclède estate, June 20, 1779, Instrument #264, St. Louis Archives, MHMA.

14. Foley and C. David Rice, *The First Chouteaus,* 25; Billon, *Annals of St. Louis,* 148.

15. Billon, *Annals of St. Louis,* 148.

16. Leyba to Gálvez, July 11, 1778, in Houck, *SRM,* 1: 161–62.

keeping an eye on the turmoil brewing to the east of the Mississippi; the war between American rebels and the British crown had the potential to become more than a family quarrel.[17]

Trouble seemed to surround Leyba, with even his trip up the Mississippi to St. Louis appearing a foreshadowing of chaotic relationships and rising antagonisms. A soldier traveling with him, Joseph Piernas (no apparent relation to the former lieutenant govenor), spent the voyage gambling with the sailors manning the boat. So that Leyba would not be disturbed by the racket of their leisure activities, they went off into the woods when they could. Leyba was appalled by the men's behavior, noting that when his ensign returned from these excursions, he was in bad shape, "sometimes with his face swollen, and at others, all covered with dirt and limping." Investigating the matter, Leyba seized the men's dice and threw them away, noting with satisfaction that this action "put an end to the fighting and wagering of trousers and shirts." Piernas was clearly a troublemaker, "telling everybody" that because of Leyba's "lack of experience in the government" of Upper Louisiana, the governor had appointed him a special advisor to Leyba. "I have not paid the slightest attention to this nor to other things of the same kind which have come to my notice," stated Leyba, "partly because I consider him not the kind of man to be able to discredit me, and partly because his deceit is manifest, as everyone sees the contempt with which I treat him." Adopting a contemptuous posture toward a subordinate may have suited Leyba at the moment, but his condescension toward others became a problem for his administration.[18]

Before Leyba had much chance to settle into his new post, he was overwhelmed by indigenous visitors. July brought Indians of many tribes to St. Louis, as they made the journey to meet the new lieutenant governor. During a transition of power such as this, it seems likely that an air of pageantry and uncertainty prevailed. Numerous Indian peoples came to the village to greet the new official, simultaneously welcoming him and making their presence known, in what may have been for Leyba unsettling cultural exchanges. By July 21, Leyba had already received visits from the Kickapoos, Sacs, Mahas, Mascutens, Missouris, and Big and Little Osage. "According to reports I have received," he wrote with some worry, "about a dozen more are still to come." Some nations sent word to him that they planned to leave their dogs to guard their villages, which he understood to mean that they intended to bring their wives and children to St. Louis.

17. Bernardo de Gálvez to Leyba, March 9, 1778, in Kinnaird, *SMV,* 1: 258–60.
18. Leyba to Gálvez, July 11, 1778, in ibid., 295–96.

"The Missouri nation has done this and has been here for two weeks, eating us out of house and home," he complained. Already frustrated with the Indians of the region a month into his new job, Leyba pronounced that there were "only two ways of treating these people, either run them out with guns or feed them."[19] Lacking either the cause or the garrison to do the former, he pursued the latter course of action.

Adding an extra layer of difficulty to his interactions with Indian visitors was a shortage of presents. Although Maxent had promised him a cargo, to be delivered by Laclède, Leyba found himself empty handed. Forced to look elsewhere, he ordered local merchants, who were "taking it with very bad grace," to give him what he needed.[20] Thus, within weeks of landing in St. Louis, Leyba had begun to antagonize the local merchant class, imposing his authority in ways they saw as undermining their profits. Auguste Chouteau's experience confirmed Leyba's sense of how the war was disrupting business; he could not obtain the goods he wanted for trade with the Indians and had to bring "drinkables, coffee, and sugar" to St. Louis instead.[21] The difficulties Chouteau and others faced in doing business prompted Leyba to warn officials that shortages would encourage Indians to turn to the British for their supplies, and Leyba took the unusual step of permitting several St. Louis merchants to buy goods in British Illinois. Trying to further assist these men in their commercial endeavors, Leyba restricted the number of trade licenses, thereby pleasing a handful of rich merchants, including Chouteau, Sylvestre Labbadie, and Gabriel Cerré, while antagonizing many other, less affluent ones.[22] Such actions on Leyba's part contributed to the dislike many villagers developed for him.

The influx of Indian visitors that summer was partly fueled by the international unrest making its way to the continent's interior. War with the English was unsettling the region, Leyba believed, "causing a great number of Indian tribes to go from one side to the other without knowing which side to take." Even more compelling than uncertainty about location was fear of the Americans. "Terrified by the Bostoneses [as the Americans were called], and in order to escape their anxieties for a few days," he opined, "they come to this post under the pretext of asking for advice on their troubles, and consume many rations of bread." Feeding this many visitors posed a problem, as the official number of rations had been set in 1771, when far fewer Indians came to the village. The fewest

19. Leyba to Gálvez, July 21, 1778, in ibid., 298–99.
20. Leyba to Gálvez, July 25, 1778, in ibid., 300.
21. Foley and C. David Rice, *The First Chouteaus,* 26, citing Leyba to Gálvez, July 13, 1779.
22. Foley and C. David Rice, *The First Chouteaus,* 26.

rations distributed in any given day was fifty, and on some days as many as two hundred rations were handed out.[23] In answer to Leyba's pleas for more resources for provisions, the governor responded sympathetically but negatively. "I fear that you will have frequent visits from the Indian tribes during the war between Great Britain and her colonies," Gálvez wrote. "But I must tell you that I have no authority to increase the number" of rations. He urged Leyba to do his best to limit visits to no more than three or four days, not fully appreciating perhaps how difficult implementing such a policy might be.[24]

While disruptions in the movements of Indian peoples in the region appeared to be triggered by the Revolutionary War, the conflict between Britain and her North American colonies came much closer to home in the summer of 1778. In July, American forces achieved victories over the British in Illinois, with American military men subsequently appearing in St. Louis. On July 4, 1778, Colonel George Rogers Clark led a party of 153 Americans, who had descended the Ohio River from Pittsburgh, to a surprise victory over the British in Illinois, where Clark's men captured the post of Kaskakia.[25] Deploying his ragtag, barely clad, and poorly equipped men, Clark split his forces into two, attacking the fort and seizing the commandant from his bed. Although "there was great confusion among the inhabitants," they decided quickly "to surrender without firing a musket shot."[26] When Leyba learned of the victories at Kaskaskia and Cahokia, he responded quickly, sending letters to Americans across the Mississippi.[27] On July 6, he wrote to Captain Joseph Bowman in Cahokia to congratulate him on his arrival as well as Clark's. On July 8, Leyba sent word to Clark, adopting an extremely cordial tone toward the American officer. "Sir, if the affairs of the government, of which I have taken charge only a few days ago, permit me," he wrote, "I shall come in person to congratulate you on your happy arrival at the Kaskaskias." Such an overture must have been gratifying to Clark, although perhaps he did not find it as welcome as Leyba's news that supplies for the Americans had arrived from New Orleans; an American merchant there, Oliver Pollock, acting as agent for the United

---

23. Leyba to Gálvez, July 21, 1778, in Kinnaird, *SMV,* 1: 298–99.

24. Gálvez to Leyba, September 2, 1778, in ibid., 305.

25. For some of the correspondence regarding the mission, see "George Rogers Clark and the Kaskaskia Campaign, 1777–1778." In 1778, Kaskaskia was under the command of a Frenchman, Philippe de Rastel, known as Rocheblave, who was an officer in the French army during the Seven Years' War, who later entered British service and was appointed commandant of Kaskaskia in 1776. Kinnaird, "Clark-Leyba Papers," 95 n. 14.

26. Clark to O'Hara, July 15, 1775, Kaskaskias, Illinois, in Kinnaird, "Clark-Leyba Papers," 97; Kinnaird notes that the original was lost, 97 n. 23.

27. Kinnaird, "Clark-Leyba Papers," 93.

States and the State of Virginia during the war, had procured them and sent them upriver to St. Louis.[28]

Spanish support was crucial to the American effort, and Leyba, as well as traders in St. Louis, provided important assistance. As Lawrence Kinnaird noted, without Leyba's influence and credit, Clark's situation would have been impossible: American financial support was neglible, Pollock's supplies inadequate, and the French villages of Illinois too small and poor to support American troops.[29] Leyba's personal guarantees helped sway local traders to accept Clark's orders for merchandise, and Clark was able to make necessary purchases, as on September 5, when he bought 150 hats, 130 shirts, and 150 pairs of shoes, or two weeks later, when he ordered up seven barrels each of wine and brandy.[30] Describing the help he received from Leyba, Clark delightedly declared, "This gentleman interested himself much in favor of the States,—more so than I could have expected."[31] Leyba's tone and offers of aid must have come as a relief to the rebel officer, given how exposed, vulnerable, and distant from the eastern seaboard he and his men were.

Soon after taking Kaskaskia, the brash and bold American was in St. Louis, supping with Leyba as the Spanish commander's guest and drinking convivially with the other diners.[32] Newly arrived in the village himself, Leyba did not hesitate to pull out the stops in welcoming Clark, perhaps trying to dazzle both the American and the inhabitants of St. Louis at the same time. (Whether some found the festive air incongruous coming soon after news of Laclède's death had reached the village is impossible to know, but a new Spanish official wining and dining an American military leader would certainly have prompted comment.)[33] Gunfire salutes, lavish meals, and balls punctuated Clark's stay; such gestures highlighted Leyba's role as host, benefactor, and local authority as much as they celebrated Clark's visit and recent victory. "There was a great consuming of powder at his

28. John Francis McDermott, "The Myth of the 'Imbecile Governor': Captain Fernando Leyba and the Defense of St. Louis in 1780," in McDermott, *The Spanish in the Mississippi Valley,* 329; Leyba to Clark, July 8, 1778, in Kinnaird, "Clark-Leyba Papers," 94.

29. Kinnaird, "Clark-Leyba Papers," 93.

30. Receipt for September 5, 1778; September 17, 1778, George Rogers Clark Papers, Clark Family Collection, MHMA.

31. Kinnaird, "Clark-Leyba Papers," citing James Alton James, ed, *George Rogers Clark Papers, 1771–1781,* 8: 19.

32. According to family tradition, Gabriel Cerré was one of the guests at a Clark dinner. When Clark asked to drink a glass with him, Cerré agreed but reminded the visitor such would not have been his reception if Cerré had been at home in Kaskasia when Clark entered his home and searched it. Interview of L. C. Draper with Paschal Leon Cerré, St. Louis, October 1846, from Draper Collection of Clark manuscripts, vol. 8, in Wisconsin State Historical Society Library, Gabriel Cerré Papers, 1787–1846, MHMA.

33. On July 21, Leyba wrote that he was expecting Clark any day. "Clark-Leyba Papers," 98.

arrival as well as at his departure," Leyba told the governor. "I entertained him at meals and laid [a dinner for thirty] on his visit which lasted two days. Dances were given for him both nights and a supper to the ladies and dancers, and lodging in my house with as much formality as was possible for me."[34] In New Orleans, Governor Gálvez was delighted with Leyba's report, penning in the margins of Leyba's letter his draft response: "This gives me great pleasure and I hope that you will continue co-operating with them on your part in accordance with the instructions I sent you."[35]

Leyba's decision to host Clark was no doubt informed by what Gálvez alluded to: a set of secret instructions that ordered Leyba to "endeavor to learn all the news occurring in the English part (of Illinois)." In particular, he should seek knowledge of the war the British were waging against their rebellious colonists so as to avoid being "surprised in case of any unforeseen design" on Spanish interests and territory. If anyone from that conflict happened to seek sanctuary, whether British or American, he should be allowed it.[36] Perhaps most importantly, any news Leyba obtained should be reported promptly to the governor, and Leyba should be sure to act with "the greatest secrecy" if he had any correspondence with any American leader. In his account of the "conquest of Illinois," Clark recalled the "intimacy" that grew between himself and Leyba after his visit to St. Louis. Leyba "omitted nothing in his Power to prove his Attachment to the Americans with such openness as left no room for a doubt." From Clark's perspective, the Spaniard was a revelation. "As I was never before in company with any Spanish Gent," he remembered, "I was much surprised in my expectations; for instead of finding that reserve thought peculiar to that Nation, I here saw not the least symptoms of it, freedom almost to excess gave the greatest pleasure."[37] When he had the chance, Clark returned Leyba's hospitality, purchasing quantities of ham, fowl, and spices to present a suitable entertainment.[38]

From Leyba's accounts, it is clear he was impressed with the American. His description of the capture of Kaskaskia, presumably based on reports from Clark, celebrates the daring, bravery, and physicality of the American,

34. Leyba to Gálvez, November 16, 1778, in ibid., 102.

35. Gálvez to Leyba, draft response, January 13, 1779, penned on Leyba to Gálvez, November 16, 1778, in ibid., 102 n. 36.

36. McDermott, "The Myth of the 'Imbecile Governor,'" 329; Bernardo de Gálvez to Leyba, March 9, 1778, in Kinnaird, *SMV,* 1: 260.

37. George Rogers Clark, *Col. George Rogers Clark's Sketch of His Campaign in the Illinois in 1778–79,* 42.

38. List of articles obtained for the entertainment of the Spanish commandant, May 31, 1779, George Rogers Clark Papers, MHMA, photostat, cited in McDermott, "The Myth of the 'Imbecile Governor,'" 330 n. 14.

who arrived at the town "in hunting shirt and breechcloth, naked of foot and limb and with his bed, food, and gun on his shoulder."[39] As Clark and Leyba corresponded in July 1778, the esteem Leyba developed for the American became palpable. Writing to his superior in New Orleans, Leyba praised Clark gushingly, declaring that he "deserves the greatest courtesy from all the inhabitants of his district since they are debtors to him for his pleasant manner, clemency, and upright administration of justice. Although his soldiers are bandits in appearance, he has them under the best of control."[40] How the residents of St. Louis reacted to the sight of badly clad Americans in their midst is unknown. But the seeming lawlessness and wildness of the Americans' self-presentation, Leyba implicitly argued, was in direct contrast to their civilized, disciplined behavior. Perhaps such admirable conduct lent additional justification to the Spanish decision to aid the "the Bostoneses."[41]

The initial good impression Leyba and Clark made on each other as well as the friendliness of their relationship deepened over time. In one note, Clark asked to be especially remembered to his "two favourites," Leyba's young daughters.[42] Leyba felt so in tune with Clark that he told a superior they were in harmony. Not entirely naïve, Leyba suspected that Clark had received instructions similar to his own with regard to maintaining friendly relations across the Mississippi. In a gesture likely designed to reassure Leyba of his appreciation, Clark let Leyba see a copy of a letter he wrote to Congress, "in which he expresse[ed] himself as proud and pleased at the fine reception he had been given by the Spanish commandant of this district."[43]

Clark's visit and the developing friendship between the two men was a highlight of Leyba's first few months in office, a period otherwise occupied with the challenges presented by large numbers of Indian guests and a host of related difficulties connected to trade on the Missouri. Almost immediately after his arrival, Leyba reconfigured the commerce of the Missouri, dividing it "up into small shares, thereby filling many needs." Rather pleased with his own initative, Leyba reported that his actions "appear to have greatly pleased the public, with the expection of those who, although not totally deprived of a share, expected a larger one."[44] In early August, "before all the traders and hunters for the Missouri and tributary streams,"

39. Leyba to Gálvez, July 11, 1778, in Kinnaird, "Clark-Leyba Papers," 95.
40. Leyba to Gálvez, July 21, 1778, in ibid., 98.
41. Leyba to Gálvez, August 6, 1778, in ibid., 99.
42. Clark to Leyba, October 26, 1778, in ibid., 100.
43. Clark to Leyba, November 16, 1778, in ibid., 102.
44. Leyba to Gálvez, July 21, 1778, AGI-PC 2358, in Kinnaird, *SMV,* 1: 299.

he reiterated the government's prohibition of the Indian slave trade and announced the penalties for violating that order or any other regarding the places they were allowed to trade: confiscation of pelts and merchandise, as well as "exemplary punishment."[45] From the beginning, it seems, Leyba's relations with the local community were fraught, and his judgment and actions were called into question more than once.

Given the pivotal role he played in St. Louis, as not only the king's ranking representative but as the official who heard civil and criminal cases and dispensed justice, Leyba had no choice but to listen to the wishes and opinions of those under his command, even if he sometimes disregarded them. Villagers' complaints did prompt one of Leyba's earliest punitive actions. In early August 1778, trying to appease the populace (and perhaps suit himself in the process), he sought the governor's permission to expel Joseph Piernas, the troublemaking soldier who accompanied him from New Orleans, from St. Louis. Residents had "been insulted and badly counseled every day" by the Spaniard, as reflected in the complaint Leyba sent south, and he wanted Piernas gone.[46] Unfortunately for Leyba and the other inhabitants, the recently arrived Piernas was far from the only source of disorder and conflict in the community.

On the night of September 21, 1778, Leyba's household and the village's tranquillity were disturbed by a domestic dispute. Marie Anne Laferme, wife of Gaspard Roubien, fled to Leyba's residence in the middle of the night, desperately seeking refuge from her violent and drunken husband. According to her account, Roubien, after spending some hours tippling elsewhere in the village, had returned home to drink some more. Damning his wife, swearing at her, "and calling her by vile and foul names too indecent to repeat," Roubien grew incensed when she objected to his language. As she recalled the next day, "this enraged him" to such an extent "that he gave her a violent blow in the face with his fist." Witnessing the assault, her oldest daughter, the offspring of her marriage to Auguste Condé, a wealthy doctor who had died two years before, sprang to her mother's defense. For trying to protect her mother, the girl "received a violent box on the side of her face." Roubien called his stepdaughter terrible names as well. Becoming "transported with rage," Roubien seized a thick stick that stood near the bed, prompting his wife and daughter to scream loudly. To their great relief, their enslaved mulatto woman forced open the door, providing a chance for Laferme to flee. Running through the village streets clad only in her petticoat and accompanied by her slave,

45. Labuniere v. Beaudoin, February 23, 1779, box 1, folder 4, Litigation Collection, MHMA.
46. Leyba to Bernardo de Gálvez, August 6, 1778, AGI-PC 1, in Kinnaird, *SMV*, 1: 302.

Madame Roubien made her escape, hurrying to the government house for sanctuary.[47]

Soldiers and officers responded quickly to Madame Roubien's sudden and disheveled appearance. Private Antonio Steffanelli, the soldier standing watch, saw her approach the guard house sometime after 11 p.m. and asked her why she came "at that unseasonable hour." She said she needed to see the commandant, because "her life had been sought while in bed."[48] Unwilling to wake Leyba, Steffanelli roused Sergeant Diego Blanco instead. Going to the guard house, Blanco found Madame Roubien in tears, stating that her husband had come home drunk, had beaten her, and that she had come for protection. Her husband was breaking and destroying things when she left, and she begged the guard to send someone to collect her two daughters. Blanco summoned Leyba's mulatto slave woman, Marianne, to escort Madame Roubien upstairs to the government hall.[49] Marianne found Madame Roubien crying and asking to speak to Leyba, and so escorted her to the Leyba's bedchamber and knocked at the door. "Who is there?" asked Madame Leyba. When she learned the visitor's identity, Madame Leyba ordered Marianne to make up a bed for Madame Roubien in another room and "not to disturb the commandant at that unseasonable hour." Lying down, Madame Roubien implored Marianne to get her daughters out of the house and away from their stepfather.[50] Blanco then dispatched Marianne and a soldier, Pierre Rebouil, to the home.[51] It was Marianne who called Rebouil, telling him that Madame Roubien said her husband "desired to take her life," and feared that he might beat her daughters. Arriving at the house, the two emissaries found Monsieur Roubien pacing the gallery. He cried out, "Who is there, a negro?" When Rebouil identified himself, Roubien said, "The women have too much tongue." (Whether Roubien objected to his wife rebuking him or saw her flight to the government house as an unwarranted betrayal or act of petty treason is unknown; clearly, he wanted her silent.) On returning to the government house, the Condé sisters in tow, Rebouil found the girls' mother weeping, repeating "that her husband would kill her."[52]

Although Roubien did not oppose the removal of his stepdaughters from the house, he remained agitated and came to the government house himself about an hour later. Steffanelli, still on duty, reported his conduct, noting

47. Petition of Marie Anne Laferme, September 22, 1778, Billon Collection, MHMA.
48. Antonio Steffanelli testimony, September 22, 1778, Billon Collection, MHMA.
49. Diego Blanco testimony, September 22, 1778, Billon Collection, MHMA.
50. Marianne testimony, September 22, 1778, Billon Collection, MHMA.
51. Diego Blanco testimony, September 22, 1778, Billon Collection, MHMA.
52. Pierre Rebouil testimony, September 22, 1778, Billon Collection, MHMA.

that "he appeared to be slightly inebriated." Roubien asked whether "the governor had strangers at his house this night," to which the private said he gave the noncommittal response that he "did not know."[53] Roubien left without obtaining satisfaction, and his wife and her daughters spent an undisturbed, if not restful night, in the Leyba household. Madame Roubien "cried nearly all night, complaining that her husband led a disorderly life which was continual."[54] Early the next morning, Madame Roubien and her daughters left the government house without saying where they were going and went to the home of merchant Louis Debreuil. There, they let themselves in and took seats in the parlor. When he arose at 6 a.m., Debreuil was surprised to find the intruders and for a moment did not even recognize Madame Roubien, whose head was wrapped in a handkerchief. "Is that you, Madame?" he asked, "What troubles you?" She replied, "The wretch has almost killed me." Showing him her face, she said, "See how he has fixed me." Observing that "one side of her face was black and blue," Debreuil told her to go with him into the room where his wife was and tell them both the story.[55]

At this point, Leyba became directly involved. Whether the comings and goings in his household has disturbed his slumber is unknown, but he did, the next morning, see Madame Roubien in an official context, when she appeared before him to state her complaint. Bruised and clearly fearful, Madame Roubien told the lieutenant governor that she would no longer live with her spouse; she said that her life was in danger and her property and that of her daughters was being squandered. If not stopped, her husband's spending would reduce her "to a bed of straw." To protect her person and her estate, Madame Roubien asked Leyba for a legal separation from her abuser and urged his banishment.[56] After listening to her account, Leyba instructed Labuscière to prepare a petition for her, called for Dr. Antoine Reynal to examine her, and ordered her alleged assailant thrown into jail.

In a detailed deposition, which was read aloud to her for confirmation, Madame Roubien described "the cruel treatment" she had endured "since the unfortunate day of her marriage." The account she gave presented a grim picture of a violent, abusive relationship. A year earlier, she began, she had "the ill fortune to enter into a second marriage with Mr. Gaspard Roubien." Since that time, she had "received from him the most grievous and shameful

53. Antonio Steffanelli testimony, September 22, 1778, Billon Collection, MHMA.
54. Marianne testimony, September 22, 1778, Billon Collection, MHMA.
55. Louis Debreuil testimony, September 22, 1778, Billon Collection, MHMA.
56. Ibid.

treatment that any husband could inflict on his wife." The outrageous and scandalous terms he used, well known to the public, could not be repeated. Abusive language was not her only grievance: "in the moments of his furious passion," he had "inflicted on her bodily injury by blows with his fists and cane, that on several occasions required the interference of her slaves to protect her." She had borne his treatment as long as she could, but his excesses grew daily, and she saw, with pain, that he was wasting her property and that of her daughters, "in a manner unknown to her, but doubtless in dissipation." She feared that he would leave her and her daughters "in frightful poverty." Only by "flying from her home with the help of her slaves, and in seeking a refuge for the night, under the sacred roof" of the government house, had "she escaped the last excess of his fury."[57]

Money was not an insignificant part of this case. Madame Roubien had been a very wealthy widow when she and Monsieur Roubien wed.[58] Not only was Gaspard Roubien depleting the property, he had brought no riches to the marriage in the first place. Madame Roubien suggested that were he inclined to reflection, her husband "would remember that he entered this house with nothing but what he had on his back." With proper conduct, he might "have found a happy home, with limited means, which was a fortune to him." Instead, his "fury and evil designs," the practices of a money-grubbing, violent man, threatened "her life, her means, and those of her children."[59]

It seems the domestic nature of this dispute led to the qualified support Madame Roubien received and may indeed have contributed to her dropping the case. When Madame Roubien appeared a second time before Leyba, accompained by Debreuil and l'Ami, her uncle, she listened to her words being read aloud a second time, and confirmed their truth. At this point, Debrueil felt compelled to interrupt the proceedings. Addressing Leyba, he said, "As to myself, Sir, I tell her in your presence, that I do not intermeddle in these disputes of her husband and herself." Domestic squabbles and spousal abuse were none of his concern. Rather, he was "only

57. Petition of Marie Ann Laferme, September 22, 1778, Billon Collection, MHMA.

58. Estate inventory of Auguste Condé, October 28, 1777, Instrument #1410. A prominent and wealthy member of the community, Dr. Condé was creditor to many St. Louisans at his death. See also the marriage contract of Marie Ann Laferme and Gaspard Roubien, September 19, 1777, Instrument #2044. On settling the Condé estate, see Instruments #1815, #1815-B-C-D, June 9, 1779 (all St. Louis Archives, MHMA).

59. Petition of Marie Ann Laferme, September 22, 1778, Billon Collection, MHMA. As it turned out, this was not the first time that the domestic discord of the Laferme-Roubien household had come to public attention. A month earlier, on a Sunday, the parish curate, Father Bernard, "was obliged to go over there to settle a quarrel between the husband and wife." Antonio Steffanelli testimony, September 22, 1778, Billon Collection, MHMA.

interested on account of her daughters as their relatives, her oldest daughter feeling herself grievously insulted, her reputation being attacked."[60] Dr. Reynal's report of his examination seems to have minimized the violence of the assault as well, noting "but one slight bruise, which was discolored of about an inch and a half in diameter," and no signs of injury on her daughter. Before the day was out, Madame Roubien had dropped her petition for separation from her husband, with its request for his expulsion from the village. At the bottom of her petition was written, "After the case had proceeded so far, an accommodation was brought about on the same day." Under its terms, Madame Roubien consented to the appointment of a new guardian for her minor daughter, in place of herself, which removed the girl from her husband's reach; he made no immediate opposition to the arrangement.[61] (Years later, Roubien was in court again, wrangling with his stepdaughter Constance Condé's guardians, Louis Debreuil and Charles Sanguinet, over financial matters and fending off a new accusation of physical abuse.)[62]

What does this incident tell us about colonial St. Louis? In in the late 1770s, village households were permeable and accessible. Neighbors overheard and observed what went on, and domestic discord did not go unnoticed. Madame Roubien did not hesitate to enter the presumably unlocked door of the Debreuil residence, her slave responded to her cries for help, and Corporal Hortiz and another man overheard from across the street "all the infamous words which her husband had applied to her oldest daughter."[63] The apparatus of the law was available as a recourse, but Madame Roubien's decision to withdraw her petition raises questions about how fully she enjoyed the support of male friends and relatives. Also striking in the case are the roles of two enslaved women: one who helped Madame Roubien escape her husband's blows and accompanied her to the government house and another who was sent to the scene of violence. These women appear to have moved about the streets of the village at night easily and to have acted as important go-betweens and defenders of Madame Roubien. Finally, there is no indication that Gaspard Roubien suffered any repercussions from this or other acts of abuse besides the few hours he spent in the village jail.[64]

60. Louis Debreuil testimony, September 22, 1778, Billon Collection, MHMA.

61. Petition of Marie Ann Laferme, September 22, 1778, Billon Collection, MHMA.

62. Gaspard Roubien petition, October 23, 1786, Litigation Collection, box 2, folder 2, MHMA.

63. Petition of Marie Ann Laferme, September 22, 1778, Billon Collection, MHMA.

64. Interestingly, Roubien served as an estate arbitrator in a domestic dispute case in 1789, when Maria Genevieve Catoise and François Barrere successfully petitioned for a separation agreement.

While Leyba's role in this unhappy situation came to an end with Madame Roubien's decision to withdraw her petition, he was not free from mediating or addressing the disputes of villagers for long. Only a couple of weeks after Madame Roubien came to Leyba to make and then retract her complaint, Leyba was witness to other signs of discontent as a number of St. Louisans put in similar appearances before him in the government hall when they decided to bring their neighbors to court over squabbles large and small. In October 1778, Joseph Marchetaud Denoyer and Claude Tinon sued and countersued each other over a land deal gone wrong. When Denoyer discovered the land he had purchased in St. Louis belonged to someone other than Tinon, who had moved a couple of miles to nearby Carondelet, he demanded the return of the cow with which he had paid for the lot. Tinon denied the claim that he had not been the rightful owner, accusing Denoyer of being a stingy and lazy man, whose neglect of the property prompted its reversion to the government. Leyba found in Tinon's favor.[65]

Disgruntled villagers abounded, as Leyba discovered the next month, when he learned that several men coveted the position of sublieutenant of the militia. After he appointed fellow Spaniard and merchant Benito Vasquez to the post, another member of the militia, Pierre Montardy, requested a discharge from his duties, feeling passed over by Vasquez' promotion. Montardy had served as a sergeant in France and had held the same rank in the St. Louis militia since the Spanish had arrived. Now, he was being snubbed because Leyba preferred a man whom Montardy thought "had no other merits than that of having ben a private soldier and a servant of Don Pedro Piernas." Sounding exasperated, Leyba noted, "I afterwards learned that there were others who had their eyes on the post, but I have pacified them all, telling them not to lose hope." Perhaps Leyba's selection of one of the few Spaniards in an overwhelmingly French community added to the insult. To assuage the desire for titles, Leyba came up with a plan: with the governor's permission, he would split the militia into two companies and thereby create openings for additional officers.[66] Blundering unintentionally, whether through favoritism to a fellow countryman or insensitivity to long-standing rivalries or power dynamics, Leyba was alienating villagers as well as trying, when a solution suggested itself, to make amends.

Married in 1775 in New Orleans and soon thereafter moving to St. Louis, the couple requested to separate and end their property ties to avoid "daily quarrels, and to spend the remainder of their days in peace, and to procure the salvation of their souls, which they cannot do peaceably, living together." Billon, *Annals of St. Louis*, 251–52.

65. Testimony from Tinon v. Denoyer, October 1778, in ibid., 151–54.

66. Leyba to Gálvez, November 16, 1778, in Kinnaird, *SMV*, 1: 314–15.

Part of the challenge Leyba faced in St. Louis was, in his view, intrinsic to the character and conduct of the people. While the area itself was promising—"There is not a soil in this country which is not suitable for all kinds of crops, and there are many square leagues of beautiful meadows on these heights"—the people were problematic. Echoing a refrain first voiced by Pedro Piernas in the late 1760s, Leyba declared the settlers were "interested only in trading with the Indians" and so neglected their farming. "All are, or wish to be merchants," he pronounced, a desire that had several negative consequences. As the ranking official, he was inundated with requests for trading permits for the Missouri River. "As it is impossible to satisfy them all, it is impossible not to make some enemies," he confessed. Because so few farmed, there was always a scarcity of food in St. Louis. Perhaps even worse for Leyba, "the classes of people are so mixed up that one cannot tell who is a farmer and who is a merchant." Leyba seemed altogether at sea in dealing with the residents of St. Louis, making mistakes and enemies at every turn as he attempted to exercise his judgment and administer justice. The solutions Leyba proposed were all expensive: establish a garrison of 800 men in order to create a good market for flour that would inspire villagers to turn to cultivation, or send large numbers of black slaves to St. Louis to encourage their future owners, the *habitants,* to pursue hemp production. Only self-interest, he believed, would motivate the people to turn from commerce to cultivation.[67]

Law and order deteriorated further in the fall of 1778, when the village suffered a spate of thefts of foodstuffs and other property. Whether a lack of provisions contributed to this crime wave is unknown, but one thing is recorded: Leyba's response. In December 1778, after receiving complaints from villagers that vegetables and fruits had been stolen from their gardens, cattle from their pens, and boats from the banks of the river, Leyba decided, "in order to stop this (long standing) disorder, to place a pillory with collar" in front of the government house, the building where he lodged and dispensed justice. His goal, he informed the governor, was "to expose to public shame anyone caught in such crimes." To deter crime and seize malefactors to place in the pillory, Leyba ordered a nightly patrol to roam the village. "Perhaps these precautions or the threat of punishment alone will be sufficient to restrain the miscreants," he predicted, "as nobody has complained to me since they have been taken."[68] While no one may have complained to him of new thefts, one can easily imagine St. Louisans grumbling to each other about the new lieutenant governor. Authoritarian in the measures he

67. Leyba to Gálvez, November 16, 1778, in ibid., 312–13.
68. Leyba to Bernardo de Gálvez, December 9, 1778, in ibid., 316.

deployed to deter misconduct and seemingly arbitrary in matters of prefer-
ment, he was willing to make an example out of those he punished and
publically humiliate those under his rule. The sight of the pillory in front
of the government house may have served to remind passersby of the power
of the state, and therefore of Leyba, to treat people's bodies with violence
and their dignity with impunity. When the governor received word in New
Orleans of Leyba's innovation, he promptly countermanded it, declaring
that the lieutenant governor had gone too far with the nightly patrols, pillory, and iron collar. "I must tell you that this punishment is too terrible for
such a minor offense," Gálvez wrote. Payments and fines for damages done
should suffice, with the collar resorted to "only for grave deeds or crimes."[69]
Whether some colonists were disappointed to see the pillory taken away is
unknown; it seems likely that some might have seen its removal as another
sign of Leyba's arbitrariness or inconsistency.

Soon after adopting the pillory as a preventitive measure, Leyba saw
the threat of violence come to the village with the return in late 1778
of an Indian man, Louis Mahas, a troublesome, occasional member of the
community. Mahas, a free Indian, had been at the center of several conflicts, beginning with a bizarre shooting a few years earlier. Unable to date
the incident exactly, a witness thought it took place around the time that
Cruzat arrived in St. Louis in the spring of 1775. One morning around 8
a.m., Mahas was passing by Joseph Mainville's home, where, without any
apparent provocation, he aimed his gun at a cow in the yard and shot it.
The bullet passed through the cow, which fell over dead, and narrowly
missed hitting an enslaved black woman standing nearby. When she asked
Mahas why he fired his weapon at the cow and thus at her, he responded
only that he had done it for his pleasure and that he would pay for the dead
animal. Despite Mainville's enlistment of officials in pursuit of damages for
the destruction of his livestock, Mahas made no reparations before leaving
the village.[70] On another occasion a couple of years later, Mahas was back
in St. Louis and attacked a soldier. Angel Izquierdo, a member of the garrison, recalled going out around seven in the evening and seeing Mahas,
tomahawk in hand, stopped near a building that served as a mill. "As soon
as he saw me," remembered Izquierdo, "he ran toward me and gave me a
blow with the tomahawk that I parried with a stick." Managing to disarm
Mahas, Izquierdo hit the Indian on his left arm, leaving a permanent mark.
In testifying about the incident, the soldier recreated the conversation that

69. Bernardo de Gálvez to Leyba, March 9, 1779, in ibid., 330.
70. Joseph Mainville Deschesnes testimony, January 2, 1779, Litigation Collection, box 1, folder
3, MHMA.

ensued: "Mahas said to me, 'You hurt me.' I answered him 'Why are you attacking me? You were asking for it.'" In response, Mahas purportedly said, "'That's true, I was wrong,'" and left without another word.[71]

In the latest incident, in December 1778, Mahas had been apprehended outside of the village, near the Illinois River, where François Villet, a hunter, had encountered him near an encampment of other French hunters. As testified to in Villet's report, Mahas had grabbed Villet's rifle, announcing that he wanted to kill some Frenchmen, and fired a shot. By blocking the rifle, Villet prevented any injury, and he decided to preempt other attempts by tying Mahas up, securing the aid of other hunters to do so. The next day, after Mahas untied himself, the two returned together to St. Louis, where Mahas stayed at Villet's home; why Villet allowed someone he considered violent and dangerous to travel and stay with him is unknown. Once in St. Louis, Mahas let down his braid, telling his host that he had dressed in the French way for a long time but would henceforth dress as a warrior and do his hair accordingly. Alarmed, Villet feared for the residents of St. Louis and urged Leyba to expel Mahas from the village.[72] He was joined in this request by several others, including Labuscière and Sylvestre Labbadie, who petitioned Leyba to banish Mahas. From their perspective, Mahas was a walking source of disorder and danger inappropriate for the village confines. A former slave, Mahas had lived in and around St. Louis for six or seven years, accused of crimes including stealing, running off cattle, debauching slaves with alcohol, insulting residents, and threatening to take French and Spanish scalps. The petitioners wanted the man gone, "for the peace and safety of our people."[73]

As 1779 dawned, in response to the request of leading citizens that he expel the unwelcome Indian, Leyba had Mahas thrown in jail and ordered an investigation, which uncovered a history of violence. A parade of villagers came through the government house, presenting their stories as Leyba sat and listened. On January 1, 1779, the first villager to testify swore that Mahas, when a slave in Canada, had been sold to an English merchant whom he had killed before fleeing south to St. Louis.[74] After hearing that testimony, as well as accounts of Mahas's earlier visits to St. Louis, Leyba not only banished the Indian man from the village forever but ordered that he be sent to the capital to be dealt with by the governor.[75] Mahas's

71. Angel Izquierdo testimony, January 2, 1779, Litigation Collection, box 1, folder 3, MHMA.

72. François Villet testimony, January 2, 1779, Litigation Collection, box 1, folder 1, MHMA.

73. Petition of Joseph Labuscière, Silvestre Labadie, and François Bonrozier to Leyba, December 30, 1778, Litigation Collection, box 1, folder 3, MHMA.

74. Noel Langois testimony, January 1, 1779, Litigation Collection, box 1, folder 3, MHMA.

75. Leyba sentence, January 3, 1779, Litigation Collection, box 1, folder 3, MHMA.

belongings were inventoried, revealing a small stock of bear butter, a knife, a rifle, a number of pelts, and almost one hundred pounds of meat; the contents of a straw bag in his possession, described intriguingly as full of various knickknacks of Indians, are unknown.[76] If Mahas had been sent quickly to New Orleans, that might have ended the case as far as St. Louisans were concerned. But while Mahas was imprisoned in the village jail, he managed to file off the iron shackles on his feet, make a hole at the bottom of the wall, and escape.[77] When Leyba learned of the flight from Sergeant Diego Blanco, he went to examine the cell himself but learned nothing of any use. Mahas was never apprehended.[78]

Only a few days before Mahas fled the village jail in late January 1779, violence came directly into Leyba's home when Marianne, an enslaved black woman who was a member of his household, was assaulted by the enslaved mulatto woman Lorine, who belonged to Gaspard Roubien. A third woman, a mulatto slave named Louison, was also involved. The incident provoked an unusual legal proceeding, with Leyba recusing himself from hearing the case on the grounds of his relationship to the victim. Several enslaved women were called as witnesses to what transpired. Each had to receive explicit, written, signed permission from her owner before she could give a deposition, and each had to raise her right hand, make the sign of the cross, and swear to God and promise to the king that she would speak the truth. According to these women's testimony, an ordinary social interaction had turned violent. The scene they sketched was as follows.

On the morning of January 21, 1779, with the weather freezing, Marianne had gone to do the Leyba family's washing at the *Rivière du Moulin,* or Mill Creek. Laundering her items in a hole cut in the ice, she talked with some other enslaved women from the village who were similarly engaged. Fanchon, a black slave woman belonging to Widow Dodier, said that Marianne had exchanged some words with Louison, apparently wanting to do her wash at the spot Louison occupied. As tension between the two women grew, heated words were soon followed by blows, and the women slapped each other in the face. Roubien's slave Lorine approached Marianne, said something to her, and began to hit her. Although Marianne fought back, Lorine, "being the strongest," threw Marianne "into the water and would have drowned her, if she, the deponent [Fanchon] had not gotten her out." Still spoiling for a fight, Lorine went after Marianne, striking her again and throwing her into the fire the women kept to warm themselves. By her own account, Fanchon

76. Inventory of Louis Mahas, January 23, 1779, Litigation Collection, box 1, folder 3, MHMA.
77. Billon, *Annals of St. Louis,* 158; Mahas case, January 27, 1779, Litigation Collection, box 1, folder 3, MHMA.
78. Mahas case, January 27, 1779, Litigation Collection, box 1, folder 3, MHMA.

intervened again, extricating Marianne from the flames and pulling Lorine off of her.[79] Next to testify was Melanie, a black slave woman belonging to Father Limpach, whose statement largely confirmed Fanchon's, including her role as Marianne's rescuer. In response to questioning, Melanie said she had no knowledge of any previous problems between the two.

One white villager also testified, a fourteen-year-old boy, Joseph Coté. Like the enslaved women, he, as a minor, had to have the permission of another, in this case his father, François Coté, before he could speak to the court. He had been sent to the *Rivière du Moulin* to heat up water for Fanchon and witnessed Louison and Marianne exchanging slaps and addressing each other with "injurious words." He said that Lorine, laundering a short distance away, got up and attacked Marianne. When Marianne tried to defend herself, Lorine upped the assault, throwing Marianne into the water and then into the fire, "where she gave her several blows on the stomach and on the head." The boy said he saw Fanchon pull Marianne from the blaze "with burning skirts," and then Marianne left, heading back to the village in tears.[80]

With several witnesses corrobating the attack, de Volsey, who was hearing the case in lieu of Leyba, ordered the surgeon, Dr. Reynal, to examine Marianne. Having gone to the government house and been escorted to a bedroom to see her, the doctor offered a grim report: he found Marianne in bed and gravely ill from the assault, burning with fever, bruised, and complaining of pain in her side and elsewhere. Somewhat qualifying his remarks, he testified that the color of her skin made it difficult to observe any other than one main contusion. Given, however, that she was suffering from a fever and spitting up blood, Reynal treated her according to standard medical practices of the day, by bleeding her in the foot. Although that treatment had not alleviated her pain or fever, Reynal expected that she would recover fully. His assessment made clear that there was no question that a violent assault had occurred and that a member of the lieutenant governor's household had been seriously affected.[81]

Whether the punishment meted out reflected the injuries Marianne suffered or the potential financial loss to her owner is not clear. As Lorine's masters, Gaspard Roubien and his wife Marie Anne Laferme, only a few months before involved in an assault case of their own, were held responsible for all legal costs as well as for the physician's bill for caring for Marianne, from "the moment of his first examination until the day of her complete recovery." For Lorine, without any financial resources of her own,

79. Fanchon testimony, January 23, 1779, Litigation Collection, box 1, folder 2, MHMA.
80. Joseph Coté testimony, January 23, 1779, Litigation Collection, box 1, folder 2, MHMA.
81. Antoine Reynal testimony, January 23, 1779, Litigation collection, box 1, folder 2, MHMA.

the guilty sentence meant corporal punishment. De Volsey ordered 100 lashes with a whip, fifty to be administered at four that afternoon in the village square and fifty more at the same time and place on the following day. He further prohibited Lorine from committing a second offense toward either Marianne or anyone else, "either by bad words or acts of violence under pain of a more severe punishment."[82]

The link between Lorine v. Marianne and the domestic abuse case of the Roubiens is only part of what is interesting about this incident. In the first place, it is difficult not to wonder whether Lorine was also battered by the wife-beater Roubien and whether the culture of violence to which she was exposed did not influence her to perpetrate a physical assault herself. She and Marianne had certainly interacted before, as on the night when she helped Madame Roubien flee to the government house where Marianne lived and labored. Without a doubt, slavery bred brutality, and indeed was a system of institutionalized, legally protected violence. The previous lieutenant governor, Francisco Cruzat, could write with no apparent sense of the injustice he was perpetrating, that he had sold one slave in hopes of obtaining a replacement who would not require harsh treatment in order to serve well, one whom Cruzat would not need to "order about and whip all the time, which [he] absolutely detest[ed]."[83]

Secondly, the disparity in the punishments accorded Lorine and Gaspard Roubien for assaults on women in the village is striking. Lorine was likely stripped to the waist before being publicly whipped, receiving a brutal hundred lashes over the course of two freezing January days. In contrast, Monsieur Roubien escaped any physical or financial repercussions for his violent behavior. The comparison underlines both the vulnerability of enslaved women and married women before the law, and their analogous status as subject to the will of their masters, or, as the French noted of the relationship between husband and wife, *le mari est seigneur*—the husband is lord. Finally, as in the Roubien case, one gets a sense of the enslaved women of St. Louis moving about the village unsupervised and independently as they went about their labors and followed their masters' orders, both day and night. A final irony is the role of Pierre François de Volsey, as cavalier of the royal and military order of St. Louis and adjunct captain of the infantry, assuming Leyba's place. Only a few weeks later, he was at the center of a complicated and contested domestic abuse case himself, responding to his wife's accusations of long-standing mistreatment with counteraccusations of her infidelity.

82. De Volsey sentence in case of Marianne v. Lorine, January 23, 1779, box 1, folder 2, Litigation Collection, MHMA.

83. Cruzat to Vallé, November 11, 1776, quoted in Ekberg, *Colonial Ste. Genevieve,* 220.

Violence against and disputes about property rather than persons prompted other contentious cases in St. Louis. Several weeks after Lorine's attack and Mahas's escape, in early March 1779, Sylvestre Labbadie took his neighbor Alexis Marié to court, suing him for encroaching on his land and destroying fruit trees on it. The property dispute developed when Marié tried to claim property he believed to be his, a strip of land that neither of the lot's previous owners had used, on which Labbadie had planted an orchard. When Labbadie objected, Marié moved back his fence and took out the trees, claiming them as his own. A villager overheard Labbadie declare the trees worthless and say that he could do whatever he wanted to with them. Given that testimony and other depositions, Leyba pronounced Labbadie's case against Marié unfounded and ordered him to pay the expenses of the trial.[84]

Despite losing that case, Labbadie did not hestitate to bring another suit several weeks later, this time joined by his brother-in-law Auguste Chouteau, against three men they accused of infringing illegally on their trading rights with the Oto Indians. Given the plaintiffs' standing in the community, it is perhaps not surprising that Leyba did as they wished, ordering the seizure of the defendants' pelts. When the case went against Labbadie and Chouteau, however, Leyba had the other traders' goods returned to them.[85] On another occasion that year, Auguste Chouteau turned to the court for redress, trying to prevent his fellow villagers from fishing in the pond by his mill. Having recently purchased both the mill and the pond, he objected to others presuming to fish in it. Chouteau believed that their actions mocked "the customs and laws, which consider the fish in a pond to be immobile and attached to the place, and properly belonging to the owner." With no such law in effect, Leyba did not hesitate to rely in this case, as he had in others, on custom. Other residents, "trustworthy people," informed him that fishing in the pond had "always been common to all the residents." Given that long-standing practice, Leyba denied Chouteau's petition.[86] While such apparent impartiality in these cases was no doubt appreciated by some, the decisions did not signal a dramatic change in Leyba's reputation.

The destruction of the trees and the language that prompted it in the Marié-Labbadie case suggested that speech could be as injurious to

---

84. Marié v. Labbadie, March 6, 8, 10, 1779, Litigation Collection, box 1, folder 6, MHMA.

85. Labbadie and Chouteau v. François Larche, Pierre LeCompete, and Jean-Baptiste Duchesne, June–July 1779, Litigation Collection, box 1, folder 11, MHMA.

86. Chouteau and Leyba, quoted in Banner, *Legal Systems in Conflict*, 62–63.

villagers' hopes and reputations as acts of overt violence could be to their lives, and Leyba was called upon repeatedly to adjudicate such matters, as in the quarrel between Mesdames Montardy and Denoyer, discussed earlier, and the case of Joseph Robidou. In the Robidou affair, damaging speech that described violent acts was at the heart of the matter. In January 1780, Joseph Robidou sued Louis Robert and Luc Marly for damaging his reputation by spreading unfounded rumors about him. The problems emerged after Robidou, a newcomer from Canada, asked for permission to marry the young woman he had been courting, Mademoiselle Bequet, daughter of the village blacksmith. The father asked for three days to consider the young man's request, and Robidou was surprised when he was refused approval. Monsieur Bequet had heard reports that there were some in Robidou's family "who had sold their souls to the devil."[87] The news came to him from a relative who suggested Bequet needed "to pay attention to this alliance, to know where this Robidou comes from, as it is usually done."

The rumors in circulation were shocking: that Robidou's uncle in Canada had murdered both his wife and his employer and had fled to Cahokia, where he had kidnapped another man's wife and absconded with her to the post of Vincennes, and that other relations had desecrated an image of Christ. Outraged, flabbergasted, and seeking redress, Robidou demanded that his accusers substantiate their charges. Leyba asked Robidou and the rumormongers to produce character references and proof of their accusations. Before long, fifteen men on both sides of the Mississippi had provided sworn testimony as to the conduct of the Robidou family. While seven men asserted that the Robidous were an honest family, eight attested to members of the family having committed crimes. In addition to the charge of spousal homicide, about which one man claimed to have credible knowledge, there were descriptions of gross acts of profanity and sacrilege.[88] Several suggested that knowledge of the Robidous' outrageous behavior was widespread in Canada and had been the recent subject of a priest's pulpit commentary in Fort Chartres.[89] Purportedly, Charles and François Robidou, accomplices in a heinous crime, had fled their home, leaving behind the burning remains of a crushed Christ in the fire.[90] Two other

87. Joseph Robidou testimony, January 28, 1780, Litigation Collection, box 1, folder 15, MHMA.

88. Pierre Borgne St. Belfeu testimony, January 28, 1780, Litigation Collection, box 1, folder 15, MHMA.

89. Luc Marly testimony, January 31, 1780, Litigation Collection, box 1, folder 15, MHMA.

90. Michel Godimière testimony, January 30, 1780, Litigation Collection, box 1, folder 15, MHMA.

deponents had heard of a deadly assault case involving a Jacques Robidou near Milwaukee.[91] While such statements could only have further upset the spurned suitor, they were not proof of his family's guilt. With all the testimony in hand in early February 1780, Leyba concluded that the statements produced by both sides canceled each other out, making it impossible for him to determine their truth; he could not pronounce a judgment. In the short term, he imposed silence on the parties involved but allowed Robidou a year to obtain proof from "authentic documents from the clerk's office and the archives of Canada, fully and duly legalized," in order to clear his family name.[92]

While all these suits, instances of mutual recrimination, acts of violence, and public conflicts were paraded before Leyba as he sat in the government house and listened to the villagers' complaints, external crises and difficulties were affecting the community as well. Repeatedly, Leyba attempted to deal with problems in trade and shortages of presents, both issues exacerbated by the international conflict among European powers and the war engulfing the East Coast. In October 1779, Leyba complained that he had received no presents that year, that he had distributed all he had, and that, as a result, there remained "nothing of this kind for next year."[93] As it turned out, the New Orleans merchant responsible, Maxent, was away on a military expedition in Florida, and so had failed to send any goods to Leyba (the second year in a row he had failed to provide Leyba with the presents he needed). On learning the news, the governor contacted Madame Maxent to act in her husband's stead to send the requisite presents for the Indians to St. Louis as soon as possible.[94]

Closer to home, Leyba's temporary solution to the shortage of presents caused discord among the traders and engendered hostility and criticism toward him. So that he would have something to distribute to visiting Indians, Leyba permitted five traders "to bring in some goods from the other side," which remedied the immediate problem. Because the goods were very expensive, Leyba tried to enable the merchants to make some profit by granting them permits to trade with the Indians. "For this reason I have not," he informed the governor, "made a wide

91. François Chevalier and Joseph Deloge testimony, January 30, 1780, Litigation Collection, box 1, folder 15, MHMA.

92. Leyba, February 2, 1780, Litigation Collection, box 1, folder 15, MHMA.

93. Leyba to Bernardo de Gálvez, October 28, 1779, no. 365, AGI-PC 1, in Kinnaird, *SMV,* 1: 361.

94. Bernardo de Gálvez to Leyba, draft response accompanying Leyba to Bernardo de Gálvez, February 19, 1780, no. 365, AGI-PC 1, in Kinnaird, *SMV,* 1: 361.

distribution of permits."[95] What seemed like a sensible decision in his mind only served to antagonize other men of commerce in the village. One disgruntled trader, Jean Baptiste Martigny, whom Leyba denied a permit, protested that the lieutenant governor gave trading licenses only to those merchants who could afford to pay him "a considerable sum," with the result that all the lucrative posts along the Missouri had gone to Auguste Chouteau, Sylvestre Labbadie, and Gabriel Cerré.[96] (Trade with the Indians was greater in 1779 than it had been in previous years, with Chouteau and several other St. Louis merchants acquiring enormous quantities of furs.)[97]

The next week, on All Saints' Day, another trade-related dispute arose in the village, when a rogue trader from the American side, Joseph Buteau, was found selling rum in violation of government orders. Traveling on the Cuivre River north of St. Louis, Buteau had been discovered with a canoe full of goods, including flour, pelts, tobacco, and several barrels of rum; they were seized while he managed to escape. On November 7, at Leyba's orders, village bailiff François Demers went to the church door, where he proceeded "in a loud and intelligible voice and by public proclamation" to summon Buteau to appear in the village, answer the accusations against him, and begin serving a sentence in the prison.[98] Not too surprisingly, Buteau did not step forward, and after waiting some time, Demers withdrew. On two subsequent Sundays, Demers repeated the public performance at the church door with the same result. Finally, Leyba concluded that Buteau's seized goods should be sold before they spoiled and sentenced Buteau, in his absence, to six months in prison and a significant fine.[99] The case suggests how difficult controlling trade and access to Indian markets actually was. As with Ducharme several years before, the vastness of the territory and the limited resources of the Spanish made it possible for traders to evade government regulations and punishments. Such incursions from unlicensed competitors must have been a sore point with the frustrated merchant class of St. Louis.

By this point, in the fall of 1779, Leyba's own position in the community had grown considerably worse. Over the course of the previous

95. Leyba to Bernardo de Gálvez, October 28, 1779, no. 367, AGI-PC 1, in ibid., 361.

96. Foley, *Genesis of Missouri,* 38; Jean Baptiste Martigny to [Gálvez], October 30, 1779, as quoted in Nasatir, *BLC,* 1: 71. Nasatir noted that during Leyba's tenure, no new Indian tribes were added to the list of those for whom merchants received trade permits.

97. Nasatir, "The Anglo-Spanish Frontier in the Illinois Country," 35.

98. Joseph Buteau case, November 5, 1779, Litigation Collection, box 1, folder 10, MHMA.

99. Joseph Buteau case, sale, and Leyba sentence, December 15 and 16, 1779, Litigation Collection, box 1, folder 10, MHMA; Banner, *Legal Systems in Conflict,* 33.

fifteen months, his attempts to follow the governor's orders by assisting the Americans had, despite his happy relations with Clark, led to disastrous consequences, both financial and emotional, for him. "The coming of the Americans to this district has ruined me utterly," he declared. When St. Louisans had proved unwilling to trade their goods to the Americans for worthless currency, Leyba pledged his own credit, feeling he had no choice in the matter. "What was there for me to do with your Lordship's orders except to come to their aid in view of the fact that even the principal leader, however many American documents he brought, had not a shirt to cover his nakedness?" he asked. Leyba's assistance enabled the Americans to obtain the supplies they needed, but Leyba "was left as hostage," becoming the target of numerous creditors, with debt and humiliation stalking him. "The result of this is that I am now overwhelmed with trouble," he confessed, "not only for what I owe and cannot pay, but also by the chance that your Lordship may not approve my measures (this is what tortures me most) although all were intended to show you my blind obedience."[100]

Leyba's financial difficulties were destroying his personal life. His own health was suffering, his young daughters faced an impoverished future, and his wife, he believed, had died from the shock. She had come with him "to this exile with so many hardships" with hopes of returning one day to Spain. But "she saw her hopes frustrated by the labyrinth of debts" surrounding her husband. "Overcome by such a great melancholy," she died after an illness of five days. The "unexpected blow" of catastrophic debt "had been too much of a shock." In light of the loss of a "beloved wife," property loss was of "little importance." But Leyba feared, rightly as it turned out, that he would not long survive his spouse and implored the governor to assist him for the sake of his "innocent little girls," his "weeping little daughters." Grief-stricken, distressed, and debt-ridden, Leyba was likely in no state of mind to appease merchants peeved by what they saw as favoritism in granting trading permits. Nor was he likely to have the stores of patience required for adjudicating what must have seemed at times trivial disputes among villagers. He concluded his pleas with a last justification: "Whatever I have done has been purely an act of hospitality, fitting between any nations."[101]

What Leyba characterized as "hospitality" did not strike the British, who noticed the assistance afforded by the Spanish regime in St. Louis, in the same way. In January 1779, Henry Hamilton, lieutenant governor

---

100. Leyba to Gálvez, October 18, 1779, in Kinnaird, "Clark-Leyba Papers," 111–12.
101. Ibid., 112.

and superintendent of Indian affairs for the British in Detroit, contacted Governor Gálvez. Assuming a courteous tone and adopting the guise of one sharing important news, Hamilton subtly let the new governor know he was aware of illicit Spanish aid and threatened that a failure to stop it would lead to potentially deadly consequences. "The Rebel Americans," he informed Gálvez, had gained a "footing in the Illinois Country," and he felt it his "duty to dispossess them as soon as convenient."[102] Hamilton's job would be difficult if the rebels had aid. Under Gálvez's predecessor, Hamilton wrote, New Orleans merchants had sent gunpowder and other supplies to the rebels. While the previous governor might have been unaware of the practice, Gálvez must, insisted Hamilton, prohibit it. Hamilton coupled this request with a threat of force.

If the trade were allowed to continue, the "several Nations of Savages" who accompanied Hamilton's troops as allies might "forget what instructions" they had received regarding Spanish subjects. Anyone who remained ignorant of the British being in legal possession of the territory would receive no mercy, and those who succored rebels "in arms against their lawful Sovereign" would have to "blame their own Conduct, if they should suffer any inconvenience in consequence."[103] Any sense of alarm Gálvez felt would have deepened on receiving Leyba's next report, which was filled with dread. In Leyba's view, Hamilton was "a depraved man" with "countless Indians at his service and great ill will toward the Spaniards because, he says, they protect the rebels." Hamilton had access to good intelligence about St. Louis and its pathetic, indeed nonexistent fortifications, causing Leyba to be "somewhat on the alert." With only sixteen men, including the drummer, Leyba had an inadequate garrison and could not count on St. Louisans for much aid, either. There were scarcely forty militiamen capable of bearing arms in the winter of 1779, he reported, "since at this season they are all trading on the Misury, hunting," or in New Orleans. If an attack against St. Louis or Colonel Clark "were only by royalist troops, there would not be the least fear," Leyba declared. "But the practice in Indian wars is to attack not where one should but where there is the least risk; and for that purpose this side is more desirable than the American," because the Americans possessed troops—190 men—and were stationed "in a good log fort with seven cannon."[104]

In short, the presence of Indian allies with the British forces made the Americans east of the Mississippi safer from their enemies and left the

102. Hamilton to Gálvez, January 13, 1779, in ibid., 103.
103. Ibid.
104. Leyba to Gálvez, April 24, 1779, in ibid., 108.

Spanish west of the river decidedly more vulnerable. Calling the matter to the governor's attention, Leyba hoped for some aid, but none was forthcoming. Indeed, Leyba may have been surprised, given the earlier instructions he had received regarding aiding the Americans, when Gálvez urged him to promote neutrality. As Gálvez wrote, "I should say that I deeply regret not being able to aid you and that I hope your zeal and energy will not spare measures to avoid all conflict by remaining neutral to both parties so as to keep peace and harmony with them." If neutrality proved impossible, Galvez expected Leyba to act in a manner that would "preserve the honor" of Spain.[105] Fortunately for Leyba and St. Louis, the likelihood of Hamilton carrying out of threats disappeared when George Rogers Clark's forces recaptured Vincennes on February 24, 1779, and sent Hamilton as a prisoner of war to Virgina.[106] The American victory staved off the immediate likelihood of a British attack on St. Louis; however, the settlement remained pivotal to control of the west.

As long as St. Louisans offered aid and succor to Americans and the Anglo-American conflict continued, Leyba and the residents of the village could not rest easy. The situation took a took for the worse in early 1780. On February 9, Auguste Chouteau returned to St. Louis from New Orleans, where he had been engaged in the final settlement of Pierre Laclède's estate, with weighty news that forced Leyba and the *habitants* to consider something more threatening than occasions of slander, petty disputes, and favoritism on the lieutenant governor's part: Spain had officially joined forces with France and America against Britain.[107] The previous summer, Spain had cut off diplomatic relations with and then declared war on England. As John Francis McDermott summed up the British response, "Immediately Lord George Germain, British secretary of state for the colonies, ordered General Frederick Haldimand, commanding British forces in Canada, to reduce the American and Spanish establishments on the Mississippi."[108] Living in an outpost of the Spanish empire, St. Louisans were now officially involved in the increasingly global conflict. With the news that Chouteau brought, the once distant storm clouds of war gathered ominously on the horizon, and the inhabitants of the small, undefended village looked to the future with alarm.

105. Draft response from Gálvez to Leyba, March 23, 1779, penned on Leyba to Gálvez, February 5, 1779, in ibid., 105 n. 41.

106. McDermott, "The Myth of the 'Imbecile Governor,'" 336.

107. Foley and C. David Rice, *The First Chouteaus*, 27.

108. McDermott, "The Myth of the 'Imbecile Governor,'" 339.

Chapter 8

"L'Année du Coup"

THE "LAST DAY OF ST. LOUIS" AND THE REVOLUTIONARY WAR

On February 17, 1780, Patrick Sinclair, the lieutenant governor of Michilimackinac, a British post in the Great Lakes, predicted that a planned attack on Spanish interests in the Illinois Country—with St. Louis as the centerpiece of a three-pronged offensive—would prove a certain success.[1] Once Britain and Spain were officially at war, Sinclair had been assigned by his superiors to plan the expedition against American and Spanish settlements on the Mississippi. Sinclair expected that taking St. Louis would pose no particular challenge as it lacked much in the way of defense, with "only 20 men and 20 brass Cannon" to ward off invaders. Perhaps more importantly, the fact that Indians found "Easy admission" to the village meant that "the reduction of *Pencour* [St. Louis], by surprise," was assured.[2] With such an expectation in mind, Sinclair organized a group of 750 men, "including Traders, Servants, and Indians" to attack "the Spanish & Illinois Country." That force set out on May 2, heading south to Chicago to meet another group there.[3] Joined by a third contingent, the allied British-Indian forces proceeded to attack several settlements on both sides of the Mississippi, with St. Louis the central target. Fortunately for St. Louisans,

---

1. Michilimackinac's location on the southern shores of the straits of Mackinac, the span of water linking Lake Michigan and Lake Huron, made it important to British maneuvers.

2. Patrick Sinclair to Frederick Haldimand, February 17, 1780, "Documents Relating to the Attack upon St. Louis," 41; Sinclair was lieutenant governor of Michilimackinac; Nasatir, "The Anglo-Spanish Frontier in the Illinois Country," 311 n. 63.

3. Patrick Sinclair to Frederick Haldimand, May 29, 1780, in "Documents Relating to the Attack upon St. Louis," 42.

the information Sinclair had in February, which underpinned his plans for the offensive, had grown stale by late May, when his forces descended on the village. Due to the efforts of the commanding officer, Lieutenant Governor Leyba, and the villagers' own resourcefulness, St. Louis was no longer an undefended, easy target when English and Indian forces arrived. And while *l'année du coup,* or "the year of the blow" as villagers named it, did destroy the tranquility of the community and witness the bloodshed of many St. Louisans, it did not signal the conquest and devastation that the allied British-Indian forces envisioned.

Over the course of the 1760s and 1770s, the western reaches of colonial settlement increasingly preoccupied British officials. Engaged in an uneasy dance of competition for supremacy over the fur trade of the Missouri and Mississippi Rivers, the British and the Spanish eyed each other warily. Their officers on either side of the Mississippi observed each other's moves as colonists engaged with Indian trading partners and parried each other's thrusts as they trespassed on the other's territory, all the while exchanging letters full of diplomatic niceties and veiled threats. From the Spanish perspective, the British presence and the vast quantities of merchandise British traders offered to the Indians of the area undermined Spanish efforts to maintain the trading connections and indigenous alliances the French had cultivated and enjoyed. For the British, the Spanish occupation of western lands was an ongoing reminder that they were hemmed in, their North American empire inhibited from expanding. The Spanish control of New Orleans, and thus command over the trade that flowed through it, rankled the British.

Competition for trade along the Upper Mississippi was especially fierce, with both powers vying for dominance with the Sac (or Sauk) and Fox nations, in the area that is today Iowa.[4] Indigenous rivalries complicated the situation. While the Spanish considered both the Sac and Fox in their camp, the hostilities between these tribes and the Little Osage and Missouri peoples threatened to undermine peaceful trading and thus Spanish interests. Despite British efforts to enlist Sac and Fox support, the

---

4. Nasatir, "The Anglo-Spanish Frontier in the Illinois Country," 295. These two tribes were among those who visited St. Louis regularly to receive presents, "Report of the Various Indian tribes receiving presents in the district of Ylinoa or Illinois, 1769," in Houck, *SRM,* 1: 44; in 1777, the Sac were described as "well inclined to this district" and as not dealing "with the hunters of the English district, notwithstanding the more liberal presents generally given them from there." "Report of the Indian Tribes who receive presents at St. Louis, dated November 15, 1777," in Houck, *SRM,* 1: 146.

tribes "remained in reality attached to the Spaniards."[5] On the British side of the Mississippi, the Kickapoo and Mascuten were also favorably disposed toward the Spanish. Over the course of the 1760s and 1770s, British officials considered attacking New Orleans and Louisiana, if a war with Spain should "afford the opportunity."[6]

In the 1770s, as European imperial conflicts expanded the scope of the American Revolution beyond a limited war between colonies and mother country, earlier competition between these powers for the rich fur trade with the Indian peoples of the region gave way to a more belligerent stance. The ties between Spain and France, Britain's ancient enemy, increased the tension in the Illinois Country. With British colonists having declared their independence in 1776 and France promising to support the rebels' cause with the treaties of Alliance and Amity and Commerce in 1778, the American war assumed a European dimension. Then, in April 1779, France and Spain entered into a treaty with the declared aim of possessing the entire Mississippi valley. Given that intention, it is not surprising that Spanish efforts to serve as a mediating power between England and France failed. By the end of June 1779, Spain broke off relations with England and then declared war in early July.[7] Still smarting from the loss of Florida at the conclusion of the French and Indian War in 1763, Spain was deeply anti-British. Anything that could be done to undermine Britain's colonial empire and maritime might was appealing.

Spain did not hesitate to support the American cause, covertly at first and then more openly as the Revolutionary War progressed. As early as the summer of 1776, Oliver Pollock, an agent for Virginia, obtained gunpowder from Louisiana's Governor Unzaga in New Orleans. Unzaga's successor, Gálvez, similarly offered to aid the rebels: New Orleans was open to Americans while British vessels that plied the Mississippi were captured and confiscated by Spaniards.[8] When rebellious Americans successfully attacked British forts in Illinois in 1778, the Anglo-American family quarrel arrived on the doorstep of Spanish Illinois. With French traders in St. Louis and New Orleans—acting with the tacit approval of the Spanish

5. Nasatir, "The Anglo-Spanish Frontier in the Illinois Country," 297, 324.

6. Carter, *Great Britain and the Illinois Country*, 142. Military leaders made plans for invading Louisiana, sending General Thomas Gage in New York secret orders to prepare to do so in 1771, when a conflict over the Falkland Islands threatened to erupt into war. Gage planned to approach New Orleans via the Ohio and Mississippi rivers, sending artillery and other supplies to Fort Chartres. Gage to Lord Hillsborough, August 6, 1771, 143, 144; Nasatir, "The Anglo-Spanish Frontier in the Illinois Country," 292.

7. Nasatir, "The Anglo-Spanish Frontier in the Illinois Country," 308. Spain formally declared war on July 8, 1779.

8. Ibid., 299–300.

government—supplying valuable goods to rebel American forces, Great Britain decided it could no longer countenance the Spanish presence. The British military began to plot ways to destroy Spain's hold on the interior of the continent in hopes of simultaneously eliminating an unwanted competitor and depriving rebellious colonists of crucial military aid. If the British effort had succeeded, St. Louis might have been destroyed in May 1780 or suffered huge casualties and damage. Fortunately for the residents of the village, a constellation of circumstances in their favor enabled them to thwart the attack of a far superior force and survive.

Leyba deserves significant credit for creating and coordinating the defensive strategy that saved the village.[9] The intelligence that he received in early 1780 dictated that he take immediate steps to prepare for hostilities. On February 9, Pierre Chouteau had arrived in the village with news of Spain's declaration of war on the British the previous summer. Then, in March, a trader identified as John Conn, who was traveling down the Mississippi, brought word of imminent danger: an attack was in the works against the Illinois Country. With the Mississippi River the international border between Spain and Great Britain, Spanish settlements and possessions on its western shores were logical targets. According to the report of William Brown, a wandering hunter captured by Indians during the attack on St. Louis and subsequently questioned by the British, "The Spaniards began to fortify Pencour" on the basis of Conn's report; only arriving in St. Louis in March himself, Brown may have been unaware when exactly fortification efforts began.[10] Regardless of the precise timing, it is clear that Leyba reacted to the reports he received in early 1780, notifying the governor in New Orleans that he had heard that large numbers of Indians, led by a Frenchmen, were heading toward St. Louis to attack or destroy it, and he was planning construction of defensive towers around the village.[11] (A recent interpretation suggests that there may have been a move on the part of some St. Louisans to divert an attacking Indian party by sending a large present, a gesture that Leyba did not allow.)[12]

9. A key essay that identified crucial documents and revised earlier views of Leyba as inept at best and complicit in the attack at worst is McDermott's "The Myth of the 'Imbecile Governor.'" Scholars, including this author, are greatly indebted to McDermott's scholarship in this piece and many other works. Carolyn Gilman recently explored the battle and narratives of it in "*L'Année du Coup:* The Battle of St. Louis, 1780," part 1 and 2.

10. Nasatir, "The Anglo-Spanish Frontier in the Illinois Country," 310 n. 60; testimony of William Brown, reproduced in "Documents Relating to the Attack upon St. Louis," 44; McDermott, "The Myth of the 'Imbecile Governor,'" 340.

11. Leyba to Gálvez, March 9, 1780, in Nasatir, "The Anglo-Spanish Frontier in the Illinois Country," 25–26.

12. Gilman, "*L'Année du* Coup," part 2, 198–99.

Summoning the residents to his home, the government house at the center of the community, Leyba expressed his concerns about the dangers they faced in a village "open on all sides to the enemy and without defense."[13] Although Leyba did not enjoy thoroughly positive relations with the villagers, it is likely that they were willing to follow his lead and indeed expected him, as the ranking official, to take charge in this crisis. Proposing that they get to work as quickly as possible building some defenses, Leyba urged everyone to contribute funds to support the project and collected 600 *piastres,* a sum he praised as coming from residents afflicted by "extreme poverty and misery." To supplement these contributions, Leyba provided 400 *piastres* from his own pocket; thinking of his daughters' future stopped him from pledging more. The residents also donated about 400 working days to the effort to construct defensive works. The first tower, thirty feet in diameter and thirty to forty feet high, was soon underway, rising on a commanding spot on the western edge of the village, close to its center, where the church and government house both stood. The lane leading to it became known as *Rue de la Tour* (Tower Street).[14]

On April 17, Father Limpach blessed the first stone of the new Fort San Carlos, as it was christened, in the presence of Leyba, militia officers Martigny and Vasquez, and several other villagers.[15] After the tower was built, however, and a second one begun, Leyba realized there was not enough money to construct the three others he had proposed. Improvising, Leyba ordered Pierre Picoté de Belestre, a former French officer who had become a member of the Spanish garrison, to oversee an alternate defense project: the digging of two long trenches, 750 and 1,250 yards in length, around the tiny village.[16] While planning these defensive works, Leyba also moved to increase the firepower of St. Louis. In early April, he had received word that a party of Indians was nearing the ruined fort on the Missouri, where there were five abandoned cannons. To prevent the seizure of the weapons, he sent the captain of the militia and a detachment to retrieve them and bring them back to St. Louis, "in order to put them in security and to be of service in case of need."[17]

13. Leyba, June 8, 1780, AGI-PC, 193, in Nasatir, "The Anglo-Spanish Frontier in the Illinois Country," 316.

14. The tower was located at what it today the intersection of Walnut and Fourth Streets; Musick, *St. Louis as a Fortified Town,* 28.

15. Ibid.; McDermott, "The Myth of the 'Imbecile Governor,'" 340.

16. Leyba to Bernardo de Gálvez, June 8, 1780, in Nasatir, "St Louis during the British Attack," 1: 244; McDermott, "The Myth of the 'Imbecile Governor,'" 343 n. 34. The size and locations of the trenches are discussed in Musick, *St. Louis as a Fortified Town,* 29.

17. Leyba to Bernardo de Gálvez, June 8, 1780, in Nasatir, "St. Louis during the British Attack," 1: 243; Musick, *St. Louis as a Fortified Town,* 27.

As preparations in St. Louis continued, enemy forces began to move. Without regular British troops available, Sinclair enlisted traders and Indian allies. Trader Emmanuel Hesse was appointed by Sinclair "to assemble the Minomines, Puants, Sacks & Rhenards," collect all the corn and canoes he could, and wait at the confluence of the Mississippi and Wisconsin rivers at Prairie du Chien.[18] After Indian men from several nations, including the Ottawa, Dakota, Kickapoo, Chippewa, Potawatomi, and Winnebago, had arrived, the party readied itself for the next stage of the journey. Wabasha, a Dakota chief, and Matchekewis, a Chippewa chief, both received British general's commissions and uniforms.[19] When the combined British-Indian war party left on May 2, it split into three parts: one destined for St. Louis, one for Ste. Genevieve and Kaskaskia, and the third for other Spanish and American interests. As George Rogers Clark summed up the situation, the Illinois settlements counted St. Louis as their seat of government and were "much threatened by the British Gentlemen at Detroit."[20] A week later, on May 8, a seriously ill Leyba learned that an enemy force of 900 men was nearing St. Louis.[21]

Faced with the increasingly real prospect of being attacked by a huge force that could easily overwhelm the village's inadequate defenses and small number of men capable of bearing arms, Leyba did everything he could to forestall disaster, sending word on May 9 to civil and military authorities in Ste. Genevieve. At that point, he was already so ill that he could not write himself and so dictated his letter, "using a strange hand." Leyba ordered to St. Louis two boats with swivel guns and thirty militiamen each, and provisions for all for twenty-four days; he also recalled all trappers within twenty leagues of St. Louis and forbid any in the village to leave.[22] On May 13, Lieutenant Silvio Francisco de Cartabona de Oro, the commandant of Ste. Genevieve, arrived with the sixty men requested. Thus, within four or five days, an additional 150 men had arrived, "all good

18. Patrick Sinclair to Frederick Haldimand, February 17, 1770, "Documents Relating to the Attack upon St. Louis," 41. At this time, Hesse, a Pennsylvania native, was a trader at Prairie du Chien. He previously had served as an officer in the "King's Royal American Regiment." Rickey, "The British-Indian Attack on St. Louis," 36; Musick, *St. Louis as a Fortified Town*, 24.

19. Rickey, "The British-Indian Attack on St. Louis," 37; on Wabasha, see Gilman, "*L'Année du Coup*," part 1, 142.

20. George Rogers Clark to Oliver Pollock, May 11, 1780, quoted in McDermott, "The Myth of the 'Imbecile Governor,'" 343. More details regarding American efforts to coordinate with Leyba may be found in McDermott's essay.

21. Leyba to François Vallé, May 9, 1780, in Nasatir, "St. Louis during the British Attack," 1: 242. In his report of June 8, 1780, Leyba refers to having learned on May 9 of a force of "300 Englishmen and 900 savages," in ibid., 245.

22. Leyba to François Vallé, May 9, 1780, in Nasatir, "St. Louis during the British Attack," 1: 242; Leyba to Bernardo de Gálvez, June 8, 1780, in ibid., 1: 245.

shots," according to Leyba, and, equally important, willing to stay in the village until May 31. With these reinforcements in place, Leyba then sent an officer with forty men in three pirogues to scout out the enemy. Under orders to go no more than ten or twelve leagues north of St. Louis, the party was joined by two canoes of men who had been sent twenty leagues out. On May 23, the latter group spotted the approaching enemy. Hurriedly, they all returned to the village.

Meanwhile, the residents of both banks of the Mississippi had begun to prepare. Some took steps to build up their defenses and others to safeguard their property. In Illinois, American officer John Rogers, a cousin of George Rogers Clark, tried urgently to get more clothes for his men, so they would be ready for the fight.[23] "A Soldier well Cloathed is worth two Naked ones," he wrote, asserting that appropriate dress inspired the men with courage "whereas a Naked man is Cowd and ashamd of himself."[24] In nearby Cahokia, merchant Charles Gratiot decided to send his goods to St. Louis, where he thought they would be safe, and left home to seek out Colonel George Rogers Clark to implore him to return to help repel the feared attack.[25] He and his fellow residents found themselves in a "deplorable situation," afraid of being attacked "by considerable parties of savages," and unable "to work at the cultivation" of their fields.[26] Gratiot's assistant, Ducheneau, went to St. Louis and left his employer's wares in the hands of Charles Sanguinet, who tricked the illiterate man by giving him a receipt saying he was holding the goods as payment for a debt and not just for safe keeping for Gratiot.[27]

The resulting dispute over Gratiot's goods, a private and relatively petty matter, came before Leyba in May, when he was seriously ill and preoccupied with the specter of a more ominous conflict. After Gratiot discovered the deception practiced on Ducheneau and thus by extension on himself, he sued Sanguinet. Ordered to appear before Leyba to answer the charges against him, Sanguinet complied but provided evasive, noncommittal responses. As a result, with petitions of both men in hand, Leyba enlisted others in settling the dispute: "We order both parties to appoint each one arbitrator, who will meet at 8 o'clock a.m. on Monday next, at Mr. Cerré's house in the post of St. Louis" to assess the value of the goods in question.

23. George Rogers Clark Papers, 1771–1784, 2: 12 n. 2.

24. John Rogers to George Rogers Clark, May 9, 1780, George Rogers Clark Papers, Clark Family Collection, MHMA.

25. Billon, *Annals of St. Louis,* 178.

26. Charles Gratiot to George Rogers Clark, April 11, 1780, quoted in McDermott, "The Myth of the 'Imbecile Governor,'" 343.

27. See Billon, *Annals of St. Louis,* 177–90, for all the suit documents.

Although an attempt to follow Leyba's orders was made, Cerré reported back that the ordered appraisal did not proceed as planned. "When about to commence," he stated, "Messrs. Gratiot and Sanguinet presented themselves—the one declaring to us that no one in the world but himself, had the right to value his goods, and the other having challenged the arbitrator appointed by the adverse party." Faced with such challenges to their roles, the men assigned to assess the goods "unanimously renounced the arbitration, and returned back all proceedings therein between those parties to the judicious enlightenment and decision" of the lieutenant governor.[28] Leyba ordered the parties to come to the government hall on Friday, May 26, to hear his decision.

Two days later, while this squabble between two prominent local merchants continued to be a subject of much interest, word arrived that the enemy was nearing. An advance lookout group sent out by Leyba reported that the attackers were only twenty-six leagues away from St. Louis.[29] As the combined force of English troops and Indian warriors from several tribes neared the village, its inhabitants must have grown increasingly anxious, indeed terrified about what was coming. But the daily business of the community continued, and on the morning of May 26, many of the principal merchants of St. Louis assembled in Leyba's chambers to hear the results of the Gratiot-Sanguinet suit. Leyba declared Sanguinet entirely in the wrong, ordered him to pay all legal costs, and commanded that he restore all of the goods in question to Gratiot.[30] Within hours, the significance of the commercial dispute had faded into irrelevance. St. Louis was under fire.

Almost simultaneously, the combined English-Indian offensive hit both sides of the river. Jean Marie Ducharme, the trader involved in a 1772 trading incident on the Missouri and likely embittered by the confiscation of his goods on that occasion, led an Indian party against Cahokia, on the east bank of the Mississippi. That left Hesse with a force of about 650, which included roughly two dozen British and Canadian traders, to cross the river and attack St. Louis, approaching the village from the north.[31] In the early afternoon, the invaders attacked, encountering at St. Louis a defensive force of twenty-nine professional soldiers and 281 other men, far more than the twenty men the British had anticipated back in February.[32] From an account written decades later, it is difficult to pinpoint how exactly the

28. Ibid., 189.
29. Foley, *History of Missouri,* 1: 28.
30. Billon, *Annals of St. Louis,* 189–90.
31. Rickey, "The British-Indian Attack on St. Louis," 41.
32. DeLeyba, June 8, 1780, AGI-PC, 193, and Navarro to Gálvez, in Nasatir, "The Anglo-Spanish Frontier in the Illinois Country," 317, 319.

attack began. One interview presented a plausible, if potentially roman-
ticized, version: "At the first alarm, just about mid-day, and many of the
people at their dinners, a man ran through the town crying 'to arms!' 'to
arms!' and the people jumped from their tables greatly alarmed. The alarm
gun was shot from the tower to warn the people who were at work out in
the fields, and the women and children out after strawberries." While it is
difficult to imagine large numbers of villagers out in the fields when scouts
had only days before announced the approach of the invaders, it is also
true that work could not be put on hold indefinitely and food had to be
obtained, and there were indeed casualties outside of the village proper.[33]

Leyba's contemporary account, dictated because he was too sick and
weak to write it himself, is riveting. His French secretary prepared it, as
the only Spanish soldier capable of writing in Spanish was an unsatisfactory amanuensis. Leyba opened simply enough by saying that the "enemies
attacked the fortifications on the north." As he described what followed,
Leyba sketched a terrifying encounter. Certain of "finding the post without any fortification," the enemy began "to advance like madmen, with an
unbelievable boldness and fury, making terrible cries and a terrible firing."
A guard posted on the tower alerted Leyba immediately, and the troops and
militia sprang into action, hastening to the defensive works, so that "not
a single man [was] left in the houses," Leyba reported. All the women and
children hurried to the government house, where Leyba placed Lieutenant
Cartabona and twenty men to protect them. Within its walls, the mood
and scene were no doubt dramatically different than they had been shortly
before, when the resolution of the Gratiot and Sanguinet suit was the main
business at hand. Terrified children likely clung to their mothers' skirts,
while the adult women tried to comfort them even as they feared for their
own lives, and those of their husbands, fathers, brothers, and sons outside.
Audible throughout the village, the "confusion and the lamentable cries of
the women and children" were horrible and disturbing. Admiringly, Leyba
noted that "it was only due to heroic courage that the arms did not fall
from the hands of the fathers of families," and that they stayed at their posts
rather than rush to their loved ones' sides.[34]

From his position in the tower, overseeing village defenses, Leyba ordered
the cannons recently retrieved from the ruined fort on the Missouri to be

33. "Interview of L. C. Draper with Pascal Leon Cerré, St. Louis, October 1846," from Draper
Collection of Clark manuscripts in Wisconsin State Historical Society Library, reprinted in
"Documents Relating to the Attack upon St. Louis," 52.
34. Leyba to Bernardo de Gálvez, June 8, 1780, in Nasatir, "St. Louis during the British Attack,"
246.

fired. More useful for their noise and shock value than their accuracy, the cannon fire "very much surprised the savages, who did not expect such a maneuver." Making a claim that was for a long time doubted but has since been supported by the research of John Francis McDermott, Leyba asserted the centrality of his leadership in successfully staving off the enemy. "If it had not been for the rapidity with which I acted, together with all the people on the fortifications," he declared, "it would have been the last day of St. Louis." Leyba did not, however, assert that all the glory belonged to him alone. "Our soldiers and inhabitants have shown marvels of bravery," he reported proudly. So courageous and daring were they in their defense of the village that he had to prevent them from making "a sortie against the enemy." If he had allowed them to venture beyond the village, they would, he was certain, have fallen to "the great number of the enemy, who awaited only this moment in order to force open and enter the village."[35]

Frustrated in their efforts to draw St. Louis' defenders into the open and stunned by the cannon fire, the attacking forces abandoned their assault on the village and turned their attention to its surroundings. The Indian forces scattered over the countryside, where they found several farmers and their slaves who had been sowing maize and had failed to make it to safety. Proceeding to attack, according to Leyba, the Indian men "destroyed the fields" and acted savagely toward all the livestock they found: oxen, cows, horses, pigs, and hens. In Leyba's official casualty list, he included domestic animals as a distinct category, noting the deaths of twenty oxen and thirty horses. Worse, "what was most pitiable and lamentable," the Indian warriors killed a number of people working in the fields and took others prisoner. With a grand total of roughly 300 troops, militia, and armed inhabitants at his disposal, Leyba could do nothing to save those outside the village, and he bemoaned the fate that befell them. It was a "horrible spectacle," he wrote, "to see these poor corpses cut into pieces," their entrails removed and their limbs and heads "scattered all over the field." Clearly traumatized by the day's events, Leyba confessed, "In detailing this to you, I find myself very deeply grieved with great pain. It is the *Champs de St. Louis* where was exercised, in less than two hours, the most unheard of barbarity." His only comfort was that divine providence and the bravery of the village's defenders had saved those within St. Louis "from the fury of those barbarians, animated by the English."[36]

On receiving Leyba's report, a high-ranking official in New Orleans sent an even more outraged and embellished report of purported Indian

35. Ibid.
36. Ibid., 247, 250.

atrocities to Spain. "If these hungry wolves had contented themselves with destroying the crops, if they had killed all the cattle which they could not take with them," averred Martin Navarro, "this act would have been looked upon as a consequence of the war." But property destruction had not been the end of the story. Navarro predicted that "when the learned world *(mundo filosófico)* shall know that this desperate band slaked their thirst in the blood of innocent victims," dishonor and ignominy would cling to them. Characterizing the Indian fighters as ferocious perpetrators of unwarranted violence, Navarro declared that they "sacrificed to their fury all whom they found, cruelly destroying them and committing the greatest atrocities upon some poor people who had not other arms than those of the good faith in which they lived." In his view, Great Britain bore responsibility for the actions of the Indian fighters and thus might "add to its glorious conquests in the present war that of having barbarously inflicted by the hands of the base instruments of cruelty, the most bitter torments which tyranny has invented."[37] Such language perpetuated contemporaries' perceptions of Indian peoples as solely responsible for wartime atrocities, despite the barbaric acts committed by other combatants.

Among those caught outside the fortifications when the battle began was an enslaved African, Louis, who belonged to Gabriel Cerré. Pascal Leon Cerré, seven at the time of the attack and a resident of St. Louis only since 1779, provided a much later account of some dramatic moments on the day, with the truth perhaps somewhat embellished. His report of Louis's near-miraculous escape from death is one such example. Pursued by an Indian man armed with both gun and tomahawk, who was gaining rapidly on him, Louis purportedly turned to see the warrior close at hand with his tomahawk raised and quickly threw himself "flat upon the earth" in hopes of evading the blow. The Indian, who was "unable to suddenly check his speed, stumbled over him, and in the fall dropped his gun." Seizing the weapon, Louis shot his attacker "and brought in the gun as a trophy of victory." According to Pascal Cerré's childhood memory, another enslaved man fared worse than Louis. Mortally wounded by the Indians, he "hid himself in a sink-hole not far from the path." At his side was a dog, which "kept with him until after his death, when, as was supposed, his hunger forced him to leave and go to town." For the next three days, back in the village, the dog howled and started off repeatedly in the direction of the sinkhole. After the dog's master, Monsieur Cerré, had someone follow the dog, the dead man was discovered. Of the seven enslaved Africans taken

37. Martin Navarro to Joseph de Gálvez, August 18, 1780, in Houck, *SRM*, 1: 168.

prisoner by the Indians, five belonged to Cerré and were returned to St. Louis the following year.[38]

Enslaved persons were not the only St. Louisans harmed. Two other men outside the village fell victim to the attack. Jean Baptiste Riviere recalled years later how the Indians had captured him as he lay asleep in a cabin on the Grand Prairie and took him to Chicago as their prisoner. Perhaps his unconscious state saved his life, for his companion Jean Marie Cardinal was killed while trying to flee to safety.[39] William Brown, an Irishman who had been living in North America for twenty-four years, was among those captured during the battle of St. Louis. As the battle raged, "he was taken Prisoner by the Winipigoes, within three hundred yards of the Lines lately thrown round a Stone House at Pencour"; the unidentified stone structure was likely the government house. His report highlighted the losses incurred. "Thirty three scalps were taken on the West side and about Twenty four prisoners, blacks, and white people," he testified. "A great number of Cattle were killed on both sides of the River and the Inhabitants were very much spared by all the Indians excepting the Winipigoes and Scioux. They only scalped five or six who were not armed for the Defence of the Lines."[40]

Although Brown's estimates of the day's damages were inaccurate, it is clear that the casualties and losses suffered during the Battle of St. Louis were severe. Leyba's report listed the deaths of fourteen whites and seven enslaved villagers, injuries to six whites and one slave, and the capture of twelve other whites and thirteen slaves. Madame Chouteau's household experienced a significant loss, with one slave killed and five others taken prisoner.[41] For a village of less than 700 people, the death and capture of forty-six individuals constituted a loss of roughly 7 percent of the population.[42] After the attack was over, Father Limpach oversaw the burials of some of the slain later that day.[43] Forty-six other whites had been captured

38. The younger Cerré was born in Montreal in April 1773; Cerré's recollections contain some inaccuracies. "Interview of L. C. Draper with Pascal Leon Cerré, St. Louis, October 1846," from Draper Collection of Clark manuscripts in Wisconsin State Historical Society Library, reprinted in "Documents Relating to the Attack upon St. Louis," 51 n. 1, 53. According to Pascal Cerré, the five slaves belonging to his father returned from their captivity "of their own accord from regard for their master or owner" while the others "were never recovered."

39. Testimony of Jean Baptiste Riviere dit Baccane in Theodore Hunt, testimony before the Recorder of Land Titles, 1825, cited in Foley, *Genesis of Missouri,* 44.

40. Testimony of William Brown, in "Documents Relating to the Attack upon St. Louis," 44, 46.

41. Leyba, "Estado que manifiesta los muertos, herid⁵, y Pricioner⁵," June 8, 1780, AGI-PC 113, in Nasatir, "St. Louis during the British Attack of 1780," 1: 250.

42. McDermott, "The Myth of the 'Imbecile Governor,'" 346.

43. Musick, *St. Louis as a Fortified Town,* 43.

elsewhere along the Mississippi. Another contemporary estimate noted the deaths of eighteen people around St. Louis, nine hunters burned to death by the Kansas Indians, two people killed on the American side of the Mississippi, and fifty-seven people captured.[44]

Why did the attack fail? From the British perspective, Indian and French treachery was to blame. "There is no doubt can remain from the concurrent testimony of the Prisoners, that the enemy received Intelligence of the meditated attack against the Illinois." On the day itself, the "Sacks and Outagamies under their treacherous leader Monsr Calvé" fell back early. Another Frenchmen, "a Monsr Ducharme" who had also traded with the Sacks, "kept pace with Monsr Calvé in his perfidy" and further undermined the assault. "Unsuccessful as it was, from misconduct & unsupported," the attack would "still have its good consequences." Trying to put a brave face on the surprising outcome of the battle, Sinclair suggested that many of the Indians who participated were now "rivitted in our Interest." Indian losses were limited, too, with one chief and three men killed and four others wounded "the only sufferers." Moreover, traders who failed to enlist in the effort had lost any grounds for complaining about the decline in commerce. In contrast, the "Rebels" lost an officer and five men at Cahokia; five others were taken prisoner there. Sinclair's estimates of the losses at St. Louis were greater: sixty-eight killed and eighteen "Blacks and White People made Prisoners." In addition, many hundreds of cattle were destroyed and forty-three scalps taken.[45]

Those east of the Mississippi survived the attack well. One officer credited George Rogers Clark. Having heard of a threatened invasion, Clark hurried back in "time enough to save the country from Impending ruin, as the Enimy appeared in great force within twenty four hours" after his return. "Finding that they were likely to be disappointed in their Design, they retired after doing some mischief" on the Spanish shore. Even the damage on the Spanish side of the river would have been prevented, in one officer's view, "if unfortunately the high wind had not prevented the signals being heard."[46]

What the British described as Sac treachery was, from the Spanish perspective, a key to survival. The Sac and Fox had "prevented a company of six hundred men, who formed part of the invading expedition, from taking

---

44. McDermott, "The Myth of the 'Imbecile Governor,'" 347.

45. Patrick Sinclair, July 8, 1780, "Documents Relating to the Attack upon St. Louis," 48–49.

46. Col. John Montgomery to the Hon. the board of Commissioners for the settlement of western accounts; dated February 22, 1783, New Holland; Palmer, ed., *Calendar of Virginia State Papers and Other Manuscripts,* 441–44.

part in the attack."[47] In the weeks leading up to the battle, the Sac and Fox had been vacillating, with many of them either neutral or pro-American. Arguably, they had participated only at the threats and insistence of Hesse, who had arrived with his forces at their village of Saukenuk in May; of the close to 1,000 Indians participating in the attack, about 250 of them were Sac and Fox warriors.[48] As one scholar noted, such "reluctant allies" may have hindered more than helped the British cause. Soon after the battle, some prisoners escaped due to Indian assistance. In June, Sac and Fox Indians returned to St. Louis, "bringing three *habitants* and three slaves who had been captured by the royalists." Such aid should have been rewarded, yet Leyba had fallen sick and was too ill or unable to give their tribes "the necessities for subsistence," which was "the only requisite necessary for holding their friendship."[49] It is likely Leyba actually had nothing to give them. A report a few weeks later noted that the king's storehouses in St. Louis were "without gunpowder, without munitions of war, and entirely empty of merchandise sent by the King for the nations friendly to Spain."[50] As a result of this failure to act, Leyba fell into "discredit with some of the inhabitants of St. Louis."[51] (For his actions in the defense of St. Louis, Lebya was posthumously promoted from captain to lieutenant colonel; the king was "greatly pleased at the vigorous defense" he made and conferred the new position as "proof of his sovereign gratitude.")[52]

Although May 26 had not proved "the last day of St. Louis," neither did it signal the end to hostilities between the Spanish and British or to fears of renewed attacks. In the weeks after the battle, rumors circulated in the village that another assault was imminent. Worried that "enemies are continually in the vicinity," awaiting a favorable moment to surprise the post "and totally destroy it," Leyba felt compelled to keep the Ste. Genevieve militia in St. Louis and contracted with merchant Gabriel Cerré to provide them with daily rations of "six ounces of salted bacon or eight ounces of fresh meat, one and one-half pounds of bread and one ounce of salt."[53] Reports that 800 Sioux were joining other Indians on the Missouri River in anticipation of a second offensive terrified the residents. Many people wanted to abandon St. Louis altogether.

47. Nasatir, "The Anglo-Spanish Frontier in the Illinois Country," 324.

48. Rickey, "The British-Indian Attack on St. Louis," 37.

49. Nasatir, "The Anglo-Spanish Frontier in the Illinois Country," 324.

50. Cartabona to Gálvez, July 2, 1780, in McDermott, "The Myth of the 'Imbecile Governor,'" 349 n. 44.

51. Nasatir, "The Anglo-Spanish Frontier in the Illinois Country," 324.

52. Martin Navarro, August 18, 1780, to Joseph de Gálvez, in Houck, *SRM,* 1:167–70; McDermott, "The Myth of the 'Imbecile Governor,'" 348.

53. Leyba proclamation, May 30, 1780, in Nasatir, "St. Louis during the British Attack," 252.

About fifteen days after the attack, Leyba, coordinating with the Americans, agreed to form a detachment to "avenge in so far as possible the evil" the "English and savages" had committed; he hoped that the men would accomplish enough to keep the village and its surroundings safe "during the remainder of the summer."[54] Shortly thereafter, on June 14, the expedition of 300 men, with 200 men from the eastern shores of the Mississippi—100 troops and 100 volunteers—and 100 men from St. Louis, ventured forth, searching out Indian communities to enact revenge and wage a preemptive strike against a second assault. With the men from St. Louis under the command of Picoté de Belestre, they traveled north up the Illinois River and marched one hundred miles to the Sac and Fox village of Saukenuk on the Rock River. Hoping to "chastise" their "common enemies," the French-American force found the village abandoned. As Belestre reported, "We were not able to accomplish anything more than to burn their cottages" and destroy their maize and pumpkin crops. As a parting gesture, they left a written note with "some threats to pay them a visit in a couple of months with a much stronger army."[55] While this force was away from St. Louis, the Ste. Genevieve militia stayed in place to protect the village. Meanwhile, Leyba grew sicker and weaker, turning over the reins of government on June 20 to Ste. Genevieve's commandant, Cartabona, who had been in St. Louis for several weeks at this point. "Continuous suffering," said Leyba, "has obliged me to place the daily affairs in the command of Lieutenant Cartabona."

Sadly, Leyba's illness was only one aspect of the misery that awaited him in the aftermath of the battle. The people of St. Louis mistrusted him and disliked him. Rather than enjoying the gratitude of a population his efforts and personal resources had helped save, he faced the anger of a frightened and struggling community. Apparently, some felt that decisions on the day of the battle, when he had forbidden any sallies beyond the village's fortifications, had been unwarranted. During the days and weeks immediately following the attack, the traumatized residents of St. Louis lashed out at Leyba. Anonymous letters sent to New Orleans charged him with a laundry list of abuse, corruption, and greed. One signed *"Le Peuple Des ilinois,"* the people of Illinois, accused Leyba of, among other crimes, allowing a sergeant to keep a public house outside the barracks, where he lived with a black woman; of cheating the carpenter who built his wife's coffin;

54. Leyba to Gálvez, June 20, 1780, in ibid., 253, 254.
55. McDermott, "The Myth of the 'Imbecile Governor,'" 347–48; Picoté de Belestre, July 10, 1780, in Nasatir, "St. Louis during the British Attack," 260; Rickey, "The British-Indian Attack on St. Louis," 45.

of keeping too great a share of the Missouri trade to himself; and of depriving visiting Indians of presents and provisions in order to enrich himself. Another anonymous missive, signed *Virtutis, Veritatisque Amicus* (a friend of courage and truth), charged Leyba with selling gunpowder to Indians for private gain, thereby causing deadly shortages on the day of the attack.[56] In this account, courageous villagers manned the trenches, crying out for powder and bullets that never came, and seeking the leadership of Leyba, who, instead of responding, remained shut up in the tower. As McDermott has abundantly demonstrated, such charges were unfounded; no evidence has ever been located to prove that Leyba acted reprehensibly, either by accepting bribes or selling needed gunpowder. Nevertheless, Leyba went to the grave a despised and maligned man. He died on June 28 and was buried the same day, interred in the church next to his wife, who had died the previous September.[57]

In a letter written a few days after Leyba's death, thirty of St. Louis's most prominent men, including Auguste Chouteau, signed a statement to Cartabona, enlisting the temporary commandant's assistance in presenting their case to the governor. They desperately wanted and needed immediate aid. Characterizing the village as "at the moment of its ruin," the inhabitants described themselves as destitute, "without gunpowder, without munitions of war and being entirely devoid of merchandise sent by the king for the nations friendly to Spain—the inhabitants there are entirely exhausted." According to this missive, Leyba had made the situation worse by refusing to give presents to the Indians and prohibiting the inhabitants from providing their own "to preserve the friendship of the savages." As a result of Leyba's inaction and the agitation of the British, who would stop at nothing in their quest to take new territory, the villagers were "still surrounded by cruel and destructive enemies," and they had heard that a joint English-Indian force of 1,500 men was on its way from Detroit. Other Indian parties were on the move, and 800 Sioux and Missouri warriors were purportedly hurrying to take possession of the village with "fire and blood."[58] Promptly, Cartabona sent the villagers' plea, with his endorsement, to Governor Gálvez in New Orleans.

The palpable fear that suffused the inhabitants' letter to Cartabona was likely increased by a disturbance that took place in the village a few days before, on the day of Leyba's death. La Balafre, a Little Osage chief, had

56. Nasatir, "The Anglo-Spanish Frontier in the Illinois Country," 324–25.

57. Billon, *Annals of St. Louis,* 196, 205.

58. Inhabitants to Cartabona, July 2, 1780, in Nasatir, "St. Louis during the British Attack," 255, 256.

come to St. Louis under the pretence of petitioning for clemency for various crimes; instead, he allegedly spent his visit stealing horses and silver and was promptly thrown in the village jail when the thefts were discovered. A few days later, La Balafre tried to escape, "assaulting the sentinel and seeking a way to disarm him in spite of the vigilance of the guard who, with considerable difficulty, arrested him on the street." The incident could only have added to the jittery nerves of the village's inhabitants. For forty days that summer, La Balafre remained imprisoned in St. Louis. In his misery, La Balafre turned to further violence. According to the official report, written by Francisco Cruzat, who replaced the interim commander Cartabona in late September, La Balafre's wife had been permitted to join him in quarters assigned to the two of them. One day in early August, as they lay side by side, he kneed her in the chest, grabbed the knife she carried, and stabbed her with it, twice in the throat and once in the chest. As she lay bleeding, La Balafre grabbed a musket and tried to hit a soldier, Domingo Alonso, over the head. The barracks erupted in noise, and the troops ran to see what was amiss. La Balafre fought desperately, like someone "who looks not to his life." When he was finally subdued and tied up, La Balafre began a hunger strike. For the next six days, "he refused food and drink, uttering a thousand oaths, making great threats in the name of his nation, and injuring his face and all his body by striking himself against the floor and wall." Three days after his wife was stabbed, she died. Three days later, La Balafre himself died, as the official account claimed, from his self-inflicted wounds: "This caused his death, as Your Lordship may well imagine, more than any mistreatment which he received." When no members of the Little Osage expressed outrage at the events, Cruzat was surprised, having anticipated they would seek revenge for the death of their chief, "to which he himself contributed," by assassinating residents of the village and stealing their horses.[59]

But when the Little Osages arrived in St. Louis to greet Cruzat, the new lieutenant governor, a few days after he took charge on September 24, several weeks after the deaths of La Balafre and his wife, there were no apparent problems. Conscious of the critical situation in the region and the need of the Spanish to seek assistance from the Little Osages and their allies in quelling the Kansas nation, Cruzat "treated them with kindness and made presents to them as usual."[60] Whether the Little Osages were as unaffected as Cruzat maintained seems implausible; more likely is that they were engaged in a careful calculation of their own diplomatic and military needs when they came to the village to obtain resources.

59. Cruzat to Gálvez, November 12, 1780, in Kinnaird, *SMV,* 1: 394.
60. Ibid.

In St. Louis itself, Cruzat quickly took measures to quell the disorder he believed was disrupting public harmony and order. Eight days after he arrived, an alarm spread through the village when someone spotted Indians, thought to be hostile, on the move. Although nothing happened, Cruzat had quickly had ammunition distributed to the militia and ordered the slaves in the community to be at the ready.[61] The people were jittery, and any threat to the security of the village had to be confronted. In the first ordinance Cruzat issued in his second term, the lieutenant governor noted "with displeasure" that people were busily violating established prohibitions on distributing alcohol to Indians. "Reckless of public tranquility," he opined, such individuals "give themselves up to drinking with the savages, in the hope of obtaining through this means their own private objects." Personal greed that led to public disorder was unacceptable. "Consequently, we strictly forbid every person, of whatever occupation, rank, condition, and sex, from giving any liquor to the savages," no matter what the pretext.[62] Trying to establish a system for keeping the people informed, Cruzat put in place a plan for community alarms. In the second ordinance he issued for St. Louis, Cruzat ordered that by day, the colors would be hoisted, and two cannon shots discharged, "one fired from the government building, and the other from the Exchange," accompanied by drums beating a general alarm. If during the night, "a cannon shot is heard, with the general alarm by the drums, every man shall repair immediately to the intrenchment assigned to him."[63] With such clear instructions, villagers would know how to respond if a genuine emergency occurred.

Reports of Indian movements were rife in the summer and fall of 1780. In November, Cruzat reported hearing of such plans from the visiting Fox Indians and their chief. "I have learned that a great number of Indians of different nations and even of the same nations who came to attack us last spring," he wrote, "are now getting ready to come next spring with the idea of soliciting our clemency and alliance." To receive them appropriately, Cruzat would need vast quantities of merchandise: "particularly gun powder, cloth, blankets, brandy, guns, vermillion, and other indispensably necessary articles." When additional Fox Indians and some of their principal chiefs arrived a couple of days later, Cruzat felt bound to inform the governor of their intentions. "They are coming to request that they be received under the protection of the Spanish flag," he stated, "and that they be treated as our allies and friends." While it was "true that some of them permitted

---

61. Cruzat to Gálvez, November 11, 1780, AGI-PC 2-563 (Price compilation, MHMA).
62. Cruzat ordinance, October 7, 1780, in Houck, *SRM,* 1: 240.
63. Cruzat ordinance, October 29, 1780, in ibid., 1: 241.

themselves to be won over last spring by the English," the great body of the nation had always maintained itself in a position of neutrality, and "not separated itself from our friendship." In addition to this news, one chief, Antayà, told Cruzat of English movements of men and materials. They were "employed constantly in taking provisions and munitions of war . . . with the idea of making an expedition against these settlements this spring."[64]

The presence of these and other Indian visitors discomfited Cruzat and his fellow St. Louisans, who were no doubt still shaken from the May attack and fearful of its repetition. In describing his position and the situation in St. Louis, Cruzat grumbled about the demands on his time: "The continued visits which I receive from the nations of Indians most of the time even prevent me from sleeping the requisite hours." As a result of their constant visits and the intricate negotiations he had to pursue in heading a government "left in a most disordered condition because of the death of Don Fernando Leyba," Cruzat had no time to report on many other issues.[65] Busy with the Indians, Cruzat also had to deal with unhappy villagers who complained that the Indian visitors were tearing down the stockades surrounding their courtyards to use as firewood. To address that problem, Cruzat signed a contract with Benito Vasquez for necessary fuel for the visitors; he hoped that the governor would approve of the additional expenditure.[66]

As the fall went on and the visits continued, Cruzat noticed a recurring theme in his conversations with the Indians: the chiefs all had British medals, for which they wanted Spanish replacements. The British had been dispensing flags and medals to the tribes of the Missouri to cement alliances, and now the Indians were surrendering these items to the Spanish. When Auguste Chouteau left for New Orleans that fall, he carried with him thirteen British medals that the Sac tribe had given up as well as a number of English flags. Frustrated, Cruzat could not satisfy his Indian guests, as he had insufficient quantities of Spanish banners and medallions.[67] Lacking adequate quantities of other gifts as well, he tried "to satisfy then more by astuteness than by presents." Even though he gave as many presents as he could, he guessed that "they never reach the hundredth part of those which our enemies are distributing among them."[68] Cruzat believed that presents had a critical role to play, and his inability to compete with the British

---

64. Cruzat to Gálvez, November 14, 1780, in Kinnaird, *SMV,* 1: 398, 399.
65. Ibid., 399.
66. Cruzat to Gálvez, November 14, 1780, AGI-PC 2-585, MHMA microfilm.
67. Cruzat to Gálvez, December 2, 1780, in Houck, *SRM,* 1: 175.
68. Cruzat to Gálvez, December 19, 1780, in ibid., 1: 175.

in this regard was affecting the allegiances of some nations, according to what some chiefs told him. The Spanish simply could not deliver, and the consequences were calamitous. Cruzat complained that even the flag meant to be hoisted in the village on feast days and for Indian visits had deteriorated so much that it was too worn and tattered to fly; he needed a new, large flag that would inspire veneration for the Spanish crown rather than disdain.[69]

Rumors of peace in the east heightened fears in St. Louis. Just before Christmas, Cruzat heard that an American in Kaskaskia had received a letter stating that the Americans and the British had come to terms and founded a close alliance for defense and offense. More imminently alarming was the report that Colonel Clark was returning to the area with 600 men and no good intentions. Cruzat predicted that if the Americans broke off their alliance with Spain, they would work against the Spanish, unite with the English in Canada, and launch a campaign against the region, which, once in their possession, would be very difficult to reclaim.[70] Given such concerns, it is not surprising that the Spanish retained a larger militia than they had previously. When the roll was taken on December 20, 1780, the two companies of militia amounted to 214 men, each with three sergeants, eight corporals, and ninety-six enlisted men; such notable villagers as Auguste Chouteau, Pierre Montardy, Eugene Pourré, and Benito Vasquez were officers. Among the ranks of the enlisted men were traders, rowers, farmers, shoemakers, and merchants who were born in Canada, Illinois, France, and New Orleans, with a handful hailing from the eastern colonies and Italy.[71]

Fears of renewed attacks and a desire for revenge fueled a drive to launch a counteroffensive, and an expeditionary force of St. Louisans left the village on January 2, 1781, marching north, with residents of Cahokia and friendly Indians at their side. It must have been a difficult journey, as bitter weather had set in early that winter and continued unabated for months. Cruzat selected Captain Eugene Pourré, "a person acquainted with the languages of the Indians" as interpreter of the expedition, "accompanied by the great chiefs Heturno and Nqguiquen, with a detachment of sixty-five militia soldiers and about sixty Indians of the Otoguay, Sotu, and Putuatamy nations." The men traveled by boat until ice forced them to continue on foot, and then marched twenty days overland, attacking the British fort at St. Joseph, Michigan, completely by surprise. Their victorious return to St.

69. Cruzat to Gálvez, January 18, 1781, AGI-PC 2-689, MHMA microfilm.
70. Cruzat to Gálvez, December 22, 1780, in Houck, *SRM*, 1: 178.
71. Militia roll, December 20, 1780, in ibid., 1: 182–89.

Louis on March 6 after an 800-mile roundtrip journey must have triggered relief and celebration.[72]

Before the expedition had returned, to counter unwarranted panic and fears of Indian attacks, Cruzat issued two ordinances designed to improve village security. On February 9, 1781, the lieutenant governor issued an order, his third, prohibiting anyone from "retailing to the public false tidings and unreliable reports, in the hopes of alarming and disturbing that very public." The specific rumors Cruzat had in mind are unknown, but he clearly wanted to stop people from engaging in loose talk generally. "These persons, uneasy, restless, and giddy, thrust themselves in to stir up the people, for the malicious pleasure of disturbing the public tranquility," he complained. Anxious to remedy the abuse, "so opposed to the general peace," Cruzat decided to forbid anyone "of whatever sex, rank, occupation, and condition," from communicating to the public "or even to a single individual, any news—whether true or false, favorable to the state, or otherwise—before he has privately announced it to the government." Since the king's representatives alone should "make public that which concerns the nation," anyone who opposed or violated the ordinance would be deemed in rebellion against the government and sent to New Orleans to be prosecuted.[73] Two weeks later, Cruzat ordered that villagers bear arms at all times. As "treacherous blows" sometimes came from Indians who "seemed most trustworthy," Cruzat insisted that "every person, whatever his rank, occupation, and condition," must not "leave his dwelling by day or night (whether or not there be savages in the village) without being well armed." In his mind, given the state of war and their vulnerable position, "one [could not] take too great precautions against the emergencies to which one is daily exposed."[74]

All told, the situation in St. Louis in the months following the May attack was fairly desperate, with fear, severe shortages, and an unusually harsh winter compounding the troubles of the villagers. From November 1 to April 14, the weather was exceptionally bad. A lack of goods and supplies in the royal storehouse forced Cruzat to buy goods from local merchants.[75] As a consequence of serving day and night in the defense of their village—a duty the inhabitants claimed Leyba had forced on them—the residents had

72. Foley, *History of Missouri,* 1: 31; Kinnaird, *SMV,* 1: xxix, 432–33; Nasatir, "The Anglo-Spanish Frontier in the Illinois Country," 56, 59, quotation to Nasatir, 56, citing Cruzat to Miró, August 6, 1781.

73. Cruzat ordinance, February 9, 1781, in Houck, *SRM,* 1: 241–42.

74. Cruzat ordinance, February 25, 1781, in ibid., 1: 242.

75. Cruzat to Miró, August 8, 1781, quoted in Nasatir, "The Anglo-Spanish Frontier in the Illinois Country," 63.

neglected their occupations and grown impoverished. Despairing of "paying their small debts" and unable "to sustain their desolate families," they implored Cruzat to support a request for financial assistance from the governor. They wanted wages "for these three months of labor and of painful guard." Some twenty-one prominent members of the community, men like Pierre Chouteau and Benito Vazquez, signed their names to the request, and an additional eighteen illiterate men put their marks on it.[76] In August 1781, summing up the months since he had returned to the region, Cruzat wrote that Indian incursions, "inspired by the British," had turned the settlements of Spanish Illinois, "most especially St. Louis," into a "new theater of sorrow and horrible tragedies."[77]

Disorder grew as the spring 1781 progressed into summer. It became clear that soldiers in the village were running up debts with local merchants that they could not pay.[78] Villagers in search of some distraction instituted horse races, in the process antagonizing Cruzat. Noting that his predecessors had forbidden horse racing in the village as a practice "diametrically opposed to public safety," Cruzat criticized the continued violations. Trying to stamp out such habits, Cruzat prohibited anyone, whether on horse or in any horse-drawn vehicle, from going through the villager "faster than a trot," for any reason whatsoever, and further ordered the villagers to keep their plows, carts, and other possessions off the streets.[79]

Additional threats to public harmony stemmed from the village's enslaved population, in Cruzat's view. "The abuses which are daily creeping in through the unruly conduct of the slaves at this post of St. Louis," he declared, were "owing to the criminal indulgence of some masters who are too little solicitous for their authority and for the public welfare." Reiterating his predecessors' prohibition on assemblies of slaves, Cruzat added more severe punishments for transgressors and "strictly forbid all the slaves to leave their cabins at night or otherwise" after the beat of tattoo signaled the soldiers' retirement to their quarters. Not only could slaves not leave their cabins, they could not receive any slaves besides those belonging to the same master, and all were ordered "to detain those who are strangers" and confine them. Slave dances, "either by day or night, in the village or elsewhere," were likewise outlawed, unless "an express permission from the masters and the consent of the government" had been obtained.[80] Cruzat's

76. Inhabitants to Cruzat, undated, in Nasatir, "St. Louis during the British Attack," 258–59.

77. Cruzat to Gálvez, August 18, 1781, quoted in Nasatir, "The Anglo-Spanish Frontier in the Illinois Country," 55.

78. Cruzat ordinance, May 24, 1781, in Houck, *SRM*, 1: 243.

79. Cruzat ordinance, June 10, 1781, in ibid., 1: 243–44.

80. Cruzat ordinance, August 12, 1781, in ibid., 1: 244.

prohibitions suggest that enslaved villagers were moving around the streets of St. Louis at all hours, pursuing their own social interactions.

The movements of St. Louis's enslaved inhabitants had become problematic in part because of a matter of dress. A few days after he issued his ordinance prohibiting slaves' assemblies and imposing a curfew, Cruzat raised the subject of costume. "It has come to the knowledge of the government," he pronounced, "that the savages, both free and slaves, and the negroes who belong to this post often dress themselves in barbarous fashion." What he meant by "barbarous" was quite specific: these members of the community adorned themselves "with vermilion and many feathers which render them unrecognizable, especially in the woods." To a colonial populace terrified of the prospect of another Indian attack, the sight of enslaved Indians and blacks adopting indigenous attire that served to disguise their identity must have been deeply unsettling for them and potentially dangerous for their Indian and black neighbors and slaves. These men, "thus metamorphosed," might surprise others, "who, taking them for enemies, would shoot at them." To prevent that tragedy, Cruzat strictly forbid "all savages, whether slave or free, and all negroes of this said post to clothe themselves in any other manner than according to our usage and custom, either in the village or when they go into the woods or fields." Whether those targeted by the ordinance had only recently adopted indigenous elements of dress is unclear. Equally elusive are their reasons for doing so: did they turn to such dress when going outside of the village confines in an attempt to protect themselves by disguising their colonial affiliation? Did they wish to put their masters on notice by symbolically linking themselves to the powerful forces that had attacked the village the previous year? Regardless of the underlying intentions that informed their co-opting indigenous dress, these Indian and black residents of St. Louis clearly disturbed the white members of the community.[81]

The ordinances Cruzat issued in the months after his September 1780 arrival in St. Louis suggest a community in disarray in many regards. Internal sources of disorder were on the rise, or at least perceived to be increasing, and the ongoing threat of external assault contributed to a climate of fear. In the fall of 1781, Cruzat tried to put in place additional measures for insuring public order and private well-being. Noting that too many villagers died without wills, he ordered that anyone who lived with a sick person declared by the surgeon to be "in danger" must report the situation. Doing so would enable Cruzat to visit the sick individual and urge the writing of a will, a measure that would prevent the legal disputes and

81. Cruzat ordinance, August 15, 1781, in ibid., 1: 245.

underhandedness that too often resulted when someone died intestate.[82] One gets a sense of a village where social structures were falling apart. In November 1781, Cruzat addressed carelessness related to personal property, reiterating his command that villagers not leave any carts, plows, sledges, or other items in the streets. Animals were on the loose, too. "The kids and goats in the village cause injury to the inhabitants," Cruzat declared and ordained "that all persons who wish to have these animals must keep them shut up in their own yard or stable." Further, anyone who killed an animal that destroyed a garden or other property would be not be held responsible for the act. Fines and two weeks in jail awaited those who continued to "dare to disobey" Cruzat's orders.[83]

Fortunately, the fall of 1781 also saw the first signs of good news with regard to the region's Indian peoples. On November 28, a trader who had been captured by the British a few days before the May 1780 attack returned to St. Louis, accompanied by important chiefs of the Wisconsin and Mitasa tribes. These leaders, whom Cruzat identified as Sac and Fox Indians, came to ask Cruzat for his permission for them to trade for the time being with the British, as he had no goods for them. Banking on the future benefits of showing good will, Cruzat agreed to allow them to do so.[84] This encounter was the first of a wave of positive interactions with the Indian peoples of the area. On March 5, 1782, Cruzat welcomed to St. Louis four chiefs and forty Indians belonging to the Shawnee, Delaware, Chickasaw, and Cherokee tribes, giving them "four large blue and white necklaces, which are the customary symbols of peace among all the Indians." Writing to the new governor of Louisiana, Esteban Miró, Cruzat reported that the chiefs represented 130 tribes from the territory between the Mississippi and Ohio Rivers who wished to establish "a firm and sincere peace with the Spaniards." Traveling for a year as they visited all the tribes and urged unity, the chiefs declared that they had succeeded in "separating them completely from the affiliations they had previously had with the English." From Cruzat's perspective, the visit was a triumph; these tribes had not visited St. Louis before, with one brief exception. With the good will of these nations, "our boats which go down from this capital may have free passage in the Misisipy." With that aim in mind, Cruzat gave presents (obtained from local merchants) to his guests and "treated them with distinction."[85] Breaking off ties to

---

82. Cruzat ordinance, October 14, 1781, in ibid., 1: 245.
83. Cruzat ordinance, November 16, 1781, in ibid., 1: 246.
84. Nasatir, "The Anglo-Spanish Frontier in the Illinois Country," 67.
85. Cruzat to Esteban Miró, March 19, 1782, in Houck, SRM, 1: 209–10.

the English and building peaceful relations with the Spanish, the Indian peoples who visited St. Louis in the spring of 1782 brought very good news to the beleaguered officials and ushered in a sense of greater peace for inhabitants of the village.

Relations with Indians were not the only factor governing journeys between St. Louis and the capital. The hostilities of the Revolutionary War led to displacements of both Indians and colonists, and some of these people targeted the Mississippi and its travelers. Thus, while Cruzat was busy with Indians in Upper Louisiana, his wife, their four children, and their four slaves fell victim to pirates on the Mississippi as they traveled north to join him in St. Louis. A group described as rebels and Natchez fugitives—comprised of Englishmen from Connecticut who wanted to reestablish English rule, Chickasaw Indians, and blacks—waylaid the large barge on which Madame Cruzat and her party were passengers some seventy to eighty leagues from the Arkansas post.[86] One of those captured, Labbadie, said the pirate band included 100 whites and 200 Indians and believed that the group's overall forces included 300 whites and 250 Chickasaws. Purportedly, they told Labbadie that they expected more English forces to arrive and assist in the conquest of the Illinois territory.[87] According to Madame Cruzat, who testified about the incident after her release, the pirates demanded she, Labbadie, and the rest of their companions "surrender themselves as prisoners of the King of Great Britain." Forced to comply, the captives were marched to a makeshift prison made of trees, with "no light except through [a] breathing hole at the top" while Madame Cruzat and her children were taken to a hut; only she and the children were left unbound.[88] Throughout the ordeal, Madame Cruzat kept her wits about her, preventing "one of the inhuman brigands" from striking her with a tomahawk.[89] Held as a prisoner for nineteen days and then ransomed, Madame Cruzat made her way with her children to New Orleans before eventually journeying upriver to St. Louis.[90]

The kidnapping of Madame Cruzat and her family meant one thing to Spanish authorities: St. Louis, the other posts of the region, and trade were all at risk. Their enemies would "cause all the trouble they can in order

86. Esteban Miró to Bernardo de Gálvez, May 4, 1782, in ibid., 1: 213; Bernardo de Gálvez to Joseph de Gálvez, August 5, 1782, in ibid., 1: 211.

87. Labbadie to Miró, May 22, 1782, in Kinnaird, *SMV,* 2: 14–15.

88. Madame Cruzat [Nicanora Ramos] deposition before Esteban Miró and Andres Lopez de Armesto, May 30, 1782, in Houck, *SRM,* 1: 222, 223; Silvestre Labbadie deposition, July 5, 1782, in Kinnaird, *SMV,* 2: 26.

89. Silvestre Labbadie deposition, July 5, 1782, in Kinnaird, *SMV,* 2: 25–26.

90. Madame Cruzat [Nicanora Ramos] deposition, May 30, 1782, in Houck, *SRM,* 1: 221–31.

to cut communication on the Mississippi." With roving, armed pirates, and rebels downriver at Natchez, Spanish posts were vulnerable to attack. At the very least, shipments of goods to Upper Louisiana could easily be stopped, depriving posts like St. Louis of the goods needed "to cajole the Indians and keep them peaceful and quiet and friendly."[91] In order to forestall such calamities, Governor Miró prepared to send 200 men to Natchez, "to protect the richest possessions of this province, and to drive away that harmful party of English, which has united on the upper part of the river."[92] Rumors circulated that there were new British plans afoot to attack Spanish Illinois.[93]

In St. Louis, news of Madame Cruzat's kidnapping triggered a council of war in the government house, during which the state of defense was the primary topic. Undoubtedly deeply worried about his wife and children, Cruzat had to focus on the matter at hand: the vulnerability of St. Louis and Ste. Genevieve. "It is well-known," he stated, "that I am without any goods with which to make presents to the numerous parties of Indians who gather constantly at this town." Coming from far and wide, these Indian visitors were newcomers, many of them known only a short while before for their devotion to Spain's enemies. "In time of peace they were never in the habit of coming to this town," he wrote. Although local merchants could provide some of the needed goods, the expense was prohibitive. "Even brandy is hardly to be found in this town," he lamented, "although it is one of the articles most essential to satisfy the aforesaid Indians." At a loss for a solution, Cruzat declared he did not know "what may result from this lack of drink and the limited presents," particularly at a time when Spain's enemies were "making the greatest efforts to strengthen themselves by giving the most splendid presents." With Ste. Genevieve entirely undefended, St. Louis was especially weak, as it "obtains all its supplies" from its neighbor to the south. Delivering these observations to the officers of his garrison and soliciting their feedback, Cruzat determined not to demobilize the militia, as he had been ordered to do, and to add fifty men to defend Ste. Genevieve.[94]

Throughout the early 1780s, the inhabitants of St. Louis were acutely aware of their vulnerability in relation to potential attacks on a number of fronts. Through his many efforts—to enforce law-abiding behavior, restore order, better arm and protect the village, and build relationships

91. Martin Navarro to Jose de Gálvez, June 4, 1782, in Kinnaird, *SMV,* 2: 18–19.
92. Martin Navarro to Jose de Gálvez, June 5, 1782, in Houck, *SRM,* 1: 232.
93. Kinnaird, *SMV,* 2: 34–42.
94. Cruzat to officers of garrison, War Council, July 9, 1782, in ibid., 40–41.

with merchants and indigenous peoples concurrently—Cruzat worked to promote a greater sense of stability, security, and peace in the village, which continued to face challenges and external pressures as Europeans and Americans sought land and opportunity in the West. As one historian noted, "Because of its failure at the inception, the far-flung plan of the British to hem in the rebellious American Colonies on the west came to naught."[95] Eventually, with the peace treaty that ended the Revolutionary War in 1783, the threat of British hostilities faded. The Americans, however, the newest power in the region, became a source of instability. Still reeling from the losses and trauma of 1780 and facing chronic shortages, the residents of St. Louis began the postwar period on a different footing. Their circumstances had altered, and not for the better. Spain's ability to succor the community had been brought into serious question. Meanwhile, travel on the Mississippi River, the lifeline of their community and source of their merchandise, seemed less safe than it had been in the 1770s. Across the river in Illinois, once entirely francophone settlements were being increasingly overrun by English-speaking, Protestant, and above all, land-hungry Americans.

95. Musick, *St. Louis as a Fortified Town*, 45.

Chapter 9

The Struggles of the 1780s

Eventually, with the end of the Revolutionary War, the threat of British hostilities receded, and the newest power in the region, the United States, brought a fresh source of anxiety and instability. The erstwhile friendship between Spain and America, established so quickly and warmly in St. Louis between Leyba and Clark, lasted only as long as the war. Once the war was over, officially concluded by the 1783 peace treaty, and it became clear that Americans were a more numerous, active, and expansive presence on the eastern banks of the Mississippi than the British ever had been, Spain's pro-American fervor was replaced with concern about competition and territorial boundaries. In 1784, Spain announced that it would not permit free navigation of the Mississippi, a gesture designed, as William Foley described it, to deter "western American settlements by shutting off their only commercial outlet."[1] In the first years after the war, the American presence in Illinois, combined with a host of other difficulties—from epic floods, chronic poor harvests, and widespread sickness to a wave of arson and the threat of an Indian slave uprising—made St. Louis in the 1780s a village always seemingly on the brink of a disaster comparable to that of the May 1780 attack. In the face of myriad challenges, the villagers and the colonial officials who attempted to govern them struggled to keep the community going. Throughout the decade, the difficulties administrators encountered served as a reminder that Spain did not exercise its authority unchallenged; dissension within the territory, powerful indigenous actors, and unstable foreign and domestic diplomatic relations all plagued Spain's attempts to rule.

1. Foley, *History of Missouri,* 1: 33.

The worries that Spanish officials expressed about American aggressiveness and expansion were shared by the region's indigenous inhabitants. The war between Britain and her rebellious colonists had been a devastating one for American Indians. Whether particular nations supported the British or the Americans or maintained neutrality throughout the conflict, all Indians were losers in the aftermath of the American Revolution. The peace treaty that concluded the war contained no recognition of indigenous territorial rights, and the newly minted Americans showed little compunction about such niceties as Indian nations' long-standing occupation of the land. The former colonists were a land-hungry, restless people, ready and willing to lump all Indians together and treat them as conquered enemies without rights.[2]

In response to American actions against them following the conclusion of the Revolutionary War, Indian leaders sought alliances with Spain. In August 1784, 260 Indians from the Iroquois, Shawnee, Chickasaw, Choctaw, Cherokee, and Loup nations came to St. Louis, stayed for six days, and asked for Spanish aid against the newcomers. Reporting the visit, Cruzat noted that there were many important chiefs, who presented him with large, symbolic collars of porcelain beads, and he met with them in a great council, "with all the formalities customary on such occasions." They spoke to him of their plight, addressing him as their Spanish father: "From the moment we had the misfortune of losing our French father and learned that the Spaniards were to be our neighbors," Cruzat quotes the chiefs, "we had a great desire to know them and to establish with them a sincere friendship which would assure to us their affection."[3] Depictions of peaceful and friendly relations between the Indians and the French were followed by representations of equally harmonious ties between the Indians and the Spanish.

The English and then the Americans destroyed all hope that the Indian peoples had of peaceful coexistence, the Indian chiefs told Cruzat. "The Master of Life willed that our lands should be inhabited by the English, and that these should dominate us tyrannically, until they and the Americans, separating their interests, formed two distinct nations." That event proved "the greatest blow that could have been dealt," short of the Indians' "total destruction." With the split between the English and the Americans, and the victory of the latter in the recent war of independence, a new threat arose. "The Americans, a great deal more ambitious and numerous than the English, put us out of our lands," forming great settlements and invading Indian lands along the Ohio River "like a plague of locusts." In presenting

2. See Calloway, *The American Revolution in Indian Country.*
3. Cruzat to Miró, August 23, 1784, in Kinnaird, *SMV,* 2: 117–19.

their plight to Cruzat and describing the hunger and war that Americans brought to Indian villages, the chiefs asserted that the Americans also urged the Indians to question the Spanish and doubt their promises, saying to them, "Why do you want to go to see the chiefs of a poor nation that will never give you anything?" Despite repeated American assertions of Spanish weakness, the Indians had nonetheless come to seek aid directly, offering Cruzat peace and a military alliance in exchange.[4]

Faced with a group of prominent chiefs making such extraordinary overtures, Cruzat embraced the opportunity. Addressing the "worthy chiefs and warriors of the six nations" at the council, Cruzat expressed "extreme pleasure" at their visit and promised that no harm would ever come to them from Spanish hands. He accompanied his speech with a present in order to give "these Indians a concept of our nation diametrically opposed to what they might have acquired from the insinuations of the Americans." Both Spanish and Indian participants in the council appeared pleased, and the Indians stayed in the village to enjoy Cruzat's hospitality. Cruzat reported with satisfaction that after six days, the Indians "left in a very good humor, giving vent to praises of the Spaniards."[5]

This sign of peace and the successful visit must have been a balm to Cruzat, given the other problems plaguing St. Louis in August 1784. Food shortages compounded the suffering of the many people falling sick. "Since the establishment of the village of St. Louis," Cruzat wrote, "no year has seen so many sick people as now," with every house a "veritable hospital." Already sick for more than a month himself, Cruzat was fulfilling his duties, he said, only with a great deal of difficulty. All of Cruzat's family had fallen ill as well, suffering violent fevers, and two-thirds of the troops were sick. With neither surgeon nor medicine on hand to relieve the afflicted, Cruzat sent repeated pleas for aid to New Orleans. He noted that the scarcity of flour had driven prices very high, and the poor inhabitants had been reduced "to eating corn instead of bread, a sad food for the sick." (A widespread prejudice against bread made from anything other than wheat flour lay behind such views; European colonists typically characterized corn as better suited to animal fodder.) Cruzat implored the governor "to pity the deplorable state" of St. Louis and to send a surgeon, well supplied with medicines, as soon as possible. Even if the doctor could not destroy the disease, perhaps he might be able to lessen its effects.[6] Cruzat described the heart-wrenching suffering of the villagers, saying that the fevers had begun with the onset of summer

4. Ibid., 117.
5. Ibid., 118–19.
6. Cruzat to Miró, August 23, 1784, AGI-PC 10-275, MHMA microfilm.

and were so widespread that no one could avoid them. His own house had become the site of lamentations and sorrow.[7] When the governor received these letters a few weeks later, he acknowledged how critical the situation was, but told Cruzat he had no funds for a surgeon's salary; nonetheless, he promised he would do his best to send one.[8] But no physician arrived in time to save Cruzat's daughter Josette. The four-year-old died on October 12, the second of his offspring to die in St. Louis; the first, an infant son, had died in September 1775 during Cruzat's first term in office.[9]

The shortages and illnesses of 1784 were followed by the terrible spring of 1785, when the Mississippi breached its banks and flooded the country-side. "The inundation was so extraordinary," noted an official, "that the old-est persons of these settlements" declared that they had never seen "another one like it."[10] Built on limestone bluffs well above the Mississippi's chan-nel, St. Louis was spared the worst of the flood. But in what became known as *l'année des Grands Eaux*, "the year of the Great Waters," the Mississippi's rise nearly destroyed Ste. Genevieve.[11] Most of the villagers were forced to flee their homes, and the village itself was basically abandoned. Louisiana's governor summed up the "sad and unhappy situation" of the country, due to bad weather over the previous five years, "and, especially, during the present season." He reported that the waters of the Mississippi had entirely submerged Ste. Genevieve, noting that the village's inhabitants had "been obliged to retire with great haste to the mountains," abandoning "their houses which were inundated, and their furniture and other possessions which they had in them."[12]

The high water not only devastated Ste. Genevieve's housing stock, it flooded the fields, ruining the crops that sustained both that village and St. Louis and further undermining the economy of the region. In the latest of the "continuous accidents" plaguing the country, acres of wheat surround-ing the village were entirely destroyed, a serious blow that signaled the sixth year in a row of bad harvests and high prices in Upper Louisiana; the state of the area was "deplorable."[13] On the eastern shores of the Mississippi, the floods spread far in the alluvial plain, causing widespread damage. A court in Cahokia pronounced the "unhappy conditions of the time" so disastrous

7. Cruzat to Miró, August 28, 1784, AGI-PC 10-287, MHMA microfilm.

8. Miró to Cruzat, 24 September 1784, AGI-PC 31-662 (Price compilation, MHMA).

9. Billon, *Annals of St. Louis,* 232.

10. Miró to Conde de Gálvez, July 10, 1785, in Houck, *SRM,* 1: 236.

11. Auguste Chouteau described April 1785 as the onset of *l'année des Grands Eaux.* "Testimony before the Recorder of Land Titles, St. Louis, 1825, in McDermott, ed., *Early Histories,* 92.

12. Miró to Conde de Gálvez, July 10, 1785, in Houck, *SRM,* 1: 236.

13. Cruzat to Miró, August 23, 1785, AGI-PC 11-581, MHMA microfilm.

as to warrant the suspension of normal procedures. "When there are neither crops nor money; and considering furthermore the loss of the cattle
occasioned by the inundations and contagious disease," it made no sense for
creditors to be able to have the property of debtors seized and sold.[14]

In the midst of the crises created by floods and food shortages, Cruzat
found himself dealing with ongoing challenges from Indian visitors.
In August 1785, he complained about the Kickapoos, "who come constantly to this town," and worried about how to deal with them and other
nations. Cruzat was predisposed to favor the Kickapoos, given that they
were among those tribes that refused to join in the 1780 attack on the village. Nonetheless, their behavior did little to reassure the villagers. On one
occasion, they captured a white hunter and took his merchandise. After
his release, the man came directly to St. Louis, spending some time there
and fitting himself out to embark on another hunt.[15] Another visitor that
August, an Arkansas Indian man, was murdered in the village by a companion, acting with no apparent motive.[16] Such incidents likely agitated
the frayed nerves of villagers.

More worrisome than the constant visits of unwelcome tribes were the
reports Cruzat received of plans for an Indian attack. An Indian leader,
Leturno, a principal chief of the Ottawa, came to St. Louis in August 1785
to talk with Cruzat about rumors of a big collar reportedly circulating
among various nations. Such collars were beaded in particular ways to convey various messages; the one in question supposedly encouraged Indians
of various nations to unite to wage war against the Spanish, French, and
Americans. Not having seen the collar himself, Leturno offered to find
out what he could. Two weeks later, Lachez, "the principal chief of the
Mascouten nation" appeared in St. Louis and informed Cruzat that he
himself had received the rumored collar from a group of Abenaki Indians.
According to Lachez, the Abenaki party was traveling to numerous villages
to urge Indians to join forces in case of a white attack. Cruzat passed the
chief's account along to the governor in New Orleans, noting that Lachez
told him the Indian nations "are all in readiness to defend themselves."
But the Indians' plans were not just defensive: "Lachez went even further
to say that the English governor of Detroit had told him not to bury the
tomahawk very deep, which is equivalent to saying that they should keep
themselves in readiness for an attack." Other visiting Indians conveyed the

14. "At a court," October 1, 1785, in Alvord, *Cahokia Records,* 202–3.
15. Cruzat to Miró, August 13, 1786, in Kinnaird, *SMV,* 2: 133–35.
16. [Unknown] to Cruzat, January 12, 1786, referring to incident of previous August 15, AGI-
PC 117a-78, MHMA microfilm.

same information to Cruzat.[17] Thus, even though the Revolutionary War was over, the threat of hostilities was not, and the specter of another Indian attack on the village loomed ever larger.

A few weeks after Cruzat had written to the governor about the problems with Indian visitors and the reports of anti-Spanish sentiment on the part of the region's Indians, a series of fires erupted in the village.[18] For much of the fall of 1785, it appeared that St. Louis was at risk of going up in flames. In late September, fires occurred daily, without Cruzat "being able to discover the cause." Since there had been no problems with fires previously, noted Cruzat, there were no procedures in place to deal with them. Accordingly, the lieutenant governor took steps to protect the village both from the blazes and from what he feared was the underlying cause: a potential Indian attack. Cruzat appears to have thought that if a fire began and the villagers dropped everything to rush to battle it, an enemy might take advantage of the emergency and chaos to launch a deadly assault. To preclude this outcome, Cruzat ordered that once a bell was rung or drums were sounded to signal the general alarm, all the *habitants* and other residents (the white men of the community) were to rush to the site of the fire, "each one carrying his gun or other defensive weapon." The precaution of bearing arms might thus "forestall any feint or ambush on the part of the enemy." All villagers who owned slaves were instructed to send them "without distinction of sex" to the scene of any fires, armed with "axes, spades, and mattocks" (a tool similar to a pickax) to combat the spreading flames.[19] Given that there was some suspicion about the possible involvement of the enslaved in setting the fires, Cruzat's order that other slaves be sent to help douse them seems on the surface surprising. Surrounded, however, by armed colonists, as they were likely to be, slaves bearing tools to fight fires were not a major threat; indeed, Cruzat may have thought it better to have slaves bearing axes at fire scenes and supervised by white villagers bearing arms rather than elsewhere.

Not long after the wave of fires began in late September 1785, the village was further disrupted by the sudden flight of a number of its inhabitants. Apparently, in November, eight Indians living in St. Louis, seven men and one woman, "deserted" the homes of their masters, taking with them horses, guns, blankets, and ammunition, as well as "several negro slaves," and set two or three fires as they left, "with a view of destroying

---

17. Cruzat to Miró, December 4, 1784, in Kinnaird, *SMV,* 2: 157.

18. See Jill Lepore, *New York Burning: Liberty, Slavery, and Conspiracy in Eighteenth-Century Manhattan,* for a fascinating analysis of the wave of arson that hit the city and the subsequent trials and punishments of those named as conspirators.

19. Cruzat ordinance, October 1, 1785, in Houck, *SRM,* 1: 246–47.

the village."[20] One can only imagine how the incident affected the rest of the villagers. The runaway Indians, clearly living for a time in close proximity to other St. Louisans, did more than desert the post. They took an unknown number of black slaves with them, perhaps invoking the prospect of freedom and offering their friendship and aid to those seeking to make their way outside the confines of colonial settlements. For a time, it seemed that members of an interracial group of were plotting to insure St. Louis's destruction, arming themselves and committing arson. While they did not succeed in their aim, they must have obliterated whatever peace of mind white villagers and Spanish officials had in the years after the attack of 1780. With incidents of arson, rumors of other Indians keeping themselves "in readiness for an attack," and runaways hiding in the vicinity, St. Louisans appeared to be under attack from all sides.[21] The environs of the village were affected as well. In November and December, according to one account, the fugitive Indian slaves wrought havoc in the countryside. A number of homesteads, including that of an American and his wife on the Meramec River, were pillaged, and at least one settler was murdered.[22]

After a month's absence from St. Louis, four men from the group of fugitives left their hiding place and approached the village. Stealing into St. Louis under the cover of night on December 27, they purportedly intended "to try to persuade some female slaves to abscond with them."[23] Before they could achieve this aim, two of them encountered an enslaved black man, Baptiste. As it turned out, when Baptiste (a much-trusted slave belonging to Madame Chouteau) discovered the fugitives at his mistress's barn on the hill at the rear of the village, he sought to capture rather than join them. Persuading the Indians to stay a while, he hurried to tell Joseph Papin, Madame Chouteau's son-in-law, as Papin had been the master of one of the runaways. Papin gave Baptiste a bottle of rum to take back to the barn, telling him to use the liquor to keep the Indians there until he could get assistance. While Baptiste did so, Papin organized a party to seize the Indian fugitives. A corporal and ten other troops were also sent to assist. In the darkness that cloaked the ensuing encounter, soldiers "bound and secured them [the Indians], and marched them to the public jail of the village."[24] Before they had accomplished that goal, however, gunfire had been exchanged, and

20. Joseph Papin to Cruzat, January 5, 1786, in Billon, *Annals of St. Louis,* 234–36; Cruzat to Miró, April 1, 1786, AGI-PC 13-24, MHMA microfilm.
21. Cruzat to Miró, December 4, 1785, in Kinnaird, *SMV,* 2: 157.
22. Joseph Papin to Cruzat, January 5, 1786, in Billon, *Annals of St. Louis,* 235.
23. Ibid., 234–36.
24. Pedro Torrico testimony, December 27, 1785, in ibid., 237.

someone among the village contingent had shot Baptiste fatally, straight through the chest at close range. The physician who examined his corpse thought death had been instantaneous.[25] The evening, which proved fatal for Baptiste, must have been terrifying for everyone else in the village as well, with shouts and gunshots punctuating a dark winter night.

Baptiste's death in December 1785 prompted an interfamily squabble, as Madame Chouteau decided to sue her son-in-law for his role in the loss of an important slave. "His services were invaluable to me," she told Cruzat. "His good qualities, ability, his attachment to the family, the care he took continually of my interests, not only in his own work, but over-looking the others," she asserted, was such "that I could safely trust him with the management of all my slaves." In her view, Baptiste's death, "in the flower of his age," was a blow from which she would not easily recover. Although she stated that "no money [could] remunerate [her] for his loss," Madame Chouteau requested that Papin pay her a significant sum. Her legal standing was, she believed, clear, and she maintained that her son-in-law Papin was entirely at fault. Without any authority to send Baptiste "on his dangerous expedition" and without Madame Chouteau's knowledge or permission, Papin had entirely ignored his mother-in-law's rights over her property and had failed utterly to "reflect on the danger to which he exposed" Baptiste.[26]

Faced with a lawsuit involving two of the most prominent members of the community, Madame Chouteau and Joseph Papin, Cruzat trod care-fully. Initiating a formal inquiry, he listened to testimony from seven indi-viduals involved in the incident. (The places of origin of those involved in the case serve as another reminder of the demographic mix that defined colonial St. Louis. The soldiers hailed from the Canary Islands, mainland Spain, and France, while the residents came originally from Fort Chartres and New Orleans.) He also appointed three merchants—Gabriel Cerré, Louis Dubreuil, and Charles Sanguinet—to assess the financial loss Madame Chouteau suffered. Appraising the "qualities, intelligence and value" of Baptiste, the three men arrived at a figure of six hundred silver dollars "as a full compensation for his loss."[27] Whether he had a family among the vil-lage's enslaved women and children, who grieved his loss, is unknown. At the very least, the other enslaved members of Madame Chouteau's house-hold, both Indian and African, would have been deeply affected by his death.

---

25. Dr. Antoine Reynal inquest report, December 28, 1785, in ibid., 233; Chouteau-Papin Collection, MHMA.

26. Petition of Madame Chouteau, December 29, 1785, in Billon, *Annals of St. Louis*, 233–34.

27. Ibid., 241.

For his part, Papin defended the actions that led to Baptiste's death by claiming official authority. Deputized to act by the government, he had powers that trumped whatever property rights his mother-in-law had in Baptiste. "In a contest sanctioned by the authorities, and supported with zeal by the soldiers and militia," Papin and his neighbors did their best, he insisted. On the night in question, having just gathered at Papin's house, and having heard reports that the fugitives intended to come there, the civilian party was ready for action when Baptiste arrived. According to Papin, it was Baptiste's idea to get a bottle of rum to detain the fugitives. While Baptiste returned to the barn, Papin sent another member of the Chouteau clan, his brother-in-law Sylvestre Labbadie, to report what was afoot to Cruzat and to seek reinforcements. Immediately, Cruzat dispatched two detachments to take different paths to Madame Chouteau's barn. Claiming that he instructed all "not to fire unless in defense of his own person," Papin divided the men and soldiers up and sent them by separate roads in order to "surround easily the spot where the criminals were." When they arrived at the barn, they were "immediately assaulted not only by our enemies in front, but by a general discharge of gun shots on both sides of our own people." The only one to fall victim to the friendly fire was "the unfortunate negro" who died "without the satisfaction of witnessing the glorious end of the action." Laying the blame for Baptiste's death solely at his feet was, Papin believed, deeply unfair. "After having exposed myself to the greatest danger for a matter of public concern, acting only by express orders," Papin asked, "would it be just that the whole burden should fall on me?" Public-minded men should not be forced to bear the costs of public security alone, he protested. As far as he could see, he should not have any responsibility for paying for a slave "who volunteered himself," particularly when he, Papin, had a legitimate "right to command."[28]

Although Papin was passionate in his own defense, it seems clear from soldiers' testimony that he was not a particularly adept commander. According to one soldier, he and four other troops had hurried to a deep trench near the barn, lying in wait there to apprehend the Indian fugitives if they attempted an escape. Pedro Torrico testified that although he could see nothing of what happened, he could hear the confusion, "a tumult of voices and gunshots."[29] Another soldier, Juan Antonio Diaz, was better positioned and provided more damning testimony. Diaz reported that Baptiste and an armed Frenchmen entered the barn, where a shot was fired. When no one appeared at the door, Papin, Labbadie, and others rushed in, "discharging

---

28. Joseph Papin to Cruzat, January 5, 1786, in ibid., 234–36.
29. Pedro Torrico testimony, January 9, 1786, in ibid., 237.

their firelocks at the same time." Who fired the weapon that killed Baptiste is unknown, but what does seem clear is that confusion and poor discipline among the part-time soldiers, village militia members like Papin, added to the danger and may have directly caused Baptiste's death.[30]

Ultimately, Cruzat passed the buck in the Chouteau-Papin case, sending all of the petitions and depositions to the governor in New Orleans for examination and a final decision. Writing to Miró, he reported that he had three of the fugitive Indians, responsible for different crimes, under guard in the public jail; he ultimately sent them to New Orleans.[31] He also expressed his view that Baptiste's death resulted entirely from confusion and that the owners of all the Indian runaways should bear the costs, perhaps in part as a reminder that holding Indian slaves had been outlawed. Everyone needed to be informed again that it was illegal to "hold as a slave any Indian," as his predecessor Piernas's publication of O'Reilly's announcement had made clear.[32] Although Cruzat was mistaken about the specific provisions of the decree outlawing slavery, suggesting it prohibited all Indian slavery, not just acquiring new Indian slaves, his comments are instructive. He seemed to believe that St. Louisans had been willfully ignoring the law and were now reaping what they had sown, with the loss of life and property the obvious result. While it is impossible to say whether most or all of the runaway Indian slaves involved had been acquired illegally, that was likely the case for at least some, as O'Reilly had banned enslaving or purchasing Indians sixteen years before, in 1769. To insure that no villagers could claim ignorance regarding the laws and Indian slavery in the future, Cruzat reissued O'Reilly's 1769 decree. Adding an important preamble, Cruzat explained his decision to publicize O'Reilly's proclamation in the context of what had transpired regarding Baptiste and the fugitive Indians. Regarding the Indians, he noted that they had "been held as slaves by various habitants of this post despite the ordinances which were published in the month of May" 1769. He reminded the people that "all Indians, of both sexes, who are detained as slaves" after that date "shall be accounted free and recognized as such."[33]

Meanwhile, in New Orleans, Governor Miró determined a solution to the dispute over Baptiste's death that was probably to the liking of neither side. Madame Chouteau was to be compensated financially for Baptiste's

---

30. Juan Antonio Diaz testimony, January 9, 1786, in ibid., 238.

31. Cruzat to Miró, February 18, 1786, AGI-PC 12-97, MHMA microfilm; Cruzat to Miró, April 1, 1786, AGI-PC 13-27, MHMA microfilm.

32. Cruzat to Miró, April 1, 1786, AGI-PC 12-188, MHMA microfilm.

33. Cruzat ordinance, June 23, 1787, in Houck, *SRM,* 1: 249–50.

death, a victory of sorts for her, but her son-in-law was found only partly liable, and not for ordering Baptiste to follow his instructions. As one of the owners of the fugitives, Papin bore the costs of damages for Baptiste's death along with the owners of the other runaways, including Madame Chouteau herself.[34] To inform all the concerned individuals of the governor's decision, Cruzat summoned the Chouteau brothers-in-law Papin and Labbadie, their mother-in-law Widow Chouteau, along with Alexis Marie, Antoine Vincent, Charles Vallé, and Widow Genevieve Rouquier, as owners of the fugitive Indians mentioned in the suit, to appear before him. Shortly thereafter, each of the owners delivered his or her portion of Baptiste's appraisal value to Cruzat, who handed it over to Madame Chouteau. With that financial transaction, the legal dispute came to an end. Whether the litigation permanently soured Widow Chouteau's relationship with either Joseph Papin or Sylvrestre Labbadie is equally unknown. She was, it seems, a formidable person, willing to enlist the apparatus of the law in protecting her interests regardless of the potential for jeopardizing family ties.

In the midst of dealing with Baptiste's death and the controversy and heightened emotions that it engendered, Cruzat faced his own terrible losses in early 1786. On February 1, a daughter died, the third of his children to perish in St. Louis.[35] Less than three months later, yet another death struck the Cruzat family. After receiving final sacraments from the village priest, Madame Cruzat, Nicanora Ramos, the survivor of a kidnapping, a woman who had buried three of her young children in the St. Louis churchyard, died. She was interred in the church, under the first bench of the main aisle, on April 15.[36] Announcing her death to the governor, Cruzat wrote that his house was in a "sad state," after "God took his wife to the next world."[37] St. Louis had not proved a happy colonial posting for Spanish officials and their families, with death cutting a wide swath through both Leyba's and Cruzat's families; Piernas had lost two children as well during his years in St. Louis.[38]

While his private life lurched from one devastating loss to another, Cruzat remained busy with the pressing matters of governance in St. Louis: administering justice, settling disputes, and dealing, always, with the Indians, who continued to come to the village for aid, in part because the American presence remained a problem for the Indian peoples of the region.

---

34. Final decree, Miró, July 31, 1786, in Billon, *Annals of St. Louis,* 241.
35. Ibid., 232.
36. Houck, *SRM,* 1: 231 n. 18.
37. Cruzat to Miró, May 16, 1786, AGI-PC 12-269, MHMA microfilm.
38. Billon, *Annals of St. Louis,* 244.

In July 1786, Cruzat recorded receiving daily news of Indian nations on the American side of the Mississippi attacking and killing the white newcomers, because they were "so decidedly displeased and irritated" by the Americans. In Kaskaskia, Potawatomi Indians killed and scalped two villagers "at their very door." The notary from Cahokia reported that seven Americans settled near that village had been killed by other Indians. "So not a day passes without news of these attacks," Cruzat told the governor. "The most curious thing is that the blame for them is placed on the English royalists who, they say, incite them to it."[39] In August 1786, a principal Abenaki chief, accompanied by fifty-seven men, appeared in St. Louis, seeking permission to relocate his people to Spanish territory after having fled homes in the Ohio River valley. Cruzat told him he had "no objection to his doing so." According to Cruzat, the chief let him know that this agreeable response "gave him much satisfaction in view of the dislike which his people feel toward the Americans."[40]

Indian animosity toward Americans was one matter; the official Spanish stance toward the Americans was quite another. Over time, a profound shift occurred, with first the Mississippi River and then Spanish territory itself being opened to the people of the new nation. In 1787, Spain permitted Americans to send produce downriver after they paid duties on it. In a more momentous decision, the Spanish government opened Louisiana to American immigration.[41] Governor Miró hoped that Anglo-Americans could be converted and assimilated. But Americans, presumably reluctant to embrace a Catholic king's rule only a decade after they had cast off the Protestant British monarchy, were initially slow to embrace that option. An alternate plan, proposed by the notorious American military commander James Wilkinson, entailed recruiting colonists for Louisiana from Kentucky's Anglo-American population. Although required to take an oath of allegiance to Spain, such settlers would not be required to practice Catholicism. Although Spain adopted elements of Wilkinson's proposal, the general failed to promote the cause of immigration, and few Americans chose to relocate.[42] As Foley notes, between December 1, 1787, and December 31, 1789, only 293 Americans "availed themselves of the opportunity to settle in Spanish Illinois, and that figure included 106 black slaves who had no choice."[43] More floods and illness swept through the

39. Cruzat to Miró, July 19, 1786, in Kinnaird, *SMV,* 2: 173–74.
40. Cruzat to Miró, August 23, 1786, in ibid., 185–86.
41. Foley, *History of Missouri,* 1: 33; Din, "The Immigration Policy of Governor Esteban Miró."
42. Din, "The Immigration Policy of Governor Esteban Miró," 157–59, 165–73.
43. Foley, *Genesis of Missouri,* 63; "Statement of Inhabitants who have come to the American side

region in 1788, discouraging new immigration of Americans who might have been otherwise drawn by the fertility of the land.[44] Efforts to encourage relocation gained a boost in the spring of 1789, when Colonel George Morgan and a party of explorers visited St. Louis in March. There to meet with the lieutenant governor, Morgan wished to discuss his plans for a new American settlement in Spanish territory, one where colonists would have religious freedom and be able to bring in their property duty free. After the lieutenant governor provided him with horses, guides, and provisions, Morgan and his followers left the village and traveled south, selecting a site for their new settlement and naming it New Madrid. When he went on to New Orleans to discuss his plans with Governor Miró, the governor's critical reaction to the proposal—particularly the American cast to the new settlement—ultimately dampened Morgan's enthusiasm for pursuing it.[45]

Spain's relationship with the new United States clearly required careful negotiation, and Spanish officials in St. Louis took steps to promote harmony. In 1787, Cruzat sent word to General Harmar, the American commandant at Kaskaskia, to come for a visit. Accepting the invitation, Harmar crossed the Mississippi on August 21 and was "very politely entertained" by Cruzat in the new government quarters he had acquired in 1783.[46] When Harmar left, he enjoyed a distinguished escort: Cruzat's son and the principal inhabitants of the village accompanied him to the river landing. Harmar's overall impression was a favorable one, and he pronounced St. Louis "the handsomest & genteelest village [he had] seen on the Mississippi," far superior to Ste. Genevieve.[47]

While working to preserve peaceful and productive ties with the Americans, Cruzat was also busy dealing with the indigenous peoples of the region, some of whom engaged in conduct that the Spanish in St. Louis found highly objectionable, including a series of thefts and murders. In October 1787, a major gathering of Big Osages and prominent villagers was held in St. Louis. Joining principal chief Clermond and several other important Indian leaders were a number of white St. Louisans, including Auguste Chouteau, Benito Vasquez, and Pierre de Volsey. Under discussion were recent difficulties between the two peoples, with the colonists accusing the Osages of permitting their people to commit murders and outrages

to settle in the District of Illinois," December 1, 1787, to December 31, 1789, in Kinnaird, *SMV,* 2: 290.

44. Peyroux to [governor], November 20, 1788, AGI-PC 201-959, MHMA microfilm.

45. Houck, *HM,* 1: 312; Foley, *History of Missouri,* 1: 36–37.

46. Billon, *Annals of St. Louis,* 245.

47. Harmar, August 1787, Houck, *HM,* 1: 311 n. 27; Josiah Harmar to Henry Knox, November 24, 1787, in Thornbrough, ed., *Outpost on the Wabash,* 49.

against Frenchmen. One Indian leader, Jean Lafon, rejected the charges, saying that no one present was involved in the crimes, which he declared were committed by young men who were out of control. Unpersuaded by this response, Cruzat asked if Lafon would accept a similar explanation if Spanish subjects murdered Osage Indians. As an insurance policy against such future depredations, Cruzat suggested that the tribe send two of its chiefs to New Orleans, there to live for two years, and then to be relieved by other chiefs, in a kind of elaborate hostage rotation.[48]

Before he had achieved any real resolution to these troubles, Cruzat was replaced by Captain Manuel Perez, who arrived in St. Louis in November 1787 to assume the post of lieutenant governor. (Perez held the position until 1792.)[49] The inventory of government effects Cruzat transferred to the new lieutenant governor highlights the importance of Indian relations in Spanish policy for the region. In lengthy lists of goods in the government storehouses, Cruzat included a "report of the merchandise, brandy, powder, balls, and other effects in [his] charge at present, belonging to the presents which must be given to the Indian tribes, who are the dependents of this western district of Ylinneses." Notable was the large quantity of liquor: 1,400 jugs of brandy, made from sugarcane, in fourteen casks. Ammunition was high on the list as well, with 1,350 pounds of powder in nine chests, 2,500 musket flints, and 2,700 pounds of balls. Whether such goods were destined for use in hunting or warfare, they were clearly important and prized by Indians. Much of the rest of the material destined for presents addressed the needs of daily life for clothing, cooking, and farming: 88 blankets, 116 shirts, 408 combs, 180 pairs of scissors, 500 sewing needles, and 25 hoes, as well as scores of other goods. Among the more ceremonial and status-oriented wares were lace-trimmed shirts and hats for chiefs, vermillion, silk ribbon for medals, several silver medals and banners, and plumes.[50]

Very soon after Perez assumed office, he encountered the challenges presented by Indians in the area, when Tanclel, the principal chief of the Mascouten nation, and a group of thirty Mascouten warriors attacked settlements in nearby American territory in December 1787. After striking

48. Council with the Big Osages, Lafon's statement, October 16, 1787, AGI-PC 200-1074; Council with the Big Osages, Cruzat's response, October 16, 1787, AGI-PC 200-1075, MHMA microfilm.

49. Cruzat purchased a house diagonally opposite to Laclède's first house and store to serve as his home and the center of government business and lived in it until November 27, 1787, when his tenure as lieutenant governor concluded. Billon, *Annals of St. Louis,* 245–46.

50. Cruzat, inventory of effects, November 27, 1787, in Houck, *SRM,* 1: 265–68. Other interesting items included 338 hawk's bells, seven mirrors, seventy-eight thimbles, and sixty steels for striking fire.

the nations of the Illinois and Kaskaskia, among whom Tanclel and his men killed five men and six children and took eight prisoners, Tanclel came to St. Louis to see Perez, his war party with him. Known for going to war "every year," Tanclel had "carried out his usual custom in the month of December." When he met Perez, the Mascouten leader informed the new lieutenant governor of his reasons for pursuing violence. "This chief, as he confessed to me . . . ," wrote Perez, "says he can do no less than make war on some nations as long as he lives, because in the time of French domination they did harm to the French whom he and his nation have always loved as well as the Spaniards." Feared by other nations, "because they say he always comes out well in his attacks," Tanclel was not—at least not yet, Perez seemed to imply—a problem. "He shows us much affection," reported Perez, "and up to now has never done any harm to our district."[51]

Whether or not Mascouten attacks in American Illinois posed any immediate threat to Spanish interests, it is clear that Indian conflicts and hostilities—both among tribes and with colonists in Spanish Illinois and Americans across the Mississippi River—were an ongoing and important feature of the period. In March 1788, reports of new crimes committed by the Great Osages spread. Right after concluding peace talks with Perez and receiving presents from him, a party of Big Osages purportedly left St. Louis and "ransacked the house" of Charles Gratiot, two leagues outside the village, and stole a number of horses. Declaring that the Big Osages had "just given new proofs of their perfidy," an official in Ste. Genevieve informed the governor that members of the tribe had committed a brutal murder. On March 8, Jean François la Buche, a French hunter, had left his fifteen-year-old mulatto son, Pierre la Buche, to return to the spot where he had earlier left his seven-year-old son. About an hour after his father left, Pierre heard gunfire coming from the direction of the camp and ran to investigate. On arriving some fifteen minutes later, he "found just the head of his father, scalped down to the eyes. His long beard had not been touched." The terrified boy "took flight at this sight, without seeing his young brother."[52] It seemed that every month brought news of more murders. Six miles north of the village, on Bellefontaine Road, an English family who had been working on a plot of land for a St. Louis merchant was attacked by a group of Indians, whose tribe was not known. On June 23, 1788, the husband, wife, son, and two daughters of the Keen family were killed, and a teenaged son and two-year-old daughter managed to escape.[53]

51. Manuel Perez to Estevan Miró, February 27, 1788, in Kinnaird, *SMV,* 2: 244–45.
52. Peyroux de la Courdinière to Miró, March 12, 1788, in ibid., 246–47.
53. Billon, *Annals of St. Louis,* 248–49.

(Their inventory of livestock and other household goods contained a striking reminder of their English origins: two teapots and eleven teacups and saucers made of faience, a fine imported porcelain prized by consumers.)[54]

As the spring of 1788 wore on, more Indian movements meant that St. Louis was increasingly a center of indigenous activity. In May, 260 Indians belonging to the Iroquois, Shawnee, Chickasaw, Chocktaw, Cherokee, and Loup tribes came to St. Louis to seek aid against the Americans. As Kinnaird notes, "This was only a beginning. Before long, parties of Shawnees began to drift into Spanish territory." Others, like the Cherokee, came to St. Louis to request permission to move into the area.[55]

In reporting news of Indian visits to St. Louis to the governor, the lieutenant governor emphasized the Anglo-American background to Indian actions. At the end of May 1788, a lesser chief of the Cherokee, accompanied by other members of his tribe, arrived in St. Louis and presented Perez with two collars "as a symbol of the message" sent "by the great chief of this nation." The message was straightforward: a request for permission "to come and establish himself in this part of the lands of the King of Spain." The request was also delivered by letter; Cherokee Indians at L'Anse à la Graisse had asked St. Louis merchant Eugenio Alvarez to put the results of a council they held on the subject into writing. Telling the petitioners that he needed the governor's permission before he could approve any move, Perez passed on to Miró what the Cherokee had explained about themselves and their motives, that they were "a good nation," which others might wish to emulate by migrating, "for they are disgusted with the Americans and English." After giving the delegation presents, including the muskets, powder, and balls that they requested, Perez alerted the governor that if the Cherokees were permitted to resettle, the budget for presents would have to be increased. "If the number of presents to be sent is as small as I have just received," complained Perez, "it will not be enough for two-thirds of the nations to whom it is necessary to give presents now." Citing "the great number of parties who are constantly coming in increasing numbers," Perez echoed the concerns and complaints of his predecessors: it was ever more difficult to discharge the duties involved in Indian diplomacy with an undersupplied warehouse and inadequate budget.

The paucity of Spanish presents increasingly jeopardized peaceful relations with the Indians. With palpable frustration, Perez emphasized the difficulty of keeping Indian peoples as friends. "How can this union be

54. Keen inventory, June 23, 1788, instrument #2412, box 23, folder 2, St. Louis Archives, MHMA.

55. Kinnaird, *SMV*, 2: xxix; Cruzat to Miró, August 23, 1784, 117–19.

maintained," he demanded, "when there is scarcely the wherewithal to make them small presents?" Increasing numbers of Indian parties were coming to St. Louis, each of forty to fifty men, not counting the women they brought, and at the head of each was a chief who expected a present. With the amount of presents reduced two-thirds from previous years, satisfying the guests was growing ever more difficult. "It is impossible to content them and give them proofs of our disposition to live in good friendship with them," Perez insisted. Trying to blame the shortage of gifts on problems in New Orleans, where a March 1788 fire destroyed 856 buildings and a great deal of other property, Perez lamented his inability to persuade Indian visitors of Spanish goodwill. "They believe that our friendship is changing," he wrote, as demonstrated by the smaller gifts.[56]

Concerned about the prospect of losing Indian friendship, Perez cast a worried eye at St. Louis's fortifications. Built of wood, they were in poor shape, as Perez reported in December 1788, due to the rapid decay that the climate caused in timber constructions. The only exception to this rule, local residents informed him, was cedar, but the nearest cedar groves were quite distant from St. Louis. Only the tower of San Carlos, part of the fortifications constructed on the village outskirts for its defense in the spring of 1780, remained intact. Recommending that the fortifications be rebuilt in stone, Perez was likely pleased when the governor approved the plans and authorized the funds for the project.[57]

While Indians were petitioning for permission to relocate to Spanish territory, the Spanish were taking steps to encourage more French migration from American territory. In October 1788, the American commandant Hamtramck, whom Cruzat had hosted in St. Louis in August 1787, intercepted a letter from Perez, addressed to the French inhabitants of Illinois. Obtaining it from the Indian man who was carrying it in exchange for a bottle of rum, Hamtramck managed to get the letter "before any of the people saw it." In it, Perez invited all the French residents of Illinois to cross the river and offered them land "for nothing."[58]

Although Perez's letter did not reach its intended recipients, many settlers in American territory were contemplating a move to Spanish lands. According to a petition of Kaskaskia residents in September 1789, addressed to the commanding officer, Major Hamtramck, the villagers were deeply worried and upset about their future. Citing their "deplorable

56. Perez to Miró, December 1, 1788, in Nasatir, *BLC,* 1: 128–30.
57. Perez to Miró, December 2, 1788, in Houck, *SRM,* 1: 271–72; Miró to Perez, June 3, 1789, in ibid., 1: 274.
58. Hamtramck to Harmar, October 13, 1788, in Thornbrough, ed., *Outpost on the Wabash,* 125.

situation" and "absolute necessity," they urged him to take steps to prevent their "total ruin." Offering their analysis of the situation, the petitioners wrote that "the Indians are greatly more numerous than the white people, and are rather hostilely inclined: the name of an American among them is a disgrace." With uncultivated lands, little commerce, absconding debtors, and few livestock, the settlers had little ability to mount "any effectual resistance." Convinced that a lack of a visible presence on the part of the U.S. government lay at the root of their problems, they declared that "ever since the cession of this territory to Congress, [they had] been neglected as an abandoned people." Adding to the difficulties was the understandable fact that "the greater part" of the residents had "left the country on this account to reside in the Spanish dominions." Others were following, and the petitioners were "fearful, nay certain, that without [Hamtramck's] assistance, the small remainder will be obliged to follow their example."[59] One resident, John Edgar, a native of Ireland, wrote a direct appeal to Hamtramck, underlining the Kaskaskia settlers' fears of daily destruction at Indian hands. "It is well known," he maintained, "that the minds of the Indians are continually poisoned by the traders on the other side," that is, Spanish territory. Having waited five years "in hopes of a government," he would not wait much longer for U.S. officials and support to materialize. If by March 1790 no government or aid had arrived, his path would be clear: "I shall be compelled to abandon the country, & I shall go to live in St. Louis." Although his "inclination, interest & love for the country" made him want to stay in U.S. territory, fears that his life and property would "fall a sacrifice" would more than justify a move to Spanish St. Louis. In concluding this combined threat and plea, Edgar asked Hamtramck to write to the commandant in St. Louis about him and his plight, a measure he hoped would contribute to the safety of Kaskaskia's white inhabitants.[60]

The potential wave of migration from the eastern shores of the Mississippi to St. Louis seemed an echo of the first wave of settlement in the mid-1760s, when French residents in the newly British territory found the Spanish side more appealing. Now, in the late 1780s, the American side was plagued by a lack of government support and security problems, and many settlers began to think that relocating to St. Louis was their only option. A sign of the difficulties facing residents was the move of Father Jean Antoine Ledru in the fall of 1789. "Unable to reside in a country of anarchy," described by one inhabitant as "the most miserable in America," the cleric had accepted

---

59. Kaskaskia residents' petition, September 14, 1789, in ibid., 190.
60. John Edgar to John Francis Hamtramck, October 28, 1789, in ibid., 199.

a position as curate in St. Louis. Once staunchly attached to the people on the eastern shore of the Mississippi, Ledru had often declared "that he would not remove from this side, even after St. Louis was offered him."[61] Hesitant to leave Kaskaskia, Ledru reported he was encouraged to come to St. Louis by the priest there, Father Limpach.[62] One villager believed that inadequate support from Kaskaskians made it impossible for the priest to obtain even necessities, "so that he was in a manner compelled to accept of the offer made him." The resident who bemoaned his loss, John Rice Jones, doubted that any priest would fare better until a government had been fully established in American Illinois.[63] Without support from the state, neither the church nor the community would flourish.

In Jones's view, the efforts of Spanish officials in St. Louis to encourage American immigration were at least partly to blame for the troubles in American Illinois. The Spanish government, he believed, was pursuing every means "to depopulate" the region across the river, making it difficult for the residents of American territory to stay put. "One step towards it is taking their priests from them," Jones asserted, "well knowing that the people will not remain where there are no pastors." He suspected a concerted plan was in place to build up the population of St. Louis and its environs at the Americans' expense. Writing to the highest-ranking American official in Illinois, Jones claimed to have heard "Mr. Chouteau, one of the most capital merchants on the Spanish side" explain the policy. Jones said that Chouteau told John Edgar that the lieutenant governor, Perez, had received orders directly from New Orleans, ordering him to "make every difficulty possible with the people of this side, so that they might thereby be forced to go to live on the other." Efforts to entice Edgar to move across the river included offers of free land, no taxes, and permission to work lead mines and salt springs. Although Edgar had thus far refused all such proposals, Jones feared that his fellow settler could not hold out much longer. Echoing the sentiments of Edgar's letter to Hamtramck, Jones expressed his certainty that Edgar would soon leave, "If by March next no gouvernment or regulation arrives, he will remove to St. Louis where his life & property will be in safety." Edgar's emigration would be a death knell for Kaskaskia, argued Jones: "this village will be effectually ruined as a settlement."[64]

61. John Rice Jones to Hamtramck, October 29, 1789, in ibid., 200.

62. Ledru to [unknown], November 20, 1789, AGI-PC 203-124 (Price compilation, MHMA).

63. John Rice Jones to Hamtramck, October 29, 1789, in Thornbrough, ed., *Outpost on the Wabash*, 200.

64. Ibid., 202.

Escalating fears of Indian attacks contributed to the unease in American territory, adding another incentive for those who considered relocating to St. Louis. In Kaskaskia, residents were in a state of terrified anticipation in the fall of 1789. In October, they kept watch around the clock for over three weeks, "for fear of the menaces of the Indians," whom they suspected were being incited "by the white men" across the river. Villager John Rice Jones declared that danger seemed all around, "as almost every person that comes from *Misère* and St. Louis" brought accounts and letters portending that Kaskaskians were going "to be massacred in the village." For his part, Jones believed most of the stories "fabricated on the other side" with the goal of frightening the villagers into moving, as "no other plan has had the desired effect."[65] Whether the plaintive pleas of Jones and Edgar made an impression on U.S. government officials is unknown, but a sizeable American contingent arrived in Illinois the spring of 1790. A Spanish official in Ste. Geneviève spotted an American galley loaded with troops heading upriver for Cahokia in April and learned from an American officer that a newly appointed American governor would reside at Kaskaskia. Large numbers of Germans were expected to arrive as well, encouraged to immigrate by all manner of enticements.[66]

As the 1780s drew to a close and a new decade dawned, the outlook for St. Louis and its residents was not rosy. The winter of 1789, though not as difficult as the previous two, seemed "too long" because of great quantities of snow and ice. Faced with a scarcity of foodstuffs and extremely high prices for the few provisions available, "the country [found] itself in great misery," reported the lieutenant governor in March 1790. The deaths of many livestock and the thefts of many horses by the Little Osages added another "heavy affliction" to those already suffered by the "poor settlers." After the weather had begun to warm up, villagers began sowing their fields, but so much rain fell in March that the ground was too muddy for them to continue. "The worst thing is that the season is becoming too far advanced," opined Perez, "and, if this year there is not a fair harvest, the misery and need will increase, so that these poor people will not be able to live for lack of what they need for their maintenance."[67] When the typical renewal of springtime failed to materialize, prospects for the future seemed even dimmer.

---

65. Ibid., 203.
66. Peyroux de la Courdenière to unknown, April 9, 1790, AGI-PC 203-239 (Price compilation, MHMA).
67. Perez to Miró, March 24, 1790, in Kinnaird, *SMV,* 2: 315–16.

Chapter 10

St. Louis in the 1790s

THE ENEMIES WITHIN AND WITHOUT

In 1791, when François Louis Hector, the baron de Carondelet, replaced Esteban Miró as governor of Louisiana, the appointment foreshadowed a change in the diplomatic and military posture of Spain in America. More inclined to resort to military action, the baron de Carondelet began his tenure in office by making plans for the defense of the Louisiana territory, both Lower and Upper, against all the forces marshalled against it. During nearly three decades of putative control of the region west of the Mississippi, Spain had continually brooked challenges to its authority and fended off the aggressiveness of other powers desirous of expanding into its territory. Throughout the period, with a brief exception during an Anglo-Spanish alliance in the mid-1790s, Spain had feared a British invasion, first from the east, across the Mississippi River, and later from the north, from Canada. British traders entered Spanish lands seemingly at will and provided goods to indigenous peoples in the Upper Mississippi and Missouri River valleys in such quantities that authorities doubted that the residents of Spanish Louisiana, particularly the French traders and merchants of St. Louis, could compete. Another source of potential danger was France, whose officials had been contemplating strategies for regaining the territory ever since ceding it to Spain in the 1760s. The French threat had a strong internal component, with colonists in Lower Louisiana petitioning the French National Assembly for reannexation in the early 1790s and Republican clubs proliferating.[1]

1. Nasatir, *Spanish War Vessels on the Mississippi*, 4.

Since 1783, the Americans had become a problem as well. Collaboration during the Revolutionary War aside, Spain saw the new nation as a clear and growing challenge. In 1784, Spain closed the Mississippi River to all except its own people. For Americans who considered access to the river a necessity and a right, Spanish domination of the river and the port of New Orleans presented an ongoing source of irritation and an obstacle to economic development. Pinckney's treaty of 1795, also known as the Treaty of San Lorenzo el Real, solved part of the problem, with Spain granting free navigation of the Mississippi and the right of deposit to Americans for three years.[2]

Reports from St. Louis suggested that dangers to the settlement and to Spanish interests were rife, driven by the competition of English traders from without and the threat of the Osage Indians from within. In the spring of 1791, shortly before Carondelet took office, Lieutenant Governor Manuel Perez had sent a plea to New Orleans, urging that new forts be built to block English traders from traveling up the Missouri. "Without these measures," he predicted, "it would appear to me that we may as well renounce the Missouri within a short time." Perez foresaw future disorders and disruptions in Spain's other New World possessions, namely Mexico, unless some immediate steps were taken. "It is evident that the English, and particularly the Americans, speak of nothing else but the kingdom of Mexico, and are always trying to find a road that will lead them to it," he warned. "Great ambition" on the part of these active enemies would fuel their aggression.[3]

The easy access of British competitors to trade goods hurt Spanish interests as well.[4] On at least one occasion, Indian visitors to St. Louis expressed their displeasure at the inferior presents offered by the Spanish. "They refused and mocked at the ones received from us," wrote the lieutenant governor, "showing us what they have received" from the English "in silverware, fine material, coats bordered with silver and gold, etc."[5] The ability of English traders to compete with those living in Spanish territory was well documented. In 1792, one official reported that at least 150 canoes

2. Ibid., 7.

3. Perez to Miró, April 5, 1791, in Kinnaird, *SMV,* 2: 410–11, also in Nasatir, *BLC,* 1: 145–46.

4. English traders seemed a separate species of men, according to some. Perez's successor described them as "men of iron," who were "hardened by the rigorous climate," and able to subsist on an unpalatable diet of unhulled corn and deer fat. Trudeau further stated, in a claim unsupported by other sources, that some of the English traders turned to even less appealing fare if the need arose: cannibalism was reputedly common enough that Trudeau could announce that "rare is the year when some of the men are not eaten on account of the lack of provision." Zenon Trudeau report, May 18, 1793, in Kinnaird, *SMV,* 3: 158.

5. Trudeau to Carondelet, July 10, 1793, in Nasatir, *BLC,* 1: 185.

manned by Englishmen and full of goods had descended from the post of Michilimackinac.[6] At the time Perez wrote, in the spring of 1791, the infusion of British trade goods into the Missouri basin was particularly problematic, as Spain had prohibited trade with the Big Osage in response to murders of settlers in which members of the tribe were implicated. Angered by the punitive trade sanction, some of the nation had tried to take Pierre Chouteau's merchandise when they encountered him wintering on the Kansas river. They also planned to come to St. Louis with a large party that summer in order to protest directly to Perez.[7]

Although the prohibitions of trade were meant to force the Osage Indians to renounce violence against colonists and usher in peaceful relations, the actual effect of the sanctions was to roil the situation further. In November 1791, a party of four notable leaders of the Osage and thirty-two other men of their tribe came to St. Louis to see Perez. Their goal was to persuade Perez, on behalf of the principal chiefs and the entire nation, to reinstitute trade. Unmoved, Perez parried their request, declaring "that they were not to hope for anything if they did not agree to send a chief and one or two" other important men to the capital to serve as hostages and "answer for any insults which their nation might commit." Responding that no nation would accede to such a demand, the Osages departed St. Louis, clearly unhappy with the results of their council with Perez. Informing the governor that the Osages did not assault any settlements as they left, Perez also reported that they had gathered some two hundred warriors at the Missouri River to await traders heading to other Indian nations, planning to waylay and rob them as they passed. A fort had to be built soon, Perez believed, or the Missouri trade would be at an end.[8] Pessimistic about Spain's future in Upper Louisiana, the lieutenant governor was relieved of his duties in St. Louis the following summer. Like his predecessors, Perez had suffered personally because of his posting. In his view, five harsh St. Louis winters had broken his health. After he left his post and had returned to New Orleans, Perez petitioned for retirement on the grounds of illness. Surgeons in the capital attested to treating him for a chronic diarrheal condition they viewed as of long standing, an ailment occasionally accompanied by "loss of sight and hearing."[9]

For Zenon Trudeau, Perez's replacement as lieutenant governor, coming to St. Louis presented an immediate set of challenges, some of them

---

6. Trudeau to Carondelet, November 12, 1792, in ibid., 1: 162.
7. Perez to Miró, April 5, 1791, in ibid., 1: 143–44.
8. Perez to Miró, November 8, 1791, in ibid., 1: 149–50.
9. Jose Fernandez and Joseph Labie, April 3, 1793, in Houck, *SRM,* 1: 372.

outlined in detailed instructions he received from Governor Carondelet. When Trudeau took office in July 1792, he had orders written in late March to begin repairs on the outmoded fortifications. Much needed to be replaced, rebuilt, or expanded. Preserving the old stone tower that had saved St. Louis in the battle of 1780, Trudeau had a new fort constructed around it, with the work completed by the spring of 1793. (Although Trudeau thought the St. Louis garrison needed two hundred soldiers to be manned adequately, Spain never allocated more than fifty troops regularly to the post throughout its rule.)[10] Trudeau's other instructions for his term as lieutenant governor in St. Louis suggested the challenges he would face in straddling the needs of the multiple constituencies under his command. First on the list was relationship building with the local residents, namely treating everyone with impartiality and justice. From Carondelet's orders, it is clear that interpersonal skills were crucial. For example, treating the local curate "with attention and civility" was important, for if Trudeau managed to keep "the civil jurisdiction in good harmony with the Ecclesiastical," St. Louis would be "well administered" and the government "respected."[11]

Among Trudeau's other charges was the instruction that he protect agriculture and increase the population of Upper Louisiana. While working to accomplish these goals, he had to be sure not to admit "vagabond persons and persons of evil customs, corrupted in manners and outcasts of the nations, especially Americans or English." At the same time, he was instructed to preserve "peace and good harmony" with the English and Americans, bearing in mind "that the latter are much more terrible at present for the Dominions of His Majesty than the English." To stave off the threats these groups presented, Trudeau was instructed to do his best to maintain the Indians' "fear and mistrust" of the Americans, while encouraging them to live in harmony with the English "without, however, permitting their traders in this part of the River." In short, Trudeau had a series of nearly impossible tasks before him.[12]

Villagers, including the merchants and traders, faced many trials of their own, which fueled their distrust of Spanish authorities. Many men in the community were dissatisfied with the status of trade, and their unhappiness had to be quelled. In response to "the most bitter complaints" of villagers against the monopoly former commandants had made of trade privileges—"selling them at excessive prices that have

10. Musick, *St. Louis as a Fortified Town,* 77–80; Trudeau to Carondelet, July 25, 1792, cited in Nasatir, *Spanish War Vessels on the Mississippi,* 306–7.
11. Carondelet to Trudeau, March 28, 1792, in Nasatir, *BLC,* 1: 151.
12. Ibid.

almost ruined" St. Louis, an establishment that should have been "one of the most powerful of these provinces"—Carondelet ordered Trudeau to take an entirely different approach with the local mercantile community. On arriving, Trudeau was to make a public proclamation, posted in St. Louis and surrounding settlements, that "all trade, without exception, is free and permitted to all vassals of His Majesty." Only a small annual fee, payable to Trudeau, would be required for a trading license.[13] Many St. Louis traders responded enthusiastically to Trudeau's announcement of free trade. The proclamation, posted during Trudeau's first week in office, inspired expressions of appreciation for the incoming lieutenant governor. Reporting the local reaction to the governor in New Orleans, Trudeau wrote that "the inhabitants are very grateful for the favor," which they believed promised to return them to "the old happiness with which they lived formerly."[14]

Whether the Indian visitors present in St. Louis at the time of Trudeau's free trade proclamation thought it beneficial to them is unclear. What is certain is that an Osage leader, "the principal chief of the Osage nation," who had been in St. Louis for two months waiting for the new lieutenant governor to arrive, wanted some trading concessions. While he apologized for the actions of the Osages, the chief attributed most of the crimes that had led to the trade embargo to the Little Osages and requested that Trudeau authorize traders to visit his people. According to Trudeau, the chief said that "he felt his nation would be more willing to listen to his council, if it saw that [the Spanish] granted him consideration." In short, he claimed that if he was able to obtain merchandise for his people, he would gain more authority and influence over their actions and decisions. Finding the argument a compelling one, Trudeau agreed to send traders. He did not, however, free an Indian prisoner whose release the Osage chief had requested. But Trudeau reported a good outcome to the encounter: "I gave him a small present and he will leave tomorrow, satisfied with having obtained some traders."[15]

Issues of mercantile discontent and Indian trade were not the only challenges St. Louis faced in the early 1790s. In the languishing community, simply finding sufficient numbers to staff the fort, inhabit the village, and populate the region presented a real problem. Indeed, in these years, St. Louis suffered a population decline, with the census of 1791 showing a total population of 1,088 and that of 1795, four years later, only

13. Ibid., 1: 152.
14. Zenon Trudeau to Carondelet, July 25, 1792, in ibid., 1: 155.
15. Ibid., 1: 156–57.

976.[16] In the winter of 1791–1792, the main cause of death appears to have been extreme cold: Foley notes that the lieutenant governor's "offhand comment that most of the twelve persons who had died in St. Louis were slaves strongly suggests that inferior clothing and housing left them more exposed to the elements."[17] A couple of years later, mortality due to lung ailments was a significant factor: Trudeau noted a high death rate due to "colds in the chest," some of which presumably were pneumonia. "That is the only dangerous illness that is experienced in the country," he reported, "and during the past winter, they have been almost general among the work people." Trudeau's explanation of the high mortality rate underlines the poor state of medical treatment available. So many became victims, he asserted, "because of the badly-founded preconception of some against bleeding, and the lack of a bloodletter for others."[18] The trickle of immigrants did little to boost the population. In May 1794, Trudeau told the governor that the new immigrants were few and far from desirable. "It is very difficult for me to attract here Germans, Dutch, and French royalists as you desire," he explained. Those who did come to settle in Upper Louisiana were from Canada, traders rather than cultivators and somewhat disinclined to marry. The few who did settle down constituted "the only increase" in the population.[19]

Efforts to encourage immigration to Upper Louisiana proved far more successful with Americans from the western reaches of the United States, whom Spain hoped would become loyal subjects, than with other Europeans. Americans did possess abilities and traits the Spanish admired. In August 1795, Trudeau expressed a positive opinion of American newcomers who had been crossing into Spanish territory with his permission: "A certain number of these men, the good cultivators, can do nothing but great good for our inhabitants, who need an example to put aside their old methods of cultivation, and to substitute a better one."[20] By the end of the Spanish period, with the exception of large settlements like St. Louis, Americans far outnumbered the French and Spanish occupants of the territory.[21]

16. Houck, *SRM,* 2: 373–78; Houck, *HM,* 2: 58; Nasatir, *Spanish War Vessels on the Mississippi,* 305.

17. Foley, *Genesis of Missouri,* 115 n. 44; Perez to Miró, February 16, 1792, cited in Din and Nasatir, *Imperial Osages,* 221.

18. Zenon Trudeau, report to Baron de Carondelet, dated November 21, 1791 (date is wrong, as census is for 1794–1795, and should likely read 1795), in Houck, *SRM,* 1: 322.

19. Zenon Trudeau to Carondelet, May 27, 1794, in Nasatir, *BLC,* 1: 214.

20. Zenon Trudeau to Carondelet, August 30, 1795, in ibid., 1: 347.

21. Nasatir, *Spanish War Vessels on the Mississippi,* 15; on colonization and countercolonization efforts, see 13–14.

As early as 1783, a Spanish official had predicted that the United States would become "a giant, a colossus formidable" to the countries that helped the states achieve independence from Britain.[22] French residents of the region feared the Americans as well. In 1792, a French inhabitant of Kaskaskia, Bathelemi Tardiveau, wrote to the Spanish prime minister to propose a new French colony in Upper Louisiana. Having lived fifteen years among the Americans in Illinois, Tardiveau felt he had acquired valuable insight into their character and was firmly persuaded of the need "to erect a barrier between this bold people and the Spanish possessions." While American immigrants had much to offer to Spain, namely "their inventive genius, and their inclination to the arts," they should not be allowed to populate the Louisiana territory in too great numbers. "Separated among foreigners, and, above all, separated from one another," he opined, "they are docile and submissive to authority and are the ones that trouble themselves least about their independence." If, however, they formed a body, no matter how small in number, "that instant they become restless and no great time elapses before they aspire to take possession of the reins of government." As far as Tardiveau could see, "prudence, therefore, excludes the idea of peopling Louisiana with American immigrants."[23]

The danger Americans presented stemmed from their restlessness along with their willingness to move and resettle in new lands. Early attempts to encourage American immigration to Louisiana faded under Carondelet, who instead turned to other policies to shore up Spain's American possessions, such as negotiating alliances with southern tribes whom he encouraged to resist the Americans.[24] In 1793, Governor Carondelet informed his superiors in Spain that if Americans settled on the shores of the Mississippi and Missouri, nothing could prevent them from crossing the rivers and penetrating Spanish territory. "Our provinces there being in great measure abandoned [unpopulated] cannot oppose any obstacle to them," he declared, urging that massive plans for defending Spanish Illinois needed to be pursued, with galleys sent upriver, new fortifications constructed, and an enlarged garrison put in place at St. Louis.[25]

While the Americans—both across the Mississippi and within Spanish territory—were one source of worry, Indians close at hand presented

22. The prediction came from Pedro Pablo Arbarca y Bolea, Count de Aranda, the prime minister of Charles III; Houck, *SRM*, 1: 359 n. 1.

23. Tardiveau to Count de Aranda, July 17, 1794, in Houck, *SRM*, 1: 360; Kinnaird, *SMV*, 3: 60–66.

24. Foley, *History of Missouri*, 1: 38.

25. Carondelet to Count de Aranda, 1793, in Houck, *SRM*, 2: 13.

another kind of trial. In early 1793, Lieutenant Governor Trudeau complained about thefts committed by Little Osage Indians and their leaders' travesty of a response to the crimes. After some of the tribe stole twenty horses in Ste. Genevieve, fourteen of their leaders, "the most rascally chiefs," came to St. Louis to see Trudeau and "to weep, as is their custom, and give up their medals." Trudeau doubted their sincerity, claiming the chiefs "feigned the greatest sorrow" about not being able to stop the robbery or recover the horses "without exposing themselves to losing their lives." Waiting to respond to the visiting Indian leaders until the next day, as was customary, Trudeau found the situation in the village dramatically altered. Learning of the presence of the Little Osage leaders, over two hundred armed men from the Sac, Fox, Kickapoo, and other Indian tribes, "surrounded the house where the Little Osages were quartered and staged a demonstration threatening to kill them."[26] St. Louisans must have been deeply disturbed to see such a large, armed, and agitated party of warriors in the streets of the village.

Trudeau believed that if he had not intervened personally, placing himself at the head of the guard, the Osage men would have been killed. A ten-day stalemate commenced. That night, Trudeau had the Osages moved to the troops' quarters, where they hid in the loft. On the next day, when he tried to convince the two hundred armed Indians that their quarry had left, they responded roundly that they knew the Osage were with Trudeau's soldiers. Trying to persuade them he could not allow those who came to see him in peace to be injured, Trudeau told the men of the multi-tribe assembly that "first they would have to kill [him] and [his] troops as well as all the inhabitants before spilling other blood under the royal flag." Whether or not they were aware that Trudeau had volunteered their lives in this fashion, the residents of St. Louis must have found this standoff excruciatingly stressful. When words failed, Trudeau turned to other tactics and found success with alcohol. Dispensing *aguardiente* in generous quantities, he saw the visiting war party become drunk. "Taking advantage of the obscurity of the tenth night to have the Osages escape," Trudeau's solution to the problem was to help them flee the village. Fearful of their enemies, the Osages threatened Trudeau that if any of them perished, the traders along the Missouri River would suffer the consequences. To calm their fears and ensure their safety, Trudeau accompanied them out of town.[27] Whether rogue Osages attacked settlers in outlying areas or their leaders came to St.

---

26. Trudeau to Carondelet, March 2, 1793, in Nasatir, *BLC*, 1: 167–69.
27. Ibid.

Louis, inciting neighboring Indians to react, it was clear that the Osages were a destablizing force in the region.

By the spring of 1793, the Spanish decided that enough was enough. Carondelet sent word to Trudeau in St. Louis, instructing him to form a general expedition against the Osages. Other than ammunition, the expedition should not cost the crown anything. In other words, Carondelet was intent on war and on waging it on the cheap.[28] The key means of doing so would be enlisting the aid of tribes hostile to the Osages. Officials hoped to "incite the Indian nations to strike a general blow" against the main Osage town.[29] To promote this strategy, the lieutenant governor urged one of his main Indian agents, Louis Lorimier, to tell members of several tribes, who had presented a memorial of their complaints against the Osages the previous fall, that it was the ills they had suffered at Osage hands that prompted Spain to pursue war, "in order to procure for them tranquility in our territories."[30] Framing the decision to go to war as an action on behalf of tribes beleaguered by the Osage, officials of the Spanish government were "persuaded that [the tribes] will be disposed to make war of themselves at the moment when the order is given to close the Misuri." The tribes, Trudeau believed, needed to understand that the Spanish were denying themselves important trade "in order to put them in a position to avenge themselves upon those who have insulted and outraged them."[31] Trudeau predicted that the Osages, deprived of Spanish aid and "harrassed" by other nations, would "certainly come to their senses."[32] Writing to Lorimier directly, Governor Carondelet urged him to assist in the coming attack on the Osages. "The general good demands that this perfidious tribe should be absolutely destroyed," he insisted.[33]

The authorities feared that once word of Spain's intentions spread, the Osages would spring into action, and so delayed announcing the governor's plans. According to Auguste Chouteau's estimate, the combined fighting force of the Big and Little Osages was 2,200 men, a formidable body.[34] In April 1793, Trudeau wrote to the capital that he would postpone publicizing the war message until July. By doing so, he hoped to accomplish two aims. First, traders still on the Missouri would have time to return to St.

---

28. Carondelet, undated message draft appended to Ignacio Delino to Carondelet, March 24, 1793, in Kinnaird, *SMV,* 3: 145.

29. Zenon Trudeau to Carondelet, April 10, 1793, in ibid., 149.

30. Zenon Trudeau to Louis Lorimier, May 1, 1793, in Houck, *SRM,* 2: 51.

31. Trudeau to Lorimier, June 2, 1793, in ibid., 2: 52.

32. Trudeau to Lorimier, May 1, 1793, in ibid., 2: 51.

33. Carondelet to Louis Lorimier, May 8, 1793, in ibid., 2: 51.

34. Auguste Chouteau to Carondelet, May 18, 1794, in ibid., 2: 106.

Louis and so avoid being exposed to possible retaliation by the Osages. Equally important, other traders would have time "to go and provide the rest of the nations with arms and ammunition before the Osages have learned of it. Thus the war against them may be more general and successful."[35] Efforts to enlist Indian allies in a coming war against the Osages continued throughout the summer of 1793. In St. Louis, residents declared their view that their need for trade and the government's desire for war were at odds. In June 1793, when war was finally declared, thirty-eight St. Louis merchants, among them Auguste and Pierre Chouteau, immediately responded by petitioning Carondelet to restore trade.[36]

Regardless of the opposition of leading citizens, the logistics of waging a war against the Osages presented another daunting obstacle to Spanish ambitions. Planning the timing of an attack proved difficult, given the seasonal migration patterns of the Osages. In September 1793, Trudeau thought the moment had already passed for that year. "Before we reach that tribe," he suggested, "they will already be away on their winter hunting." Only when the village was reunited and its fields in good order, sufficient to furnish the Spanish attackers with provisions for their return journey, should an assault be launched. An expedition could meet with success, Trudeau estimated, from the beginning of May until August 10.[37]

At the same time Trudeau was facing the prospect of all-out Indian war, he had to deal with some immediate nuisances in St. Louis, namely internal conflict between villagers and the parish priest. Father Le Dru had been making outrageous statements about the girls and women of the village, injurious to their reputations. Incensed, members of the public demanded Trudeau launch an inquiry, a request he denied, imposing silence instead. Observing the general outcry against him, Le Dru stated his own desire for an inquiry, evidently hoping to clear his name. Acceding to these importunings, Trudeau uncovered information that displeased the litigious and outspoken priest, who proceeded to launch a verbal attack on Trudeau.[38] Another priest, Father Didier, was having a difficult time as well. His personal enemies in the village, namely Jacques Clamorgan and Gaspard Roubien (the abusive husband of Marie Anne Leferme), had tried to stir up antipathy toward him but had been unsuccessful largely because Roubien was so widely disliked and distrusted. They accused the priest of living in

35. Zenon Trudeau to Carondelet, April 10, 1793, in Kinnaird, *SMV,* 3: 148–49; also in Nasatir, *BLC,* 1: 171–73.

36. Merchants of St. Louis to Carondelet, June 22, 1793, in Nasatir, *BLC,* 1: 181–84.

37. Zenon Trudeau to Louis Lorimier, September 10, 1793, in Houck, *SRM,* 2: 55.

38. Zenon Trudeau to Carondelet, September 28, 1793, AGI-PC 208a-446, MHMA microfilm.

a morally compromising condition, in a household with young, unmarried women. In his defense, Didier retorted that he had taken charge of the girls during a brief spell when their father was away and felt he could not turn them out when their father failed to return. Didier was exhausted; he had done all he could to reanimate the faith of villagers and instill in their hearts religious principles, love of the king, and subordination to the laws—and calumny was his only reward.[39] Like many of his predecessors in positions of authority in St. Louis, life in the village had worn him out.

The same day that Trudeau reported on priestly misconduct, he sent a pessimistic missive to the governor on the prospects for victory in the war on the Osages, citing a likely manpower shortage as the first obstacle to success. Estimating the number of white men capable of enduring the fatigue of a march, Trudeau came up with a figure of no more than two hundred. None would volunteer, he expected, because there were not enough whites to guarantee success, and perhaps more to the point, whites did not trust Indians as allies. Moreover, the ongoing presence of Osage Indians in St. Louis would dissuade many from leaving the village. In late September 1793, Trudeau reported that chiefs of the Little Osages were continually coming to St. Louis to see him. Showing up unarmed and suggesting a truce, they asked him for necessities, especially gundpowder. He believed that their dependence on guns—available only through trade—for hunting game would be crucial to the effectiveness of the embargo. For their part, the Osages tried to convey to Trudeau how much they were suffering. They expressed their determination, "men, women and children, to come and die of hunger in this town of St. Louis" unless Trudeau showed mercy toward them. The mother of the principal chief came to St. Louis on her own, sent, she said, by her son, to tell Trudeau "either to kill her or feed her." With some frustration, Trudeau wrote, "She is still in my house and refuses to leave, and claims that her whole tribe will do as she did."[40]

When Indians killed some villagers at St. Ferdinand, several miles outside of St. Louis, people quit cultivating their fields, and some colonists began to evacuate the region. Trudeau understood their fear; settlers working in remote fields were exceedingly vulnerable to attack. "As regards the barbarians," Trudeau wrote, referring to the Indians, "we must annihilate them or give up irritating them."[41] Neither option seemed particularly likely or appealing. One can easily imagine a heightened state of anxiety pervading St. Louis, with widely known plans for war against the Osage

39. Father Didier to [governor], April 24, 1794, AGI-PC 209-656, MHMA microfilm.
40. Zenon Trudeau to Carondelet, September 28, 1793, in Kinnaird, *SMV,* 3: 206–7.
41. Trudeau to Carondelet, September 28, 1793, in Nasatir, *BLC,* 1: 199.

and members of the tribe circulating among the residents at the same time. Moreover, no ready solution that would satisfy all parties existed.

The fall of 1793 also witnessed a new mercantile effort in St. Louis.[42] A group of traders who met that October determined that there were nine trading posts that should be divided among twenty-nine recognized traders.[43] The following May 3, 1794, the merchants met at the government house and agreed to the distribution of licenses, twenty-five parts to St. Louis merchants, three to traders from Ste. Genevieve, and one part to the lieutenant governor.[44] Two days later, St. Louis merchants met again at the government house to organize the "Company of Explorers of the Upper Missouri."[45] Part of what fueled such efforts was the overall state of trade; over the previous few years, the profits from the fur trade had declined precipitously, from a 400 percent return on investments to a 25 percent return.[46] Another impetus was the ongoing drive, as Nasatir put it, to "penetrate to the South Sea via the Missouri River."[47]

Although many merchants signed the agreement to participate in the new company, which was to be led by Jacques Clamorgan, some objected almost immediately. Merchant and lieutenant of the militia Joseph Robidou complained that Clamorgan was perhaps least suited of any St. Louis trader to head the enterprise, given the great disorder and confusion of his own business affairs.[48] Clamorgan pressed ahead nonetheless, choosing St. Louis's part-time schoolmaster, Jean Baptiste Trudeau, to head the first expedition up the Missouri. Like many who ventured up the river, Trudeau encountered difficulties and was stopped by hostile Indians.[49] His journal, full of observations about his adventures and the Indians he met, included some scathing commentary about white men's pursuit of the sexual favors

42. Trade recommendations, October 15, 1793, in Kinnaird, *SMV,* 3: 191–98.

43. Foley, *History of Missouri,* 1: 40.

44. Trade agreement, May 3, 1794, in Kinnaird, *SMV,* 3: 278–79.

45. Petition of Jacques Clamorgan to Zenon Trudeau, May 5, 1794, in Houck, *SRM,* 2: 149–57; articles for the incorporation of the Missouri Company, in Nasatir, *BLC,* 1: 218–27; Nasatir, "Jacques Clamorgan."

46. Trudeau to Carondelet, May 31, 1794, in Nasatir, *BLC,* 1: 229–30.

47. Nasatir, "Anglo-Spanish Rivalry on the Upper Missouri," 370.

48. Joseph Robidou to Zenon Trudeau, May 12, 1794, in Billon, *Annals of St. Louis,* 287; Houck, *HM,* 1: 329ff.; Foley, *Genesis of Missouri,* 71; Distribution of Missouri Trading Posts, May 1–3, 1794, Trudeau to Carondelet, April 18, 1795, Nasatir, *BLC,* 1: 209–11, 320–21.

49. Foley, *History of Missouri,* 1: 41; Trudeau's journal, June 7, 1794–March 25, 1795, May 24, 1795–July 20, 1795, in Nasatir, *BLC,* 1: 259–311.

of Indian women, as well as what he characterized as the debauched state of the women themselves. "Our young Canadians and Creoles who come here are seen everywhere running at full speed, like escaped horses, into Venus' country," he pronounced.[50]

The desire to explore the far reaches of the Missouri prompted a wave of expeditions in the 1790s, which had limited commercial impact but larger significance for acquiring knowledge of the land and its peoples. Over the course of several years, numerous traders attempted to explore the length of the Missouri.[51] Clamorgan's Missouri company fueled several such excursions, including Jean Baptiste Truteau's 1794 journey. Another company expedition was led by James Mackay, a native of Scotland, in 1795. As his deputy, Mackay chose a newcomer to St. Louis, John Thomas Evans, a young man from Wales who hoped to locate a tribe of Welsh Indians on the upper reaches of the Missouri.[52] According to the members of a London literary society, the Gwneddigion, the Welsh under Prince Madoc had discovered the New World in 1170. As the literary group's emissary, Evans was charged with finding the Welsh-speaking descendants of that group.[53] Like many other explorers, Evans did not fare well. On arriving in St. Louis, he had been briefly thrown in jail, taken for a spy.[54] When he made it to the Mandan post, nearly 800 miles from the mouth of the Missouri, he was disappointed to discover that the Indians whom he supposed to be Welsh were not his lost countrymen. After encountering numerous hardships, both he and Mackay made it back to St. Louis in 1797. Shortly after his return, Evans experienced some sort of a breakdown, suffering from what he described as a "nervous fever" and spending "several days neither asleep nor awake."[55] His health did not improve with time. In 1799, Louisiana governor Gayoso de Lemos, who had taken Evans into his home, informed Mackay that "poor Evans" was very ill from drinking too much; he did so when out of the governor's sight. "The strength of the liquor has deranged his head," the governor reported, "he has been out of his senses for several days." With care, Evans was improving. "I hope he will get well enough to

50. June 1795, "Trudeau's [Truteau's] Journal," *South Dakota Historical Collection* 7 (1914): 460–61; Nasatir, *BLC,* 1: 257–59.

51. See Nasatir, *BLC,* 1: 87–88; Houck, *SRM,* 2: 183.

52. Edward Williams to William Pritchard, August 15, 1792, AGI-PC 213-1006, MHMA microfilm.

53. W. Raymond Wood, *Prologue to Lewis and Clark,* 42. A native of Waunfawr, in North Wales, Evans was influenced by the 1791 book, *An Enquiry into the Truth of the Tradition Concerning the Discovery of America by Prince Madog ab Owen Gwynedd about the Year 1170.* Evans thought the Mandans might be the group he sought. Wood, *Prologue to Lewis and Clark,* 42–44.

54. Raymond Wood, *Prologue to Lewis and Clark,* 44.

55. John Evans to Samuel Jones, July 15, 1797, in ibid., 192.

be able to send him to his own country," Gayoso de Lemos wrote.[56] Back in Wales, a magazine carried the bad news from Evans's expedition to find Welsh Indians: there were no such people in existence. While Evans may have not achieved what he set out to do, he and Mackay kept journals and created maps that provided crucial information to Lewis and Clark.[57]

Traders who ventured beyond the range of European settlements to explore the west ran tremendous risks. In July 1792, Pedro Vial, en route from Santa Fe to St. Louis, had a terrifying encounter with Kansas Indians, who captured him and his companions, cut off their clothes, and kept them as naked captives. According to Vial's account, a former Indian slave from St. Louis, "who talked excellent French," recognized him and saved his life. After nearly two months of captivity in the tribe's village on the Kansas river, Vial met a French trader who provided him with clothes. On September 16, Vial and his companions left the Kansas in a pirogue belonging to three traders on their way back to St. Louis, where the men arrived on October 6.[58] All of these voyages added to the store of knowledge about the rivers and peoples west of St. Louis, information which later explorers used to good advantage.

More important than the collective efforts of St. Louis merchants to organize the Missouri trade and explore the river's farthest reaches was the commercial ambition of one man, Auguste Chouteau, to control and profit from trade with the Osages. On May 18, 1794, Chouteau, then in New Orleans, urged Spanish officials to approve the construction of a new fort among the Big Osages. He promised to build the fort at his own expense in exchange for six years of exclusive trade with the Osages and $2,000 annually to sustain a garrison of twenty men.[59] Accompanying him to lobby for the carefully designed plan were six Osage chiefs.[60] Leaping at the opportunity Chouteau's offer presented, the governor agreed to Chouteau's terms, appointing his younger brother Pierre Chouteau to serve as the fort's commandant. Ever politic, Chouteau named the outpost "Fort Carondelet," after the governor.

For the Osage, Chouteau's plan represented a far more welcome development than the Spanish war plans of the previous spring. A fort and trading

56. Gayoso de Lemos to James Mackay, American State Papers, Public Lands, Public Lands, VI, 719; U.S. Documents 24th Congress, 1st Session, House Document 59 (series 288), 33; Nasatir, *BLC*, 2: 599; Nasatir, "John Evans," 238–39.

57. Raymond Wood, *Prologue to Lewis and Clark*, 195, 6, 98.

58. Account of Pedro Vial, 1792, in Houck, *SRM*, 357–58.

59. Auguste Chouteau, May 18, 1794, in Houck, *HM*, 2: 210; Chouteau contract, in Houck, *SRM*, 2: 106–8.

60. Foley, *Genesis of Missouri*, 69; Houck, *SRM*, 2: 106–10.

post located at the site of their main settlement would provide them with vastly superior access to arms and other manufactured goods. Not surprisingly, other tribes objected to the apparent favoritism shown the Osage. A Miami chief, Pacane, charged that Chouteau's trade with the Osage served to sustain them while their people committed various crimes. If any member of the Miami nation misbehaved at all, he complained, the whole tribe was maligned and treated badly. Pacane insisted that the situation was "quite the contrary for the Osages when they steal, pillage, and kill. They get nothing but caresses, and are supplied with everything."[61] Despite such objections, Chouteau obtained official approval for his plan for Fort Carondelet, and peace spread througout the region with surprising speed. Trudeau delightedly reported that all was quiet: "It has been a long time since the country has enjoyed such a great tranquility." For their part, the inhabitants of St. Louis seemed "truly satisfied" that no expedition against the Osage took place.[62]

Despite such good news, Lieutenant Governor Trudeau was far from content. Perhaps because he was able to report peace, Trudeau felt he could raise less weighty, but nonetheless pressing, matters with the governor. Writing to his superior in New Orleans, he complained that his situation in St. Louis was miserable because his household was a mess. For the two years he had resided in St. Louis, he had been lodged "like a carriage," with neither the space nor the comfort he needed. With only four rooms, the house he occupied was scarcely his to inhabit. One room was constantly used by visiting Indians, a second contained the merchandise shipped to St. Louis as presents for the Indians, a third was full of the public archives, and the fourth, the one room he had for himself, served as a multifunction space: hall, living room, bedroom, kitchen, and even sickroom for his slaves. The sitaution was untenable, the house was in a state of disrepair, and its owner had no intention of maintaining it.[63]

One of the first tests of the new peace came in September 1794, when a large party of Osages arrived in St. Louis. Going first to the home of Auguste Chouteau, they were accompanied by their host to the government hall. The purported reason for their visit was to convey to Trudeau that they held no grudge against the Spanish for the deaths of three of the chiefs who had accompanied Chouteau to New Orleans earlier that summer and who had been killed by an attacking Indian party while they were

61. Journal of Pierre Louis Lorimier, August 26, 1794, in Houck, *SRM,* 2: 92.

62. Zenon Trudeau to Carondelet, June 8, 1794, in Nasatir, *BLC,* 1: 231.

63. Trudeau to Carondelet, June 30, 1794, AGI-PC 197-694, MHMA microfilm (Price compilation MHMA).

en route to Upper Louisiana. When they met in council the following day, the Indians expressed their agreement to the construction of a fort in their territory.[64] The party of Little and Big Osages requested his consent for holding a dance in the village for two days, which Trudeau gave, noting that no one had never seen these groups so peaceful; he gave them permission and reported that there was not the least disorder.[65] At the same time, to expedite the planned fort's construction, Chouteau took advantage of the group's homeward journey to send men and livestock with them.[66] The satisfactory outcome to this meeting promoted a continued peace.

Over the course of the next several months, the construction of the fort had a calming effect in the region. After some time among the Osages, Pierre Chouteau returned to St. Louis and reported that all was as tranquil as it ever had been. Chouteau told Trudeau that the Osages regarded the fort and livestock as their own and believed they had gained power over their enemies.[67] By August 1795, the palisade of the fort was scheduled for completion, with construction on all of the buildings well advanced.[68] By the end of the year, it seemed clear that the fort had been a resounding success. Carondelet was satisfied with his decision to approve the plan of Auguste Chouteau, "a rich man, very friendly to the name of Spaniard." In December 1795, Carondelet wrote to his superiors that he was satisfied with the results and pleased to report that the effort had been "rewarded by the most complete success." Not only were the fort and associated buildings completed, but the Indians had let Spanish settlements "alone during this year—so much so that they have not committeed one murder, and on the other hand have restored various arms and horses which their war-parties had stolen." With the return of peace, the residents of the region had gone back to cutivating their fields and working their lead mines. Meanwhile, a little colony had sprung up around the fort. In a statement reflecting his racist assumptions about settlers, Indians, and their respective cultures, Carondelet suggested that "intercourse with these colonists will end in rendering the habits of those savages more gentle, so that within a few years they will be as useful as they have been [hitherto] a cause of injury and fear to all their neighbors."[69]

Peaceful relations with the Osages did not signal an end to the military or diplomatic challenges facing the residents of St. Louis and the rest of Spanish

64. Auguste Chouteau to Carondelet, September 17, 1794, AGI-PC 209-654, MHMA microfilm.
65. Zenon Trudeau to Carondelet, September 8, 1794, AGI-PC 197-707, MHMA microfilm.
66. Auguste Chouteau to Carondelet, September 17, 1794, AGI-PC 209-654, MHMA mirofilm.
67. Zenon Trudeau to Carondelet, April 18, 1795, in Nasatir, *BLC,* 1: 320.
68. Trudeau to Carondelet, July 20, 1795, in ibid., 1: 343.
69. Carondelet to Luis de Las Casas, December 2, 1795, in Houck, *SRM,* 2: 101–2.

Louisiana. Relations with the United States were an ongoing problem. In 1794, a threatened invasion of Spanish Louisiana by Americans raised alarms.[70] In January, George Rogers Clark accepted a commission from French citizen Edmond Genet, who issued a call for volunteers to open the Mississippi to duty-free navigation. In return for their efforts against Spanish control, all the Americans who volunteered were promised large land grants.[71] The situation remained tense until October 1795, when the Spanish government changed its stance toward the United States. The minister of foreign affairs, Manuel de Godoy, decided to stave off the possibility of an Anglo-American alliance by settling Spain's differences with the United States. As a result, the Treaty of San Lorenzo, also known as Pinckney's Treaty, granted free navigation on the Mississippi River for three years to Americans, who also gained the right to deposit their goods at New Orleans.[72] Foley notes that the treaty's provisions "dismayed Governor Carondelet, because they cancelled the effect of his arduous efforts to check American encroachment along the Mississippi."[73] At the same time, Spain was involved in a war with England that prompted Carondelet to turn his attention to the defense of Upper Louisiana, a region vulnerable to British invasion from Canada.

Meanwhile, Spain began a diplomatic dance with France over Louisiana. As Foley explains, Spain had sought to use its Louisiana territory as a diplomatic tool, but the French had initially expressed little interest in regaining the land. With the French Revolution, however, the situation changed, and enthuasiasm for recovering Louisiana increased. During the 1790s, repeated discussions of retrocession took place, with Spain "prepared to surrender the colony" but "determined to await the most opportune moment to unload it to ensure receiving a good price for it."[74] Such a move would clearly have been welcomed by some residents of New Orleans. How the inhabitants of St. Louis viewed the prospect of retrocession became a matter of concern to Spanish officers, who began to suspects elements within the village population of disloyalty and pro-French agitation. On two separate occasions, Spanish authorities launched investigations into the political sentiments of St. Louisans.

Ironically, it may have been Lieutenant Governor Trudeau's remarks about St. Louisans' mood that first raised doubts about their attachment to Spain. In January 1793, King Louis XVI of France lost his head to the

70. Carondelet to de Las Casas, April 7, 1794, in Houck, *SRM,* 2: 25.

71. Foley, *History of Missouri,* 1: 38.

72. Nasatir, *Spanish War Vessels on the Mississippi,* 7; the treaty also established the boundary of the United States and West Florida at the 31st parallel.

73. Foley, *History of Missouri,* 1: 42.

74. Ibid., 1: 44.

guillotine, after being found guilty of treason by the National Convention of the revolutionary French government. When news of the king's execution reached St. Louis months later, it "affected all the old French," according to Trudeau. While acknowledging that St. Louisans had been touched by Louis XVI's death, Trudeau made a point of reassuring the governor that the inhabitants of Upper Louisiana were loyal to the Spanish crown. He based his assertion not on the fact that "there never appears an incendiary paper" but on the grounds that people were "truly attached by gratitude" to a sovereign who showered them with graces.[75] With revolutionary songs and other overt pro-French sentiments rife in New Orleans in 1795, Carondelet may have been inclined to be dubious about Trudeau's claims.[76]

Concern about the climate of opinion in St. Louis informed an official visit in the fall of 1795, when military man and future Louisiana governor Manuel Gayoso de Lemos journeyed to the village and filed a detailed assessment of its inhabitants.[77] On Friday, October 30, 1795, as his ship reached St. Louis, a salute from the tower was fired, and he had his men fire a salvo in response.[78] He stayed in St. Louis for eleven days and developed an overall assessment of St. Louis that was largely favorable.[79] Commenting upon its "beautiful aspect" due to "its advantageous position," Gayoso de Lemos found St. Louis full of "quite large and attractive houses," with inhabitants "dedicated to agriculture and commerce."[80] Although previous reports had led him "to believe that the majority of the inhabitants of St. Louis were disloyal" to the Spanish government, he was pleasantly surprised by what he found. "I cannot help but state the contrary now that I have fully investigated their opinions," he wrote. Confident that he had been thorough in his investigation, he assured the governor, "There is no individual with whom I have failed to deal." Visiting St. Louisans in their homes and observing them at their gatherings uncovered "nothing that might be remotely reprehensible," in his view. "To the contrary, all manifest their great affection toward the King."[81]

75. Zenon Trudeau to Carondelet, October 2, 1793, in Nasatir, *BLC,* 1: 204.

76. Liljegren, "Jacobinism in Spanish Louisiana," 62–63.

77. Carondelet was apparently influenced by reports of unrest in St. Louis, based on gossip, that reached from officials in New Madrid, which suggested St. Louis was full of *canailles,* or scoundrels; ibid., 85, 88, 89.

78. Gayoso de Lemos, diary, October 30, 1795, in Nasatir, *Spanish War Vessels on the Mississippi,* 304.

79. Zenon Trudeau to Carondelet, in Nasatir, *BLC,* 1: 370.

80. Gayoso de Lemos, report, November 24, 1795, in Nasatir, *Spanish War Vessels on the Mississippi,* 333.

81. Manuel Gayoso de Lemos to Carondelet, in Holmes, ed. *Documentos Ineditos para la Historia de la Luisiana,* 269–70.

Displaying some sensitivity to the whims of fashion and the political significance of clothing choices, Gayoso de Lemos raised the issue of how the women of St. Louis dressed. Having attended "an Illuminating Assembly at Mr. Chuteau's house," he observed "the fashions of the Ladies" closely. "I have not seen a single tricolor ribbon nor decoration that might betray the sentiments of their families." In short, no one sported a symbolic declaration of affiliation with France and its revolutionary regime. There was one potential exception, he spotted, in the "tricolored dress" of Mr. Robidou's wife. "But I attributed this to the poor taste of the lady," he wrote, "furthermore it was older than the French Revolution, and her husband and she are persons of good character."[82] While Madam Robidou's dress might have been an offense against fashion, it was no crime against the state.

Another crisis of confidence in St. Louisans' allegiance to Spain occurred several months later, after the September 1796 visit of a French general, Georges-Victor Collot. The seemingly too-enthusiastic welcome villagers accorded Collot raised fears among the Spanish that threats to their rule came not only from external agents but from enemies within, in this case, potentially traitorous residents. Sent by the French government's minister to the United States, Pierre Adet, to gather information about the continent's interior, Collot spent nine months traveling through North America.[83] Leaving Pennsylvania in March 1796, he and the other members of his party, which included two trained cartographers, descended the Ohio and then ascended the Mississippi to St. Louis. As they journeyed along waterways, including the Illinois and Missouri Rivers, and stopped at settlements, they made detailed observations and notes about military installations and topographic features.

In St. Louis, Collot saw much that pleased his appraising eye, both as a military man and a Frenchman. He described the population of St. Louis as about 600 inhabitants, "of whom two hundred, all French, are capable of bearing arms." Characterizing St. Louisans as "less degenerate than the race which dwells on the American side," Collot praised the villagers for their attachment to France. "They appear to be excellent patriots, whose lives and fortunes are devoted to France; families of laborers in easy circumstances, and prosperous merchants," he opined. The people would be altogether happy, he declared, if not "for the viciousness" of the Spanish administration, which controlled the fur trade in unfair ways. Even more to the point, Collot expressed his opinion that the weak garrison, numbering

82. Ibid.
83. Neil A. Hamilton, "A French Spy in America," 22–28.

only seventeen men, and dilapidated fortifications meant "that Spain had the intention of abandoning Upper Louisiana."[84]

If Spain abandoned St. Louis, France stood to gain much from its setting and location. The physical landscape was appealing, and its location near the confluences of the Ohio, Illinois, Mississippi, and Missouri Rivers made the settlement an ideal jumping off place for military ventures. In his journal and on his map, Collot envisioned French fortifications at St. Louis and campaigns being launched from the town. In the atlas that accompanied his posthumously published journal, plate 27 showed a "Plan of St. Lewis. With the Project of an intrenched French Camp."[85] Indeed, Collot was certain that St. Louis would become the key military post for stopping British incursions. Clearly, Collot thought the village's location of immense importance strategically and of even potentially greater value commercially. "This place will stand in the same relation to New Orleans," he predicted, "as Albany to New York." All the produce transported on the great rivers of the region would be gathered there, including all the furs of the Missouri, "a source of inexhaustible riches for more than a century."[86]

Perhaps Collot asked too many questions of his hosts during his stay in the village, for it appears that when he left St. Louis, he did so stealthily, under a cloud of suspicion that also came to envelop many of the villagers.[87] When he reached New Orleans, Collot, despite carrying letters of introduction from a French government minister, was detained on the grounds of making a relief plan of the river and of most Spanish posts along it.[88] Apparently, in an effort to persuade the governor that he was hiding nothing, Collot confided to Carondelet that St. Louisan Jean-Marie Papin had inquired with interest about the retrocession of the territory to France.[89] Carondelet's sense of the problems created by Collot's visit expanded when rumors began to circulate that some residents of Upper Louisiana had taken Collot's visit as a sign that retrocession of the territory to France was imminent and had purportedly expressed delight at the prospect with drinking and singing. Some St. Louisans tried to persuade authorities that such demonstrations meant nothing, and that there was in fact no reason to suspect the fidelity of the village's residents.[90] A number

---

84. Collot, *A Journey in North America,* 1: 247–51.
85. Collot, *A Journey in North America,* 3: plate 27.
86. Ibid., 1: 247–51.
87. Hamilton, "A French Spy in America," 27.
88. Carondelet to Miguel José de Asana, in Houck, *SRM,* 2: 133–34.
89. Liljegren, "Jacobinism in Spanish Louisiana," 94.
90. François Vallé to Carlos Howard, April 15, 1797, AGI-PC 214-812, MHMA microfilm.

even signed a formal protest, objecting to the government's view of them as supporters of France.[91]

In New Orleans, reports of Collot's reception in St. Louis took on an ominous significance when coupled with reports of new pro-French societies being founded in the aftermath of his visit. A reputed enemy of the Spanish government had decided to form one such *Sanscoulottes* club in St. Louis after Collot left the village. The instigator, Louis Cogniard, called meetings and held public balls, during which revolutionary songs, designed to "influence the most loyal vassals to rebellion," were heard. Supposedly, the group had even marched through the streets of the village one September evening, armed with musical instruments, stopping at the homes of notable inhabitants, including the priest, to wish them a happy new year.[92] Under the new calendar of the revolutionary French republic, in use by the French government since 1793, the autumnal equinox was the first day of the new year.

Fears of incipient rebellion in St. Louis, combined with worries that the contagion of revolution would spread to other parts of Upper Louisiana, prompted Carondelet to send Lieutenant Colonel Carlos Howard to Spanish Illinois on a "confidential commission."[93] Once settled, Howard was supposed to call an assembly of St. Louisans and inform the leading citizens who attended it how displeased the Spanish government was with their ingratitude, an attitude they they "exhibited to excess" both by manifesting "improper joy over their ill-founded hopes of a change of government" and by forming a secret society and "singing scandalous and revolutionary songs in contempt of the Government."[94] Whether or not he followed these instructions exactly, Howard clearly managed to arouse a good deal of defensiveness on the part of St. Louisans.

St. Louisans objected to what they saw as an inaccurate portrayal of them as seditious supporters of France. Writing to Howard, a number of inhabitants insisted they had only welcomed Collot as an expression of hospitality.[95] Lieutenant Governor Trudeau echoed the protest offered by St. Louis residents. After Howard arrived in St. Louis on April 27, he had given Trudeau a letter from the governor, dated the previous November, that suggested

91. Remonstrance of inhabitants to Carlos Howard, May 12, 1797, AGI-PC 2365-434 (Price compilation, MHMA).

92. Carondelet to Miguel José de Asana, in Houck, *SRM,* 2: 134.

93. Carondelet to Carlos Howard, secret instructions, November 26, 1796, in Houck, *SRM,* 2: 123–32; Carondelet to Miguel José de Asana, in ibid., 2: 134.

94. Carondelet to Carlos Howard, secret instructions, November 26, 1796, in ibid., 2: 125.

95. Remonstrance of inhabitants to Carlos Howard, May 12, 1797, AGI-PC 2365-434 (Price compilation, MHMA).

"Indian of the Nation of the Kaskaskia," 1796. Plate 20 from Georges
Henri Victor Collot, *A Journey in North America*, Huntington Library

that Carondelet harbored suspicions of Trudeau's conduct. He "was greatly
affected to learn that a man so fastidious and attached to his duties" as he
was could be "suspected of having failed." Deeply offended by the implications of the governor's letter, Trudeau declared himself relieved by Howard's
presence, as it would give him an opportunity to restore the governor's good
opinion of him and justify his conduct "in an unequivocal manner." Trudeau
asked whether it was wrong of him to show hospitality to a French officer

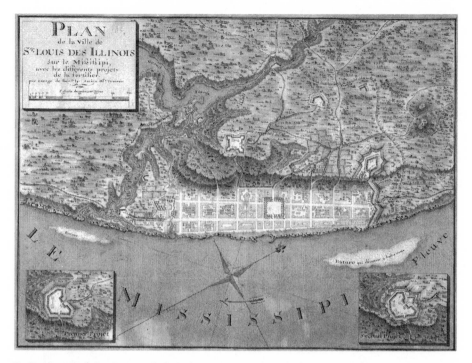

St. Louis, 1796, by George de Bois St. Lys, "Plan de la Ville de St. Louis des Illinois sur le Mississippi avec projets de la fortifier," Missouri History Museum, St. Louis

with good papers, carrying a recommendation from the Spanish minister in Philadelphia. Despite the good treatment he accorded the French general, Trudeau showed him nothing he should not have, as proved by a false report Collot carried, that was in direct contrast to an accurate one Trudeau had in his possession and had refrained from showing Collot.[96]

Charging Howard with investigating the mood and actions of the incendiaries in St. Louis, Carondelet also ordered the officer to send the troublemakers to New Orleans, removing them from St. Louis without alarming the rest of the community, if possible.[97] As chief troublemakers, Carondelet identified Papin, nicknamed Lachance, a stonemason from Canada who had settled in St. Louis in the 1760s, and Cogniard. It was important to "cut off without delay the beginnings of a sedition, so dangerous that if they spread to the other settlements of which San Luis of Ilinoa is the capital their

96. Zenon Trudeau to Carondelet, May 26, 1797, in Nasatir, *BLC*, 2: 519.
97. Carondelet to Carlos Howard, secret instructions, November 26, 1796, in Houck, *SRM*, 2: 123–32; Carondelet to Miguel José de Asana, in ibid., 2: 134.

reduction would be extremely difficult and costly." Papin and Cogniard, along with any suspect men, were to be arrested and sent to New Orleans for trial, where Carondelet expected to "inflict exemplary punishment on those who shall be found guilty."[98] Howard was ordered to assume control of Upper Louisiana's military as well.[99]

Carondelet outlined a careful plan for spying on St. Louisans. Firstly, he instructed Howard to misrepresent the purpose of his mission to Upper Louisiana. On arriving, he should "spread the report" that the object of his expedition was to "protect San Luis de Ylinoia against an invasion of the English in case war is declared." Since the Spanish barracks in St. Louis were too small to accompany the large number of troops Howard was bringing with him, the residents of the village would have to provide them with accommodations. "The citizens will be obliged to give quarters in their houses to all the troops who cannot find room in the fort," ordered Carondelet, "or else to provide a building for them at the expense of the community." While this measure might be a necessity given the inadequate housing stock of the government, it had the benefit of facilitating close observation of St. Louis residents. When explaining the need for quartering troops with the villagers, Howard was to make St. Louisans "understand that this force has accidentally [temporarily] been stationed there with a view to their protection and defense."[100] (Such language calls to mind the British quartering acts of the 1760s and 1770s, which deeply angered colonists along the eastern seaboard and were listed among their grievances in the Declaration of Independence.)

Like Gayoso de Lemos, Howard found reports of a rebellious St. Louis populace greatly exaggerated and saw the need for protection against the British as a much more alarming and immediate concern. When he arrived with his vast forces—five vessels, weapons, and over one hundred soldiers—there was no need to "reestablish the calm" that Governor Carondelet believed had been "disturbed by some hot-heads since the departure of General Collot."[101] Sedition, treason, and revolutionary songs were nowhere in evidence. Acceding to the pleas of St. Louisans to consider the behavior of men like Papin and Coignard nothing more than drunken exuberance, Howard took the two men into probationary custody but promised to seek their release; in July 1797, Carondelet pardoned the

98. Carondelet to de Asana, December 1, 1796, in ibid., 2: 134–35.

99. Carondelet to Delassus, November 27, 1796, in Houck, *SRM*, 2: 122.

100. Carondelet to Howard, November 26, 1796, in ibid., 2: 125.

101. Carondelet to Howard, secret instructions, November 26, 1796, in ibid., 2: 123; Foley, *Genesis of Missouri*, 77; Nasatir, *Spanish War Vessels on the Mississippi*, 137–40.

two fully.[102] Concluding that there was no danger of a local insurrection, Howard determined that the main danger was an external one, the threat of a British attack from Canada. During his stay, Howard decided to combat the British threat by bolstering St. Louis's inadequate defenses with four additional stone towers and a blockhouse.[103]

As the decade drew to a close, the defense of St. Louis became increasingly a preoccupation of authorities in both Lower and Upper Louisiana. Carondelet worried that if St. Louis fell into foreign hands, the enemy would become "the masters of all Upper Luisiana, that is, from the Misuri River to California, and from the Misisipi River to Nogales."[104] Efforts to take on the British were not successful, with Howard's troops, aided by Sac and Fox warriors, conducting a failed raid against Prairie du Chien in the summer of 1797.[105] Nor did other expeditions fare much better. A Spanish vessel stationed in St. Louis, *La Flecha,* sent out several times to patrol the Mississippi River to the north, was forced to retreat to St. Louis out of fear of a Sioux Indian attack in 1802.[106] As the British threat grew, the dangers Collot had seemed to present faded in comparison. Carondelet eventually received a rebuke for having arrested Collot. According to a senior minister, the common interest of France and Spain in staving off British territorial gains in North America canceled out the possibility that Collot's "military examination" of the province was in any way harmful to the Spanish. So certain was the official of France's good will that he was sending a French engineer to St. Louis to assist in making plans for the defense of the village.[107]

In 1796, the population of St. Louis jumped upward, with 418 new people added in one year, an increase made up largely of Canadians, French creoles from American territory, and Americans. As Foley notes, "the vast majority of immigrants who came to Upper Louisiana had been Frenchmen from Canada and the settlements east of the Mississippi, but after 1796 almost all of the newcomers were American."[108] One of the more noticeable

102. Liljegren, "Jacobinism in Spanish Louisiana," 96.

103. Foley, *History of Missouri,* 1: 43.

104. Carondelet to Count de Santa Clara, April 21, 1797, in Houck, *SRM,* 2: 231.

105. Foley, *History of Missouri,* 1: 43.

106. Nasatir, *Spanish War Vessels on the Mississippi,* 141–42.

107. Carlos Martinez de Yrujo to Carondelet, March 13, 1797, in Houck, *SRM,* 2: 230–31; Carondelet to Count de Santa Clara, April 21, 1797, in ibid., 2: 231.

108. Foley, *History of Missouri,* 1: 44.

Americans to pass through St. Louis was Moses Austin, who visited in the fall of 1797. Clearly wanting to make an impression, he entered the village "with as large a retinue, and as much parade as possible." Leading his party from horseback, "clothed in a long blue mantle, lined with scarlet and embroidered with lace," Austin rode to the governor's residence trailed by his servants, guides, and others.[109] Interested in the lead mines of Upper Lousiana, Austin sought economic opportunity in the Spanish territory. His ostentatious arrival in the village may have been designed to convey to officials there that he was a man of substance, a leader who could be trusted to develop whatever opportunities Spain was willing to grant to him.

In January 1798, Trudeau offered an economic appraisal of St. Louis and its 948 inhabitants "of all ages and sexes." These people consumed little from the capital, except for brandy, coffee, soap, iron, and items for the Indian fur trade. Describing the village's "very few farmers," Trudeau noted that those who did cultivate the land lacked sufficient knowledge or willingness to innovate to do it well. He thought that their preference for common farm lands, enclosed and at a distance from their homes, was both outmoded and counterproductive. Inadequate maintenance of the fences surrounding the fields meant that animals routinely destroyed significant quantities of crops. However, the biggest hindrance to development was not the farming style, in Trudeau's view; rather, it stemmed from the Indian peoples of the region. Obliged to oppose and resist hostile Indians, villagers at times dared not go to their farms. "That introduced among them a passive idleness," he believed, "which gave them over to the tasting of spirituous liquors and drunkness," a proclivity harmful to all the villages and directly responsible for "the total ruin" of new settlements. According to Trudeau, although Auguste and Pierre's Chouteau fort among the Osages and exclusive trade with the two tribes had resulted in peace with the Big and Little Osages for three years, other tribes were restive and inclined to treat isolated white settlers badly.[110]

Given the stagnation and underdevelopment of St. Louis and its environs, Trudeau predicted that the main changes in the region would come from American sources. Residing on the eastern bank of the Mississippi, the American population was increasing rapidly. Estimating that American Illinois had a population of three thousand, Trudeau predicted that a hundred thousand people would occupy the territory in a decade's time, and he conceded the future to the Americans. "The more I consider the location

---

109. Houck, *HM*, 1: 369; Schoolcraft, *Travels in the Central Portions of the Mississippi Valley*, 241–42.

110. Zenon Trudeau report on Spanish Illinois, January 15, 1798, in Houck, *SRM*, 2: 249–52.

"French Habitation in the Country of the Illinois." 1796. Plate 21 from Georges Henri Victor Collot, *A Journey in North America*, Huntington Library

of these settlements and seek the possible means for increasing their population," he wrote, "I see no other means than that of the United States, who alone can supply a great number of families." The voyage from New Orleans to St. Louis was simply too costly, and the Americans wanted to settle the lands west of the Mississippi more than any other newcomers did. Those who had done so over the previous year had made a good impression, behaving "very well," improving land, and constructing mills. With some ambivalent admiration, Trudeau noted that "their houses are already better than those of the Creoles and Canadians, who were settled in villages thirty years ago." The time for an interpreter who could help communicate with the Americans was at hand; French, Spanish, and various Indian languages were no longer sufficient to administer Upper Louisiana.[111]

Signs that St. Louis was faltering abounded. In February 1798, reports reached New Orleans that the parish church of the village was practically in ruins. Its timbers were rotted, and it was dangerous to enter. Funds had to be found for its restoration. "Its repair is urgent," wrote a bishop to the new governor, Gayoso de Lemos, "since if it falls, and the faithful become

111. Ibid., 2: 255–56.

accustomed to not attending it, it will be difficult to get them to return to the habit."[112] Whether the inhabitants were unwilling to put up the funds for renovating the church or too impoverished to do so is not clear. Trudeau estimated that fewer than fifteen citizens "could be considered in easy circumstances" and urged the governor to reconsider a tax on trade with the Indians as a means of raising funds for reconstructing the church.[113] The governor had previously rejected imposing taxes on liquor sales, billiards, and companies that had exclusive trading privileges on the Missouri. In the meantime, the capital of Upper Louisiana had as its only church a neglected and dilapidated structure, an eloquent symbol of the weakness of institutions that underpinned successful colonies elsewhere.

Although money was short for the church, St. Louisans did reach into their pockets for defense. With fears of an English invasion of Upper Louisiana and an American invasion of Lower Louisiana circulating in the fall of 1799, the residents of St. Louis began to make voluntary contributions to support the Spanish war effort. (As a result of the French Revolution, Spain and Britain had briefly become allies against the revolutionary government in 1793, until Spain broke that alliance by signing a separate peace treaty with France in 1795, an act that left Britain and Spain once again at odds with each other.)[114] Twenty-seven men, including leading merchants like Auguste and Pierre Chouteau, Charles Gratiot, and Jacques Clamorgan, as well as one of the men suspected in the *sanscoulottes* scandal of a few years before, Louis Cogniard, pledged and immediately paid in animal pelts, a significant gift in "patriotic voluntary subscriptions." Whether motivated by concerns about the security of St. Louis or a desire to allay Spanish suspicions about their loyalties, the "well-to-do people of this city" tendered concrete expressions "of patriotism."[115]

A series of administrative changes took place in 1799, leaving the inhabitants of St. Louis once again dealing with a government seemingly uncommitted to their welfare. In July, Governor Gayoso de Lemos died in New Orleans, and the marquis of Casa Calvo was sent from Havana to replace him. Next, Carlos Dehault Delassus took over as lieutenant governor of St. Louis from Zenon Trudeau, whose administration ended on August 29.[116] Throughout the 1790s, Spain's commitment to administering Upper Louisiana seemed to parallel the feeble condition of its physical facilities.

112. Luis Penalyver y Cardena, bishop of Louisiana, to Manuel Gayoso de Lemos, February 14, 1798, in ibid., 2: 222.

113. Didier to [Carondelet], April 15, 1797, quoted in Nasatir, *BLC,* 2: 559 n. 9.

114. Nasatir, *Spanish War Vessels on the Mississippi,* 7.

115. Voluntary subscriptions, October 12, 1799, in Houck, *SRM,* 2: 298–300.

116. Billon, *Annals of St. Louis,* 350, 295.

Scene near St. Louis. Watercolor on paper by Anna Maria Von Phul, 1818, Missouri History Museum, St. Louis

In the early fall of 1799, storms so damaged the inadequate government buildings that the barracks was ruined and both the kitchen and dungeon flooded.[117]

As bleak as the prospects for development in St. Louis seemed in some regards, there were hopeful signs. Charles Gratiot celebrated the growth of the population "in spite of the impediments" imposed by the government. Ferries were constantly carrying families and animals across the Mississippi, and new settlements were springing up everywhere. If the pattern continued, Gratiot predicted that agriculture would soon become the basis of the economy.[118] The 1799 census showed that St. Louis had 925 inhabitants.[119] The following year, the census of 1800 showed an increase of 114 to 1,039 residents. Animals outnumbered people, with 1,834 cattle

117. Eugenio Alvarez to Carlos Dehault Delassus, October 10, 1799, in Houck, *SRM,* 2: 267.

118. Charles Gratiot to James Swan, November 30, 1799, Charles Gratiot Letterbook, 1797–1817, Charles Gratiot Papers, MHMA.

119. Houck, *HM,* 2: 209.

and 186 horses.[120] To contemporaries, the winter of 1799 and 1800 was *l'année du Grand Hivèr,* the year of the great winter. Years later, Auguste Chouteau recalled that the thermometer fell to 32 degrees below zero during that winter.[121]

As the spring of 1800 neared, the colonists of Upper Louisiana were shocked by news of an Indian attack on a family settled near the Meramec River. Delassus sent word to the commandant of the settlement of Carondelet, just to the south of St. Louis, to take the militia with him and investigate. When they reached the site, a horrific spectacle greeted them. They first spied the decapitated body of an adult man, riddled with musket shots. A few feet away was another headless corpse, that of a boy of eight or nine; in the mouth of the severed head was a piece of maple sugar. A dead cow and calf also lay on the ground, decapitated as well. Inside the house, the men from Carondelet found beds cut to pieces and utensils broken and scattered around the house. Not knowing the names of the man and boy, the militia buried their bodies before leaving. Soon, the identities of the murdered pair were known. A fourteen-year-old, John House, who had escaped with a wound from a musket shot, told authorities that Indians had killed his father Adam and brother Jacob. He and his two young sisters were given shelter elsewhere.[122]

The March murders, attributed to the Osages, became a matter of diplomatic concern, with Spanish officials feeling it necessary to respond to the deaths of settlers in territory under their administration. In August 1800, Delassus received a letter from the governor advising him to authorize Paw-Hiu-Skah, also known as *Les Cheveux Blancs* (or White Hair), the chief of one branch of the Osage, to destroy another branch, the Arkansas Osage band thought responsible for the deaths of Adam and Jacob House. Three days after receiving this letter from the governor in late August, and likely before he had a chance to send a missive to Chief White Hair, Delassus met the Osage leader in St. Louis, where White Hair had decided to visit to discuss the incident. With him were two hundred armed men of his own tribe, as well as La Chesniere, the chief of the suspect Arkansas Osages, and "many of his band."[123]

As a result of Chief White Hair's initiative, a dramatic council took place between St. Louis leaders and Osage leaders in late August 1800.

120. Resumen del Padron General de los Establecimientos de la Alta Luisiana, December 31, 1800, in *SRM,* 2: 414 (foldout after 414).

121. Auguste Chouteau, "Testimony, Before the Recorder of Land Titles, St. Louis, 1823," in McDermott, ed., *Early Histories,* 93.

122. Billon, *Annals of St. Louis,* 298.

123. Delassus to Casa Calvo, September 25, 1800, in Houck, *SRM,* 2: 301.

The Osage party was hosted by Pierre Chouteau, whom the lieutenant governor thought allowed the Indians to treat his quarters as if they were their own. The day after the Osages arrived, Delassus received them "in the presence of all the militia officers of this post, and of the most notable habitants." Delivering over the ringleader of the March attack, White Hair acknowledged that he and his men had come armed, but they had done so only because they were at war with other Indians and needed means to defend themselves. Under his command, no one had "dirtied the road" of Spanish territory. White Hair promised, "While we remain here no one of them will insult thy people." The chief expressed his hopes that Delassus would be able to persuade La Chesniere and his followers to unite with White Hair's branch of the Osage "and cease their raids against the whites." Tellingly, Chief White Hair mentioned that Pierre Chouteau had already advised the Arkansas band of the need to mend their ways. Other chiefs reiterated the same points, and Pierre Chouteau urged that Delassus allow the man responsible for leading the attack on the House family to speak. Agreeing, Delassus listened as the Osage man accepted responsibility for the murders and voluntarily surrendered himself to save his tribe from Spanish vengeance. After listening to the chief's speech, Delassus ordered the murderer clapped in irons and taken to the fort, told the assembled Indians to return for his response the next day, and then invited White Hair, La Chesniere, Pierre Chouteau, Auguste Chouteau, and two other men to dinner.[124]

The next day's meetings proved equally dramatic, with the parties presenting their respective positions, airing their grievances, and making their demands for the benefit of each other and for the large assembled audience. Part of the meeting included gift giving, with Delassus authorizing the distribution of presents to celebrate the council and urge the reunion of White Hair's branch of the Osage with a splinter group that had broken from them and was widely considered responsible for various thefts and atrocities. Presented in the government hall, the presents were distributed under Delassus's supervision and before the officers of the militia, who signed the list of goods as witnesses to what had transpired. The hand of the Chouteau family was visible in this encounter, too. Auguste Chouteau supplied the king's storekeeper, Eugenio Alvarez, with the items distributed, including such weapons of war and the hunt as 100 muskets, 100 pounds of powder, and 300 pounds of bullets. Ceremonial goods included 15 pounds of vermillion and 200 pounds of tobacco. Among the items

124. Ibid., 2: 301–3, 306.

useful for daily life were 300 flints, a gross of awls, a gross of flint-steels, six kettles, fifty hatchets, and two gross of large knives. Rounding out the list of presents were fifty white shirts, large quantities of cloth and ribbon, and four dozen mirrors.[125]

In addition to Delassus's distribution of presents and reproving speech, in which he expressed some anger about Pierre Chouteau's trade with the Osage, the day's council witnessed a remarkable address by Pierre Chouteau himself. Speaking to the hundred people in the room and an audience outside as well, Chouteau blamed the imprisoned Indian and others present for lying to him, telling him they were going hunting when they were "doing evil" instead. He defended his own conduct and declared his subordination to the Spanish. At the end of Chouteau's speech, the Indians shouted their approval of his words. Speaking next, Chief White Hair told Delassus he was doing all he could but could not force the reunion of his tribe with the splinter group. According to Delassus's report, the Osage leader stated, "They refuse to listen, and the reason is that, although I am chief of my tribe, as thou of thine, thy means fail me." In other words, he had no officers or soldiers who blindly obeyed his commands. Nonetheless, both he and La Chesniere pledged to do all they could to urge peace and unity.[126] As on many other occasions, the difference between Native American consensus building and European-style authoritarian rule was thrown into sharp relief.

Clearly the champion of the tribe, Chouteau petitioned Delassus on behalf of the Osage to allow them to stay in St. Louis for a few days. Now unarmed, they wished to seek peace with other tribes and conduct their negotiations in the village, with Delassus as the mediator. Uniterested in playing that role, Delassus explained, "I have not cared to be a party in their treaties of peace under any consideration." In lieu of participating himself, he urged the Osage to pursue peace for their own well-being and permitted Pierre Chouteau "as they venerate and respect him," to be present at their councils. Delassus noted that the Osages made no move whatsoever without consulting Chouteau. Calls to other tribes were issued, and members of the Shawnee, Abenaki, Kickapoo, and Miami nations all came to St. Louis for a grand council. With Chouteau present, the tribes agreed to adopt "a general peace." That remarkable development was celebrated promptly. "That night, in testimony thereof, they all danced together" and left St. Louis a few days later.[127]

125. Ramon de Lopez y Angulo to secretary of state, July 13, 1801, in ibid., 2: 309–11.
126. Delassus to Casa Calvo, September 25, 1800, in ibid., 2: 304–5.
127. Ibid., 2: 306.

What Delassus found most striking about everything that transpired during the Indians' week-long visit to St. Louis, with its intertribal negotiations, dances, and councils, was the role played by the Chouteau brothers. The lieutenant governor was "greatly surprised at seeing the confidence" the Osage placed in Pierre and his brother Auguste, "and the manner in which they get along with them." Without a doubt, the government owed the Chouteaus a debt of gratitude. Since the moment the brothers had constructed their fort and trading post among the Osages and "kept this tribe under their care," Osage raids had greatly diminished. Moreover, no one else in St. Louis was prepared to show the generous hospitality the Chouteaus did, regardless of how much profit they stood to make from the Indian trade. They hosted the Osages at their houses, which Delassus was certain must have cost a great sum. In Delassus's view, the quiet and calm that prevailed during the Indians' visit was directly attributable to the Chouteau brothers. "I had taken all the precautions necessary for the public quiet, in case that they had any hostile intentions," he wrote, "but not one of them committed the slightest act of license and that, I repeat, is due in great part to the Messrs. Chouteau." Almost as an aside, Delassus asked the governor if he should give the Osage man being held for the murders of the House father and son his liberty; he urged that the release take place if and when the two branches of the Osages reunited.[128]

In the aftermath of the Osage visit and intertribal councils in St. Louis, Delassus mused about the future of commerce with the Indians, doubting the merits of the free trade so desired by many local merchants. In his view, free trade generated problems, and government-managed trade created solutions. As an example, he cited the impact that August and Pierre Chouteau had had. Since assuming exclusive control over the Osage trade, the brothers had employed a large number of people who earned their living at the post. That economic contribution was more than matched by the greater tranquility in the region that the brothers had facilitated. The Osage raids had diminished over time. "Now, when anything happens," he informed the governor, "the Osage nation gives satisfaction for it every way that can be expected." Stolen horses were returned. On the two occasions murders were committeed, the Osages turned in the perpetrators. Prior to the Chouteaus' control of the trade, "all who engaged in it were ruined as a result of it." In short, everyone—Osage Indian, white trader, colonial settler, government official—benefitted.[129]

---

128. Ibid., 2: 305.

129. Carlos Dehault Delassus to Marques de Casa Calvo, November 29, 1800, in Nasatir, *BLC*, 2: 622–24.

Chief White Hair (Paw-Hiu-Skah) of the Osages. Portrait by
Charles B.J.F. de St. Mémin, New-York Historical Society

Whether trading privileges should be exclusive or free trade should
exist for all remained a source of local discord. Jacques Clamorgan's leadership of the Missouri Company was very contentious, with a number of
members, as well as the lieutenant governor, charging the St. Louis merchant with gross ambition, personal greed, and incompetence. In June
1798, Zenon Trudeau described Clamorgan's conduct as outrageous and
his most recent letter as "made up of the absurdities of a veritable mad-
man, who enriches himself with dreams." Given that the company was
not doing a fourth of the business Clamorgan claimed, it seemed clear to

Trudeau that the merchant's plans and complaints stemmed from either "the most daring knavery or the most complete madness."[130] One of Clamorgan's chief accusers of malfeasance was Joseph Robidou, who presented a memorial against him to Trudeau, and whom Trudeau thought justified in fearing Clamorgan's schemes and malice. Since there were too few formal complaints to launch an investigation, Trudeau could do nothing, but he had no doubt Clamorgan was guilty of everything imputed to him. "The downfall of his commercial firm and his total ruin, notwithstanding all his schemes," Trudeau believed, had to convince the governor that Clamorgan's exclusive privilege for the commerce of the Upper Missouri "ought to be annulled."[131]

In October 1801, a number of St. Louis men, including Manuel Lisa, signed statements protesting exclusive trade.[132] A newcomer to St. Louis, Lisa made a splash in the village, visiting billiard halls and other public places to proclaim loudly that free trade was on its way. The lieutenant governor thought him imprudent and seditious.[133] In an unsigned response to statements signed by Lisa and others, some members of St. Louis' mercantile community argued that free trade would be disastrous and implied that those who advocated it had little basis for being counted among the trading class. Their signatures were "useless." By including such men, who lacked industry, talent, and reputation, those who complained revealed their desperation. Successful in gathering a group of supporters to the cause of free trade, Lisa repeated the complaint of October 1801 the following June. The sole goal he and his fellow traders had was to obviate "the repeated public wrongs" occasioned to the people of St. Louis by Auguste Chouteau's exclusive trading privileges. "This individual alone [reaped] the benefit from a branch of trade" that all inhabitants were interested in "for their subsistence." If Chouteau's rights were cancelled, the community would thrive, agriculture would flourish, money would circulate, "and other things useful to the public good" would result.[134]

---

130. Zenon Trudeau to Gayoso de Lemos, June 20, 1798, in ibid., 2: 567.

131. Trudeau to Gayoso de Lemos, November 15, 1798, in ibid., 2: 582.

132. "List of the individuals who have signed the three representations against the exclusive trades," October 7, 1801, in ibid., 2: 644.

133. Carlos Dehault Delassus to J. Manuel de Salcedo, May 13, 1802, in ibid., 2: 674.

134. Manuel de Lisa and others to J. Manuel de Salcedo, June 4, 1802, in ibid., 2: 677–79. When Lisa discussed a trade infraction on the part of another man, he took it upon himself to investigate and bring the case before the lieutenant governor. Delassus's response, "Are you the Judge to take information?" prompted Lisa to complain that Delassus was prejudiced against him. Manuel de Lisa and others to Carlos Dehault Delassus, March 14, 1803, in ibid., 2: 717.

As the new century dawned, St. Louisans continued to face many of the same challenges that they had over the previous years, such as internal conflicts over trade and ongoing tensions with the region's indigenous population. What lay before them was an unpredictable and dramatic change, one perhaps foreshadowed by the immigration of large numbers of Americans into Spanish territory. Their days as subjects of European monarchs were numbered, and an American future awaited.

Conclusion

"The Devil Take All" or "A Happy Change"?

THE END OF EUROPEAN RULE AND THE AMERICAN TAKEOVER

As a new century dawned, the inhabitants of St. Louis and its environs were in a strange, in-between state, adrift from the authorities that had governed the past and not yet integrated into the new sources of power in the region. The convergence of different groups and ambitions in the area—particularly the increasingly visible and influential presence of the Americans across the Mississippi—brought new pressures, opportunities, and fears to colonial and Indian peoples plagued by years of bad harvests, floods, harsh winters, poor trade, and hostilities. Each group had reason to worry about what the future would bring. For the mercantile residents of St. Louis, the vigorous and industrious Americans presented the possibilities of regional economic development as well as competition. Far outnumbering Spanish troops and officials throughout the eighteenth century, these French speakers faced the prospect of needing to learn the language and habits of the more numerous newcomers to the east. For years, they had negotiated in Spanish, French, and various Indian languages, and now English would be indispensable.[1] For the indigenous inhabitants of Upper Louisiana, the Spanish side of the Mississippi seemed increasingly a haven from the violence and territorial aggressiveness of the westward-moving

---

1. Awareness of a contemporary trilingual environment existed back in France. In a letter to her doctor son, who relocated to St. Louis from France, Madame Saugrain wondered about the languages spoken in America, asking "Do they speak Spanish where you live? If such is the case all your children will naturally speak French, English and Spanish, which will be useful to them, especially to the boys." Madame Saugrain to Dr. Antoine Saugrain, February 14, 1802, Saugrain-Michau Papers, box 1, folder 1, MHMA.

Americans. Population pressures from the Americans in the east contributed to disruptive relocations of tribes. And for the handful of Spanish officials and soldiers stationed at the northeasternmost point of Spain's North American empire, St. Louis served as a reminder of the limits to that country's imperial reach and coffers, with inadequate supplies, poor facilities, and an understaffed garrison all exposing the inability of administrators to fulfill the diplomatic and defensive responsibilities of the post. Thirty-six years after it was founded by Pierre Laclède, St. Louis remained a place where imperial ambitions faltered and official efforts to exercise authority were frustrated.

Although no one publicized the fact at the time, officials in Spain had decided to relinquish the Louisiana territory to relieve the strain of an over-extended budget and to cut their losses by letting go of a colony that had never fulfilled its promise. In 1800, Spain legally retroceded Louisiana to France, ending, on one level, the period of its involvement initiated by the secret 1762 Treaty of Fontainebleau. As Foley argued, "The treaty pleased both nations. With Louisiana now in his possession, Napoleon could proceed with his plans to build an empire in the New World. On the other hand, Spain believed she had rid herself of an increasingly costly burden."[2] Although Spain agreed to transfer the territory back to France, there were no immediate steps taken to do so, and Spanish administrators remained in charge in both Lower and Upper Louisiana. News of the Louisiana transfer to France reached St. Louis in late 1802, presenting the local population with a serious subject for contemplation.[3] In early 1803, while in New Orleans on business, Pierre Chouteau met with the French official in charge of the transfer and returned to St. Louis convinced by their conversations that the retrocession of Louisiana to France would have positive repercussions for his family.[4]

Some change clearly needed to happen. St. Louisian Charles Gratiot, who was married to a member of the Chouteau family, foresaw imminent ruin. A well-traveled merchant—born in Switzerland, he had lived with relatives in London for a time and moved to Canada in 1769, Cahokia in 1777, and then St. Louis in 1781—Gratiot worried about the future.[5] Pronouncing the country "in a most distressed" situation in early 1803 due to declining Indian trade, poor harvests, and inadequate currency, Gratiot feared that "if

2. Foley, *HM*, 1: 45.

3. Foley and C. David Rice, *The First Chouteaus*, 88.

4. Pierre Clément Laussat to Pierre Chouteau, April 30 and August 24, 1804, Delassus Collection, MHM, cited in ibid.

5. Musick, *St. Louis as a Fortified Town*, 33 n. 29; Billon, *Annals of St. Louis*, 481–90.

Charles Gratiot, Sr. (1752-1817), Missouri History Museum, St. Louis

a happy change" did not take place soon, the best inhabitants would desert.[6] His sense of uncertainty, or even impending doom, was likely shared by many. At that point, of course, St. Louisans had little idea of the profound changes that lay in store for them.

Although Napoleon's dreams of an American empire had prompted him to recover the Louisiana Territory from Spain with the 1800 Treaty of San Ildefonso, the French were unable to assume full control of the land, its people, and its administration. An important factor was war with England. In an effort to stave off a British attack on Louisiana, France kept news of the retrocession from Spain, with whom Britain was at peace, a secret.[7]

6. Charles Gratiot to Guy Bryan, April 5, 1803, Charles Gratiot, letterbook, 1797–1817, Charles Gratiot Papers, box 3, MHMA.
7. Worsham, "Raising the Stars and Stripes over Louisiana Territory," 41.

But Napoleon's "western design" for renewing France's New World empire foundered on the shores of Hispaniola, where a slave uprising ultimately gave birth to the first black republic in the western hemisphere.[8] Bogged down militarily in the Haitian revolution and sinking under massive debts, the French government proved receptive to overtures from American officials sent to Paris to try to purchase New Orleans.

Securing that port and the trade that flowed through it been been a concern of the United States government since the country's inception. Use of the Mississippi and the Gulf of Mexico appeared key to the trading ambitions of the nation. Early in his presidency, Thomas Jefferson had sent a delegation to France to try to insure American access to the Mississippi. In October 1802, Spain closed the port of New Orleans to all foreign nations, a decision that threatened to hamper American commerce significantly.[9] By the end of April 1803, American negotiators in Paris had received a dramatic surprise. Instead of agreeing to sell New Orleans and its immediate environs for the $10 million the Americans offered, French officials made a remarkable counteroffer: the United States could buy all of the Louisiana Territory for $15 million. Seizing this unexpected opportunity, the Americans signed the Treaty of Cession on May 2, 1803, hoping that their actions would meet with congressional approval back home.[10] Acquiring the Louisiana Territory basically doubled the size of the country, its lands eventually forming part or all of fifteen states.

Meanwhile, back in New Orleans, plans were underway for the retrocession of the territory from Spain to France. Almost no sooner than word arrived in Spanish Louisiana of the French recovery of the land, the prospect of French rule had dissipated, buried by financial problems and imperial exhaustion. Transfer of the territory from Spain to France and then to the United States took time to accomplish and happened more quickly in Lower Louisiana. In November 1803, French officials formally took possession of Louisiana from Spanish administrators in New Orleans. On November 30, sixty French colonists escorted Pierre Clément Laussat, the official French representative, to the New Orleans City Hall, while a military salute was fired from a boat in the river. Spanish troops lined the central plaza while drums rolled.[11]

French possession of Lower Louisiana, however, was short-lived, with the formal transfer of control of the territory to the United States taking

8. Dubois, "The Haitian Revolution and the Sale of Louisiana."
9. Foley and C. David Rice, *The First Chouteaus,* 88.
10. News of the cession reached the United States in July; Foley, *History of Missouri,* 1: 65.
11. Sayad, "Louisiana Purchase," 34.

place just a few weeks later, on December 20, 1803. The commander of the American army, James Wilkinson, and Misssissippi territorial governor William C. C. Claiborne participated in the ceremony, assuming authority over Lower Louisiana or, as it was renamed, the District of Orleans.[12] According to a writer for the *Moniteur,* a New Orleans newspaper, a thousand people watched in silence as the French flag was lowered in front of the government headquarters. The American flag was raised at the same time, and the two fluttered for a moment together. According to the reporter, many in the crowd had tears in their eyes, and an air of sadness reigned.[13] The transition of power in Upper Louisiana, which the United States labeled the District of Louisiana, would have to wait. (The dividing line between the two districts was roughly the southern border of Arkansas.)[14]

Although the formal transfer of authority in St. Louis did not take place until the spring of 1804, signs of the imminent change were visible in a flurry of activity in the winter of 1803. Shortly after news of the Louisiana Purchase reached the United States, Jefferson had authorized funds for an expedition he had long envisioned. Its charge was to discover the resources contained in the vast territory encompassed by the Missouri River and its tributaries, ideally reaching the ocean via one of the west's great rivers. During the 1790s, numerous traders and explorers had ventured northwest from St. Louis, but none had reached the source of the Missouri or found the elusive water route to the Pacific. The territory they wished to travel encompassed unknown peoples, unfamiliar (to European colonists and American citizens) topography, and vast lands and resources, such as potentially valuable new species and minerals. To head the expedition that would explore the Missouri River as it meandered through the Louisiana Territory, Jefferson appointed his fellow Virginian and friend Meriwether Lewis.[15] As his co-leader, Lewis selected William Clark, a native of Virginia whose family had resettled to Kentucky and who had significant experience in the American west.[16] In December 1803, the two captains of the newly founded Corps of Discovery reached Upper Louisiana. Having heard reports that the Spanish lieutenant governor intended to stop them, Lewis hurried ahead to St. Louis. On December 7, he met Carlos Dehault Delassus and explained his commission but found a frosty reception.

---

12. Worsham, "Raising the Stars and Stripes over Louisiana Territory," 41.

13. New Orleans *Moniteur,* December 29, 1803, cited in Sayad, "Louisiana Purchase," 32.

14. Worsham, "Raising the Stars and Stripes over Louisiana Territory," 41.

15. A good introduction to the expedition is the handsomely illustrated companion volume to the Missouri History Museum's Lewis and Clark exhibition: Gilman, *Lewis and Clark.*

16. Foley, *Wilderness Journey,* 49–51.

Delassus was unwilling to allow the Americans to enter Spanish territory and camp on the Missouri River, where they wished to establish a base in preparation for their journey. Delassus explained that he was opposed to any such expedition until he received permission from higher-ups; he soon had to reverse his stance.[17] Delassus's hesitation was not surprising, given the Spanish government's concerns about how aggressive and grasping the Americans could be.[18] In the interim, Lewis and Clark decided to set up camp across the Mississippi River in American territory, at Wood River, opposite the mouth of the Missouri River.[19] As they made their way to that spot, they drew the attention of St. Louisans. "The admiration of the people were So great," reported Clark, "that hundreds Came to the bank to view us." For their part, Lewis and Clark briefly stopped at the landing along the riverfront to pay their respects to the inhabitants.[20] One can only imagine the rumors that flew through the village with the Americans' arrival, quick departure, and continued progress upriver.

Early in the new year, Delassus learned the details of the upcoming territorial transfer, which involved American officer Captain Amos Stoddard taking formal possession on behalf of the United States. Anticipating Stoddard's arrival and trying to maintain everything in readiness for the transfer, Delassus issued an order to the Spanish garrison of St. Louis on February 23, 1804, in which he commanded the men "keep themselves in full uniform, and with strict regard to personal neatness." Until the day of "the delivery of the fortifications to the United States," no one was permitted to absent himself from the quarters.[21] The appearance of his men had been preying on Delassus's mind for some time. In August 1803, he had requested funds to repay a loan from Auguste Chouteau so that he would have some money to pay his soldiers. He wanted them to "have a decent appearance during the Transfer ceremony," yet he had received no money in months, nor had the soldiers received wages.[22] Delassus also had high

17. Nemesio Salcedo to Pedro Cevallos, May 8, 1804, enclosure with dispatch no. 4, from Carlos Dehault Delassus, December 9, 1803, referring to Lewis's visit of December 7, 1803, in Nasatir, *BLC,* 2: 731; Foley, "Friends and Partners," 272; William Clark to Jonathan Clark, December 16, 1803, in Holmberg, ed., *Dear Brother,* 61.

18. Nemesio Salcedo to Pedro Cevallos, May 8, 1804, in Nasatir, *BLC,* 2: 731. An official who anticipated that "Captain Merry Weather" was likely to stray beyond the territory he was entitled to explore proposed arresting him and his party if they entered Spanish territory in New Mexico.

19. Foley, *History of Missouri,* 1: 72–73.

20. William Clark to Jonathan Clark, December 16, 1803, in Holmberg, ed., *Dear Brother,* 61; Foley, "Friends and Partners," 272.

21. Billon, *Annals of St. Louis,* 352, 357–58.

22. Sayad, "Louisiana Purchase," 36.

expectations for the troops' conduct, requiring that each man "so comport himself as to uphold the reputation of the Spanish troops so justly acquired and extolled for ages past." He flattered himself that his men's conduct in St. Louis would "earn for themselves the respect and esteem of the American troops."[23] Whether or not the troops managed to maintain the order and polish Delassus commanded, it seems likely that his orders added to an air of anticipation in the village.

The first official meeting between the ranking Spanish and American officials took place in February 1804. From across the river in Kaskaskia, Stoddard sent greetings to Delassus, to which Delassus promptly responded in kind, and then the American came to St. Louis on February 24 to meet the outgoing offical and other members of the village community and to begin making plans.[24] Twenty people escorted Stoddard as he made his way into the village. In the presence of "some of the most respectable inhabitants" of St. Louis, Delassus made a speech. "In the King my master's name," he began, "I now salute you as the commissary of the French Republic; and permit me to Congratulate the United States of America on the purchase they have made of this fine and rich Territory." Presenting to Stoddard the officers under his command and the residents, he promised the American that these inhabitants, who had demonstrated "zeal and fidelity" to Spain were "now ready to receive the new Laws" of the United States.[25] Equally gracious, Stoddard thanked his host for the "wholly unexpected" reception, which he declared "a favorable omen" for "future harmony."[26] In receiving the American officer, Delassus pulled out the stops to welcome him, throwing a "great Dinner" at his home to accompany the speeches and introductions and hosting Meriwether Lewis and William Clark as well. The following day, Delassus entertained Stoddard again, throwing "a most Sumpcious Dinner" for a large party that again included Lewis and Clark, the latter of whom noted the "great Deel of formality and parade" on display.[27] Although the Spanish and American leaders started to set up the details for the official ceremonies to take place as soon as

---

23. Billon, *Annals of St. Louis,* 357–58.

24. Stoddard to Delassus, February 18, 1804; Delassas to Stoddard, February 20, 1804, Stoddard Papers, box 1, folder 3, MHMA.

25. Carlos Dehault Delassus, speech, February 24, 1804, Stoddard Papers, box 1, folder 3, MHMA.

26. Amos Stoddard, response to Carlos Dehault Delassus speech, February 24, 1804, Stoddard Papers, box 1, folder 3, MHMA.

27. William Clark to Jonathan Clark, February 25, 1804, in Holmberg, ed., *Dear Brother,* 76–77; Foley, "Friends and Partners," 275.

possible, Delassus fell ill and Stoddard's men were delayed in transit by the ice-blocked river.[28]

In the weeks leading up to the transfer, Stoddard asked Delassus for advice about the inhabitants of St. Louis and other parts of Upper Louisiana. He requested that Delassus prepare a list of the residents of the region in his employ, providing their names and a decription of the tasks they performed for the government. In describing forty-three men in government service, Delassus attributed varying levels of usefulness to them, from the fifth man on the list, Joseph Robidou, for whom the complete description as "an infirm old man, almost blind," made clear that he was of no potential assistance to the incoming government, to the sixth, Pierre Chouteau, whom Delassus characterized as "the most suitable officer of this post" to handle business related to the Indians of the Missouri River basin. "A very zealous officer," observed Delassus, Chouteau had served as the commandant at Fort Carondelet, where he managed trade with the Osage with unprecedented skill. "He is respected and feared, and I believe loved by this nation," he added.[29] Others were noted variously as illiterate, talented, given to drink, or devoted to service.

During the winter of 1803 and early 1804, while Lewis and Clark assembled men and provisions, they built relationships with the people of St. Louis as well. Clark was, in fact, renewing acquaintances, having first visited St. Louis in September 1797 when he came to know many of the local elite and attended a ball at the residence of Pierre Chouteau.[30] In the months before their departure, Lewis and Clark spent a great deal of time with Auguste and Pierre Chouteau—translators at hand—exchanging information and establishing connections that would prove mutually beneficial.[31] Hospitality at Pierre Chouteau's home played a role in their developing ties. As Clark noted gratefully later that spring, "On our several visits to St. Louis, in the course of the Winter and Spring, we have made the house of this gentleman our home."[32] In January, Lewis sought to acquire as much information as he could, turning to Auguste Chouteau for answers to a series of questions he had about Upper Louisiana. Ranging

28. Amos Stoddard to Governor William Claiborne and General James Wilkinson, March 26, 1804, Stoddard Papers, box 1, folder 5, MHMA; Billon, *Annals of St. Louis,* 354; Foley, *History of Missouri,* 1: 71.

29. Billon, *Annals of St. Louis,* 365–66.

30. Foley, "Friends and Partners," 271–72; Foley, *Wildernesss Journey,* 42.

31. Foley, "Friends and Partners," 274.

32. William Clark to William Croghan, May 2, 1804, Clark Papers, MHMA, cited in Foley, "The Lewis and Clark Expedition's Silent Partners," 132.

from straightforward statistical queries about the population—numbers of slaves and other nonwhite peoples, numbers of emigrants from the United States—Lewis sought Chouteau's insights and opinions about the potential of the area, the habits of its residents, and the basis of their wealth.[33] The Chouteau brothers gave the leaders of the expedition practical assistance, such as a look at the 1800 census and the loan of a map of the Missouri River.[34] In turn, the brothers gained welcome business as Lewis and Clark purchased from them the supplies needed for their journey. In short, the Americans were made welcome in St. Louis, attending balls, enjoying local hospitality, and spending time with the village elite.[35] (Although only a handful of English speakers resided in St. Louis at the time, estimates held that Anglo-Americans constituted roughly two-thirds of the non-Indian population of Upper Louisiana in 1803.)[36]

While people like the Chouteau brothers were looking to the future, busy building the relationships that would enable them to continue enjoying positions of influence under the new regime, government officials like Delassus were occupied with the immediate matter of making that transition happen as smoothly as possible. On March 8, 1804, Delassus had an announcement posted that signalled the end to an era in St. Louis. He informed the public that at 11 a.m. or noon the following day, the transfer ceremony would take place.[37] In a detailed "Order of the Ceremony" directed at the troops, Delassus commanded the soldiers to follow a set routine: march to a drumbeat at double time until within thirty feet of the flag pole in front of the government house, then line up in formation to its right, maintaining silence and "keeping that severe military appearance so becoming to Spaniards." Once the sergeant in charge saw Delassus exit the government building, he was to order the soldiers to execute a maneuver with their weapons while a drummer played on. Once Delassus received the official papers, the drummer was to stop.[38]

The next day's spectacle brought a number of impressive sights and sounds. Most of the inhabitants of St. Louis assembled in the street in

33. Meriwether Lewis to Auguste Chouteau, January 4,1804, in Billon, *Annals of St. Louis,* 384.

34. Foley, "Friends and Partners," 273.

35. Moulton, ed., *The Journals of the Lewis and Clark Expedition,* 2: 174.

36. Amos Stoddard estimated that two-thirds of the inhabitants of Louisiana were American, many from New England, and one-third was French. Stoddard to [mother] Mrs. Phoebe Benham, June 16, 1804, Stoddard Papers, box 1, folder 9, MHMA.

37. Delassus, "Notice to the public," March 8, 1804, Delassus–St. Vrain Collection, box 2, folder 6, MHMA; Sayad, "Louisiana Purchase," 36.

38. Delassus, "Orders for the 9th of March 1804," Delassus–St. Vrain Collection, box 2, folder 6, MHMA.

Auguste Chouteau, Missouri History Museum, St. Louis

front of the government house to watch the strangers approach. With the American soldiers were a number of officers including Captain Meriwether Lewis, whom many in the village had already met. Waiting at the government house was an official welcoming party that included Lieutenant Governor Delassus and some of the most prominent members of the community. In advance, Delassus had ordered that at the moment Stoddard entered the government house to receive possession of the territory, a salute would be fired from all the cannon at the fort. A soldier, standing at the corner of the gallery of the government house, would wave his hat to the sentinnel at the fort, thereby signalling him that the salutes should begin.[39]

39. Billon, *Annals of St. Louis*, 358.

Speaking to the assembled crowd, Delassus delivered a brief proclamation to open the transfer ceremony. "Inhabitants of Upper Louisiana," he
began, "By the King's command, I am about to deliver up this post and its
dependencies." With his words, the villagers' days as the colonial subjects
of a Catholic European monarch were at an end; incorporation into the
American republic was at hand. "The flag under which you have been protected for a period of nearly thirty-six years is to be withdrawn," Delassus
stated. "From this moment you are released from the oath of fidelity you
took to support it." With these words, Delassus severed the official ties that
linked the villagers on the banks of the Mississippi to the Spanish king and
court thousands of miles away. Declaring that St. Louisans' "fidelity and
courage" in Spain's defense would "never be forgotten," Delassus concluded
by wishing his audience "perfect prosperity" in the future.[40] Turning to
Stoddard, Delassus addressed the American officer, who then played his role
by delivering brief remarks to Delassus and the villagers. Stoddard noted
that the assembled St. Louisans responded emotionally to the ceremony.
"The change excited the sensibilities of many people," he acknowledged,
drawing "tears from the eyes of all—but there were not tears of regret."[41]
Stoddard's take on the outpouring of emotion seems unlikely to be accurate; one can imagine the moment provoking a range of reactions, from
regret, humiliation, and loss to anticipation and anxiety over the future.[42]

Military salutes, the raising and lowering of flags, and document signing
completed the formal event. Standing by at the fort on the hill at the edge
of the village, Spanish troops fired a salute as Delassus had planned. Eleven
cannon salvos accompanied the lowering of the Spanish flag.[43] American
troops then marched to the fort and exchanged salutes with their Spanish
counterparts. The Spanish flag that had flown above St. Louis for decades
was lowered for the last time. For the next twenty-four hours, the possession
of the territory was French. For the francophone inhabitants of St. Louis,
most of whom were ethnically French and many of whom still had close ties
to family in France, the days of transition must have been poignant ones,

40. Proclamation of Delassus, March 9, 1804, in ibid., 355; Delassus, "Orders for the 9th of
March 1804," Delassus–St. Vrain Collection, box 2, folder 6, MHMA; Delassus to Inhabitants of St.
Louis, March 9, 1804, Delassus–St. Vrain Collection, box 2, folder 6, MHMA.

41. Stoddard to Claiborne and Wilkinson, March 26, 1804, Stoddard Papers, box 1, folder 5,
MHMA; Foley, *Genesis of Missouri,* 139 n. 29.

42. Decades later, Marie LaRue, a young woman at the time, recalled that "all of the French and
Spanish inhabitants of that day, herself among the number, shed tears of misgivings and regret at
their deep humiliation"; *St. Louis Republican,* January 21, 1878, cited in Vogel, "Social Life in St.
Louis," 85.

43. Sayad, "Louisiana Purchase," 37.

reminders that the country from which they originally hailed never had nor ever would officially govern their village. The point could only have been driven home by the lack of any French official on hand to oversee the ceremonies. To save money, the French commissioner in charge of the transfer had appointed Stoddard to act as France's agent, receiving Upper Louisiana from the Spanish as France's representative. He then in effect delivered it to himself, as the official representing the United States.[44] Lewis acted as a witness for the U.S. government, signing the transfer documents along with two prominent St. Louisans: surveyor Antoine Soulard and translator Charles Gratiot. Altogether, they signed six copies, three in Spanish and three in English.

Regardless of the feelings of the parties involved, there were numerous celebrations of the transfer. The Spanish official, Delassus, threw a dinner and ball in Stoddard's honor on March 9.[45] On the next night, after the American flag had been raised, the Chouteaus hosted an unofficial celebration, signalling the open hand and welcome of the local elite to the incoming American regime.[46] For his part, Stoddard spent significant resources to treat St. Louisians as well. In the large house that he rented in St. Louis, Stoddard hosted a dinner and ball, spending over $600 that he had borrowed from Pierre Chouteau for the occasion. Although he hoped he would be reimbursed, he considered the money well spent regardless: "Even if I am denied a compensation for these *particular expenses,* I shall not regret them for the pleasure I have given and received is adequate to them."[47]

On the day after the transfer, Stoddard assumed control of the government for the United States, and his men raised the American flag. Anticipating some hostility, Stoddard was delighted to report that his expectations had been disappointed. "I have not been able to discover any aversion to the new order of things," he wrote. "On the contrary a cordial acquiescence seems to prevail among all ranks of people."[48] The country was "beautiful beyond description," he told his worried mother, and the French residents considered it "a duty as well as a pleasure to make themselves agreeable

44. Pierre Clement de Laussat was the French commissioner. Foley, *History of Missouri,* 1: 71.

45. Stoddard to [mother] Mrs. Phoebe Benham, June 16, 1804, Stoddard Papers, box 1, folder 9, MHMA; Foley, *Genesis of Missouri,* 140 n. 32; Foley, *History of Missouri,* 1: 72; Sayad, "Louisiana Purchase," 38; Foley and C. David Rice, *The First Chouteaus,* 92.

46. Sayad, "Louisiana Purchase," 39.

47. Stoddard to [mother] Mrs. Phoebe Benham, June 16, 1804, Stoddard Papers, box 1, folder 9, MHMA; Sayad, "Louisiana Purchase," 38.

48. Stoddard to Secretary of War [Gen. Dearborn], March 10, 1804, Stoddard Papers, box 1, folder 4, MHMA.

to the United States."[49] Whether his assessment was accurate or not, it is likely that villagers understood clearly that the aggressive, ambitious people who had been coming to the area for years were not temporary visitors. The Americans wanted all of the Louisiana Territory: the Mississippi, New Orleans, the Missouri, and all the trade and resources its tributaries and ports promised. Thus, regardless of what may have been their private concerns about the newcomers, the pragmatic merchants and farmers looked to an American future and wisely made the officials of the new government welcome. On March 10, Stoddard issued a circular address that outlined at length the benefits the newly minted Americans were to derive from becoming part of the United States. Outlining the reciprocal duties of a government and a people, Stoddard pronounced, "You are divested of the character of Subjects, and clothed with that of citizens." Whether promises of inclusion and rights in "a great community" moved the residents of the region, Stoddard's decision to confirm all the land grants made by his predecessors eased the fears of some St. Louisans and made them more amenable to the shift.[50]

Stoddard had reason to be concerned about the reaction to American rule on the part of the region's indigenous inhabitants as well. A few days after the transfer ceremony, Delassus, at Stoddard's request, prepared a speech to be delivered to many tribes in St. Louis and its environs, in which he announced the shift from the Spanish to the American government. Addressing the Delawares, Abenakis, Sacs, and others, Delassus began by announcing that the tribes' "old fathers, the Spaniard and the Frenchman," had grasped the hand of the new father, "the head chief of the United States."[51] Now in control of all the territory formerly claimed by the French and Spanish, the United States would "defend them, and protect the whites and red skins" who lived on these lands. "You will be as happy," he told his likely skeptical audience, "as if the Spaniard was still here."[52] Singling out Takinousa, a chief, Delassus reminded the Indian leader that he had distinguished him with a medal and letters attesting to his loyal services to Spain and that he had recommended Takinousa to the Americans on the

49. Stoddard to [mother] Mrs. Phoebe Benham, June 16, 1804, Stoddard Papers, box 1, folder 9, MHMA.

50. Amos Stoddard, circular address, March 10, 1804, Stoddard Papers, box 1, folder 4, MHMA; Foley, *History of Missouri,* 1: 71–72.

51. Billon, *Annals of St. Louis,* 362–63.

52. Indian peoples were not consistently referred to in any one way. In this instance, Delassus used "peaux rouge." Ibid., 362; original in Delassus, draft of oration to the Delawares, Abenakis, and Saquis nations regarding the transfer of Louisiana to the United States; Delassus–St. Vrain Collection, box 2, folder 6, MHMA.

Auguste Chouteau purchased Laclède's original house in 1789, renovated it, and lived in it until his death in 1829, State Historical Society of Missouri, Columbia

grounds of his service and desire "to maintain a sincere friendship with the whites."[53]

Delassus tried to cast the transfer ceremony celebrations of the previous week as symbolic rituals intended for the Indians' benefit. "For several days past we have fired off cannon shots to announce to all the nations that your father the Spaniard is going," said Delassus. "His heart is happy to know that you will be protected and sustained by your new father." In the haze of the weapon fire was, he claimed, a message. Delassus hoped "that the smoke of the powder may ascend to the master of life, praying him to shower on you all a happy destiny and prosperity in always living in good union with the whites."[54] Invoking Indian cultural beliefs and linking them to harmonious relations with whites, Delassus attempted to shore up the position of the American newcomers. Whether Delassus's Indian auditors found any element of his speech reassuring is impossible to determine. What does seem likely is that they listened warily, doubtful that the Americans came with a strong desire for peaceful cohabitation and trade. Many came into St. Louis to see Stoddard. "They crowd here by hundreds to see their new father, and to hear his words," the American officer reported, somewhat

53. Billon, *Annals of St. Louis,* 363.
54. Ibid.

worried that the Indian peoples in the village expected presents and would commit hostile acts if no gifts were forthcoming. Unauthorized to provide anything beyond provisions, Stoddard was relieved that Lewis was able to offer the Indian visitors whiskey and tobacco.[55] Some Indians in St. Louis may have been more immediately interested in the preparations under-way for Lewis and Clark's expedition, since journeys up the Missouri River had previously signalled attempts to open or develop commercial ties with indigenous peoples.

As the spring wore on, St. Louis witnessed a bustle of activity leading up to Lewis and Clark's departure. Over the course of the previous decade, several men and expeditions left St. Louis to explore the upper reaches of the Missouri. Although repeatedly failing to achieve all of their aims, the men who undertook those journeys had acquired valuable information that added to the store of knowledge Lewis and Clark amassed before setting out. On May 14, supplies and vessels readied for the jouney, Clark and forty men of the expedition left Camp Dubois with a keelboat and two pirogues and headed up the Missouri, reaching St. Charles on May 16.[56] There, they waited for Lewis, still in St. Louis making final arrangements for the trip. Staying in the home of Pierre Chouteau, Lewis finished his business a few days later and made plans to leave.

On Sunday, May 20, Lewis "bid an affectionate adieu" to his hostess and to some of his "fair friends of St. Louis." Meeting up with Captain Stoddard, Auguste Chouteau, Charles Gratiot, "many other respectable inhabitants of St. Louis," and two other American officers, who had all decided to accompany him to St. Charles, Lewis set out to join his "friend companion and fellow labourer Capt. William Clark." The journey took Lewis, the American officers, and the leading Frenchmen of St. Louis through what Lewis described as "a beatifull high leavel and fertile pra-rie" that encircled the village and then into woodlands that led to the Missouri. A violent thunderstorm in the early afternoon interrupted their progress, forcing the party to take shelter in a cabin. Lunching while they waited for the rain to stop, the men finally concluded that the succession of clouds scuttering across the sky meant that the morning's fair weather was unlikely to return. Determined to reach St. Charles that day, Lewis decided to go on, accompanied by most of the men in the party.[57] Arrving in early evening, they met Clark. The next day, a little past three in the

55. Stoddard to Governor William Claiborne, March 26, 1804, Stoddard Papers, box 1, folder 5, MHMA.

56. Moulton, *The Journals of the Lewis and Clark Expedition,* 2: 60.

57. Ibid., 2: 240–41.

afternoon, Lewis and Clark's crew of forty-five began their journey. Among those present to bid them farewell was Amos Stoddard, who recalled traveling with Lewis to St. Charles, in the company of "most of the principal Gentlemen in this place and vicinity," and the sight of the corps of discovery as it pulled away from the shore. "He began his expedition with a Barge of 18 oars, attended by two large perogues; all of which were deeply laden, and well manned."[58]

As the vessels pulled away, the well-wishers on the bank, a number of them the most prominent French residents of St. Louis, gave out three cheers.[59] Men with long-standing commercial involvement in the fur trade of the Missouri River basin, they may have watched the corps leave with mixed feelings: hopes that the journey would go well and fears that the expedition signalled an end to their control over the trade. As Foley put it, the moment of "the expedition's departure symbolized the true beginning of a long and successful partnership uniting the old French inhabitants and the American newcomers in a common effort to develop the trans-Mississippi frontier."[60]

One of those missing in the crowd that day was Pierre Chouteau, then en route on his own remarkable expedition in the opposite direction. Some time before, the younger of the Chouteau brothers had learned from Lewis that Thomas Jefferson wished to meet and confer with Indian leaders of the Louisiana Territory. Chouteau "promptly volunteered to escort a delegation of Osage chieftains to the federal capital," an offer Lewis accepted.[61] Clark wrote an effusive letter of introduction for Chouteau, which he carried with him on his journey. In it, Clark described "Peter Chouteau" as "an inhabitant of St. Louis, a gentleman deservedly esteemed among the most respectable and influential citizens of Upper Louisiana." His promptness, fidelity, and service to the wishes of the new American government merited the gratitude of his fellow citizens. "Besides Mr. Chouteau's personal merits," wrote Clark, ". . . he has a still stronger claim on my particular friends," arising from the "marked politeness and attention" that he, his wife, and family had shown to Clark and Lewis during their sojourn in St. Louis.[62]

58. Amos Stoddard to Dearborn, May 21, 1804, in Nasatir, *BLC,* 2: 741.

59. Foley, *History of Missouri,* 1: 73; May 21, 1804, Moulton, *The Journals of the Lewis and Clark Expedition,* 2: 244.

60. Foley, "The Lewis and Clark Expedition's Silent Partners," 137–38.

61. Meriwether Lewis to William Clark, February 18, 1804, cited in ibid., 135.

62. William Clark to William Croghan, May 2, 1804, cited in ibid., 132–33; William Clark to Jonathan Clark, May 3, 1804, in Holmberg, ed., *Dear Brother,* 81–82; Lewis likely wrote a similar letter on which Clark modeled his letter of introduction; Clark to Wiliam Croghan, May 2, 1804, cited in Foley, "Friends and Partners," 276.

The week before Lewis departed, Chouteau, twelve Osage Indian chiefs, and two Indian boys left St. Louis for the new capital of the United States, Washington, D.C., where the president personally welcomed the delegation, the first of three to visit during the course of his tenure in office.[63] There, they attended a session of Congress, dined with dignitaries, and witnessed a variety of spectacles designed to convey to them the power of the United States. From the surviving accounts of the delegation's visit, it appears that Washington's residents were deeply impressed by the Indian leaders. For both the Osages and Chouteau, the capital of the United States must have seemed vastly different from St. Louis, the leading settlement of the newly designated District of Louisiana.

While Chouteau believed that the Osage delegation's visit helped secure the tribe's allegiance to the United States, the journey had other repercussions around St. Louis. Factional conflict among the Osages increased during the absence of Chief White Hair, one of the delegation, and took years to die down. Rival tribes, especially the Sac and the Fox, were deeply unhappy with the American government's favorable treatment of the Osage. Their displeasure fueled Indian attacks on American settlers in 1804. As Foley and Rice conclude, "At least temporarily, the first visit to the capital increased tensions along the frontier." Despite these problems, the 1804 journey had the potential to achieve positive change, at least from the Osage chief's perspective. Chief White Hair said, "I have come with my head down. I hope to return with it raised. I have long since been sold as negroes are sold. I hope that is done, and that we shall not have to at all times await petty Frenchmen coming to our villages to give bad counsel."[64]

For his part, Pierre Chouteau returned to St. Louis as the first appointed Indian agent of the United States for Louisiana, a sign of his ability to improve on the opportunities the new regime offered. Back in St. Louis in time to celebrate the arrival of the new American governor of the territory, future U.S. president William Henry Harrison, in October 1804, Pierre attended the welcoming ball his brother Auguste held in Harrison's honor.[65] Writing from Montreal in 1804, one of the Chouteaus' extended family wished his St. Louis relations well under the new regime. "You are now citizens of the United States," he noted. "I hope that you like this unexpected change."[66]

63. Foley, "The Lewis and Clark Expedition's Silent Partners," 133. Foley and Charles David Rice, "Visiting the President," 7, 8.

64. Foley and Charles David Rice, "Visiting the President," 14, 8.

65. Sayad, "Louisiana Purchase," 39; Foley and C. David Rice, *The First Chouteaus*, 94.

66. Pierre-Louis Panet to Auguste Chouteau, May 18, 1804, quoted in Gitlin, *The Bourgeois Frontier*, 45.

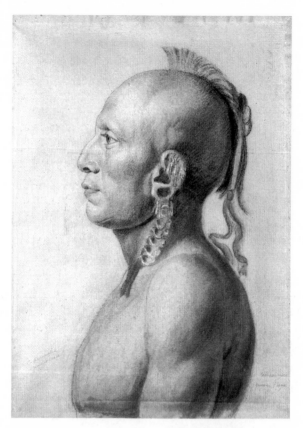

Cashunghia, who traveled to Washington, D.C., as part
of the Osage delegation. Portrait by Charles B.J.F. de St.
Mémin, New-York Historical Society

In 1804, the year of the transfer, when the village was officially absorbed
into the expanding United States, St. Louis remained a small community.
On the few streets running parallel to the great river stood 130 wooden
structures and 51 built of stone; most of the buildings were residences.[67]
The spot, described early on as a pretty one, safe from the river's floods on
limestone bluffs, remained appealing. As a Frenchman, François Perrin du

67. Billon, *Annals of St. Louis,* 76. See "St. Louis: The Town as Seen by Lewis and Clark," on
the National Parks Service web site, *The Lewis and Clark Journey of Discovery,* for an interactive map
showing structures and background information on their inhabitants in 1804, http://www.nps.gov/
archive/jeff/lewisclark2/Circa1804/Circa1804Main.htm.

Lac, who visited St. Louis just after the turn of the century had enthused, the village stood on one of the healthiest and most beautiful locations on the banks of the river. The fertile fields and vast prairies surrounding it promised much. Blessed with an impressive fur trade, St. Louis should have, he thought, become "a considerable city, under any other government than that of Spain." Addicted to commerce and largely uninterested in agriculture, the villagers were, in Perrin du Lac's view, "less ignorant and more polished" than those of Ste. Genevieve. In short, St. Louis had tremendous resources in its people, land, and trade and potential that he thought would never be realized while Spain remained in charge.[68]

In the fall of 1804, the last Spanish lieutenant governor of Upper Louisiana finally left St. Louis. During the course of the previous several months, since the arrival of Stoddard and American troops, Delassus had taken steps to address the concerns and behavior of the various groups most directly affected by the transfer: the residents of St. Louis, the troops of the Spanish garrison, and the Indian peoples of the surrounding territory. All had reason to expect that the American takeover would lead to significant and not altogether desirable changes for their lives. Months after participating in the formal transfer of the territory to the United States, Delassus finally prepared to vacate his home and post. As had his predecessors, he prepared inventories of legal documents in the local archives and documented the business he had conducted on behalf of the crown. In a gesture Foley suggested reflected "a sense of frustration born of nearly four decades of unrealized Spanish expectations," Delassus editorialized in the official records. At the end of a list of licenses granted for the Indian trade between 1799 and 1804, for the "Year 1804," Delassus wrote one thing only. Across the page, in a large hand, switching from the French in which he had recorded licenses granted in previous years, Delassus wrote in Spanish, *"El díablo se lo llevo todo"* or "The devil take all!"[69] Whether that parting comment was meant to describe the incoming Americans, sum up the condition of the Spanish empire, or express the sheer exasperation felt by its author, it is an evocative epitaph for Spanish rule in St. Louis. Where his predecessor Leyba worried that St. Louisans were too obsessed with the lure of "the world, the flesh, and the devil," Delassus no longer seemed to care, figuratively consigning the inhabitants of the village to

68. Perrin du Lac, *Voyage dans les deux Louisianes,* 187–88.

69. Trade licenses, 1801–1804, in "Indian Trade and Fur Companies, 1801–1802," Native American Collection, box 1, folder 3, Native American Collection, MHMA; Foley, *Genesis of Missouri,* 79 n. 78; "Summary of Distribution of Trade Licenses by Delassus, 1799–1804," in Nasatir, *BLC,* 2: 590–93.

Carlos Dehault Delassus, lieutenant governor, Missouri History Museum, St. Louis

oblivion. Shortly thereafter, Delassus left the community that had been his home for several years, encountering Pierre Chouteau traveling upriver with William Henry Harrison, the incoming territorial governor of the district for the United States.[70]

Whether Delassus's parting remark of sarcasm and disgust or Gratiot's hopes for "a happy change" more aptly captured what the coming years held for the erstwhile colonists of St. Louis was uncertain and depended on a great many factors. What was clear, and indisputably so, was that an important chapter in the community's history had come to an end. The connections between what went on in the government quarters in St. Louis and in European courts became a thing of the past. Anyone with a critical mind might have anticipated that the days of French as the dominant

70. Carlos Dehault Delassus diary, November 17, 1804, cited in Foley and C. David Rice, *The First Chouteaus*, 91.

language were numbered, and the French creole cultural life of the community would inevitably encounter competition.[71] Adaptability had been the key to the successes of people like the Chouteaus, who accepted new regimes and officials with apparent ease; such a trait would be indispensable for accommodating the more numerous Americans, who approached their new territory with more energy and resources than their predecessors had ever been willing to expend. What lay ahead for the residents of St. Louis and the indigenous inhabitants of the region, as they looked to an American future, had yet to be written. What remained the same were the rivers—the Mississippi and the Missouri—the great waterways that drew settlers, channeled trade, inspired expansion, and made St. Louis the gateway to the West.

71. In St. Louis, over the subsequent decades, French increasingly became a private, domestic language; as Jay Gitlin notes: "If the francophone merchants of this bourgeois frontier played a unique and significant role in the history of American expansion, it is ironic that the cultural landscape of the region they helped established had little room for their own distinctive culture." Gitlin, *The Bourgeois Frontier*, 139. How the French colonial past figured into subsequent narratives of the city's history is the subject of Adam Arenson's essay, "The Double Life of St. Louis."

Afterword

We shall not cease from exploration
And the end of all our exploring
Will be to arrive where we started
And know the place for the first time.

T. S. Eliot, *Four Quartets*

Born in St. Louis in 1888, Nobel Prize–winning poet T. S. Eliot was the grandson of William Greenleaf Eliot, a Unitarian minister who was instrumental to the founding of one of the city's finest institutions, Washington University. Eliot traveled far from his birthplace, eventually settling in and becoming a citizen of Great Britain. A culturally transcendent and proto-typically modern writer, Eliot carried his American past with him, and it shaped his poetic meditations on the meaning of time and history.

For someone interested in the history of St. Louis, the lines above evoke how compelling the adventure of studying the past can be and how one can come to look at the fascinating and rich stories of the place with altogether new eyes. In the introduction, I alluded to Judy Garland's delight at experiencing the wonders of the 1904 St. Louis World's Fair, right in her own backyard. While researching and writing this book, I have tried to turn the spotlight on the remarkable and neglected history of early St. Louis. Throughout the process, I have endeavored to keep in mind the goal of recovering the too-often-overlooked colonial past of the United States and the need to populate that past with people whose voices and presence have been largely lost.

A few themes emerge with clarity, notably the connectedness of the city's history to larger continental and global developments. The movements of peoples—indigenous, African, European, and American—shaped the creation of a diverse and polyglot colonial society. Without the waterways that were the highways of the past, these different groups of people would never have converged at St. Louis. The circumstances of their encounters both necessitated and facilitated a willingness to seek out common ground for communication and exchange. In turn, this adaptability enabled the elite to maintain their power and influence under successive regimes and those in subordinate positions to survive and carve out space for themselves. Throughout the period, Indian peoples shaped the trade and diplomatic initiatives of the region.

Confluence, convergence, migration, and mobility all determined the development of a community linked to political and economic factors that encompassed vast territories on both sides of the Mississippi River and indeed crossed the Atlantic Ocean. As one British official recognized in the 1760s, communication between the mother country and far western posts in America was never the problem some predicted. Such suppositions, he charged, were based on the inaccurate view that western settlements were too remote. "This is altogether founded upon an erroneous Notion of the Country," he wrote. "The great Rivers, the Lakes, the lesser Rivers & navigable Creeks, with which [the country] is everywhere intersected, afford the greatest Means both of interior Communication and foreign Intercourse, yet discover'd in the known World." That sense of connectedness—of the periphery of empire tied to its center and of the centrality of the continent's great rivers—was crucial for a global village like St. Louis.[1]

So if we reflect on Eliot's message, where does it leave us? If, as he wrote, "the end is where we start from," we return to the banks of the Mississippi, near its confluence with the Missouri, contemplating the land as Pierre Laclède did, assessing its potential and imagining the possibilities its future might hold.

---

1. Lord Shelburne, September 11, 1767, in Alvord and Carter, *Trade and Politics,* 20–21.

Bibliography

PRIMARY SOURCES

Lovejoy Library, Southern Illinois University, Edwardsville, Illinois: John
    Francis McDermott Collection
Missouri History Museum Archives (MHMA), St. Louis, Missouri:
    Archivo General de Indias (microfilm)
    Billon Collection
    Census Collection
    Chouteau Papers
    Chouteau-Papin Collection
    Church Papers
    George Rogers Clark Papers, Clark Family Collection
    Oscar W. Collot, Church Records
    Delassus–St. Vrain Collection
    Fur Trade Collection
    Gratiot Papers
    Laclède Collection
    Litigation Collection
    Poepping Family Papers
    Native American Collection
    St. Louis Archives, 1766–1804
    St. Louis History Collection
    Sanguinet-Hogan Collection
    Saugrain-Michau Papers
    Slave Papers
    Stoddard Papers
Tulane University Library: Favrot Collection

Adams, Eleanor B., and Fray Angelico Chavez, eds. *The Missions of New Mexico: A Description by Fray Francisco Atanasio Dominguez.* Albuquerque: University of New Mexico Press, 1956.

Alvord, Clarence W., ed. *Cahokia Records, 1778–1790.* Springfield: Illinois State Historical Society, 1907.

Alvord, Clarence Walworth, and Clarence Edwin Carter, eds. *The Critical Period, 1763–1765.* Springfield, Illinois: Illinois State Historical Library, 1915.

———. *The New Regime, 1765–1767.* Springfield, Illinois: Illinois State Historical Library, 1916.

———. *Trade and Politics, 1767–1769.* Springfield: Illinois State Historical Library, 1921.

Ames, Gregory, ed. *Auguste Chouteau's Journal: Memory, Mythmaking, and History in the Heritage of New France.* St. Louis: St. Louis Mercantile Library, forthcoming.

Angle, Paul M., ed. and comp. *Prairie State: Impressions of Illinois, 1673–1967, by Travelers and Other Observers.* Chicago: University of Chicago Press, 1968.

"Archaeology of the Saline Creek Valley, Missouri." Translation and compilation of Archivo General de Indias—Papeles Procedentes de Cuba by Anna L. Price. Saline Creek Valley Project, University of Missouri–Columbia, 1988 (unpublished manuscript, Missouri History Museum Archives).

Barnhart, Warren Lynn. "The Letterbooks of Charles Gratiot, Fur Trader: The Nomadic Years, 1679–1797. Edited with an historical introduction." PhD dissertation, St. Louis University, 1972.

Brackenridge, H. M. *Views of Louisiana.* Baltimore: Schaeffer and Maund, 1817.

Brown, Margaret Kimball, and Lawrie Cena Dean, eds. *The Village of Chartres in Colonial Illinois, 1720–1765.* New Orleans: Polyanthos Press, 1977.

Caroon, Robert G., ed. *Broadswords and Bayonets: The Journals of the Expedition under the Command of Captain Thomas Stirling of the 42nd Regiment of Foot, Royal Highland Regiment (The Black Watch) to Occupy Fort Chartres in the Illinois Country, August 1765 to January 1766.* Society of Colonial Wars in the State of Illinois, 1984.

Carter, Clarence E., ed. *The Territorial Papers of the United States.* Washington: Government Printing Office, 1949.

Chouteau, Auguste. "Narrative of the Settlement of St. Louis." In *The Early Histories of St. Louis,* ed. John Francis McDermott. St. Louis: St. Louis

Historical Documents Foundation, 1952.

————. "Notes of Auguste Chouteau on the Boundaries of Various Indian Nations." Edited by Gary Foreman. *Glimpses of the Past* (Missouri Historical Society) 7 (1940): 119–40.

"Chouteau's Journal of the Founding of St. Louis." *Missouri Historical Society Collections* 3, no. 4 (1911): 335–49.

Clark, Emily, ed. *Voices from an Early American Convent: Marie Madeleine Hachard and the New Orleans Ursulines, 1727–1760.* Baton Rouge: Louisiana State Press, 2007.

Clark, George Rogers. *Col. George Rogers Clark's Sketch of His Campaign in the Illinois in 1778–79,* with an introduction by Hon. Henry Pirtle of Louisville and an appendix containing the public and private instructions to Col. Clark and Major Bowman's journal of the taking of Post St. Vincents. Cincinnati: Robert Clarke, 1907.

Collot, Georges-Victor. *A Journey in North America, containing a survey of the countries watered by the Mississippi, Ohio, Missouri and other affluing rivers....* 3 vols. Edited by J. Christian Bay. Reprints of Rare Americana, no. 4. Firenze: O. Lange, 1924.

"Criminal Suit for Slander, Bernardo Shiloc vs. Chouteau (Rene) Pastrycook, 20 April 1771." *Louisiana Historical Quarterly* 8 (April 1925): 324–28.

Dart, Henry P., ed. "The Oath of Allegiance to Spain." *Louisiana Historical Quarterly* 4 (1921): 205–15.

De Finiels, Nicolas. *An Account of Upper Louisiana by Nicolas de Finiels.* Edited by Carl J. Ekberg and William E. Foley, and translated by Carl J. Ekberg. Columbia: University of Missouri Press, 1989.

"Documents Relating to the Attack upon St. Louis." *Missouri Historical Society Collections* 2 (July 1906): 41–54.

Dominguez, Francisco Atanasio. *The Missions of New Mexico: A Description by Fray Francisco Atanasio Dominguez.* Edited and translated by Eleanor B. Adams and Fray Angelico Chavez. Albuquerque: University of New Mexico Press, 1956.

Gayarré, Charles. *Histoire de la Louisiane.* 2 vols. New Orleans: Magne and Weisse, 1846–47.

"George Rogers Clark and the Kaskaskia Campaign, 1777–1778." *American Historical Review* 8, no. 3 (April 1903): 491–506.

"Un Habitant des Kaskaskias." *Invitation Serieuse aux Habitants des Illinois.* Philadelphia, 1772; reprinted facsimile with an introduction by Clarence Walworth Alvord and Clarence Edwin Carter. Providence, RI: Club for Colonial Reprints, 1908.

Holmes, Jack D. L., ed. *Documentos Ineditos para la Historia de la Luisiana, 1792–1810.* Coleccion Chimalistac de Libros y Documentos Acerca de la Nueva España, vol. 15. Madrid: Edicion Jose Porrua Turanzas, 1963.

Holmes, Jack D. L., trans. and ed. "A 1795 Inspection of Spanish Missouri." *Missouri Historical Review* 55 (Oct. 1960): 5–17.

———. "O'Reilly's Regulations on Booze, Boarding Houses, and Billiards." (October 8, 1769) in *Louisiana History* 6, no. 3 (Summer 1965): 293–300.

Holmberg, James, ed. *Dear Brother: Letters of William Clark to Jonathan Clark.* New Haven: Yale University Press, 2002.

Houck, Louis. *A History of Missouri from the Earliest Explorations and Settlements until the Admission of the State into the Union.* 3 vols. Chicago: R. R. Donnelley and Sons, 1908; reprint New York: Arno Press and the New York Times, 1971.

Houck, Louis, ed. *The Spanish Regime in Missouri.* 2 vols. Chicago: R. R. Donnelley and Sons, 1909; reprint New York: Arno Press and the New York Times, 1971.

Kinnaird, Lawrence. "Clark-Leyba Papers." *American Historical Review* 41 (October 1935–July 1936): 92–112.

Kinnaird, Lawrence, ed. *Spain in the Mississippi Valley, 1765–1794,* part 1: *The Revolutionary Period, 1765–1781.* Annual Report of the American Historical Association for the year 1945, vol. 2. Washington, DC: United States Government Printing Office, 1949.

———. *Spain in the Mississippi Valley, 1765–1794,* part 2: *Post War Decade, 1782–1791.* Annual Report of the American Historical Association for the year 1945, vol. 3. Washington, DC: United States Government Printing Office, 1946.

———. *Spain in the Mississippi Valley, 1765–1794,* part 3: *Problems of Frontier Defense, 1792–1794.* Annual Report of the American Historical Association for the year 1945, vol. 4. Washington, DC: United States Government Printing Office, 1946.

Margry, Pierre. *Découvertes et Etablissements des Français dans l'ouest et dans le sud de L'Amerique Septentrionale, 1614–1754: Mémoires et Douments Originaux,* vol. 6. Paris: Maisonneuve et Ch. Leclerc, 1888.

McDermott, John Francis, ed. *The Early Histories of St. Louis.* St. Louis: St. Louis Historical Documents Foundation, 1952.

Moulton, Gary E., ed. *The Journals of the Lewis and Clark Expedition,* vol. 2, *August 30, 1803–August 24, 1804.* Lincoln: University of Nebraska Press, 1986.

Nasatir, A. P., ed. *Before Lewis and Clark: Documents Illustrating the History of the Missouri, 1785–1804.* 2 vols. St. Louis: St. Louis Historical Documents Foundation, 1952; reprint with introduction to the Bison Book edition by James P. Ronda, Lincoln: University of Nebraska Press, 1990.

Palmer, Wm. P., ed. *Calendar of Virginia State Papers and Other Manuscripts, from January 1, 1782, to December 31, 1784, preserved in the capitol at Richmond.* Vol. 3. Richmond: James E. Goode, Printer, 1883.

Pease, Theodore Calvin, and Ernestine Jenison, eds. *Illinois on the Eve of the Seven Years War, 1747–1755.* Collections of the Illinois State Historical Library, vol. 29. Springfield: Illinois State Historical Library, 1940.

Perrin du Lac, François. *Voyage dans les Deux Louisianes, et Chez les Nations sauvages du Missouri, par les Etats-Unis, l'Ohio et les Provinces qui le bordent, en 1801, 1802, et 1803; avec un apperçu des moeurs, des usages, du caractère et des coutume religieuses et civiles des Peuples de ces diverses contrées.* Paris: Capelle et Renand, 1805.

Pittman, Philip. *Captain Philip Pittman's The Present State of the European Settlements on the Mississippi with a Geographical Description of that River Illustrated by Plans and Draughts.* Facsimile edition with an introduction and notes by John Francis McDermott. Memphis: Memphis State University Press, 1977.

Schoolcraft, Henry Rowe. *Travels in the Central Portions of the Mississippi Valley: Comprising Observations on Its Mineral Geography, Internal Resources, and Aboriginal Population.* (Performed under the Sanction of Government, in the Year 1821.) New York: Collins and Hannay, 1825.

Stoddard, Amos. *Sketches, Historical and Descriptive, of Louisiana.* Philadelphia: Matthew Carey, 1812.

Thornbrough, Gayle, ed. *Outpost on the Wabash, 1787–1791: Letters of Brigadier General Josiah Harmar and Major John Francis Hamtramck and Other Letters and Documents Selected from the Harmar Papers in the William L. Clements Library.* Indianapolis: Indiana Historical Society, 1957.

Thwaites, Reuben Gold, ed. *The Jesuit relations and allied documents: travels and explorations of the Jesuit missionaries in new France, 1610–1791; the original French, Latin, and Italian texts, with English translations and notes.* 73 vols. Cleveland: Burrows Brothers, 1896–1901.

———. *Early Western Travels, 1748–1846,* vol. 3. Cleveland: Arthur H. Clark, 1904.

Tissot, Samuel Auguste André David. *Advice to the People in General, with Regard to their Health: But more particularly calculated for those, who, by their Distance from regular Physicians, or other very experienced Practitioners, are the most unlikely to be seasonably provided with the best Advice and Assistance, in acute Diseases, or upon any sudden inward or outward Accident.* Translated by J. Kirkpatrick. London, 1765.

————. *L'Onanisme: Dissertation sur les Maladies produites par la Masturbation.* 3e ed. Lausanne: Marc Chapuis, et Compagnie, 1765.

Williams, Henry W. *Old Missouri Land Cases,* part 4, *Cutter vs. Waddingham.* St. Louis: Keemle and Hager, 1851.

SECONDARY SOURCES

Adelman, Jeremy, and Stephen Aron. "From Borderlands to Borders: Empires, Nation-States, and the Peoples in between in North American History." *American Historical Review* 104, no. 3 (1999): 814–41.

Afable, Patricia O. "Journeys from Bontoc to the Western Fairs, 1904–1915: The 'Nikimalika' and Their Interpreters." *Philippine Studies* 52, no. 4 (2004): 445–73.

Alvord, Clarence Walworth. *The Illinois Country, 1673–1818.* Centennial History of Illinois, vol. 1. Chicago: McClurg, 1922.

Appleby, Joyce, Lynn Hunt, and Margaret Jacob. *Telling the Truth about History.* New York: Norton, 1994.

Arenson, Adam. "The Double Life of St. Louis: Narratives of Origins and Maturity in Wade's *Urban Frontier.*" *Indiana Magazine of History* 105, no. 3 (Sept. 2009): 246–61.

Arnold, Morris S. *Colonial Arkansas, 1686–1804: A Social and Cultural History.* Fayetteville: University of Arkansas Press, 1991.

Aron, Stephen. *American Confluence: The Missouri Frontier from Borderland to Border State.* Bloomington: Indiana University Press, 2006.

Aubert, Guillaume. "'The Blood of France': Race and Purity of Blood in the French Atlantic World." *William and Mary Quarterly* 3d ser., 61, no. 3 (July 2004): 439–78.

Baker, Vaughan B. "'*Cherchez les Femme*': Some Glimpses of Women in Early Eighteenth-Century Louisiana." *Louisiana History* 31 (1990): 21–37.

Baker, Vaughn, Amos Simpson, and Mathé Allain. "*Le Mari est Seigneur:* Marital Laws Governing Women in French Louisiana." 7–18. In *Louisiana's Legal Heritage,* ed. Edward H. Hass. Pensacola, FL: Published for the Louisiana State Museum by Perdido Bay Press, 1983.

Banner, Stuart. *Legal Systems in Conflict: Property and Sovereignty in Missouri, 1750–1860.* Norman: University of Oklahoma Press, 2000.

Banner, Stuart. "Written Law and Unwritten Norms in Colonial St. Louis." *Law and History Review* 14, no. 1 (Spring 1996): 33–80.

Bardet, Jean-Pierre. "Early Marriage in Pre-Modern France." *History of the Family* 6 (2001): 345–63.

Barr, Julianna. "From Captives to Slaves: Commodifying Indian Women in the Borderlands." *Journal of American History* 92, no. 1 (June 2005): 19–45.

———. *Peace Came in the Form of a Woman: Indians and Spaniards in the Texas Borderlands.* Chapel Hill: University of North Carolina Press, 2007.

Billon, Frederic L. *Annals of St. Louis in Its Early Days under the French and Spanish Dominations, 1764–1804.* St. Louis: Printed for the author, 1886; reprint New York: Arno Press and the New York Times, 1971.

Boyle, Susan C. "Did She Generally Decide? Women in Ste. Genevieve, 1750–1805." *William and Mary Quarterly* 3d ser., 44 (1987): 775–89.

Brasseaux, Carl A. "Confusion, Conflict, and Currency: An Introduction to the Rebellion of 1768." *Louisiana History* 18, no. 2 (Spring 1977): 161–69.

———. *Denis-Nicolas Foucault and the New Orleans Rebellion of 1768.* Ruston, LA: McGinty Publications, 1987.

———. "The Moral Climate of French Colonial Louisiana, 1699–1763." *Louisiana History* 27, no. 1 (Winter 1986): 27–41.

Breitbart, Eric. *A World on Display: Photographs from the St. Louis World's Fair, 1904.* Albuquerque: University of New Mexico Press, 1997.

Briggs, Winstanley. "The Enhanced Economic Position of Women in French Colonial Illinois." In *L'Héritage Tranquille: The Quiet Heritage,* edited by Clarence A. Glasrud. Moorhead, MN: Concordia College, 1985.

———. "Le Pays des Illinois." *William and Mary Quarterly* 3d ser., 47 (1990): 30–56.

Brooks, James F. *Captives and Cousins: Slavery, Kinship, and Community in the Southwest Borderlands.* Chapel Hill: University of North Carolina Press, 2002.

Brucken, Carolyn, and Virginia Scharff. "Home Lands: How Women Made the West." Paper presented to the Autry Institute Workshop, December 2005.

Butler, Judith. *Bodies that Matter: On the Discursive Limits of "Sex."* New York: Routledge, 1993.

Calloway, Colin G. *The American Revolution in Indian Country: Crisis and Diversity in Native American Communities.* New York: Cambridge University Press, 1995.

————. *The Scratch of a Pen: 1763 and the Transformation of North America.* New York: Oxford University Press, 2006.

————. *White People, Indians, and Highlanders: Tribal Peoples and Colonial Encounters in Scotland and America.* Oxford: Oxford University Press, 2008.

Camp, Gregory S. "The Corps of Discovery Takes Shape." *North Dakota History* 70, no. 3 (2003): 26–35.

Carol, Anne. "Les Médecins et la Stigmatisation du Vice Solitaire." *Revue d'Historie Moderne et Contemporaine* 49, no. 1 (January 2002): 156–72.

Carter, Clarence. *Great Britain and the Illinois Country.* Washington, DC: American Historical Association, 1910.

Chandler, R. E. "O'Reilly's Voyage from Havana to the Balize." *Louisiana History* 22, no. 2 (1981): 199–207.

————. "Ulloa's Account of the 1768 Revolt." *Louisiana History* 27, no. 4 (1986): 407–37.

Chapman, Carl H. "The Little Osage and Missouri Indian Village Sites, ca. 1727–1777 AD." *Missouri Archaeologist* 21, no. 1 (December 1959): 1–67.

Christian, Shirley. *Before Lewis and Clark: The Story of the Chouteaus, the French Dynasty that Ruled America's Frontier.* New York: Farrar, Straus and Giroux, 2004.

Coleman, James Julian. *Gilbert Antoine de St. Maxent: The Spanish-Frenchman of New Orleans.* New Orleans: Pelican Publishing House, 1968.

Conrad, Glenn R., ed. *The French Experience in Louisiana,* vol. 1, Louisiana Purchase Bicentennial Series in Louisiana History. Lafayette: Center for Louisiana Studies, University of Southwestern Louisiana, 1995.

Corbett, Katherine. "Veuve Chouteau, a 250th Anniversary." *Gateway Heritage: Quarterly Journal of the Missouri Historical Society* 3, no. 4 (Spring 1983): 42–48.

Cronon, William. *Changes in the Land: Indians, Colonists, and the Ecology of New England.* New York: Hill and Wang, 1983.

Cummins, Light Townsend. "'Her Weary Pilgrimage': The Remarkable Mississippi River Adventures of Anne McMeans, 1778–1782." *Louisiana History* 47, no. 4 (Autumn 2006): 389–415.

Cunningham, Mary B., and Jeanne C. Blythe. *The Founding Family of St. Louis.* St. Louis: Midwest Technical Publications, 1977.

Dawdy, Shannon Lee. *Building the Devil's Empire: French Colonial New Orleans.* Chicago: University of Chicago Press, 2008.

————. "First you make a roux . . . with bear fat: Cooking, Eating, and Colonialism in French Louisiana," prepared for the École des hautes études en sciences sociales (International workshop on colonial

Louisiana, November 2007/April 2008), unpublished essay.

Denny, James M. "Running the Lower Missouri River Gauntlet: The First Trial of the Lewis and Clark Expedition." *Missouri Historical Review* 98, no. 4 (2004): 283–313.

Desplat, Christian. "The Climate of Eighteenth-Century Béarn." Translated by Mark Greengrass. *French History* 1, no. 1 (1987): 27–48.

———. *Pau et le Béarn au 18ᵉ Siècle: Deux Cent Mille Provinciaux au Siècle des Lumières.* 2 vols. Biarritz, France: J et D éditions, 1992.

Din, Gilbert C. "Arkansas Post in the American Revolution." *Arkansas Historical Quarterly* 40 (Spring 1981): 3–30.

———. "Captain Francisco Riu y Morales and the Beginnings of Spanish Rule in Missouri." *Missouri Historical Review* 94, no. 2 (2000): 121–45.

———. "The Immigration Policy of Governor Esteban Miró in Spanish Louisiana." *Southwestern Historical Quarterly* 73 (1969): 155–75.

———. "Spain's Immigration Policy in Louisiana and the American Penetration, 1792–1803." *Southwestern Historical Quarterly* 76 (1969): 255–76.

Din, Gilbert C., and A. P. Nasatir. *The Imperial Osages: Spanish-Indian Diplomacy in the Mississippi Valley.* Norman: University of Oklahoma Press, 1983.

Dowd, Gregory Evans. *War under Heaven: Pontiac, the Indian Nations, and the British Empire.* Baltimore: Johns Hopkins University Press, 2004.

Dubois, Laurent. "The Haitian Revolution and the Sale of Louisiana." *Southern Quarterly* 44, no. 3 (Spring 2007): 18–41.

DuVal, Kathleen. "The Education of Fernando de Leyba: Quapaws and Spaniards on the Border of Empires." *Arkansas Historical Quarterly* 60, no. 1 (2001): 1–29.

———. *The Native Ground: Indians and Colonists in the Heart of the Continent.* Philadelphia: University of Pennsylvania Press, 2006.

Ekberg, Carl J. *Colonial Ste. Genevieve: An Adventure on the Mississippi Frontier.* Gerald, MO: Patrice Press, 1985.

———. *François Vallé and His World: Upper Louisiana before Lewis and Clark.* Columbia: University of Missouri Press, 2002.

———. *French Roots in the Illinois Country: The Mississippi Frontier in Colonial Times.* Urbana: University of Illinois Press, 1998.

———. *Stealing Indian Women: Native Slavery in the Illinois Country.* Chicago: University of Illinois Press, 2007.

Ekberg, Carl J., and Anton J. Pregaldin. "Marie Rouensa-8cate8a and the Foundations of French Illinois." *Illinois Historical Journal* 84 (August 1991): 146–60.

Fausz, J. Frederick. "Founding St. Louis: A New French Frontier at the End of Empire." *Gateway: The Magazine of the Missouri History Museum* 29 (2009): 9–23.

Faye, Stanley. "Indian Guests at the Spanish Arkansas Post." *Arkansas Historical Quarterly* 4 (Summer 1945): 93–108.

Fenn, Elizabeth. *Pox Americana: The Great Smallpox Epidemic of 1775–1782.* New York: Hill and Wang, 2001.

Florence, Robert. *City of the Dead.* Lafayette, LA: Center for Louisiana Studies, 1996.

————. *New Orleans Cemeteries: Life in the Cities of the Dead.* New Orleans: Batture Press, 1997.

Foley, William E. "Friends and Partners: William Clark, Meriwether Lewis, and Mid-America's French Creoles." *Missouri Historical Review* 98, no. 4 (July 2004): 270–82.

————. "Galleries, Gumbo, and '*La Guignolée.*'" *Gateway Heritage: Quarterly Journal of the Missouri Historical Society* 10 (Summer 1989): 3–17.

————. *The Genesis of Missouri: From Wilderness Outpost to Statehood.* Columbia: University of Missouri Press, 1989.

————. *A History of Missouri,* vol 1, *1673–1820.* Columbia: University of Missouri Press, 1971.

————. "The Laclède-Chouteau Puzzle: John Francis McDermott Supplies Some Missing Pieces." *Gateway Heritage* 4 (Fall 1983): 18–24.

————. "The Lewis and Clark Expedition's Silent Partners: The Chouteau Brothers of St. Louis." *Missouri Historical Review* 77, no. 2 (January 1983): 131–46.

————. "Slave Freedom Suits before Dred Scott: The Case of Mari Jean Scypion's Descendants." *Missouri Historical Review* 79 (October 1984): 1–23.

————. "St. Louis: The First Hundred Years." *Missouri Historical Society Bulletin* 34, no. 4 (1978): 187–99.

————. *Wilderness Journey: The Life of William Clark.* Columbia: University of Missouri Press, 2004.

Foley, William E., and C. David Rice. *The First Chouteaus: River Barons of Early St. Louis.* Chicago: University of Illinois Press, 1983.

Foley, William E., and Charles D. Rice. "Compounding the Risks: International Politics, Wartime Dislocations, and Auguste Chouteau's Fur Trading Operations, 1792–1815." *Missouri Historical Society Bulletin* 34, no. 3 (1978): 131–39.

Foley, William E., and Charles David Rice. "'Touch Not a Stone': An 1841 Appeal to Save the Historic Chouteau Mansion." *Gateway Heritage:*

Quarterly Journal of the Missouri Historical Society 4, no. 3 (Winter 1983–1984): 14–19.

———. "Visiting the President: An Exercise in Jeffersonian Indian Diplomacy." *American West* 16 (November–December 1979): 4–15.

Fox, Tim, ed., with intro. by Eric Sandweiss. *Where We Live: A Guide to St. Louis Communities.* St. Louis: Missouri Historical Society Press, 1995.

Francini, Giacomo. "Divorce and Separations in Eighteenth-Century France: An Outline for a Social History of Law." *History of the Family* 2, no. 1 (1997): 99.

Gallay, Alan. *The Indian Slave Trade: The Rise of the English Empire in the American South, 1670–1717.* New Haven: Yale Universtiy Press, 2002.

Gilbert, Judith A. "Esther and Her Sisters: Free Women of Color as Property Owners in Colonial St. Louis, 1765–1803." *Gateway Heritage: Quarterly Journal of the Missouri Historical Society* 17, no. 1 (Summer 1996): 14–23.

———. "Free Women of Color as Property Owners in Colonial St. Louis, 1665–1803." Missouri Historical Society Compilations, 1995.

Gilman, Carolyn. *"L'Année du Coup:* The Battle of St. Louis, 1780, Part 1." *Missouri Historical Review* 103, no. 3 (April 2009): 133–47.

———. *"L'Année du Coup:* The Battle of St. Louis, 1780, Part 2." *Missouri Historical Review* 103, no. 4 (July 2009): 195–211.

———. With an introduction by James P. Ronda. *Lewis and Clark: Across the Divide.* Washington, DC: Smithsonian Books in assocation with the Missouri Historical Society, 2004.

Gilman, Carolyn, and Emily Troxell Jaycox. "The Chouteau Map Re-examined: A Quest in Progress." *Gateway: The Magazine of the Missouri History Museum* 29 (2009): 25–37.

Gitlin, Jay. "'*Avec bien du regret*': The Americanization of Creole St. Louis." *Gateway Heritage* 9, no. 4 (Spring 1989): 2–11.

———. *The Bourgeois Frontier: French Towns, French Traders, and American Expansion.* New Haven: Yale University Press, 2010.

Green, Lorenzo J., Gary R. Kremer, and Antonio F. Holland. *Missouri's Black Heritage.* 1980; rev. ed. Columbia: University of Missouri Press, 1983.

Gutierrez, Ramon. *When Jesus Came, the Corn Mothers Went Away: Marriage, Sexuality, and Power in New Mexico, 1500–1846.* Stanford, CA: Stanford University Press, 1991.

Hall, Gwendolyn Midlo. *Africans in Colonial Louisiana: The Development of Afro-Creole Culture in the Eighteenth Century.* Baton Rouge: Louisiana State University Press, 1992.

Hamilton, Neil A. "A French Spy in America." *American History* 34, no. 3 (August 1999): 22–28.

Hanger, Kimberly S. *Bounded Lives, Bounded Places: Free Black Society in Colonial New Orleans, 1769–1803.* Durham: Duke University Press, 1997.

Hauser, Raymond E. "The Fox Raid: Defensive Warfare and the Decline of the Illinois Indian Tribe." *Illinois Historical Journal* 86 (Winter 1993): 210–24.

Hayhoe, Jeremy. "Illegitimacy, Inter-generational Conflict, and Legal Practice and Eighteenth-Century Northern Burgundy." *Journal of Social History* 38, no. 3 (2005): 673–84.

Hodes, Frederick A. *Beyond the Frontier: A History of St. Louis to 1821.* Tucson: Patrice Press, 2004.

Hodes, Martha, ed. *Sex, Love, Race: Crossing Boundaries in North American History.* New York: New York University Press, 1999.

Holder, Preston. "The Fur Trade as Seen from the Indian Point of View." In *The Frontier Re-examined,* edited by John Francis McDermott, 129–39. Urbana: University of Illinois Press, 1967.

Holt, Thomas C. "Purity of Blood and the Social Order of Blood and Power: An Introduction." *William and Mary Quarterly* 3d ser., 61, no. 3 (July 2004): 235–38.

Hortard, Corey David. "Bombarding the City of the Dead: Who Has a Right to the Past?" MA thesis, Louisiana State University, 2003.

Hugon, Alain. "La Frontière Pyrénéenne pendant l'Ancien Régime: Un Espace sous Surveillance." La politique espangnole au debut du 18ᵉ. *Revue de Pau et du Béarn* 27 (January 2000): 121–49.

Hurley, Andrew, ed. *Common Fields: An Environmental History of St. Louis.* St. Louis: Missouri Historical Society Press, 1997.

Hurtado, Albert L. *Intimate Frontiers: Sex, Gender, and Culture in Old California.* Albuquerque: University of New Mexico Press, 1999.

Ingersoll, Thomas N. *Mammon and Manon in Early New Orleans: The First Slave Society in the Deep South, 1718–1819.* Knoxville: University of Tennessee Press, 1999.

Jacob, Margaret C. *Strangers Nowhere in the World: The Rise of Cosmopolitanism in Early Modern Europe.* Philadelphia: University of Pennsylvania Press, 2006.

Jacobs, Wilbur R. *Indian Diplomacy and Indian Gifts: Anglo-French Rivalry along the Ohio and Northwest Frontier, 1748–1763.* Stanford: Stanford University Press, 1950.

Johnson, Ronald W. "Historic Preservation in Missouri: Origins and

Development through the Second World War." *Missouri Historical Society Bulletin* 32, no. 4, part 1 (July 1976): 222–40.

Johnston, A. J. B. "Alcohol Consumption in Eighteenth-Century Louisbourg and the Vain Attempts to Control It." *French Colonial History* 2 (2002): 61–76.

Keister, Douglas, ed. *Going Out in Style: The Architecture of Eternity.* New York: Facts on File, 1997.

Kelly, John E. "The Preservation of the East St. Louis Mound Group: An Historical Perspective." *SAA Archaelogical Record* 3, no. 3 (May 2003): 20–23.

Kilgo, Dolores A. *Likeness and Landscape: Thomas M. Easterly and the Art of the Daguerreotype.* St. Louis: Missouri Historical Society Press, 1994.

Kinnaird, Lawrence. "American Penetration into Spanish Louisiana." In *New Spain and the Anglo-American West: Historical Contributions*, ed. George P. Hammond, presented to Herbert Eugene Bolton. Lancaster, PA: Lancaster Press, 1932. 1: 211–37.

Kramer, Paul A. *The Blood of Government: Race, Empire, the United States, and the Philippines.* Chapel Hill: University of North Carolina Press, 2006.

Kupperman, Karen Ordahl. *Indians and English: Facing Off in Early America.* Ithaca: Cornell University Press, 2000.

Lahey, Mary Caroline. "The Catholic Church on the Frontier of Spanish Illinois, 1763–1804." MA thesis, San Diego State College, 1966.

Labarère, Lucien. *Pierre de Laclede-Liguest, 1729–1778: le fondateur de Saint-Louis.* Saint-Jean-de-Luz, France: Ciboure Presse, 1984.

Lecompte, Janet. "Don Benito Vasquez in Early St. Louis." *Missouri Historical Society Bulletin* 26, no. 4, part 1 (July 1970): 285–305.

Lepore, Jill. *New York Burning: Liberty, Slavery, and Conspiracy in Eighteenth-Century Manhattan.* New York: Alfred A. Knopf, 2005.

Leumas, Emilie. "Ties that Bind: The Family, Social, and Business Associations of the Insurrectionists of 1768." *Louisiana History* 47, no. 2 (2006): 183–202.

Liljegren, E. R. "Jacobinism in Spanish Louisiana, 1792–1797." *Louisiana Historical Quarterly* 22 (1939): 3–53.

Magnaghi, Russell M. "The Role of Indian Slavery in Colonial St. Louis." *Missouri Historical Society Bulletin* 31, no. 4, part 1 (July 1975): 264–72.

Mancall, Peter C. *Deadly Medicine: Indians and Alcohol in Early America.* Ithaca: Cornell University Press, 1995.

Marshall, John B. "The St. Louis Mound Group: Historical Accounts and Pictorial Descriptions." *Missouri Archaeologist* 53 (December 1992): 43–79.

Martinez, Maria Elena. "The Black Blood of New Spain: *Limpieza de Sangre,* Racial Violence, and Gendered Power in Early Colonial Mexico." *William and Mary Quarterly* 3d ser., 61, no. 3 (July 2004): 479–520.

Matson, N. *Pioneers of Illinois: Containing a Series of Sketches Relating to Events that Occurred Previous to 1813.* Chicago: Knight and Leonard, 1882.

Mazrim, Robert. "The Ghost Horse Site: Pierre Laclède's First Residence in the Illinois Country?" *Gateway Heritage* (forthcoming).

———. *At Home in the Illinois Country: French Colonial Domestic Site Archaeology in the Midwest, 1730–1800.* Champaign: University of Illinois Press, 2010.

McDermott, John Francis. "The Battle of Colonial St. Louis, 26 May 1780." *Missouri Historical Society Bulletin* 36, no. 3 (1980): 131–51.

———. "The Exclusive Trade Privilege of Maxent, Laclède, and Company." *Missouri Historical Review* 29, no. 4 (1935): 272–78.

———. "Laclède and the Chouteaus: Fantasies and Facts." Unpublished manuscript in the John Francis McDermott Mississippi Valley Research Collection, Lovejoy Library, Southern Illinois University–Edwardsville.

———. "Paincourt and Poverty." *Mid-America* 5 (April 1934): 210–12.

———. "Pierre de Laclède and the Chouteaus." *Bulletin of the Missouri Historical Society* 21, no. 4, part 1 (July 1965): 279–83.

———. *Private Libraries in Creole Saint Louis.* Baltimore: Johns Hopkins University Press, 1938.

McDermott, John Francis, ed. *The French in the Mississippi Valley.* Urbana: University of Illinois Press, 1965.

———. *Frenchmen and French Ways in the Mississippi Valley.* Chicago: University of Illinois Press, 1969.

———. *The Frontier Re-examined.* Urbana: University of Illinois Press, 1967.

———. *The Spanish in the Mississippi Valley, 1762–1804.* Chicago: University of Illinois Press, 1974.

Merchant, Carolyn. *Ecological Revolutions: Nature, Gender, and Science in New England.* Chapel Hill: University of North Carolina Press, 1989.

Middleton, Richard. *Pontiac's War: Its Causes, Course, and Consequences.* New York: Routledge, 2007.

Moogk, Peter N. "'Thieving Buggers' and 'Stupid Sluts': Insults and Popular Culture in New France." *William and Mary Quarterly* 3d ser., 36, no. 4 (October 1979): 524–47.

Moore, John Preston. *Revolt in Louisiana: The Spanish Occupation, 1766–1770.* Baton Rouge: Louisiana State University Press, 1976.

Musick, James B. *St. Louis as a Fortified Town.* St. Louis: R. F. Miller, 1941.

Nasatir, A. P. "The Anglo-Spanish Frontier in the Illinois Country during the American Revolution, 1779–1783." *Illinois State Historical Society Journal* 21, no. 3 (October 1928): 291–358.

————. "Anglo-Spanish Rivalry on the Upper Missouri." *Mississippi Valley Historical Review* 16 (1929): 359–82, 507–28.

————. "Ducharme's Invasion of Missouri, an Incident in the Anglo-Spanish Rivalry for the Indian Trade." *Missouri Historical Review* 24 (1929): 3–25, 238–60, 420–30.

————. "Jacques Clamorgan: Colonial Promoter of the Northern Border of New Spain." *New Mexico Historical Review* 17 (1942): 101–12.

————. "John Evans: Explorer and Surveyor." *Missouri Historical Review* 25, no. 2 (1931): 219–39; 25, no. 3 (1931): 432–60; 25, no. 4 (1931): 585–608.

————. *Spanish War Vessels on the Mississippi, 1792–1796.* New Haven: Yale University Press, 1968.

————. "St. Louis during the British Attack of 1780." In George P. Hammond, ed. *New Spain and the Anglo-American West: Historical Contributions,* presented to Herbert Eugene Bolton. Lancaster, PA: Lancaster Press, 1932. Vol. 1: 239–61.

Norall, Frank. *Bourgmont, Explorer of the Missouri, 1698–1725.* Lincoln: University of Nebraska Press, 1988.

Norton, Mary Beth. "Gender and Defamation in Seventeenth-Century Maryland." *William and Mary Quarterly* 3d ser., 44, no. 1 (January 1987): 3–39.

Oglesby, Richard E. *Manuel Lisa and the Opening of the Missouri Fur Trade.* Norman: University of Oklahoma Press, 1963.

O'Neill, Charles Edwards. *Church and State in French Colonial Louisiana: Policy and Politics to 1732.* New Haven: Yale University Press, 1966.

Peterson, Charles E. *Colonial St. Louis: Building a Creole Capital.* Tucson: Patrice Press, 2001, reprint of 1949 edition.

Peterson, Jacqueline, and Jennifer S. H. Brown, eds. *The New Peoples: Being and Becoming Métis in North America.* Lincoln: University of Nebraska Press, 1985.

Peterson, William J. *Steamboating on the Upper Mississippi.* Iowa City: State Historical Society of Iowa, 1968.

Primm, James Neal. *Lion of the Valley: St. Louis, Missouri, 1764–1980.* 3d ed. St. Louis: Missouri Historical Society Press, 1981.

Ravenswaay, Charles van. "Director's Notebook." *Missouri Historical Society Bulletin* 18, no. 3 (April 1962): 274–76.

————. *Saint Louis: An Informal History of the City and its People, 1764–1865.* Ed. Candace O'Connor. St. Louis: Missouri Historical Society

Press, 1991.

Rickey, Don. "The British-Indian Attack on St. Louis, May 26, 1780." *Missouri Historical Review* 55 (1960): 35–45.

Rosen, Deborah A. "Women and Property across Colonial America: A Comparison of Legal Systems in New Mexico and New York." *William and Mary Quarterly* 3d ser., 60, no. 2 (April 2003): 355–81.

Rosenzweig, Roy, and Elizabeth Blackmar. *The Park and the People: A History of Central Park.* Ithaca: Cornell University Press, 1992.

Rothensteiner, John. *History of the Archdiocese of St. Louis.* St. Louis: Blackwell Wielandy, 1928.

Sailor, Rachel. "Thomas Easterly's Big Mound Daguerreotypes: A Narrative of Community." *Amerikastudien* 49, no. 2 (2004): 141–57.

Sandweiss, Eric. "Construction and Community in South St. Louis, 1850–1910." PhD diss.: University of California, Berkeley, 1991.

———. *St. Louis: The Evolution of an American Urban Landscape.* Philadelphia: Temple University Press, 2001.

Sayad, Elizabeth G. "Louisiana Purchase: Celebrations and Legacies." *Gateway Heritage: The Magazine of the Missouri Historical Society* 21, no. 2 (Fall 2000): 32–45.

Scharf, J. Thomas. *History of Saint Louis City and County, From the Earliest Periods to the Present Day: Including Biographical Sketches of Representative Men.* Vol. 1 Philadelphia: Louis H. Everts, 1883.

Schuyler, David. *The New Urban Landscape: The Redefinition of City Form in Nineteenth-Century America.* Baltimore: Johns Hopkins University Press, 1986.

Singy, Patrick. "Friction of the Genitals and the Secularization of Morality." *Journal of the History of Sexuality* 12, no. 3 (July 2003): 345–64.

Smit, William M. "Old Broadway, a Forgotten Street, and Its Park of Mounds." *Bulletin of the Missouri Historical Society* 4, no. 3 (April 1948): 153–63.

Spear, Jennifer M. "Colonial Intimacies: Legislating Sex in French Louisiana." *William and Mary Quarterly* 3d ser., 60, no. 1 (January 2003): 75–98.

St. George, Robert Blair, ed., *Possible Pasts: Becoming Colonial in Early America.* Ithaca: Cornell University Press, 2000.

Stevens, Walter B. *St. Louis: The Fourth City.* Chicago: S. J. Clarke, 1909.

Stoler, Ann Laura. "Tense and Tender Ties: The Politics of Comparison in North American History and (Post) Colonial Studies." *Journal of American History* 88, no. 3 (December 2001): 829–65.

Thompson, John B., ed. *Language and Symbolic Power.* Cambridge: Harvard

University Press, 1991.

Thorne, Tanis C. *The Many Hands of My Relations: French and Indians on the Lower Missouri.* Columbia: University of Missouri Press, 1996.

Tykal, Jack B. "Taos to St. Louis: The Journey of María Rosa Villalpando." *New Mexico Historical Review* 65, no. 2 (April 1990): 161–74.

Usner, Daniel H. *Indians, Settlers, and Slaves in a Frontier Exchange Economy: The Lower Mississippi Valley before 1783.* Chapel Hill: University of North Carolina Press, 1992.

Villiers du Terrage, Marc de. *La Découverte du Missouri et l'histoire du Fort d'Orleans (1673–1728).* Paris: Librairie Ancienne Honoré de France, 1925.

Vivier, Nadine. "Les Biens Communaux de Béarn et Pays Basque sous l'Ancien Régime et la Révolution." In Christian Desplat, ed., *Pyrénées-Terres Frontières.* Paris: Éditions du CTHS, 1996, 57–70.

Vogel, Rachel Fran. "Social Life in St. Louis, 1764–1804." MA thesis, Washington University, 1921.

Weber, David J. *The Spanish Frontier in North America.* New Haven: Yale University Press, 1992.

White, Richard. *The Middle Ground: Indians, Empires, and Republics in the Great Lakes Region, 1650–1815.* New York: Cambridge University Press, 1991.

Wood, Peter H. *Black Majority: Negroes in Colonial South Carolina from 1670 through the Stono Rebellion.* New York: W. W. Norton, 1974.

Wood, W. Raymond. *Prologue to Lewis and Clark: The Mackay and Evans Expedition.* Foreword by James P. Ronda. Norman: University of Oklahoma Press, 2003.

Worsham, James. "Raising the Stars and Stripes over Louisiana Territory." *Prologue* 35, no. 4 (Winter 2003): 40–43.

Index

Adet, Pierre, 287

Africans, 16, 19–20, 85, 117, 144, 145n., 184n., 233, 246, 308; emancipated or free, 8, 19, 19n., 143–44, 163. *See also* slavery; slaves; women

alcohol, 16, 83n., 171, 200, 247, 312; blamed for illness and death, 164–65, 170–71, 174–75, 185–88; blamed for social and sexual misbehavior, 73, 80–82, 93–96, 143–44, 154–55, 170, 175, 181, 185, 203–4, 211; conflicts over, 8, 87, 104; intoxication or "drunkeness" from, 80, 84, 86, 92–95, 111, 171, 181, 185–86, 203–4, 281, 292, 294; prohibitions, 80–81, 88, 95–96, 100, 170, 175, 181, 185–87, 190, 211, 218; prohibitions for Indians, 92, 94–96, 181, 187, 190, 218, 239, 247; prohibitions for soldiers, 80–82, 86–88, 187; as social activity, 186–87, 190, 200, 288; in trade, 84, 92, 94–96, 186–88, 190, 200, 218, 255, 265, 276, 294. *See also* presents (gift-giving)

Alonso, Domingo, 238

Alvarez, Eugenio, 121, 173, 264, 299

American expansion, 249–50, 260–61, 270, 305–6, 317

American identity in history texts, 3, 5–7

American Revolutionary War, 192, 198–99, 221, 222–31, 238–49, 261, 262n.

Arkansas Post, 27, 82

Aspe Valley (France), 13–14

Aubert, Guillaume (author), 161

Aubry, Charles-Philippe, 64, 76, 106

Austin, Moses, 294

Balboa, Joseph, 85–86

Balls. *See* dances

Banner, Stuart (author), 162, 174

Barelas, Joseph, 87

Bargas, Domingo de: inter-racial offspring,172, 174; investigation of death, 164–67, 170–75, 172n., 173n., 188–89

Barr, Julianna (author), 158

Barrera, the storekeeper, 84–87

Barrere, François, 207n., 208n.

Béarn (France), 13–15

Beaugenou, Marie, 142

Bedous (France), 11, 13, 15, 134

Belestre, Pierre Picoté de, 226, 236

Bequet, Marie, 166, 173, 216

Bérard, Antoine, 166, 171

Berard, Antonio, 128

Bissonet, Pedro, 127

Blanco, Diego, 151–52, 204, 212

Bordeaux (France), 11

Bowman, Joseph, 199

Bradbury, John, 57

Brasseaux, Carl A., 75–76

Briand, Bishop, 178

British government in American territory, 58–67, 69–70

Brown, William, 225, 233

buildings: construction of churches, 15, 177, 180, 183; construction in

About the Author

PATRICIA CLEARY is Professor of History at California State University–Long Beach and author of *Elizabeth Murray: A Woman's Pursuit of Independence in Eighteenth-Century America*. A St. Louis native, she lives with her family in Southern California.